MINICOMPUTERS IN INDUSTRIAL CONTROL

An Introduction

(

<u>E R R A T U M</u>

Title: Harrison, MINICOMPUTERS IN INDUSTRIAL CONTROL
                1st printing 1978

Reference pages 33, 34: The equations describing the "two mode"
and "three mode" controllers are transposed. The equation on
page 34 ("two mode" controller) should read as appearing on page
33. The equation for the "three mode" controller should appear
at the bottom of page 34.

This transposition will be corrected in the second printing.

The Publisher

MINICOMPUTERS IN INDUSTRIAL CONTROL

An Introduction

Edited by **THOMAS J. HARRISON**, Ph.D.

SENIOR ENGINEER
INTERNATIONAL BUSINESS MACHINES CORPORATION
BOCA RATON, FLORIDA, USA

INSTRUMENT SOCIETY OF AMERICA

MINICOMPUTERS IN INDUSTRIAL CONTROL: AN INTRODUCTION

Library of Congress Catalog Card Number 77–93080

Library of Congress Cataloging in Publication Data
Harrison, Thomas J.
Minicomputers in Industrial Control: An Introduction
    ISBN 0–87664–372–1

This book was set in Times Roman by Willmer Brothers Limited.
The designer and production coordinator was Sidney Solomon.
The copy editor was Judith Green.
Printing and binding by Capital City Press.

First Printing 1978

In Memoriam
GLENN M. HARRISON
1901–1975

Contributors

RAYMOND H. ASH, Jr., Ph.D.
  Procter and Gamble Company
  Cincinnati, Ohio

RICHARD L. CURTIS, B.S.E.E.
  Aluminum Corporation of America
  Pittsburgh, Pennsylvania

THOMAS M. STOUT, Ph.D.
  Profimatics, Inc.
  Woodland Hills, California

KIRWIN A. WHITMAN, M.Ch.E., M.B.A.
  Allied Chemical Corporation
  Morristown, New Jersey

THOMAS J. HARRISON, Ph.D.
  International Business Machines Corporation
  Boca Raton, Florida

PREFACE

This book started several years ago beside the swimming pool of a Tampa, Florida, motel during the Winter President's Meeting of the Instrument Society of America (ISA). It was Art Lumb's idea and he outlined his concept of its purpose, content, and approach to Kirk Whitman, Glenn Harvey and Frank Ryan of the ISA staff, and me. In our enthusiasm, we projected an ambitious schedule of less than a year. But, as always seems to happen in my writing efforts, the schedule was interrupted by many trips, a lot of work, and other delays on my part and that of the contributors. Much of the work was done 30,000 feet above the United States and other countries as I carried the manuscript with me on my trips and used it to put the hours in the airplane to good use. Now it is complete and I am looking back on our original purpose and goals as I compose this preface.

Our purpose was to provide a relatively brief book about the use of minicomputers in industrial control applications. It was to be a starting point for the industrial control engineer or manager who was about to get involved in a computer control project for the first time. Thus, the reader was assumed to be a technical person, but not a computer engineer or programmer, who knew the process with which he or she was concerned, but had no significant experience or training in computers and their use in an industrial process. The book was to be a tutorial, yet have sufficient depth to introduce concepts and vocabulary that would be necessary to read and understand more advanced literature on specialized topics.

We wanted the book to be complete, in the sense that it considered the entire course of events in the design, installation, and use of a computer control system from the user's point of view. That was a large order in that many books have been written on each of the subjects covered by the eight chapters in this book. It required the highest skill on the part of the contributors to distill their years of experience and specialized knowledge into the number of pages which were budgeted. With their cooperation and some tough editing, we came close to our original target without, I believe, sacrificing our goal of completeness.

The organization of the book was chosen to follow the typical sequence of events that is involved in an industrial computer project. The initial four chapters provide background information on control theory and the computer hardware and software which normally would be acquired in the learning phase associated with the study of a potential computer control project. Since the ultimate purpose of installing a computer is to make money for the company, an early consideration in the study phase is to estimate the economic benefits that are expected to accrue and compare them with the cost of installing and maintaining the computer control system. Chapter 5 provides guidance on where to look for benefits, how to estimate their value, and how to examine the profitability of the project.

If the project is economically attractive, the next step is to put a team in place to design and install the control system. Chapter 6 considers this activity, primarily from a management point of view. It discusses finding the right people to do the job, organizing them into an effective team, and keeping track of schedules and costs to ensure that the project reaches its economic goals on time. Since the design and management of software systems are often considered a particularly difficult task, special emphasis is given to this important subject.

Chapter 7 considers the physical installation of the computer. Although physical installation does not occur until well after the initiation of the project, planning for it in terms of space, facilities, electrical requirements, and the like, begins early in the project and continues until after the installation phase is complete. Once installed, the system must be thoroughly tested before being turned over to the process operator for use. Few guidelines exist in this area and this chapter draws heavily on the ISA Recommended Practice RP55. 1–1975 to provide suggestions on how to proceed with this important task. The subsequent activities of a post-completion audit and maintaining the system over its life are also considered.

Chapter 8 recognizes the new and fast-developing microcomputer and computer network technologies and their close relationship to minicomputers. These topics are currently being discussed actively in the tradepress and journals. The basic thesis of the chapter is that microcomputers and minicomputers are not significantly different in structure and use. Thus, the material in the previous chapters of the book largely is applicable in both cases.

Some differences, particularly in the area of economics, are noted and discussed. Computer networks are viewed as a natural evolution of system structure which, again, is being driven largely by economic factors.

A large number of definitions provided throughout the book are given, either explicitly or implicitly. However, the word "minicomputer" which is used often in the book and, indeed, in its title, is never defined with any degree of precision. The lack of definition is intentional and deserves some discussion.

The basic reason for not defining the term "minicomputer" is that I do not know how to do it in an acceptable way. I have read many attempts at definition and have spent many, many hours discussing it with my colleagues, but I am not satisfied with any proposed definitions.

Usually the definitions center around parameters such as size, processing power, physical packaging, and price. But, in my opinion, none is sufficient to uniquely differentiate a "minicomputer" from the other coined "classes" of computer such as microcomputers, midicomputers, medium-scale computers, large computers, and super-computers. A rack and panel cabinet construction is often cited as a characteristic of minicomputers; yet the very first computers ever built were built using this construction and these room-filling machines certainly were not "mini." Processing power, sometimes measured in terms of the number of instructions that can be executed per second, is another characteristic often mentioned; yet, some minicomputers measured on this basis are more powerful than computers which are categorized as medium-scale computers. Similarly, the price of a certain configuration is often included in the definition, but this is a moving target, in light of the rapid decline in prices caused by competition and the use of advanced integrated circuits.

Thus, defining a minicomputer is difficult and I have never succeeded in doing it to my satisfaction. In considering the problem, I have come to the conclusion that a computer is a minicomputer if the vendors and the users call it that. As much as its physical characteristics and price, the definition of a minicomputer seems to be determined by the manner in which it is offered to the user. The minicomputer is sold as a "bag of parts" for the user to assemble into an application system; that is, it is an offering of various pieces of hardware and software which can be combined in many different combinations to suit a particular application either by the vendor, a third party, or the user. This is in contrast to many other computers which are offered with a minimum number of options and a less general-purpose repertoire of software.

So, I will leave the definition of a minicomputer in this general state of imprecision. A computer is a computer, from the hand-held programmable calculator to the room-filling "number cruncher" used for esoteric research. There are, in this author's opinion, no clear demarcations between classes of computers and the fuzzy boundaries, if they exist, really are not worth defining.

The writing and production of a book of this type involves many people, all of whom cannot be individually acknowledged. My family, as I am sure is the case with the other contributors, has been patient through evenings and weekends of work and we all thank them. The staff of the ISA has been helpful in every detail of the production as have the many reviewers of the various chapters. The reviewers were coordinated by Art Lumb. Finally, the support of IBM, primarily through the use of a computer-based text editing system and the understanding of my manager, is gratefully acknowledged. I hope that this book serves the purposes for which it was written—to further the use of computers in industry as a means of improving the lives of us all.

THOMAS J. HARRISON

October 1977
Boca Raton, Florida

During the final stage of producing this book, I was notified of the death of Dick Curtis at the age of 43. I have known Dick for over ten years and worked with him on a variety of projects, most of which were related to national and international standardization. Dick was an outstanding engineer and manager with a particular interest in management methods. He was, therefore, my first choice as the author of Chapter 6 on Planning and Designing the System. Although seriously ill throughout 1977, Dick remained vitally interested in the book and participated actively, not only on his chapter, but as a reviewer for several other chapters. His contributions are found throughout this book.

Dick was an involved and tireless worker for a number of activities and committees in the Instrument Society of America and the Institute of Electrical and Electronics Engineers. Very often work in these types of organizations verges on the brink of chaos, as the limited voluntary resources and the proprietary interests of many organizations and personalities are forged into action. Dick had the ability to cut through the myriad of conflicting goals, constraints, and interests to provide the necessary leadership and clear thinking which resulted in solid progress. He will be missed by me and his many other friends and colleagues. It is my hope that his chapter in this book will be yet another significant contribution by which he will be remembered.

TJH
January 1978

CONTENTS

MINICOMPUTERS IN INDUSTRIAL CONTROL

An Introduction

1 INTRODUCTION TO INDUSTRIAL CONTROL

Raymond H. Ash, Jr., Ph.D
THE PROCTER & GAMBLE COMPANY, CINCINNATI, OHIO

Digital computers first became commonly available during the mid-1950's and created a revolutionary change in the data processing field. Their entry into real-time industrial process control has been far less dramatic and explosive; only since about 1965 has the digital computer begun to have a major effect in on-line application for manufacturing industries. Extremely rapid decreases in the cost of computer hardware (concurrent with advances in integrated circuit technology), as well as a vastly enhanced understanding of how to best use computers in manufacturing systems, have contributed to a substantial growth in the application of digital computers in the process industries over the past decade.

The term "real-time" is widely used in reference to on-line applications of computers. It is, perhaps, a misleading term (is there any other kind of time?) but is based on the idea that the computer must respond to events which occur at times over which it has no control. These times are related to random occurrences such as process upsets, response times of processes, operator commands, or the "tick" of a clock timer; thus, the term "real" (i.e., outside world determined) time. "On-line" is a term closely analogous to real-time and the two are often used interchangeably.

The functions performed by a digital computer system in an on-line process application can be broadly classified into two categories:

Control Functions are those related to manipulation of the process; that is, functions which cause the process to change in some way. For example, changing the position of a control valve changes the flow of a stream which may cause, in turn, some process temperature to change. The computer functions which determine how much to move the valve and actually move it are control functions.

Information Functions are those related to process data. Such functions include gathering, sorting, evaluating, conditioning, processing, and communicating data to an operator and others. Information functions do not change the process in any direct way.

This chapter is concerned with the fundamentals of industrial and computer control and information systems. The basic concepts of control are first examined, followed by a discussion of the various functions of an information system. The role of computers in industrial control and information systems is developed concurrently. The chapter concludes with a summary of various categories of real-time computer system applications.

CONCEPTS OF CONTROL

A process is viewed by many as a collection of interconnected hardware such as tanks, pipes, valves, fittings, motors, shafts, and couplings, with each piece contributing toward the overall production objectives of the process. Typically, this objective is to produce some product or small group of related products.

A process control engineer views the process in a very different way, however; rather than focusing on the hardware, the engineer focuses on the physical variables of the process such as temperatures, pressures, levels, flows, voltages, speeds, positions, compositions, and concentrations. He or she is interested in how these physical variables interact and how they change with time.

The fundamental control objective in process control is to keep certain key process variables as near to their desired values as possible as much of the time as possible. These key physical variables are called outputs of the process and they are selected on the basis that maintaining them at their specified values guarantees the achievement of one or more production objectives such as specified product quality, acceptable plant efficiency, satisfactory production level, safe operating conditions, or satisfactory cost of production.

The desired values, often called *setpoints*, of these process outputs are usually constant; that is, they do not change with time. Sometimes, however, some of the setpoints are programmed to follow specified trajectories as a function of time. Programmed setpoints are most frequently used during startup, shutdown, grade change in a continuous process (i.e., shifting from one product to another without intermediate shutdown), or in batch

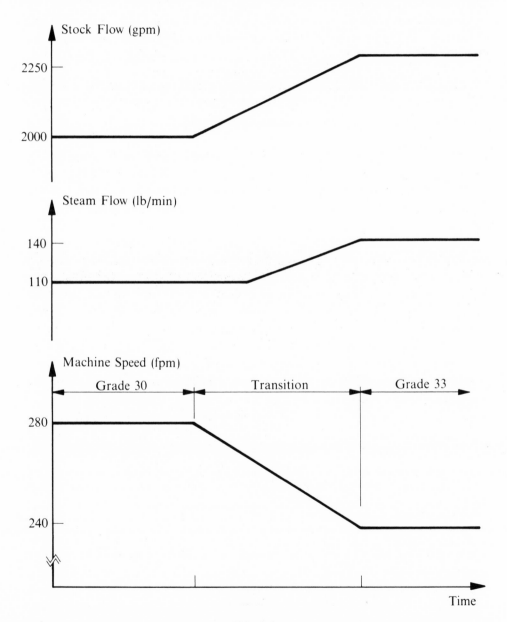

FIG. 1.1
Setpoint of Paper Machine Outputs During Coordinated Grade Change

processes. For example, in changing from one grade to another on a paper machine, it is desired to smoothly ramp the stock flow, steam flow, and machine speed from their original to their new values in a coordinated manner as shown in Fig. 1.1.

In addition to the key physical variables designated as process outputs to be controlled, another class of physical variables which are important to the control engineer are known as *process inputs*. They are the variables which, when they change, cause the outputs to change. Inputs can be classified into two categories:

Control Inputs are the process variables which can be manipulated by the controller to maintain outputs at their desired values. Control inputs are also called *manipulated variables* or manipulated inputs.

Disturbance Inputs are all the other process variables which affect the outputs. If they vary for any reason, they cause unwanted changes in the outputs. Disturbance inputs are also called *load variables* or load inputs. Changes caused by disturbances are frequently called *load upsets*.

Disturbance inputs provide the primary reason for control. If there were no load upsets, the control input could be set at the value required to keep the output at its setpoint value and nothing would ever change. In any real process, however, a disturbance variable causes one or more of the outputs to deviate from setpoint and one or more control inputs must be changed in order to return the output(s) to the desired value(s).

A block diagram, such as that shown in Fig. 1.2, is a schematic representation of the cause and effect relationship between inputs and outputs. Generally, a single block has only one process output and only one associated

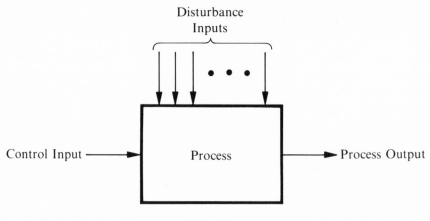

FIG. 1.2
Process Block Diagram

control input, although there may be several identifiable disturbance inputs and, perhaps, several other disturbances which are not identifiable. Each arrow in the diagram represents a physical variable; inward arrows are for "causes" (inputs) and outward arrows for "effects" (outputs). For now, the block itself is just a schematic representation of the process; later in the chapter, the relationship between inputs and outputs is quantified mathematically and the block is then used to represent this quantitative relationship.

Sensors and Actuators

Measurement is of primary importance to control, as no variable can be controlled unless its value is known. Most process variables whose values are needed are measured directly by *sensors*, instruments or devices that generate signals proportional to the value of the variable being measured. Examples are thermocouples for temperature measurements, and tachometers for shaft speed measurements. The sensors are usually associated with *transmitters* which convert the sensor output to a standard signal range representing the full range of the variable being measured. In the United States, this is most commonly either an air pressure range of 3 psig to 15 psig or an electrical current range of 4 mA to 20 mA.

There are some important process variables which are difficult or impossible to measure continuously; others only can be measured using elaborate laboratory apparatus. An example is stream composition where on-line chromatographs (often operated by computers) can provide only a periodic composition analysis (typically every 15 to 30 minutes). Other variables, such as permanganate number in pulp making, require laboratory analysis and are not feasible to obtain more frequently than every 30 minutes or so. Laboratory analysis also may add a delay between taking the sample and knowing the variable value. This periodic sampling plus delay in obtaining the measurement value compounds enormously the problems associated with control of these variables. Often it is impractical to attempt direct control of such variables.

Sometimes it is possible to calculate the value of such difficult-to-measure variables from their known mathematical relationship to other process variables which are more easily measured. For example, the reflux ratio in a distillation column is an important manipulated variable which is not directly measureable. It is easily calculated, however, by dividing reflux flowrate by takeoff flowrate, both of which are easy to measure directly. Variables calculated from formulas using other measured variables are called inferred or derived variables. The availability of a digital computer in a process application makes it much easier to perform the calculations necessary to derive such variables.

Process variables which can assume any value within a specified range are called analog variables. A great deal of information important to the control of a process, however, comes from discrete event sensors, such as switches which indicate whether a piece of process equipment is running, malfunction indicators, and counters. Such binary inputs (i.e., off or on are the only two possible values) are an important part of the total measurement system associated with a process.

Actuators. In order to keep process output variables at or near their desired values, it is frequently necessary to cause changes in the process manipulated variables. This is done via actuators, devices which can be adjusted by the control system and which, in turn, cause the manipulated variables to change. The most frequently used actuator in process industries is the valve which causes the flowrate of the stream passing through it to change when its position is changed. Pneumatically (air) operated valves are most often used for automatic control, although hydraulic and electrically operated valves are occasionally applied. A valve whose position can be changed by changing an air or electrical signal usually is called a control valve. Hand operated valves are sometimes used to control process output variables when relatively infrequent adjustment is required. Another commonly used actuator is the variable speed motor driving a pump, drive roll, or other prime mover. Changing the speed of the motor causes the manipulated variable (for example, the pump head) to change.

The Plant Subsystem. Combining the actuator and sensor with the process itself, as in the block diagram of Fig. 1.3, gives one unit of what is commonly

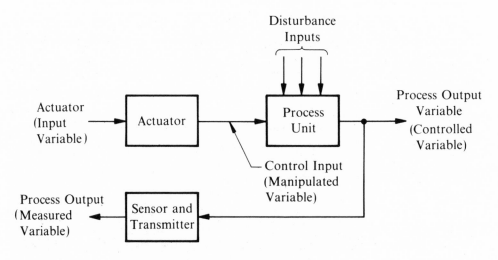

FIG. 1.3
Unit of the Plant Subsystem

called the plant subsystem. (The total process system also includes the control and information subsystem, and, in the broadest view, the operator subsystem.) There is a simple process unit associated with each key process output variable. For each process output there is one, and only one, key manipulated variable and, generally, several disturbance inputs. Each process unit has one sensor and one actuator associated with it. Together, all process units, actuators, and sensors make up the overall plant subsystem of the total process system.

Dynamic Response and Mathematical Models

The purpose of an industrial control system is to keep the key process output variables as near to their desired values (setpoints) as possible, as much of the time as possible. If a disturbance causes a process output variable to deviate from its setpoint, a change must be made in the appropriate control input or manipulated variable to cause the output to return to its desired value. Knowing how much and when to change the control input to provide the "best" response in the output is a problem which constitutes the central question of control strategy development.

The problem is complicated by the fact that almost all processes have some degree of inertia, or lag; that is, if a sudden change is made in the control input, the output variable does not follow immediately and there is a time lag before the output finally reaches its new value. A familiar example is an automobile which requires time to come to a new steady speed if the gas pedal is depressed suddenly and kept at the new position. How long this requires depends on factors such as the weight of the car, the power of the engine (characteristics of the "Process"), the number of passengers, magnitude and direction of wind velocity (disturbance or load variables), and many other factors which are either inherent to the process or external disturbances related to the environment.

A quantitative cause-effect relationship between input and output must be known to decide how much and in what manner to change the control input to correct for a disturbance-caused deviation in process output. The functional (mathematical) relationship between an input and output of a process unit is called a mathematical model of the process unit. In general, a mathematical model is any mathematical expression which, if the values of all independent variables (or inputs) are known, enables prediction of the value of the dependent variable (or output) by evaluating the expression.

As an example, Fig. 1.4a depicts a familiar water tap fed from a community water tank, assumed to be at a high elevation so that pressure remains essentially constant at the tap. The relationship between flowrate W from the tap in gallons per minute (gpm) as a function of valve opening in percent of maximum, denoted by X, is shown graphically in Fig. 1.4b. This

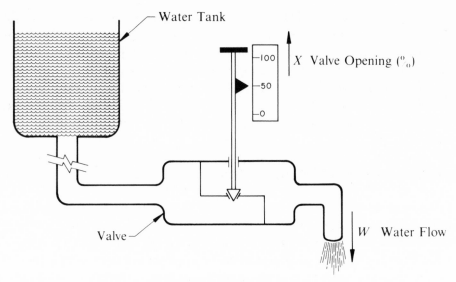

(a) Physical Configuration

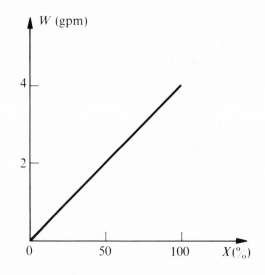

(b) Relationship Between Flow and Valve Opening

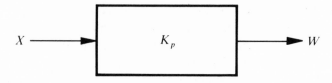

(c) Process Block Diagram

FIG. 1.4
Example Process and Block Diagram

relationship may have been obtained empirically or by calculation from the geometry of the tap and physical principles.

This arrangement can be viewed as a process unit whose output variable is water flow W and whose control input variable is valve stem position X. Thus, the block diagram for this process unit in Fig. 1.4c has X as its input and W as its output.

The relationship between X and W also can be expressed by the mathematical formula:

$$W = 0.04X \tag{1.1}$$

which is a mathematical model of the process unit. Its use enables prediction of the value of W which results from any given value of X. The actual output may vary from the predicted output due to disturbances or inaccuracies in the model.

Process Gain. Suppose that the valve is 50% open and flow is thus (0.04 × 50) = 2 gpm. If the valve is opened to 60%, the flow changes to (0.04 × 60) = 2.4 gpm, an increase of 0.4 gpm. The 10% change in stem position causes a 0.4 gpm change. This can be characterized by the parameter:

K_p = (change in output)/(change in input)
   = (0.4 gpm)/10%
   = 0.04 gpm/percent

which is called the *process gain* for this process unit. In this particular example, the process is linear; that is, the process gain K_p is a constant, independent of the stem position X.

Note that any change made in valve position X is reflected immediately as a corresponding change in W. There is essentially no process inertia in this particular process to cause a time lag between control action and output response.

Dynamic Processes. Many processes are more complex than the example process in that they exhibit some degree of inertia or lag. Such processes are called *dynamic processes.* Strictly speaking, all process units are dynamic, but some, such as in the example, respond so fast that it is convenient to view them as instantaneous processes and little or no error is made by doing so.

As an example of a dynamic process, consider the water tank shown in Fig. 1.5. There are four physical variables of interest in this process: The water level L, the flowrate of water W_i into the tank, the flowrate of water W_o out of the tank, and the position X_v of the outlet valve.

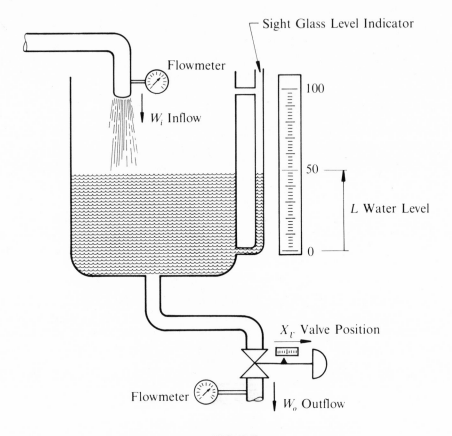

FIG. 1.5
Example Process: Water Tank and Valve

At this point, no clear-cut process unit has been defined, since it is not clear which of the four physical variables is the output variable, which is the control input, and which are disturbance inputs. Without further information, the specification of outputs and inputs is not unique; with the given hardware configuration, at least two of the variables, level L and outflow W_o, are possible outputs and they both might be. The choice of which input to use as the control input depends on what the output variable is.

When both L and W_o are outputs, two process units arise from the hardware and set of four physical variables being examined. In this case, both of the available control inputs, valve position X_v and inflow W_i, affect both outputs. This results in cross-coupling which complicates the problem of control and leads to a multivariable control problem.

Without making a specific choice of outputs and process configurations, it is possible and useful to make some observations about the behavior and cause-effect relationships of the variables. These depend only on physical laws, not on which variable is selected as the output. Observations based on physical "feel" (i.e., experience and prior observation of physical phenomena as well as knowledge of physical laws) are an important first step in the development of mathematical models as they establish the cause-effect paths.

To begin, the outflow W_o is affected by both level L and valve position X_v. For a given valve opening, increasing the level increases the outflow W_o because of the increased water pressure. Similarly, at a given level, W_o increases as X_v is increased.

The level L remains constant only if the inflow W_i and the outflow W_o are exactly the same. If they are different, then L rises or falls with time, depending on whether W_i is greater or less than W_o. Suppose that W_i and W_o initially are the same, with the level steady at some value, and W_i is then suddenly increased. Clearly, the level will begin to rise. The rate at which L increases depends on how much faster water is coming in than it is being drained and how big the tank is. If W_i exceeds W_o by 5 gpm, for instance, then one minute after the increase in W_i, there are 5 more gallons in the tank. If the tank is two feet in diameter, 5 gallons raises the level 25 times higher than it does in a 10 foot diameter tank. As L rises, W_o increases due to the increased pressure at the output. The level L continues to rise, although at an ever decreasing rate since W_o is ever increasing, until W_o exactly equals the current value of W_i. At this point, L remains constant.

This response is depicted graphically with representative numbers in Fig. 1.6. The change in Level L occurs over a time period somewhat greater than 60 minutes. The new level will be 11 feet, regardless of tank size, because it is at this level that W_o equals 105 gpm, the new inflow rate. The time required to reach the new level of 11 feet is very dependent on tank size, however. If the diameter of the tank were doubled, it would take four times as long to come to the new level, since volume increases as the square of the diameter.

This type of dynamic response is called a first-order lag or exponential response and the corresponding process unit is called a first-order process. First-order processes are the simplest kind of dynamic process and are extremely common; they are found wherever there is a single storage element (like the tank) which stores material or energy and which is supplied and drained of material or energy at rates which are dependent on the amount of material or energy in the storage unit.

The time required for 63% of the ultimate change to take place in a first-order response is called the time constant of the process. The time constant of the response shown in Fig. 1.6 is 20 minutes. For any first-order process, 86% of the total change occurs in two time constants, 95% in three time constants, and 98% in four time constants. For most practical purposes, the process has reached a steady state after four time constants. Changing the tank diameter changes the numerical value of the time constant, but still it requires four time constants for 98% of the change to occur.

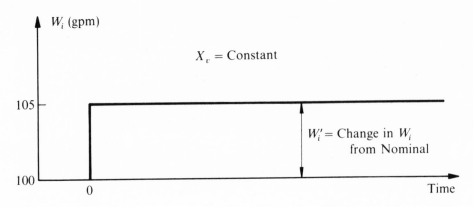

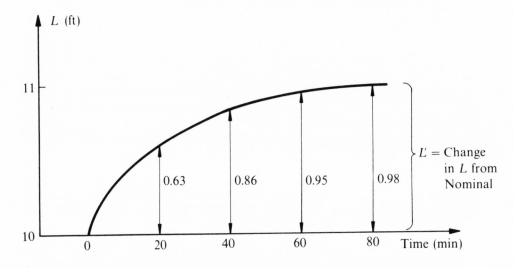

FIG. 1.6
Dynamic Response of Tank Level *L*

The time constant of a first-order dynamic process is a second important parameter of the process model. Whereas gain permits computation of the new ultimate process output value, the time constant is a measure of the time required to reach it.

When all process variables are at constant values, the process is said to be in the *steady-state*. In the example, the process is changing from one steady-state to a different steady-state. The transition period from one steady-state to another is the *transient* part of the response.

Modeling Fundamentals. Although it is inappropriate in this book to get into involved mathematics, it is useful to explore some of the basics of modeling. It is convenient for mathematical representation to work with changes of a physical variable from its nominal value. In the tank example, for instance, the level L can be represented as:

$$L = \bar{L} + L'$$

where $\bar{L}$ is the fixed nominal value (10 feet in the example) and L' is the change from that nominal value. The change L' may be positive or negative. Similarly, the inflow W_i can be represented as the sum of a nominal and change component

$$W_i = \bar{W}_i + W_i'$$

Equations can be written in terms of only the change components. The actual value at any time is determined by adding the change component to the nominal value. Any convenient set of values may be chosen for nominal values of process variables; Generally, they are a set of steady-state values corresponding to the normal process operating point.

The equation which relates the level change L' to the step change in inflow W_i' is:

$$L' = K_p \, W_i' \, (1 - e^{-t/\tau}) \tag{1.2}$$

where:

> K_p is the process gain, relating the ultimate change in level to the inflow change. In the example, $K_p = 0.2$ foot/gpm, so a 5 gpm change in W_i causes an ultimate 1 foot change in L.
> τ is the time constant (20 minutes in the example).
> t is elapsed time since the change in W_i.
> e is the base of the natural logarithm ($e = 2.71828 \cdots$).
> W_i' is the inflow change (10 gpm in the example).

Equation 1.2 is a mathematical model which predicts the level response resulting from one specific kind of change in inflow; namely, a sudden change to a fixed new value at a time when the level is at steady-state. This is known as a step change.

A more general mathematical model relating the input (inflow W_i) to the output (level L) of the process unit in Fig. 1.7 is:

$$\tau \frac{dL'}{dt} + L' = K_p \, W_i' \tag{1.3}$$

This is a differential equation because it involves the time rate of change level of $\frac{dL'}{dt}$ as well as the variable L' itself.

A dynamic process is always described by a differential equation. Differential equations are much more difficult to solve than algebraic equations, such as Eq. 1.1, which describe non-dynamic processes. Given values of the input W_i' over some period of time and the value of the output L' at the beginning of this period, it is possible to find a unique solution to the differential equation Eq. 1.3. The solution consists of a set of values of the output L' over the same time period, which can be either plotted, as in Fig. 1.6, or expressed as an equation (such as Eq. 1.2) with elapsed time as the independent variable.

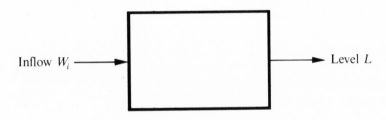

Inflow W_i ⟶ ⟶ Level L

FIG. 1.7
Block Diagram of Process Unit

Deriving the Models. It is instructive to consider how the general mathematical model is derived from physical laws and process configuration, since it provides further insight into the relationship between the physical configuration of the process and the cause-effect relationships between important process variables.

The physical law which applies and is most useful in the example is "The Conservation of Mass." "The Conservation of Mass" principle (which essentially states that "matter can be neither created nor destroyed") can be stated in the following form for modeling purposes:

$$\text{Rate of Accumulation} = \text{Inflow rate} - \text{Outflow rate} \qquad (1.4)$$

That is, the amount of material which accumulates in, for example, a storage tank over a given time period is equal to the difference between the amount put in and the amount removed during the given time period. Each side of Eq. 1.4 is expressed in pounds per hour or other similar units of mass per unit time. If there is no mixing of substances of different densities, then volumetric units (gallons per minute, for example) can also be used.

Using Eq. 1.4 in volumetric terms for the example process yields:

$$\frac{dV}{dt} = W_i - W_o \tag{1.5}$$

where $\dfrac{dV}{dt}$ is the rate of change of volume in gallons per minute, and W_i and W_o are inflow and outflow rates in gpm.

Since W_i is the input variable and level L is the output variable for this model, W_o and V in Eq. 1.5 should be expressed in terms of these variables, if possible. Assume that the tank cross sectional area A in square feet is the same at all levels. Then, the volume V in gallons is equal to CAL, where L is the level in feet and C is the conversion factor which converts cubic feet to gallons. Recognizing that C and A are constants and that $\dfrac{dL}{dt} = \dfrac{dL'}{dt}$:

$$\frac{dV}{dt} = \frac{d(CAL)}{dt} = CA\frac{dL}{dt} = CA\frac{dL'}{dt} \tag{1.6}$$

The right hand side of Eq. 1.5 also can be written in terms of deviation

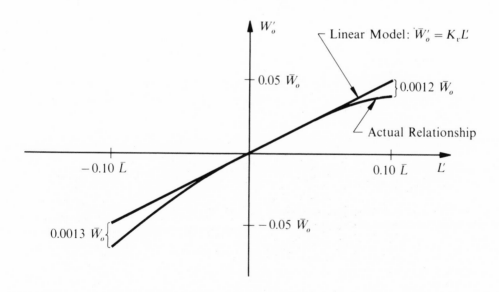

FIG. 1.8
Linear Model vs. Actual Relationship

variables as follows:

$$W_i - W_o = \bar{W}_i + W_i' - (\bar{W}_o + W_o')$$
$$= \bar{W}_i - \bar{W}_o + W_i' - W_o' \qquad (1.7)$$

In the steady-state, $\bar{W}_i$ and $\bar{W}_o$ are exactly equal to each other; thus, $\bar{W}_i = \bar{W}_o$ and from Eq. 1.7:

$$W_i - W_o = W_i' - W_o' \qquad (1.8)$$

Now consider W_o', the outflow deviation. At a fixed valve position, W_o increases as L increases. In fact, it is approximately true for deviations which are small, compared to the nominal value of the variable, that the change in outflow is directly proportional to the change in level;* that is

$$W_o' = K_v \, L' \qquad (1.9)$$

where K_v is a constant related to valve opening, pipe sizes, and other parameters of the process configuration.

Substituting the relationships of Eqs. 1.9, 1.8 and 1.6 into Eq. 1.5 and rearranging results in:

$$\frac{CA}{K_v} \frac{dL'}{dt} + L' = \frac{1}{K_v} \, W_i' \qquad (1.10)$$

which is the first order linear differential equation relating W_i' and L'.

Comparing Eq. 1.10 with Eq. 1.3 permits the following observations:

$$\frac{1}{K_v} = K_p = \text{the process gain}$$

$$\frac{CA}{K_v} = \tau = \text{the process time constant}$$

---

*Strictly speaking, flow through a pipe or a valve (at a fixed opening) increases as the square root of the pressure applied at the upstream side. Pressure is directly proportional to level in the tank, or head, so that outflow W_o varies as the square root of level L. Figure 1.8 shows the actual relationship between W_o' and L' for $\pm 10\%$ changes of the nominal level L. Note that the actual relationship bows slightly downward due to the square root relationship. However, the predicted value of change in flow from Eq. 1.9 to a $\pm 10\%$ change in level is only 2.4% different than the actual change. As a result, very little error results from the use of the linear model.

It is convenient to use linear models such as Eq. 1.9 because they result in linear differential equations which are solved more easily. Thus, it is common to approximate a nonlinear mathematical relationship with a linear model on the basis that the error between the predicted and actual behavior of the process is small for small deviations from nominal. The technique of approximating nonlinear relationships with linear models over limited ranges is called linearization.

This example illustrates how a process model is derived from basic physical laws. The particular law or principle which is applicable depends on the nature of the process. Among the more common laws are "The Conservation of Mass," "The Conservation of Energy," "Newton's Laws of Motion," and "Kirchoff's Laws of Electrical Circuits."

In almost all cases, the resulting model is a differential equation and methods are known for finding explicit solutions to large classes of differential equations. For those in which explicit solutions cannot be stated, numerical methods can often be used to develop the necessary relationships for the purposes of control.

Dead Time Processes. Another important class of dynamic process unit arises when there is a time delay between when changes occur in process variables and the time they are detected. This is characteristic of transportation processes, such as the pipeline illustrated in Fig. 1.9. In this process, dilution water is added to thick paper stock (a suspension of wood fibers in water) at the intake of a pump to adjust the stock consistency.

Suppose that the dilution water valve is initially closed with 0.05 consistency (i.e., 5% fibers by mass) stock flowing into the pump and then the valve is suddenly opened. The consistency at the pump immediately changes to, say, 0.025 but this lower consistency stock does not reach the measurement probe and is not detected until some time later. This detection delay is called the dead time, T_d, of the process and is simply the transport time of stock from the pump to the probe, equal to the distance D divided by the stream velocity v.

In this process unit with pump consistency C_p as input, and the probe consistency C_m as output, changes in the input variable C_p are exactly reproduced at the probe T_d minutes later. This presents a difficult control challenge since there is no advance indication as to coming changes in the pipeline, and they happen as rapidly as the input changes. A dead time process does not smooth out rapid input fluctuations as a first order lag process does.

Second Order Processes. Consider the process shown in Fig. 1.10a, consisting of two stirred tanks in which paper stock is first diluted and then mixed with other ingredients. A measurement probe is located downstream from the second tank. The variables of interest are the consistency of the stock at various places in the process.

Each of the tanks is a first-order dynamic process with respect to consistency; that is, if a step change is made in the inlet consistency C_i to Tank 1, the outlet consistency C_1 changes according to a first-order exponential response. In the same way, a sudden change in Tank 2 inlet consistency C_1 causes the outlet consistency C_o to change in a similar first order manner.

If Tank 1 is considered to be a process unit with input C_i and output C_1, then the two tanks together comprise a second-order process made up of two

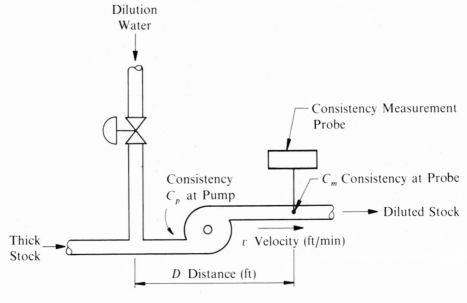

$$\text{Dead Time} = \frac{v}{D} = T_d \text{ (min)}$$

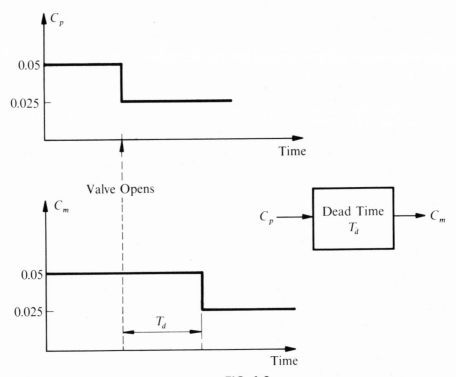

FIG. 1.9
Dead Time Process and Step Responses

cascaded first-order processes, where the output variable of the first process is an input variable to the second process. The block diagram for this cascade connection is shown in Fig. 1.10b. Since the consistency measuring probe is downstream from the tank outlet, there is a dead time T_d between outlet consistency C_o and the measured consistency C_p. This is shown in the block diagram as a third cascade process unit of pure dead time with input C_o and output C_p.

The response of each variable to a step change in inlet consistency C_i is shown in Fig. 1.10c. Taken together, the first two blocks comprise a second-order process and the C_o plot is a second-order response to a step input. The probe consistency C_p is an exact replica of C_o delayed by the dead time T_d.

The time constant of each of the two tanks is determined by the size of the tank. In general, the time constants are different. If they differ by more than a factor of 5 or so, then the response is dominated by the larger of the two and the second-order response C_o is very similar to a first-order response having the larger time constant. The C_o response illustrated in Fig. 1.10c is the response when the two time constants are approximately equal.

Higher Order Processes. For each mass or energy storage element in a system, there is one first-order dynamic element. Most real processes consist of many dynamic elements, each with a different time constant. Usually, most of the time constants are very small when compared to the largest time constant in the overall process and the largest time constant dominates the response. In addition, a large number of small time constants may combine to produce a lag that resembles pure dead time. Therefore, it is often possible to approximate the actual input-output relationship of a high-order and complex dynamic process with a simplified model consisting of a first or second-order process combined with a dead time element.

Process Noise. The above discussion and illustrative figures of process responses imply that process variables remain absolutely constant during steady-state. In actual processes, this ideal is not realized. Process variables, either inherently or as they are measured, usually exhibit noise; that is, they fluctuate, often in a completely random fashion, within a small band around their nominal value, which is the real quantity of interest.

These fluctuations may arise from process turbulence or from fluctuations in the measuring instruments, so-called "measurement noise." Process turbulence is common; for example, in tanks into which streams flow or which are vigorously agitated, the level in the tank is not well defined. In Fig. 1.5, the tank level is measured with a sight glass which provides considerable averaging. However, there may still be some noise or bounce in the sight glass level and a human reading the sight glass level naturally averages the varying reading.

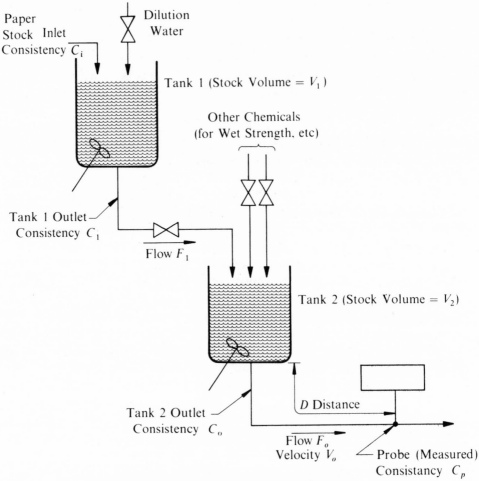

(a) Process Diagram and Variables of Interest
FIG. 1.10a

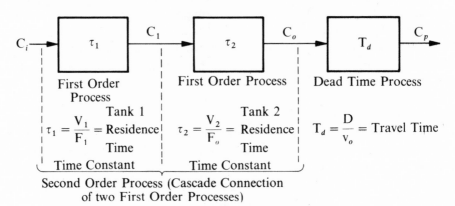

(b) Block Diagram
FIG. 1.10b

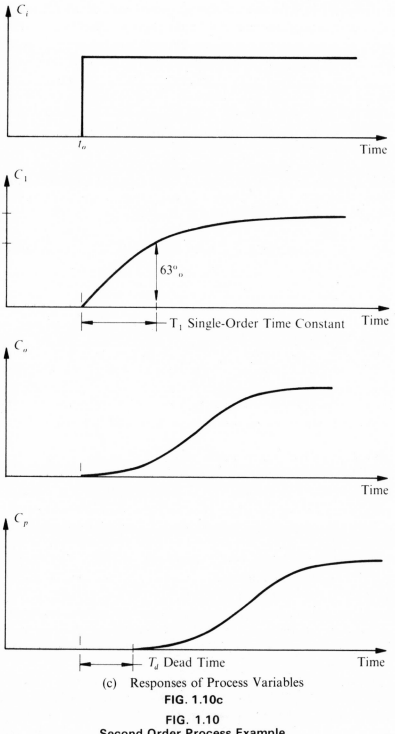

(c)   Responses of Process Variables

FIG. 1.10c

FIG. 1.10
Second Order Process Example

Regardless of the source of process noise, it is usually detrimental to control. There are a number of techniques for averaging (also called smoothing or filtering) the noise and reading only the average value of the variable. All such techniques require time, however, and delay in measurement always reduces the effectiveness of control. Too much smoothing is also detrimental in that important changes in the process variables may be smoothed out and thus missed. A good compromise between eliminating unwanted fluctuations and tracking meaningful variations in the process variable often is difficult to achieve.

Summary. The concepts of dynamic response and mathematical models have been developed here because they are fundamental; one cannot truly grasp the concepts of control without a clear understanding of what is meant by a dynamic process.

The modeling steps that have been developed above can be summarized as follows:

1. Define production objectives of the process.
2. Identify the key process variables which need to be controlled in order to meet production objectives. These are the process outputs.
3. Define the physical variables which affect the process output variables. These are the inputs. Some are disturbance inputs and some are control inputs.
4. The cause-effect relationships between the inputs and outputs are then quantitatively determined; this is the actual modeling step.

Feedback Controllers and Control Loops

The control loop is the basic unit of process control. Any industrial plant or process has dozens, hundreds, or sometimes even thousands, of control loops. Each has the purpose of keeping some process variable as near to its desired value as possible, as much of the time as possible, in spite of load upsets and without attention from an operator.

Before automatic controllers were developed, operators manually maintained process variables at their desired values. The operator periodically would mentally compare the measured value of the process variable against the desired value. If there was a difference (i.e., an error or deviation), the operator would change the manipulated variable (valve, or whatever) to reduce the error to zero.

The direction of the error indicated whether to increase or decrease the manipulated variable and the size of the error provided guidance in deciding how much to change the valve position. Also, the operator knew that it would take some time for the correction to occur (i.e., process time constant).

Through experience, the operator gained a "feel" for the process, how to manipulate it smoothly, and how often it required checking and correction.

Naturally, control in this manner was imprecise. An operator preoccupied with an emergency or other process problem easily could let a disturbance-caused deviation continue or get worse for long periods of time. In addition, each operator had an individual way of running the process and results varied accordingly. In essence, each operator developed a personal control strategy for each variable. One operator might, for example, make a single valve change of approximately the correct amount and then a later trim adjustment to correct any residual error as shown in Fig. 1.11a. A second operator might recognize that the process variable would return to target faster if the initial valve change was greater than needed (overdrive), followed by a second change at the appropriate time to the final value as shown in Fig. 1.11b. Of course, knowing the appropriate time requires additional knowledge of the process dynamics. Although both operators returned the process to its target, the cost of the two approaches may have been different. If the area under the deviation curve is proportional to the loss resulting from poor control, then the approach of the second operator minimizes the loss.

The control problem was complicated still further if disturbances occurred before the process recovered from the first load upset, and noise on the output measurement made matters even worse. For good control in many cases, almost constant attention was required, along with complete knowledge of process dynamics. Obviously, manual control was inadequate in many important instances and this led to the development of automatic process controllers.

Controllers. A controller is a device which automates the manual control techniques described above. Functionally, the controller continuously monitors the value of the process variable it is controlling, compares the value to the setpoint, calculates the difference (error), and makes continuous adjustments to the valve.

The change made to the manipulated variable is a dynamic function of error. The change is calculated from present and past values of error according to a formula or set of rules which is called the control strategy or control algorithm. Obviously, the control strategy must be designed using knowledge, of the dynamics of the process being controlled, as well as knowledge of the nature and magnitude of expected disturbances. Specification of control strategy is one of the key tasks for the control engineer. Control strategy alternatives, of both conventional and computer control, are developed in later sections.

Control Loops. Combining a controller with the process unit under control makes a control loop, the basic unit of process control. The loop block

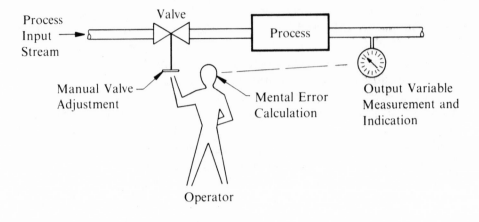

Process Input Stream

Valve

Process

Manual Valve Adjustment

Mental Error Calculation

Output Variable Measurement and Indication

Operator

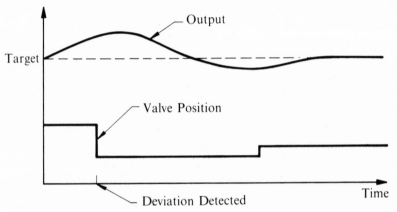

Target

Output

Valve Position

Deviation Detected

Time

(a) Operator #1: Control Strategy and Response

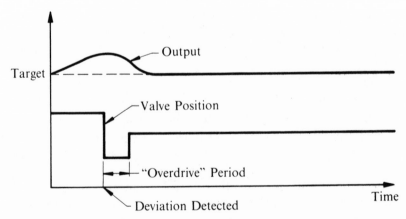

Target

Output

Valve Position

"Overdrive" Period

Deviation Detected

Time

(b) Operator #2: Control Strategy and Response

FIG. 1.11
Manual Control of a Process Variable

diagram is shown in Fig. 1.12. The process part of the loop includes the actuator and sensor and is a unit of the plant subsystem. The actuator, sensor, and transmitter are frequently referred to as process interface hardware, connecting the process to the controller.

In Fig. 1.12, the controller makes adjustments to the control input based on measurements of the output value which are continuously fed back to the controller. Hence, this approach to control is called feedback control or, sometimes, closed-loop control. The control loop is often called a feedback control loop.

Analog Versus Digital Control. An analog variable is one which can assume any value within a specified range. The literature is replete with references to analog and digital control. These are imprecise terms and refer more to the devices employed to do the controlling than to any fundamental difference in control strategy. Analog control generally means that each loop employs a packaged controller which continuously attends to the loop; that is, it monitors the process variable and determines a position for the process actuator at every instant of time. It also implies that the data processing (i.e., determining the error and computing the controller output) is done on an

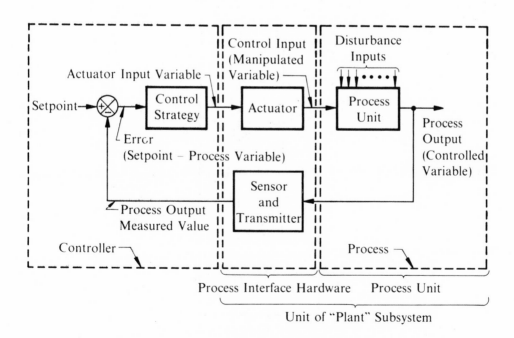

FIG. 1.12
Feedback Control Loop

analog basis. This means that the signals within the controller are all analog variables (voltages, currents or pressures).

Digital control, on the other hand, usually means that the process variable is sampled periodically and controller output to the actuators is updated at discrete time intervals. Generally, a digital computer which handles several loops on a time-sharing basis is the device doing the controlling. Control computations are done with digital hardware, such as digital adders and multipliers. Analog-to-digital (A/D) and digital-to-analog (D/A) converters are required on the input and output to the digital computer to provide compatibility with analog process signals.

Packaged Controllers. A number of manufacturers market self-contained universal analog process controllers which perform the controller functions described above. In addition to those automatic control functions, packaged controllers have provisions for manual operation; that is, it is possible to manually set the controller output to any desired value within its range. Some

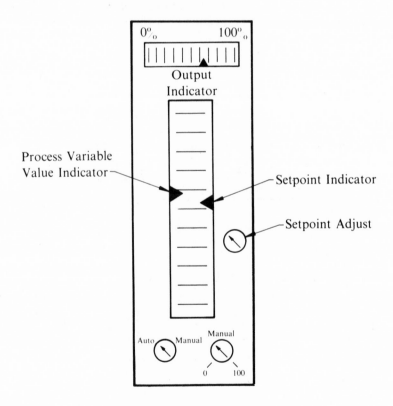

FIG. 1.13
Packaged Analog Process Controller

controllers also have the facility to continuously record one or more variables with an ink pen on a strip or circular chart.

Physically, controllers vary in size and configuration depending on manufacturer, whether or not they record, and whether they are to be located in a control panel or locally near the valve or sensor. A drawing of a typical panel-mounted controller without recording is shown in Fig. 1.13. The dimensions are typically two to three inches wide, six inches high, and 26 inches deep.

At one time, all controllers were pneumatic, operating on compressed air, with inputs and outputs spanning the standard range of 3 psig to 15 psig. Now, however, many electronic controllers are being used with inputs and outputs which are electrical current (or, less often, voltage). Several output current ranges are in use but 4 to 20 milliamperes is by far the most common and is an international standard.

Another feature available with most controllers is a remote set point which allows the setpoint to be adjusted by another device. Remote setpoint electronic controllers are used as slave controllers in cascade control loops and also with digital computers which adjust the setpoints.

Over the years, a somewhat universal control algorithm has evolved. It is called PID (Proportional, Integral, Derivative) or "three-mode" control and is tunable to the response characteristics of the process by adjusting two or three parameters in the controller. Basically, these parameters determine the amount of control action taken for a given process variable error and the speed at which the control action is taken. Parameters are adjustable over a very wide range so that the controller can provide satisfactory control for the majority of existing process units. As such, PID has become an almost universally used control algorithm for single variable analog control. The PID algorithm is described in more detail in the next section.

The control loop employing a packaged controller looks considerably different on a process flowsheet than it does in the block diagram form of Fig. 1.12. The flowsheet diagram of Fig. 1.14 shows a process unit which controls the temperature of a process stream by heating part of it with a steam heat exchanger and blending the hot stream with an unheated bypass stream. The bypass flow is controlled by a packaged controller with a pneumatically operated control valve as the process actuator. The process flow diagram shows the specific pieces of hardware and instruments, rather than the information or signal flow paths shown in the block diagram representation.

Control Strategies

In this section the basic PID control algorithm is developed in more detail. Situations in which PID control does not perform well are reviewed and some advanced control strategies for improved control in these situations are described.

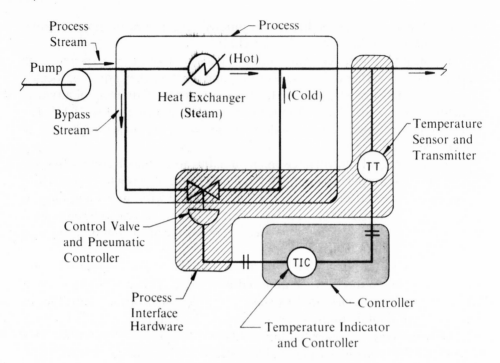

FIG. 1.14
Control Loop on a Process Flowsheet

PID Control. The PID (Proportional, Integral, Derivative) or three-mode control algorithm is the almost universally used control strategy in analog process controllers today. It encompasses a number of options, since it is possible to use only one or two of the three modes of control.

The control action (that is, the controller output to the actuator) in a PID controller is the sum of three separate terms, called modes: Proportional, Integral or Reset, and Derivative or Rate.

Proportional Control is the basic mode. It changes the output by an amount which is directly proportional to the error in the process variable: that is,

$$m = K_c \, e$$

where e is the process error (setpoint—process variable) and m is the change in controller output from the rest position. In a valve controller having only the proportional mode, this rest position is generally either fixed at 50% of the fully open valve position or manually adjustable with an adjustment called manual reset.

The constant of proportionally K_c is called the controller gain and is adjustable over a wide range (from 0.1 to 100 in most controllers). Controllers are sometimes calibrated in terms of proportional band P_B, which is the reciprocal of gain expressed as a percentage; that is,

$$P_B = \frac{100}{K_c}$$

Numerically, the proportional band is the percentage of its full range that the process variable must change to move the controller output from minimum to maximum. Thus, for example, a 50% proportional band corresponds to a gain of 2 and means that the output moves over its entire range for a 50% change in the process variable.

When gain or proportional band is a positive number, the controller output increases for positive errors and the controller is called direct acting. Some processes are such that the valve must be closed to increase the process variable value. In these cases, the controller output must decrease for positive errors and the controller is called reverse acting. Most modern controllers have a switch to change from direct to reverse acting.

With proportional-only control, the output cannot be at other than its rest position when error is zero. A permanent, nonzero error must exist to keep the output elsewhere within its range. Numerically, if the output must be kept m units away from its rest position, then a permanent steady-state error

$$e = \frac{m}{K_c} \tag{1.11}$$

must be maintained. If, for example, a valve rest position is 50% open and it needs to be at 75% to maintain the desired process variable value (a valve deviation of 25%), then a steady-state error of $25\%/5 = 5\%$ must be maintained for a controller gain of 5. This means that the controller setpoint must be set 5% higher than desired to achieve the actual desired value. This difference between the setpoint and the desired value is called steady-state offset. Equation 1.11 shows that for a given required deviation m, a higher controller gain K_c reduces the steady-state error e but it is zero only when $m = 0$.

Addition of the integral mode of control provides automatic reset, such that the output rest position is automatically readjusted to provide zero steady-state offset under all load and setpoint conditions. The integral mode moves the output an amount which is proportional to the integrated error; that is

$$m_I = K_R \int_0^t e(t)dt$$

where m_I is the change in controller output due to integral action from its original ($t = 0$) rest position, $e(t)$ is the process error as a function of time, and K_R is a gain factor. Thus, integral mode output is proportional to the area under the error versus time curve. As such, m_I is always changing as a function of time unless the error is zero. Figure 1.15 shows the error versus time curve during a typical loop response to a load upset and the corresponding controller integral mode output. The controller output remains constant only when the error is zero, and the new rest value of the controller output after the upset has settled is different from the original value. Thus, integral action has automatically reset the output to its new required position while maintaining zero steady-state error.

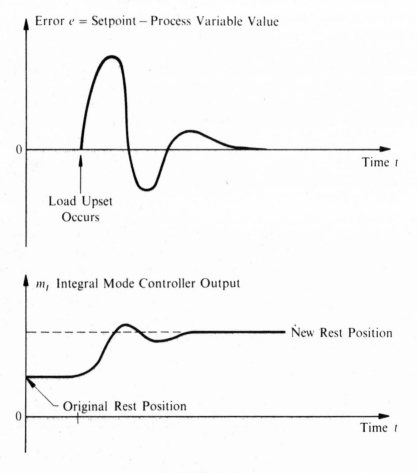

FIG. 1.15
Illustration of Integral Control Mode

The integral mode is almost always used in conjunction with the proportional mode, making a "two-mode" or PI controller. The two-mode controller is described by:

$$m = K_c\left(e + R_I \int_0^t e(t)dt + T_D\frac{de}{dt}\right)$$

The constant R_I is called the reset rate. Its units are repeats-per-minute and it is numerically equal to the number of times in one minute that the integral action repeats the proportional action if the error is constant. This idea can be clarified with the aid of Fig. 1.16. Assume that the error suddenly increases from zero to 1% at a time t_0 and remains at that value. At t_0, the controller output immediately increases by $K_c \times 1\%$ due to the proportional action. The integral action then increases the controller output at a steady rate equal to $K_c \times R_I$ percent/minute. When the controller output reaches twice its value at t_0 (in this case, $2K_c\%$), the integral action is said to have repeated the proportional action. The time required for one repeat is called the integral time T_I and is the reciprocal of the reset rate R_I:

$$T_I = \frac{1}{R_I}$$

The reset rate in commercial PI controllers is adjustable over a wide range, typically from 0.02 to 50 repeats/minute. Some controllers are calibrated directly in integral time.

The addition of the integral mode of control is a "destabilizing" factor and it generally increases the loop response time (typically 10 to 50% increase in settling time as compared to proportional only control). The integral mode has the single purpose of eliminating steady-state offset. This is so vital to so many process loops, however, that a very large majority of controllers installed have integral action.

Derivative control is a mode which improves the loop response. It is also known as rate action or anticipatory control. This mode changes the output by an amount which is proportional to the time rate of change of the error; that is,

$$m_D = K_D\frac{de}{dt}$$

where m_D is the change in controller output from rest due to derivative action, $\frac{de}{dt}$ is the rate of change of error, and K_D is a gain factor.

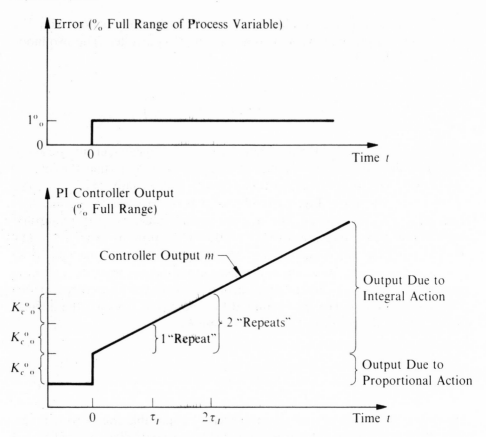

FIG. 1.16
PI Controller Output for Fixed Error Input

The effect of derivative mode is to add additional corrective action when the error is moving away from zero and to "put on the brakes" when the error is headed toward zero. Hence, the proper amount of derivative control improves response by reducing peak offset and settling time to a given load upset.

Derivative control never is used alone and seldom with just proportional control. When the derivative mode is added to PI, the complete PID control equation becomes:

$$m = K_c\left(e + R_I \int_0^t e(t)dt\right)$$

The derivative proportionality constant T_D has units of minutes. Its numerical value is the amount of corrective action (as a fraction of proportional action) taken by the derivative mode for each percent per minute rate of change of the error. It is adjustable over a wide range and on almost all PID controllers can be turned off completely.

In spite of the fact that derivative control improves response, it is not used as widely as might be expected for the following three reasons:

When the measured value of the process variable is noisy, derivative action amplifies the noise and causes more harm than good. The output is constantly modulating (which, in the case of a valve, wears it out faster) and the process constantly is perturbed by the noisy controller output. If the noise is at a much higher frequency than the rate at which real process variable changes occur, added filtering may eliminate its effect but this requires additional hardware. In addition, the added lag due to the filtering partially offsets the benefits of the derivative action.

When derivative control is used, the loop usually is more sensitive to changes in process parameters. A 10% change in a process parameter (such as gain, time constant, or dead time) in almost all cases degrades loop performance much more with a PID controller than with a PI controller.

PID controllers are more difficult to adjust properly than PI, having three parameters to adjust instead of two. The proper adjustment of controllers (called controller "tuning") is a subject about which reams of articles have been published and many good, simple-to-apply techniques have been devised. Nevertheless, many controllers are tuned using a "seat of the pants" technique and it is far more difficult to properly tune three-mode controllers by the "pants seat."

Fig. 1.17 shows the comparative responses of a typical control loop to a step change in load for no control, proportional only, PI, and PID control. It illustrates the highlights of the above discussion.

Problem Control Situations. There are a number of process situations in which PID control simply does not work very well. Poor control is recognizable by the process variable spending a lot of time far away from its setpoint. There are several imprecise words in the preceding sentence which indicates, correctly, that "poor" control is an imprecise concept. The relative quality of control can be quantified and compared by such measures as average deviation, RMS deviation, or peak-to-peak deviation over a given period of time. These measures all tell essentially the same empirical story: the width of the deviation band painted on the chart record of the process variable

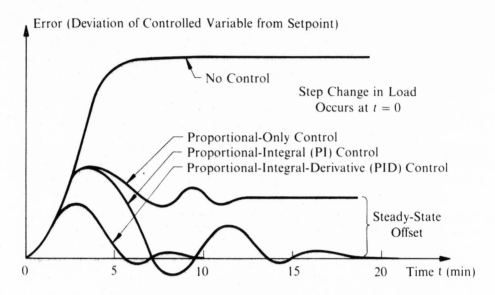

FIG. 1.17
Typical Control Loop Response to Step Load Upset

by a slow-moving recorder. The deviation of the process variable is an important and useful measure of control performance, particularly when comparing one control strategy with another for a given control loop, but it does not tell the whole story. Difficult control situations can also be recognized by some of the following behavior:

Loops which exhibit very dramatic changes in performance under different operating conditions, being very sluggish to respond at some times, wildly oscillatory (or even unstable) at other times; a highly variable deviation recording which is wide and wild at some times, narrow and well-behaved at others. These are characteristics of non-linear processes whose static and dynamic characteristics change substantially over the normal range of process operating conditions.

Loops which seem to affect each other so that when one loop is upset, the other follows, and vice-versa. These are coupled or interacting process variables.

Processes which are very sluggish and slow to respond. These are processes with problem dynamics: that is, the apparent dead time T_d is greater than the dominant time constant τ_c. The ratio T_d/τ_c is called the "Controllability factor" of the process and, the larger it is, the more difficult the control problem. Values of T_d/τ_c in excess of 1.0 signify troublesome situations where substantial improvements over PID control are possible with advanced techniques.

   Processes with a very wide deviation band relative to the desired range and accuracy of control. There are many causes for this problem, such as large disturbance inputs which act quickly on the process relative to its response time to control action, large inherent process noise, or noisy measuring instruments. It is especially troublesome if the frequency range of the noise or undesired process variation overlaps the frequency at which the loop responds to its own control action. In this case, it is not possible to remove the noise with filtering and either the sources of the noise must be eliminated or the reduced performance must be accepted.

   The approach to many of these control problems using conventional analog PID control is to tune the controller for the worst case and accept less than adequate control the rest of the time. Unfortunately, it is not always easy to recognize the worst case or to have it occur while the controllers are being tuned. An integrated, multi-product plant with a number of control loops on nonlinear, interacting process units can be a real control nightmare.

   Sometimes it is difficult to predict in advance exactly what control problems a process will have so they can be compensated in the original design. It is certainly true that many control problems are inherent in the process configuration and careful attention to control at design time is a more effective approach than solving unanticipated problems with advanced control techniques after the fact. Nevertheless, sometimes there is simply no alternative, and to make the product means to have difficult control situations. In these cases, some or all of the advanced control techniques described in the following section can be very valuable.

   "Advanced" Control Strategies. After the original development of control theory in the late 1930's and early 1940's, considerable theoretical investigation was devoted to finding better ways to do control. Many promising approaches have been developed over the years. Some proved useful immediately, but many others essentially were shelved due to lack of practical hardware to implement them. When digital computers first became available for process control in the 1960's, some hardware limitations were removed. Since that time, many of the promising approaches have been tried, proven, and applied. The following paragraphs are a brief description of the more widely known, useful, or promising of these so-called "advanced" techniques.

   Cascade Control is probably the oldest and most widely used of the advanced strategies, since it is easily implemented with analog hardware. It involves using a second controller to regulate the control input of the primary variable which is most often a flow. The second controller used in this "inner loop" is called a slave; the primary or master controller changes the setpoint of the slave controller rather than the valve position directly. Cascade control improves performance by removing the effect of a disturbance on the control input before it affects the primary variable. It also can, if properly applied, speed up the loop response and help overcome the effect of some process nonlinearities. Some installations have used double (two inner loops) or triple cascaded systems.

Feedforward Control also is used rather widely and is implementable with analog hardware, although not as readily as cascade control. Feedforward is used to reduce the effects of large, known, and measurable disturbance input variables. In concept, the known disturbance is measured and, when a change is detected, an adjustment is made to the valve to compensate for the predicted effect of the disturbance. In some cases, the valve adjustment is delayed to compensate for differences between the dynamic response time of the process variable due to the disturbance and those due to the valve. Thus, the valve is adjusted by two different sources, the feedback controller and the feedforward controller. It is possible to use more than one feedforward adjustment if there is more than one significant, measurable disturbance.

Feedforward works best if the disturbance inputs are large, relatively infrequent step changes (such as the load on a steam boiler or on a generator), rather than higher frequency random noise. When properly applied and adjusted, it can provide truly dramatic performance improvements.

Multivariable Control overcomes the problem of interaction where the controlled variable is affected by more than one manipulated variable. Interaction problems are severe in oil refining, many chemical manufacturing processes, pulp and paper, and numerous other common processes. Two loops which are coupled sufficiently to one another can lead to instability under conditions which would yield stable behavior without the coupling. Interaction problems normally are solved by detuning or desensitizing one of the coupled loops, so that it responds much more slowly than the other. This provides stability, but often at the sacrifice of performance.

A control technique known as decoupling can make each loop behave as though unaffected by any others. The approach is similar in concept to multiple feedforward strategies, in that each manipulated variable, other than the primary, is considered a disturbance input and measured changes in it are used to adjust directly the primary manipulated variable, exactly as in feedforward control. When a disturbance affects one of the loops, all the manipulated variables are adjusted such that the disturbed loop settles quickly, and all other coupled variables move very little or not at all if decoupling is perfect.

Decoupling is practically implemented only with digital computers even when as few as two loops are involved. It is a complex procedure which requires considerable design effort and computation based on accurate models during operation. The payoffs can be very significant, however.

Dead-Time Compensation techniques can vastly improve the speed of response and deviation band of the process variable in loops where the dead time is significant. Two techniques (due to O. J. M. Smith and to E. Dahlin) are in use today. They are similar in that they both employ process models. Conceptually, the manipulated variable input is applied to the model as well as the process, and the feedback control action is based on the model output with dead time eliminated. Differences between the actual process output and the predicted process output from the model with dead time are used to correct the control signal.

The techniques work exceptionally well but need a good model. As a result, process gain, dead time, and dominant time constant must be known accurately, to within about 10–20% of actual values. Gross errors in modeling can lead to poorer (even unstable) performance as compared to conventional PID control. Dead time compensation algorithms are always implemented with digital computers because of the difficulty of accurately simulating dead time with analog hardware. They are used widely today, along with multivariable decoupling, in the computer control of basis weight and moisture on paper machines.

Adaptive Control is an often used, but imprecise, term applied to a variety of control schemes. The concept common to these schemes is that the control strategy is changed in some way during actual process operation to adapt to changing process conditions, so as to realize the best control under all conditions.

Most applied adaptive control systems adjust one or two parameters in the control algorithm, based on identification of process parameters. In a typical approach, controller gain is adjusted, based on the identified value of process gain such that the loop gain (product of controller and process gain) remains constant.

Identification is an inherent part of all adaptive control approaches. It can be either indirect or direct. Indirect, or inferential, identification relies on a known relationship between the process parameter(s) of interest and a variable which is easily measured, generally the process output, input, or error. So-called nonlinear controllers, which have a variable gain as a function of error, are in this category. Direct, or on-line, identification uses sophisticated analysis techniques on the process output or error to discern the value of the process parameter of interest. Sometimes the analysis is made on actual process operating signals, whereas other techniques require deliberate perturbation of the process inputs. Perhaps because of its complexity, on-line adaptive control has not been widely applied, even though there are many situations where it could bring substantial benefits.

Optimal Control is another imprecise name applied to a variety of schemes. One class of these techniques is adaptive control, which adjusts controller parameters on-line to minimize the value of some measure of performance, typically the variance or spread of the error. Another class of optimal control utilizes a complex control strategy, which is derived off-line based on minimizing the value of a performance parameter which is a weighted average of error variance and average control effort. It requires an accurate model of the process and accurate knowledge of the statistical properties of the disturbance inputs and measurement noise, if the control strategy is to be optimal in any sense. Such names as "Kalman filtering" and "dynamic optimal control" are applied to this class of control schemes. Although they are applicable to multivariable processes, techniques from this class have not been applied, probably because of the extensive process knowledge required.

Another class, called time-optimal control methods, minimizes the time required to change from one process state to another and have been applied. They are particularly useful in large processes with long response times, where grade changes are made relatively frequently (an example is refinery distillation towers). These methods operate in much the same way as the drag racing youth, who operates either at full throttle or full braking between one traffic light and the next. They employ a control strategy based on a process model to decide when to switch from full (valve wide open), to zero (valve closed), and then to final valve position. Because the valve switches from fully open to fully closed and vice-versa, time-optimal control is often called "bang-bang" control. It was used widely in the space program and is finding its way into industrial control systems.

Predictive Control techniques usually are used in batch processes for "target," or endpoint, control. They use process models applied to measurements made during processing to predict the value of an important process variable which, for one reason or another, is not directly measurable. When the predicted value of the variable reaches its desired value, the process operation is stopped. For example, in batch pulp digesters, the current Kappa number (a measure of digesting completeness) is predicted as a function of the area under the digester temperature versus time curve. When the prediction equals the desired final value, the digester is emptied. Predictive control sometimes is combined with adaptive control such that differences between actual values measured after processing and predicted values are used to update the process model on which predictions are based. Predictive control can improve greatly the efficiency of batch processes and, as such, substantially raise the capacity of a given process facility.

These advanced control strategies represent a fairly comprehensive review of what is available and in use today. Almost all are model-based; that is, they make use of a built-in process model to determine controller output as a function or error and, sometimes, additional measurements. They are all more complex and difficult to implement than conventional PID control. Although some can be implemented with special purpose analog hardware, in many cases digital computers are the only available devices on which the strategy can be realized. The digital computer can be used to implement all of the above strategies, including conventional PID, and often it is less expensive even when analog hardware is available. In every case, digital computer implementation provides a degree of flexibility for refinements and changes far beyond that provided by analog hardware. This is because the same hardware is used to implement any of the strategies, and changes in strategy are accomplished by changes in programming.

Direct Versus Supervisory Control

The discussion thus far has been concerned with ways to keep the values of a controlled process variable as near to its setpoint as possible as much of the time as possible. The setpoints, whether fixed or changing according to some prescribed program, are determined by operators or some other means not related to the control function. As far as the control strategy is concerned, the setpoint is a given value. This kind of control is called direct control (or sometimes final control), since it is applied directly to the single variable feedback control loop as developed in the preceding text.

As noted earlier, setpoints are chosen so that the production objectives of the process will be met. In many processes the setpoint selection is made in a very imprecise way by operators and production managers, so that their production objectives are maximized, at least in some approximate way. Often there are a number of objectives, such as maximum production rate and minimum cost of energy, which are desirable simultaneously but which compete with one another. As a result, tradeoffs must be determined. The final selection generally is based on experience, trial and error, and many other factors which are difficult to quantify. Anyone who has ever worked in a processing plant knows that operators and production managers often do not agree on the "right" setpoints. A frequently observed situation is for each operator to have his own way of running the process and to see a different set of setpoints on each shift as the operators change.

Supervisory Control. The next level above direct control, in what often is called the heirarchy of control, is the supervisory control function. Supervisory control refers to a methodical, quantitative approach to determining the best setpoints for the direct controllers, either as functions of time or, more generally, as functions of the inputs to the system. Such inputs might be raw material properties, product specifications, external disturbances, and economic factors, so that system performance is maximized within whatever operating constraints might exist.

A supervisory control program has three parts:

A performance measure which is used to compare alternatives. Ideally, this is an objective function which has a single numerical value for each set of operating conditions.

A model which relates the setpoints (or, actually, the operating value of the process variables), and possibly the external factors and system inputs discussed earlier, to the performance measure.

A method or technique for determining, in a systematic manner, the setpoints which give the best performance (i.e., the highest value of the performance measure).

Hence, supervisory control is, in some loose sense, concerned with optimizing the process operation by selecting setpoints which give the best performance.

In a large class of supervisory control applications called program control, the objective is to take the process to a new operating point in the shortest possible time, consistent with whatever constraints may be required on some process variables. The measure of performance here is simply time, from the start to the new steady state. The supervisory control function specifies the setpoint trajectories as functions of time to accomplish the change in a coordinated manner. An example was given earlier in Fig. 1.1, showing setpoint trajectories for a coordinated grade change on a paper machine. Usually, but not always, the setpoints change at rates which are slow compared to the individual loop response time, so that the dynamics of individual loops need not be considered and the process variable trajectories closely follow the setpoint trajectories. Program control is used for process startup, shutdown and grade changes, and in many batch processes where the entire operation is cyclical.

Other applications of supervisory control are aimed at optimization of the performance measure under changing external or process conditions. It is assumed that, at any given time, there is a single set of setpoints which yield the best performance and that this optimal operating point changes, hopefully slowly, as external factors change. The ideal supervisory control system would find and track the optimum. Most actual applications fall far short of this ideal, but still are capable of realizing substantial benefits when compared to the imprecise techniques available to many operators.

Many sophisticated techniques have been developed for solving optimization problems of this type on digital computers. Problems of this type are called static optimization problems and the techniques for solving them are called linear and nonlinear programming methods. In practice, the solution is only as good as the model on which it is based. Some attempts have been made to do on-line model development and refinement via perturbation or hill-climbing techniques along with the optimization. There have been cautious reports of success, but the large majority of supervisory control applications in use today employ off-line optimization with a great deal of input from the operators and production managers. In many applications, there is merely an implied optimization of some not-very-well defined objective which is realized, usually very approximately, by the supervisory control algorithm.

Sequencing Control. Another category of control functions, different from the regulation and supervisory functions discussed in this chapter, is concerned with carrying out a series of process steps in a prescribed order, such as starting and stopping motors on drives or pumps and opening and closing valves. Some sequencing functions are part of almost every process computer application and, particularly in batch or production line plant automation applications, sequencing may be the only control carried out by the computer. In sequencing control, "on" or "off" are the only two possible conditions for process equipment.

Computers are also capable of implementing the logic and interlocking functions typically found where sequencing control is used. A special kind of minicomputer, called a Programmable Logic Controller (PLC), is currently being marketed by several manufacturers for sequencing and logic functions as applied to batch processes, discrete manufacturing processes, and packaging operations. The PLC originally was developed for the automobile industry and it greatly reduced costs associated with control changes for model changeovers. Rather than extensive reworking of large cabinets of electromechanical relays, the sequencing and logic can be changed completely in a PLC simply by changing the program in its storage.

INFORMATION SYSTEMS

The two broad classifications of functions performed by a digital computer system in an on-line process application are control functions and information functions. Control functions, as discussed in detail above, are related to process manipulations which cause the process to change in some way. Information functions (sometimes more broadly referred to as non-control functions) are related to process data gathering. The functions include sorting, evaluating, conditioning, processing, analyzing, storing, and presenting data to operators and others in ways which are useful to them. Information functions do not change the process in any direct way. Any changes are made by operators, based on their interpretation and evaluation of the information made available to them by the system.

Many installations of on-line digital computers have no control functions associated with them. They are "information only" systems, often called Process Monitors. An intermediate category is the so-called Operator Guide control system, in which operators take control action based on information and recommendations provided by the computer. If the information supplied to the operator is a specific suggested control action, such as a change in the setpoint of an analog control loop, it is probably appropriate to term it a control system, even though there is operator intervention. Any information needing operator interpretation (such as yields or efficiencies) before action is taken, should be included in the information classification.

Unlike control functions, information system tasks, procedures, and objectives are often easier to comprehend and far more visible than control functions. Often the most impressive part of an on-line computer facility are the many communication devices, such as printers, plotters, and CRT's (TV screen displays) presenting process data continuously in very impressive forms.

The functions of any information system, whether or not it utilizes a computer, can be classified conveniently into four categories:

(1) Data acquisition (gathering)
(2) Data storage (retention and recording)
(3) Data processing (analysis)
(4) Data communication (presentation)

Within each category, numerous functions can be included. The functions performed by any specific information system are chosen to satisfy the need of the application, and are limited only by the imagination and creativity of the system designers and users. Some of the more common functions of information systems are described briefly below.

Data Acquisition

The first step in any information system is obtaining data. The primary sources of data are process sensors and the process operators and managers, who enter data through input devices, such as keyboards, thumbswitches, and potentiometers. Discrete event sensors, such as malfunction indicators, sequencing switches, and other digital inputs, also are important sources of data.

In digital computer systems, analog data are gathered through A/D (analog-to-digital) converters and multiplexers, which are described in more detail in Chapter 3. Data acquisition functions for computer-based information systems include reading all variables at prescribed frequencies or times, and conversion of the reading to engineering units. Two additional functions usually included in this category, even though they involve some processing or calculation, are smoothing or filtering to eliminate process noise and limit checking against preset limits to detect abnormal conditions. Out-of-limits conditions are passed on to data processing routines to alarm or take other appropriate actions.

Data Storage

Retaining records of key process variable values is a second important function of an information system. In conventional non-computer process information systems, process variable values are recorded on strip or circular charts which are retained for process records. Recovery of data in this form for troubleshooting or other purposes is a tedious procedure. Furthermore, the reliability of the data collection is relatively low due to factors such as pens running out of ink and charts not being replaced on time. The recording function as an operating aid easily is provided in computer-based systems by using graphic CRT displays.

Operating logs and production records are also part of most information systems. In conventional systems these generally are maintained by operators and are subject to the same uncertain reliability as data gathered by process recorders. Emergencies easily can interfere with data being taken or recorded accurately or on time. Furthermore, almost all data taken by operators are to some extent altered by wishful thinking, as has been shown many times in comparisons with unbiased, machine-based data loggers.

These recording, logging, and reporting functions easily can be automated completely. All manner of reports are possible, at scheduled times or cued by process events such as the completion of a batch or after a reel turn-up on a paper machine. When data from past operation need to be examined for process troubleshooting, this can be done at high speed by the computer to spot appropriate conditions, print out only pertinent data, and thus significantly reduce the tedium of searching through reams of past process chart recordings and logs.

Long term automatic data storage frees the operator from routine chores and provides more reliable, more frequent, and more accurate data. In many cases, it serves as a source of backup documentation against possible future legal claims. Federal and state legislation require extensive record keeping in some product areas and computer-based information systems often are used to provide compliance at the lowest cost.

Data Processing

The real power of a computer-based information system is its ability to process data, since very little data processing is done in conventional information systems. In computer-based systems, there is almost no limit to the analysis which can be done. Some typical functions, often carried out in on-line computer systems, are described below:

Sensor correction and calibration. Many measurement systems, particularly those which employ complex analyzers for quality or composition measurements, are subject to drift or gradual changes in parameter values. These sources of errors may be eliminated by periodic calibration or standardization performed automatically by the computer. This is done by checking readings against a calibration standard and adjusting the scale factors.

Sensor correction for inherent nonlinearities or other known sources of error also is accomplished easily. Examples are linearization of thermocouple outputs, conversion of the pressure drop across an orifice to a flow reading, and correction of gas flow reading to SCFM, using associated temperature and pressure measurements.

Process Monitoring and Alarming. Limit checking to detect abnormal process conditions or malfunctioning instruments commonly is included as part of the data acquisition function. However, computer systems can do many more sophisticated functions than simple limit checking and alarming. Examples include trend analysis and warnings of possible dangerous or runaway conditions, mutli-level limit checking with different actions taken at each level (perhaps alarming at one level, switching to alternate control strategy at a second, and process shutdown at a third), and frequency analysis of process problems or incipient equipment failures.

Calculation of Inferred Variables. There are many cases where variables not directly measurable, but which can be calculated as a function of several measured variables, are valuable for control or process performance evaluation. Examples include heat flux, reflux ratios, catalyst activity, heat transfer coefficient, and material and energy balances. Performance evaluation is assisted by calculation of quantities, such as yield, efficiencies, product quality, average and spreads of process variables, costs, energy usage, and other performance measures of interest. These calculations are done easily and in a timely manner with the computer.

Process Modeling. Various advanced mathematical analysis techniques are useful in determining process parameters for control functions. Such techniques include frequency analysis and spectral density of process variables, regression (fitting of curves to process data), cross-correlation of process variables to determine coupling dynamics or to identify related causes and effects, and statistical analyses of process variables. An experienced control engineer or process analyst is needed to interpret the results of these analyses but, properly used, they can be powerful techniques in improving control or solving process problems.

Data Sorting. Data in storage can be searched and sorted against various criteria for regularly scheduled or exception reporting. The powerful sorting capabilities of a computer are, in fact, one of its most valuable assets in providing better operation through improved operator and management reporting. One-time sorts for activities related to tasks such as trouble shooting or de-bottlenecking, also are accomplished easily.

Data Communication

Presentation of information to operators and management takes various forms. In conventional installations, process indicators, such as scales and pointers, and recorders, are the primary operator communication devices with lights to indicate events such as process sequencing and alarms. In some newer installations, digital display devices are used for some process variables.

In computer-based systems, data presentation basically takes two forms: tabular lists of data or plots on either conventional recording devices or on computer devices such as CRT displays, printers, plotters, and teletypewriters. In conventional systems, there is little flexibility in selective display; generally information is available all the time, whether it is needed or not, or not at all. This has led to control rooms with instrument panels so large that it requires a number of operators just to monitor them. A real advantage of computer systems is in the selective display of data; information is displayed only when it is needed either on an operator's command or automatically in response to process conditions. Modern computer output devices, such as color CRT's and high-speed printer-plotters, provide the opportunity for truly impressive and significant advances in man-machine communications. Control panels with hundreds of indicators, recorders, and alarms, have been replaced with a single desk-size console with CRT, keyboard, and hard-copy output device. With the rapidly decreasing cost of such devices and their inherent advantages, much progress can be expected in this area within the next 5 to 10 years.

Application of digital computers to control and information system functions has been discussed in this chapter. There is hardly an industry that has not realized benefits from on-line computer applications for control and information processing.

Other Application Areas

There are a number of tasks to which on-line computer systems have been applied profitably, which are related closely to the scope of this book; for completeness, they are briefly reviewed here.

Automatic Testing. Quality control has improved by orders of magnitude with the advent of computer application to testing. Typically, every unit is tested, far more thoroughly than in pre-computer days when only spot checks and a few simple tests were made. A number of companies market circuit board testing systems, for example, which perform 9000 separate tests on a board in 5 seconds according to a testing program entered into the computer. Extensive use of computers for testing is made in the auto industry (for engines, carburetors, transmissions, tires, etc.) and a multitude of consumer goods industries.

Automatic Inspection. Related to automatic testing is the application of pattern recognition techniques to video images in order to identify defects formerly requiring a human inspector to detect visually. This has been applied to web inspection in the paper, steel, aluminium and glass industries, as well as to circuit board inspection after etching.

Laboratory Automation. Computers are being applied routinely to complex analytical laboratory instruments, such as chromatographs, mass spectrometers, and automatic titrators. They typically provide sequencing control, automatic data collection rates up to 20,000 samples per second, data analysis to determine results, and printout of reports. Increasing applications of automatic laboratory analysis also are being included with installations of on-line computers for process control and information systems.

Numerical Control. The programmed control of the cutting pattern for large, precision machine tools is called Numerical Control. It has been an established technique for years and is applied routinely to large machine tools such as lathes and punch presses. In recent years minicomputers have replaced the more conventional numerical control hardware, adding the power to generate patterns as well as follow them.

Automatic Troubleshooting. An interesting application of computers is the diagnosis of problems in mechanical, electronic, or process equipment with special testing and analysis programs. Some computers are programmed to detect process abnormalities and run an automatic diagnostic procedure in response. Computers can also troubleshoot themselves since extensive diagnostic software is available for most computers.

A FINAL THOUGHT

To add perspective, it is appropriate to conclude this introduction to industrial computer control and information systems with the warning that computers do not always realize benefits and they certainly do not do so automatically. Computers add complexity to the process that sometimes may not be needed; the potential for improvements in process operation just may not exist or it may be too small to justify the added complexity and cost of the computer system. Many on-line computer systems, particularly multitask, centralized systems which handle large processes, require full-time staffing with highly skilled personnel and this adds more people to the payroll. The support of the computer staff must come from benefits directly attributable to the computer.

Thus, with appropriate caution, it is reiterated that the potential benefits of on-line computer applications are many, varied, vast, and sometimes intangible; benefits can and should be predicted by control engineers who evaluate what is possible and by management who evaluates what they are worth. The following chapters provide additional information and insight into many of the ideas introduced in this chapter.

BIBLIOGRAPHY

Anderson, N. A., *Instrumentation for Process Measurement and Control*, 2nd Ed., Chilton Company, Philadelphia, 1972.

Coughanower, D. R. and Koppel, L. B., *Process Systems Analysis and Control*, McGraw-Hill Book Co., New York, 1965.

Dorf, R. C., *Modern Control Systems*, 2nd Ed., Addison-Wesley, Reading, MA, 1972.

Douglas, J. M., *Process Dynamics and Control*, Vol. 1 and 2, Prentice-Hall, Englewood Cliffs, N.J., 1972.

Harriot, P., *Process Control*, McGraw-Hill Book Co., New York, 1964.

Harrison, T. J., *Handbook of Industrial Control Computers*, John Wiley & Sons, New York, 1972.

Savas, E. S., *Computer Control of Industrial Processes*, McGraw-Hill Book Co., New York, 1965. (Somewhat dated but still a "classic" text.)

Shinsky, F. G., *Process Control Systems*, McGraw-Hill Book Co., New York, 1967.

Smith, C. L., *Digital Computer Process Control*, Intext Educational Publishers, Scranton, 1972.

Smith, C. L., "Digital Control of Industrial Processes," *ACM Computing Surveys*, Vol. 2, No. 3, September, 1970, pp. 211–241. (Excellent comprehensive survey article which contains an extensive, annotated bibliography.)

2 PRINCIPLES OF COMPUTER HARDWARE

Thomas J. Harrison, Ph.D.
INTERNATIONAL BUSINESS MACHINES CORPORATION,
BOCA RATON, FLORIDA

Computers are information processors. The information to be processed by the industrial control computer is derived from a variety of sources and exists naturally in a variety of forms. For example, information may be derived from the programmer in the form of programs punched into cards or tape, from the operator via a keyboard or switches on a console, from another computer via telephone lines or from a measurement sensor. The information may be numeric in nature, such as the value of a setpoint being equal to 37.1, it may be alphanumeric as in the name of a control element such as FRC-5, or it may be an analog quantity, such as the output of a thermocouple or a flowmeter. Independent of its source and its original form, however, information must be converted to a special numeric form to be processed by a digital computer. This is because digital computers internally deal only with numeric representations of information.

In the early part of this chapter the internal numeric representation used by modern computers is described. The representation is based on the binary number system which uses only the digits 1 and 0. Alphanumeric data can also be represented with only these two digits when the appropriate coding is used. An example of a coding method for this type of data is discussed. The question of how analog and other data derived directly from the process is converted into the internal numeric representation of the computer is considered in Chapter 3.

After understanding the internal representation of data and its coding, the circuits used in the computer for manipulating data, known as the computer logic, are considered by way of several simple examples. A hypothetical computer utilizing these elements is described and it is shown how it can be programmed to perform a simple valve control application.

The hypothetical computer used for illustration is much simpler than the modern minicomputer. It is, however, useful to explain the operation of the hardware. The organization and characteristics of the modern minicompeter are then described. Finally, there is a brief section discussing the costs of hardware and the comparison of various computers.

NUMBER SYSTEMS

The numeric representation with which most people are familiar is known as the decimal system. It uses the ten symbols 0, 1, 2, 3, 4, 5, 6, 7, 8, and 9, which are arranged in sequences that represent the quantity of whatever is being enumerated. Thus, for example, the symbol 237 means that there are two hundred thirty seven items in the set of things being considered. This, however, is not the only way that this quantity can be represented in a symbolic notation. For example, if we use the binary numbering system, this same quantity is represented by the symbol 11101101. This appears to be an inefficient representation since it takes eight digits to represent a number which, in the decimal system, only requires three digits. While this is true, there are valid reasons which are discussed later why the binary system is preferable for use in digital computers. Before addressing these reasons, however, let us consider the question of numeric representation in more detail.

If we consider the number 237, what we mean to express is that there are 2 hundreds, 3 tens, and 7 single units. That is:

$$237 = 200 + 30 + 7 = 2 \times 100 + 3 \times 10 + 7 \times 1$$

This can also be expressed as:

$$237 = 2 \times 10^2 + 3 \times 10^1 + 7 \times 10^0$$

where the scientific notation $100 = 10^2$, $10 = 10^1$, and $1 = 10^0$ makes it clear that the decimal notation is based on powers of 10. The base number 10 is called the radix and any decimal number can be represented in terms of powers of 10. It should also be noted that the number of unique symbols (i.e., 0, 1, 2, 3,...,9) required to express the number is exactly equal to the radix value.

There is nothing unique about the number 10 (except, perhaps, that man learned to count on his fingers and he happens to have 10 fingers) and any other number can be equally well chosen as the radix or base of a number system. Thus, for example, if base 5 is chosen:

$$237_{(10)} = 1 \times 5^3 + 4 \times 5^2 + 2 \times 5^1 + 2 \times 5^0$$
$$= 1422_{(5)}$$

Here again, note that the number of symbols necessary to express the number is equal to the value of the radix; namely, the symbols are 0, 1, 2, 3, and 4, for the base 5 number system.

In the case of modern digital computers, the radix most commonly chosen is 2, which results in what is called the binary number system. The number of symbols used in the binary number system is two; namely, 0 and 1. The 1 and 0 are called bits, a contraction of the words binary digit. The binary system of numeric representation is used because it is particularly easy to build electronic circuits to manipulate two states that represent the digits 0 and 1. A simple transistor switch can be turned "on" to represent the 1 or "off" to represent the 0. On the other hand, building an electronic circuit which is either "on," "partially on," or "off," as would be required for a base 3 representation, is much more difficult and requires more transistors. As a result, it has been determined that the optimum number system for computers is the binary, or base 2, system.

Although confusing at first, the binary system is relatively easy to understand. As in the case of the decimal system, each position within the binary numeral represents the base two raised to a power. Thus, the right-most bit has a decimal value of $2^0 = 1$, the next has a value of $2^1 = 2$, the next $2^2 = 4$, etc. For example:

$$1101_{(2)} = 1 \times 2^3 + 1 \times 2^2 + 0 \times 2^1 + 1 \times 2^0$$
$$= \quad 8 \quad + \quad 4 \quad + \quad 0 \quad + \quad 1$$
$$= \quad 13_{(10)}$$

Converting Binary to Decimal

The conversion of a binary number to a decimal number is easily performed. One merely represents the number as in the above example and sums up the decimal values represented by the positions that contain a 1 digit. As another example:

$$11001_{(2)} = 1 \times 2^4 + 1 \times 2^3 + 0 \times 2^2 + 0 \times 2^1 + 1 \times 2^0$$
$$= \quad 16 \quad + \quad 8 \quad + \quad 0 \quad + \quad 0 \quad + \quad 1$$
$$= \quad 25_{(10)}$$

Converting Decimal to Binary

The conversion of a decimal number into a binary number is somewhat more complex. One method consists of successive divisions of the decimal number by the radix 2. At each step, the remainder of the division is either 1 or 0 and this remainder is recorded. The sequence of remainders, taken in reverse order, is the desired binary number. This is demonstrated by the following example: Consider the decimal number 237 and successively divide by 2, recording the remainders:

Remainder

$$
\begin{array}{r|l}
2 & \underline{237} \\
 & 118 \quad\quad 1
\end{array}
$$

$$
\begin{array}{r|l}
2 & \underline{118} \\
 & 59 \quad\quad 0
\end{array}
$$

$$
\begin{array}{r|l}
2 & \underline{59} \\
 & 29 \quad\quad 1
\end{array}
$$

$$
\begin{array}{r|l}
2 & \underline{29} \\
 & 14 \quad\quad 1
\end{array}
$$

$$
\begin{array}{r|l}
2 & \underline{14} \\
 & 7 \quad\quad 0
\end{array}
$$

$$
\begin{array}{r|l}
2 & \underline{7} \\
 & 3 \quad\quad 1
\end{array}
$$

$$
\begin{array}{r|l}
2 & \underline{3} \\
 & 1 \quad\quad 1
\end{array}
$$

$$
\begin{array}{r|l}
2 & \underline{1} \\
 & 0 \quad\quad 1
\end{array}
$$

The remainders, taken in reverse order (i.e., from bottom to top), form the binary number 11101101.

Octal and Hexadecimal Notation

The inefficiency of the binary notation for human use is obvious from the above examples. It takes more than three bits to represent each decimal digit. For example, the decimal number 56222 is represented in binary as 1101101110011110. In dealing with such a long string of 1's and 0's, the human is very prone to making mistakes. Therefore, it is convenient to use a shorthand notation that is more convenient for human use. Two such notational systems are in common use and they are based on the fact that there is a one-to-one correspondence between three-bit binary numbers and the eight digits required in a base 8 or octal system and, similarly, between four-bit binary numbers and the 16 digits required in a base 16 or hexadecimal system. This is illustrated in the following tabulations:

Binary	Octal	Decimal
000	0	0
001	1	1
010	2	2
011	3	3
100	4	4
101	5	5
110	6	6
111	7	7

Binary	Hexadecimal	Decimal
0000	0	0
0001	1	1
0010	2	2
0011	3	3
0100	4	4
0101	5	5
0110	6	6
0111	7	7
1000	8	8
1001	9	9
1010	A	10
1011	B	11
1100	C	12
1101	D	13
1110	E	14
1111	F	15

In the hexadecimal system, sixteen symbols are required so that, in addition to the ten digits, the letters A through F are used.

As an example of how the octal and hexadecimal notations are used, consider the binary representation of the decimal number 56222 which was used above. The binary representation is 1101101110011110. To convert this to octal notation, the number is separated into three-bit groups and the appropriate octal digit is substituted:

$$1101101110011110_{(2)} = 1 \ 101 \ 101 \ 110 \ 011 \ 110$$
$$= 1 \quad 5 \quad 5 \quad 6 \quad 3 \quad 5$$
$$= 155635_{(8)}$$

Similarly, to convert to hexadecimal, the binary number is divided into groups of four bits and the appropriate symbol is substituted.

$$1101101110011110_{(2)} = 1101 \ 1011 \ 1001 \ 1110$$
$$= \quad D \quad B \quad 9 \quad E$$
$$= DB9E_{(16)}$$

It must be emphasized that the octal and hexadecimal notation is used only as a convenient notation for the human. Internal to the machine, the numbers are stored and manipulated in terms of the 1's and 0's of the binary notation

Arithmetic Operations

The addition, subtraction, division, and multiplication rules in the decimal system are well known. Similar rules which allow the same computations exist in number systems based on different radices. For example, in the binary system, the rules for addition are:

$$
\begin{array}{cccc}
1 & 0 & 0 & 1 \\
+0 & +1 & +0 & +1 \\
\hline
1 & 1 & 0 & 10 \\
\end{array}
$$

The rules of carrying to the next higher digit position are similar to those used in decimal arithmetic. For example, the sum of the binary numbers 101 (decimal 5) and 111 (decimal 7) is:

$$
\begin{array}{ccc}
1 & 0 & 1 \quad \text{(decimal 5)} \\
1 & 1 & 1 \quad \text{(decimal 7)} \\
\hline
\end{array}
$$
$$1 \ 1 \ 0 \ 0 \quad \text{(decimal 12)}$$

Multiplication is performed by a method analogous to that used with decimal arithmetic, except that the multiplication table is reduced to only four entries:

$$
\begin{array}{cccc}
1 & 0 & 0 & 1 \\
\times 0 & \times 1 & \times 0 & \times 1 \\
\hline
0 & 0 & 0 & 1 \\
\end{array}
$$

Using the same numbers as above, an example of multiplication is:

$$
\begin{array}{r}
1\ \ 0\ \ 1 \quad \text{(decimal 5)} \\
1\ \ 1\ \ 1 \quad \text{(decimal 7)} \\
\hline
1\ \ 0\ \ 1 \\
1\ \ 0\ \ 1 \\
1\ \ 0\ \ 1 \\
\hline
1\ \ 0\ \ 0\ \ 0\ \ 1\ \ 1 \quad \text{(decimal 35)}
\end{array}
$$

In a similar manner, rules for subtraction and division can be developed which parallel those used in decimal arithmetic.

ALPHANUMERIC CODING

Having a method of representing numeric data in a computer is not sufficient. Some of the data processed by the computer is alphanumeric in nature; that is, it consists of numbers, alphabetic characters, and special symbols such as punctuation marks. Examples include the names of variables, people, and places. These characters must be represented internally to the computer as strings of 1's and 0's. This can be accomplished by coding the alphabetic characters and special symbols in the form of bit strings. It is analogous to the childhood pastime of coding messages by means of numeric ciphers. Thus, for example, if we define $A = 01, B = 02, \ldots, Z = 26$, the word *CAT* is enciphered as 030120.

There are two common alphanumeric codes that were originally designed for the interchange of information between computers. These are similar to the codes used internally in computers and are used here to illustrate the coding idea. The first is known as USASCII or, more simply, ASCII which stands for American Standard Code for Information Interchange. It is defined by the American National Standard X3.4-1968, approved by the American National Standards Institute. An analogous code has been adopted by the International Organization for Standardization (ISO). This code provides a seven-bit representation of up to 128 symbols including upper and lower case alphabetic characters, special graphics, and control codes.

A second common code for interchange is known as EBCDIC, which stands for Extended Binary Coded Decimal for Information Interchange. This code is widely used in machines manufactured by International Business Machines Corporation and other manufacturers. It is an 8-bit code which

TABLE 2.1
ASCII and EBCDIC Coding Examples

	ASCII	EBCDIC
Letters		
A	1000001	11000001
B	1000010	11000010
C	1000011	11000011
a	1100001	10000001
b	1100010	10000010
c	1100011	10000011
Special Symbols		
?	0011111	01101111
%	0100101	01101100
#	0100011	01111011
!	0100001	01011010
(	0101000	01001101
/	0101111	01100001

allows for the representation of 256 numerals, alphabetic characters, special symbols, and control characters. Examples of the ASCII and EBCDIC codes are shown in Table 2.1.

Other coding systems are also in use for alphanumeric data. The common characteristic, however, is that they reduce alphabetic and other special characters to a string of binary digits. These symbolic representations are indistinguishable to the computer from the binary numbers discussed in the previous sections. The interpretation of these bit strings as alphanumeric, rather than numeric, data is entirely dependent on the programming of the computer. It is possible, for example, to algebraically add the coded representation of two letters. The result, in all probability, is meaningless but the computer hardware does not know the difference.

COMPUTER LOGIC*

Internal to the computer, the binary numbers 1 and 0 are represented by voltage or current levels. For example, in one technology in common use today, a binary 1 is represented by a voltage signal in the range of 2.0 to 5.5 volts, whereas a binary 0 is represented by a voltage level between 0 and 0.8 volts. Transistor circuits are available which can be used to manipulate these

*This and the following three sections are taken essentially verbatim from two articles written by the author and published in "Control Engineering" in November and December, 1967. Permission to use the material has been granted by "Control Engineering."

signals to perform a variety of logical functions, such as AND, OR, and Exclusive OR. These circuits are the building blocks from which modern computers are constructed.

It is beyond the scope of this book to examine the transistor circuits in detail. In the subsequent discussion, the circuits are considered only in terms of the logical functions that they perform. The inputs to these logic blocks are described in terms of the logic states 1 and 0, with the understanding that in a computer these states are actually represented by voltage levels.

Computer building blocks are conceptually the same logic elements that are used in many control systems. Examples of these logic elements and their assembly into more complex circuits are presented in Table 2.2. Relay equivalents are shown only as a reminder that there is no basic difference between computer logic elements and conventional electromechanical control devices. Electronic logic is faster; microelectronic logic has come along with decreasing cost, size, and failure rate; but early computers were made with relays.

Logic Gates

An AND gate must have a logic 1 at all of its inputs before it produces an output of logic 1. The relay example in Table 2.2 illustrates how the closing of two switches is required before the load is energized (the equivalent of producing a logic 1).

The output of the OR gate is a logic 1 if one or more of its inputs are logic 1. In the relay example, closing either relay, or both, energizes the load Z.

The NOT gate produces logic 1 if its input is logic 0, and vice versa. This type of gate is also known as an INVERTER.

In today's technology, another set of logic elements known as NAND and NOR commonly are used. AND and OR gates can be changed to NAND and NOR gates by combining them with a NOT gate. For our purposes, it is simpler to consider the AND/OR logic family as an example.

Delay Element

It is sometimes necessary to delay one switching event to insure that another switching event occurs first. The break-before-make relay is an electromechanical analog. Delay is accomplished by introducing energy storage, such as inductance in a circuit or a dashpot on the armature of a relay. In most cases, some delay is inherent in the operation of the logic gate so that separate delay elements are unnecessary. In subsequent examples, however, the delay elements are shown explicitly to aid in understanding the function of the logic circuits.

TABLE 2.2
Computer Logic Building Blocks

Element	Description	Relay equivalent
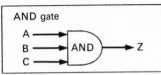	Output Z is 1 if, and only if, all the inputs A, B, ..., *and* C are 1.	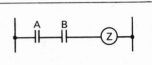
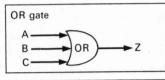	Output Z is 1 if one or more of inputs A, B, ..., *or* C are 1.	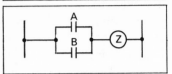
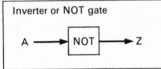	Output Z is always the opposite, or complement, of the input state. That is, if A is 1, output Z is 0; if A is 0, output Z is 1.	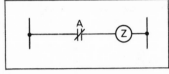
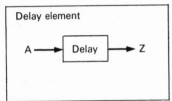	Output Z is the same as input A, but the output transitions between states are delayed with respect to input A.	Mechanical delay through placing a dashpot on the armature of relay.
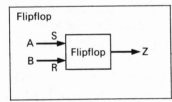	Output Z is set to 1 state by applying a 1 to input A. The flipflop remains in 1 state after input to A is removed. Output Z is reset to 0 by applying a 1 to input B, with input A being 0.	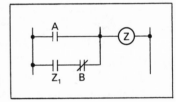
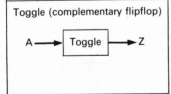	Output Z changes state each time an input pulse is applied to A. Output remains constant in each state, even when input is removed.	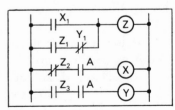

Storage Element

The logic output of a gate may be stored in a set-reset flipflop. For simplicity, a single output Z is assumed, although flipflops usually produce dual outputs of opposite logic values (1 and 0). The output Z is set to a 1 state when a 1 is applied at S, the "set" input. The flipflop remains in a 1 state even if the input is removed. The way to set the output Z to 0 is to apply a 1 at R, the "reset" input, with 0 at S.

The set-reset flipflop can be constructed from an AND, an OR, and a NOT gate as shown in Table 2.2. The equivalent electromagnetic circuit is a "lock-in" or latching relay.

A variation in storage elements is the toggle which consists of a flipflop combined with two AND gates and a NOT gate. The toggle changes its output state every time a 1 is applied.

IMPLEMENTING COMPUTER FUNCTIONS

The arithmetic, data handling, and other functions in a computer are performed by logic, delay, and storage elements such as those described above. To do this, the logic elements are combined into structures which perform specific functions such as storing a word of data or adding two numbers. In the following sections, some of the structures found in most computers are described and illustrated in terms of the basic logic building blocks. The particular representations shown here are not necessarily the only way in which these functions can be realized.

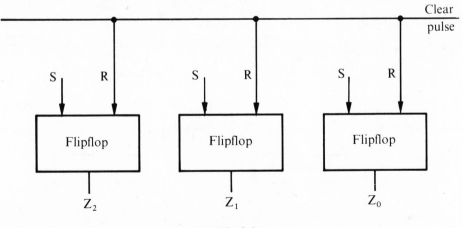

FIG. 2.1
Register Structure

Register

Many computer operations involve the register, a basic logic structure for temporary storage of binary information. The register is made up of flipflops or other storage elements, each of which can store one binary digit (bit), Fig. 2.1. The number of flipflops depends on the length of the computer word. If computer operations are based on a 16-bit word, each register requires at least 16 flipflops for proper storage capacity.

A register is cleared when all of its flipflops are in the 0 output state. This is accomplished by applying a pulse to the reset input R of all flipflops. Data consisting of 0 or 1-bits may then be read into individual flipflops through logic gates connected to "set" inputs S.

Shift Register

A register may be combined with other logic elements to permit the bit stored in each flipflop to be shifted one position, either to the right or to the left, each time a shift pulse is applied. When a binary digit is shifted one place to the left, the value of the number represented by the bits in the register is doubled. If the shift is to the right, the value of the number is halved.

In Fig. 2.2 the shift-right pulse causes each bit to be shifted by one position. If the two-bit register originally contained 10, the new content would

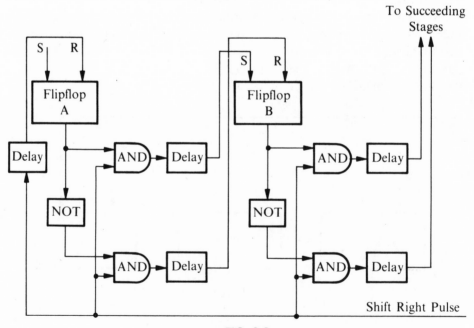

FIG. 2.2
Shift Register Structure

be 01. An additional shift would yield 00. Each shift causes the right-hand bit to be shifted out of the register. Depending on the design of the computer, the information conveyed by this bit may or may not be lost.

The output of flipflop A is applied to two AND gates, one through an inverter. The second input to each AND gate is the shift pulse. Assuming that flipflop A produced a logic 1 at the upper AND gate, the resulting logic 1 would set flipflop B at input S. The delay circuit insures that the state of flipflop B has been shifted to the succeeding stage before its new state occurs.

If flipflop A had been in the 0 state to begin with, the lower AND gate would have produced the shift signal to flipflop B. The delay circuit at the extreme left allows the shift pulse to reset flipflop A after the 1 or 0 at its output has been shifted to flipflop B. The SHIFT LEFT operation is similar.

Transfer Operation

Two registers may be connected through transfer gates as in Fig. 2.3, so that information in one register may be moved to the corresponding flipflop in another register. Each transfer gate is actuated by the output of a flipflop and the transfer pulse. If a flipflop of register 1 is in the 1 state, the corresponding AND gate produces a logic 1 in the flipflop of register 2. Assuming that all flipflops in register 2 were originally in a 0 state (cleared), a 0 in a flipflop of

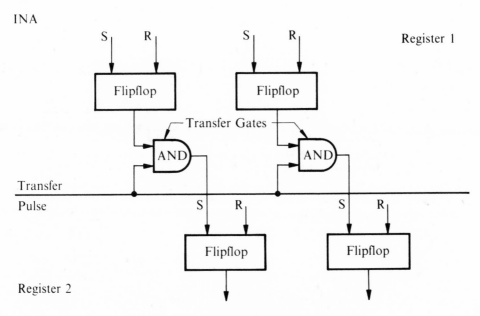

FIG. 2.3
Register-to-Register Transfer Circuit

register 1 allows the corresponding flipflop of register 2 to remain in the 0 state. The transfer operation is used whenever data words are relocated in a computer. This action is called for, explicitly or implicitly, in many instructions.

Decoding Operations

Binary information in registers or counters may represent data, addresses of data, or operation codes (OP Codes) identifying the operations to be performed on data. A decoding network like the one in Fig. 2.4 translates such binary information into a unique signal for each combination of bits stored in a register. The binary number 010, for example, may correspond to the OP Code ADD, and can be decoded into a signal which initiates the addition operation.

Figure 2.4 illustrates binary to decimal decoding. Since the register consists of two flipflops, there are four possible combinations of the bits 1 and 0. Four AND gates are provided to generate the four possible decimal outputs: 0, 1, 2, or 3.

Assuming that the register contains binary 10, the lefthand input of A1 receives a logic 1 from flipflop A; its right-hand input receives a logic 0 from flipflop B. The result is logic 0 produced by A1. The same result occurs for A3 and A4. But A2 receives a logic 1 from flipflop A, and a complemented logic 0 from flipflop B, yielding a logic 1 at its output. This corresponds with decimal 2 (binary 10).

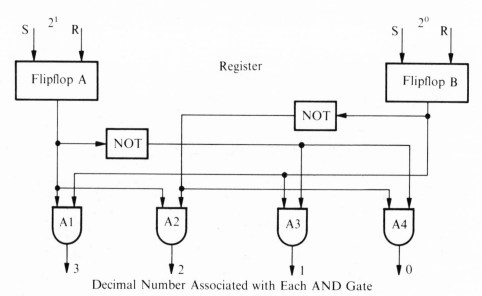

Decimal Number Associated with Each AND Gate

FIG. 2.4
Binary-to-Decimal Decoding Circuit

Binary Counter

Counters are used in basic computer operations although there may not be a specific COUNT command in an instruction set. They are used to keep track of operation sequences by counting the operations as they occur. Counters are also used in the peripheral equipment of industrial control computers to count, for example, the total number of pulses from digital transducers.

One way this operation may be implemented is the ripple counter shown in Fig. 2.5. Since it has three storage elements (toggles), it can store eight combinations of binary digits (1 or 0), corresponding to a binary count from 000 to 111, or decimal 0 to 7. The output of each toggle is connected through a capacitor to the next stage on the left, representing the next higher power of 2. The toggle-capacitor combination is a simplified version of an ac-coupled flipflop and provides a differentiating action. Only when a toggle goes through the transition from 1 to 0 will a pulse pass through the capacitor to the next toggle on the left. This condition is indicated by the 0, 1 notation at the capacitors.

The state of each toggle after arrival of each count pulse is shown in the binary count columns. The first pulse sets T1 to 1, but does not affect T2 because the transition was not from 1 to 0. The second pulse resets T1 to 0,

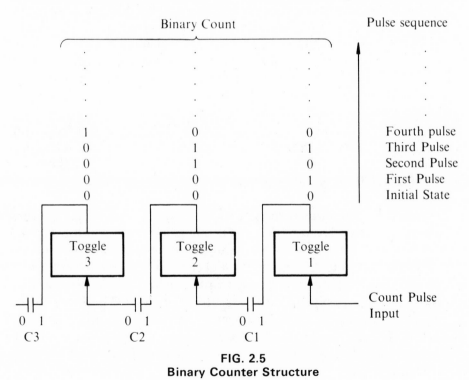

FIG. 2.5
Binary Counter Structure

and the transition of 1 to 0 causes a pulse to be transmitted through the capacitor, setting T2 to 1. The third pulse does not affect T2 but adds a count to T1. The fourth pulse changes the state of both T1 and T2, causing a count to be stored in T3, and yielding the binary numer 100 (decimal 4).

Accumulator

In the usual adder, two binary numbers are added and their sum appears at the adder output. This sum remains only as long as the adder inputs, representing the two numbers, remain. In contrast, the accumulator stores results of repeated additions. A number from an addend register is added to the augend in the accumulator and the result is stored in the accumulator. Another number may then be added to the previous result and the sum is again stored in the accumulator. The addend may come from another register, or from storage, and the status of the addend is not affected by successive adding operations.

The accumulator in Fig. 2.6 functions in two phases. First, the bits in the addend register are added without regard to carries. The second phase, slightly delayed, processes carries. In adding binary numbers, a carry to the next higher bit position is generated whenever two 1's are added.

Phase 1. An ADD pulse is applied to one input of A1 in each stage. The output of each flipflop in the addend register is connected to the second input of the corresponding AND gate A1. Any addend flipflop with a binary 1 produces a pulse at the output of A1 which passes through the corresponding OR gate 01 to its associated toggle. If the toggle is in the 0 state, it will be set to 1; if it is in the 1 state, it will be reset to 0, and a carry will be generated.

Phase 2. The requirement for a carry is indicated by a 1 in the addend flipflop and a 0 in the corresponding toggle. This is sensed by A2 in each accumulator stage. Its output produces a carry when its three inputs are a carry pulse, a 1 from an addend flipflop, and a complemented 0 from the corresponding toggle.

Going from the lower order stage to the higher order stage, the carry pulse from A2 passes through OR gate O2 into a delay circuit, before it passes through OR gate O1 to register in the toggle. Besides the delay circuit, the carry pulse is applied to A3. Should the higher order toggle be in state 1 when it receives the carry pulse, a carry to the next higher stage is necessary. A3 serves this purpose, passing its output through OR gate O2 to the next stage.

If several toggles in successive stages all store 1's, the carry will "ripple through" AND gate A3 of these stages until it finds a toggle with a 0 in it. The delay circuit in each stage permits the carry pulse to ripple through before the toggle changes state.

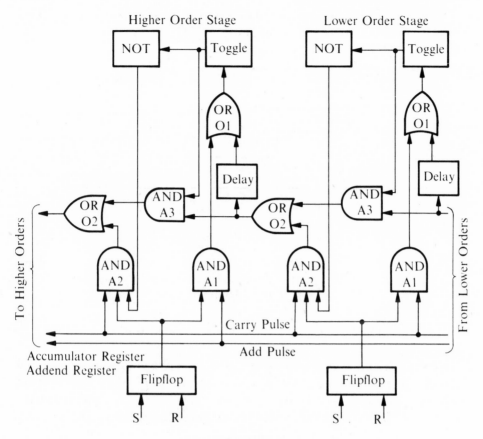

FIG. 2.6
Accumulator Circuit

VALVE CONTROL SYSTEM

In the previous section, logic blocks were combined to perform a variety of computer operations. In the following sections, these blocks are further organized into a central processing unit (CPU) of a hypothetical computer. This computer is then applied to a process control situation, drawing on a stored program of detailed instructions to carry out a sequence of steps necessary for proper control of a process valve.

In Fig. 2.7, flow through a process valve is under the control of a digital computer, in whose storage is stored a program to implement the algorithm shown. This algorithm, simplified for illustrative purposes, provides a means for changing flow through the valve in order to reduce setpoint error. In practice, many such valve operating loops could be under the supervision of

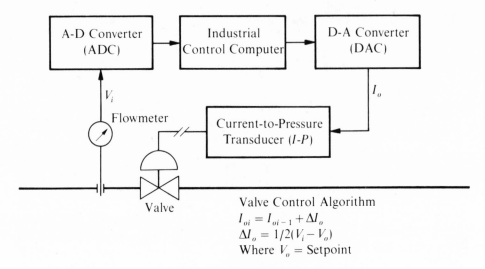

$$I_{oi} = I_{oi-1} + \Delta I_o$$
$$\Delta I_o = 1/2(V_i - V_o)$$
Where V_o = Setpoint

FIG. 2.7
Flow Control Loop Example

the same computer, responding to the same algorithm, or a variety of algorithms.

Because the flowmeter produces an analog voltage V_i, representing flow, and valve position is controlled by an analog current I_o, the digital computer requires an analog-to-digital converter (ADC) and a digital-to-analog converter (DAC) to interface with these analog signals. The ADC output in binary form is "read" periodically and its contents transferred to the accumulator in the computer. Computations performed on the value of flow result in a digital output which is transferred to the register of the DAC upon computer command. This quantity is then transformed into an analog current to actuate the current-to-pressure transducer. Pneumatic output of the transducer is transmitted to the valve, setting it in accordance with the control algorithm. For this programming example, the algorithm calls for a change in existing output current I_{oi-1} by an amount equal to one half the difference between setpoint V_o and flowmeter output V_i.

The hypothetical computer consists of counter, registers, accumulator, transfer gates, and storage as shown in Fig. 2.8. The step counter counts incoming clock pulses and sequences programmed operations. The accumulator is a multipurpose register which performs the ADD, CLEAR, and SHIFT RIGHT functions. Storage locations at the right are numbered in octal according to the stored program and data.

Computer Instruction Set

The instructions stored in the storage of Fig. 2.8 are explained in Table

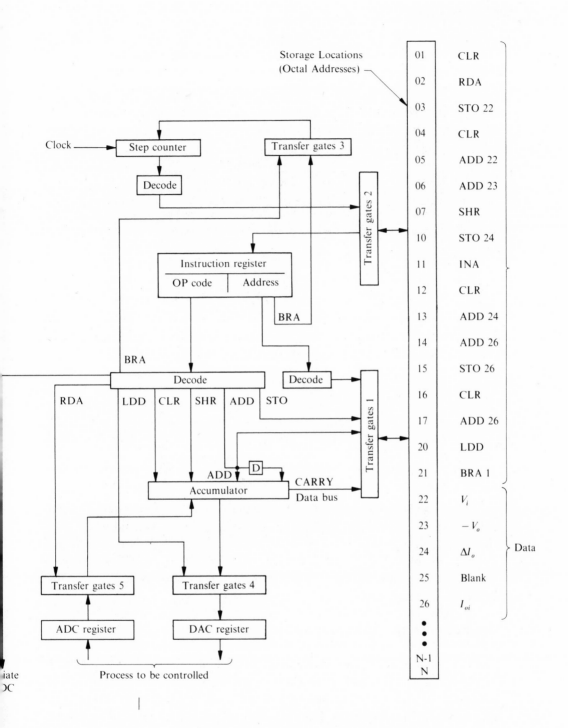

FIG. 2.8
Hypothetical Computer for Example

69

TABLE 2.3
Example Computer Instruction Codes (Octal Notation)

Mnemonic	INSTRUCTION WORD OP code	address	Meaning
CLR	01	000	Clear accumulator
ADD	02	xxx	Add contents of storage location "xxx" to accumulator
STO	03	xxx	Transfer accumulator value to storage location "xxx"
SHR	04	000	Shift to the right by one bit
BRA	05	xxx	Branch to storage location "xxx"
LDD	06	000	Load DAC register
RDA	07	000	Read ADC register
INA	10	000	Initiate ADC

2.3. An operating code (OP code) and address are specified for each instruction. The OP code indicates what operation is to be performed, and the address gives location in storage of data to be manipulated:

INSTRUCTION WORD FORMAT

	OP code	address
Using octal notation	W W	X X X
Binary equivalent	yyy yyy	zzz zzz zzz

Although the computer will actually perform its computations in binary arithmetic, this discussion uses octal notation in order to avoid writing and interpreting long sequences of bits. The three-letter symbols in the first column of Table 2.3 are mnemonics (easy-to-remember symbols) often used in programming languages. The meaning of each instruction is briefly described in the third column, and in more detail in Table 2.4.

Programming the Valve Algorithm

Each action of the computer must be specified by an instruction in the program and writing such instructions requires a detailed knowledge of the computer, of the available instruction set, and of the programming rules applicable to the computer. On the other hand, higher level programming languages are available, such as FORTRAN, that simplify program writing. An example of how FORTRAN-type programming might apply to the valve algorithm is given in Table 2.5. The meaning of each FORTRAN statement is

TABLE 2.4
Explanation of Hardware Functions Implied
by Instructions of Table 2.3

Instruction	Storage address of instruction, FIG. 2.8		
The CLEAR (CLR) instruction initiates the pulse that clears the accumulator, resetting all flipflop bits to the 0 state. This instruction does not require a specific address, as indicated by 000 in Table 2.3.	01 04 12 16		
The ADD instruction adds the number in storage location "xxx" to the number already existing in the accumulator.	05 13	06 14	17
The STORE (STO) command stores the accumulator contents in storage location "xxx", leaving the value in the accumulator unchanged.	03 15	10	
The SHIFT RIGHT (SHR) instruction in the hypothetical CPU shifts the word in the accumulator one position (bit) to the right. In an actual computer, the address or some other portion of the instruction word may specify how many times the shift right operation is to be performed. A SHIFT LEFT (SHL) instruction is also available in computers.	07		
The BRANCH (BRA) instruction causes the program to skip to the instruction in the storage location designated by "xxx". This instruction or a similar one is frequently used to transfer control to a subroutine, or to take one of two alternative program paths.	21		
The LOAD DAC (LDD) command transfers the contents of the accumulator (without affecting its contents) into the DAC register. In an actual computer, the address portion of this instruction may specify which of several DAC registers is to be loaded. This is not required in the example since there is only one DAC.	20		
The READ ADC REGISTER (RDA) instruction transfers the contents of the ADC register to the accumulator.	02		
The INITIATE ADC READING (INA) instruction always precedes an RDA instruction since a finite time is required to convert the analog value into a binary word; to await completion of the conversion would be wasteful of computing time.	11		

supplied and the equivalent symbolic program instructions are followed by the corresponding computer codes, which cause the hardware elements of Fig. 2.8 to produce desired action.

The reason for a number (such as 23) preceding a statement should be made clear. It is a number arbitrarily selected by the programmer to serve as a reference later in the program. In this case, it is used in the last statement (GO TO 23), directing the computer to return to the first statement and repeat the program.

The Compiler. Conversion of FORTRAN statements into instructions such as the octal numbers in column 4 of Table 2.5 is performed by another program known as a compiler. FORTRAN statements are punched into cards

TABLE 2.5
FORTRAN Program Example

(1) FORTRAN statement	(2) Meaning	(3) Symbolic program	(4) Computer code	(5) Computer action
23 READ ADC, VI	Read ADC register and store ADC output in a location called VI	CLR	01000	Clear accumulator
		RDA	07000	Transfer ADC register to accumulator
		STO 22	03022	Store accumulator value in storage location 22
DEL = (1/2)*(VI+VO)	Calculate $\triangle I_o = 1/2(V_i - V_o)$ DEL, VI, and VO are FORTRAN representations of $\triangle I_o$, V_i, and V_o	CLR	01000	Clear accumulator
		ADD 22	02022	Add storage location 22 to accumulator
		ADD 23	02023	Add storage location 23 to accumulator
		SHR	04000	Shift right once (multiply by 1/2)
		STO 24	03024	Store accumulator value in storage location 24
START ADC	Initiate ADC conversion	INA	10000	Initiate ADC for new reading
IOI = IOI+DEL	Calculate $I_{oi} = I_{oi-1} + \triangle I_o$ by adding the number in location DEL ($\triangle I_o$) to value in location IOI (I_{oi}) and replace the old value of IOI by the modified value	CLR	01000	Clear accumulator
		ADD 24	02024	Add storage location 24 to accumulator
		ADD 26	02026	Add storage location 26 to accumulator
		STO 26	03026	Store accumulator value in storage location 26
OUTPUT DAC, IOI	Transfer the number in location IOI to the DAC and start the conversion	CLR	01000	Clear accumulator
		ADD 26	02026	Add storage location 26 to accumulator
		LDD	06000	Load accumulator value into DAC register and initiate conversion
GO TO 23	Return to the FORTRAN statement labeled 23	BRA 1	05000	Branch to program step stored in storage location 1

or paper tape to produce a "source deck" whose data are then transmitted to the computer storage and operated on by the compiler, already in storage. The compiler interprets FORTRAN statements in terms of computer functions, expressed in binary form (computer code). The compiler also assigns storage locations to variables named in the FORTRAN program. For example, DEL is assigned the storage location octal address 24, as indicated in Fig. 2.8. (DEL, capitalizing the first three letters of "delta," is used in the program instead of ΔI_o, in order to avoid use of subscripts and symbols not legal in FORTRAN.) The compiler program also examines each FORTRAN statement to insure conformity with programming rules. The output of the compiler is a series of instructions that can be executed by the computer, corresponding to the octal instructions in column 4 of Table 2.5.

In the sample program, each FORTRAN statement generates up to five such computer instructions. In a more realistic program, a single FORTRAN statement may call for a more complicated program, such as a subroutine which may include hundreds of instructions.

The Symbolic Program. For convenience, and to assist in the interpretation of Table 2.5, the symbolic program in column 3 has been included. Symbolic language mnemonics CLR, RDA, STO 22, and so on, are abbreviations for binary operation codes. Using mnemonics makes it possible, for example, to write STO 22 for the store instruction instead of the octal code 03022, or its binary equivalent which is 000011000010010.

Using symbolic language (also called assembly language) instead of FORTRAN, the contents of column 3, Table 2.5 would constitute the program. Instead of a compiler, an assembler program would translate the instructions of column 3 into the computer code of column 4.

Unlike FORTRAN, symbolic language has a one-to-one correspondence with its machine code equivalent. The flexibility of symbolic language, as opposed to the uniform procedures characterizing a FORTRAN compiler, allows the skillful programmer to obtain an extremely efficient program. FORTRAN, however, is easy to learn and use; it does not require the detailed machine knowledge necessary when applying symbolic language.

EXECUTING THE PROGRAM

To clarify interaction between the program stored in storage and the logic hardware of CPU, individual steps are discussed in the same sequence as the listing of instruction addresses in Fig. 2.8. The number of the step is the same as the storage location (in octal) in which the instruction is stored.

Step 1: Clear Accumulator. The step counter is initially set to zero. The first clock pulse entering the step counter sets it to 1. The step counter activates transfer gates 2 and the instruction word in storage location 1 is transferred to the instruction register. This is a CLR (CLEAR) instruction which has an OP code but no address. The OP code decoder of the instruction register decodes the first two octal digits of the instruction. This activates the output line marked CLR and a CLEAR pulse is transmitted to the accumulator register. Its flipflops are reset to 0 state.

Step 2: Read ADC Register. The second clock pulse sets the step counter to 2. The decoded count activates transfer gates 2 and the second instruction RDA in storage location 02 is transferred to the instruction register. Since the RDA instruction has no address portion, only the first two octal digits (OP code 02) are decoded. This causes a pulse to be transmitted over the RDA line to transfer gates 5. The gates transfer the value of *VI* (flowmeter output V_i) from the ADC register to the accumulator.

Step 3: Store Accumulator Value in Location 22. The next clock pulse sets the step counter to 3 and causes transfer of instruction word in storage location 03 to the instruction register. This is an STO (STORE) command which has both an OP code and an address. The OP code is decoded, activating the STO line of the decode network; the address is decoded by the associated address decoder, activating transfer gates 1 to transfer data in the accumulator to storage location 22.

Step 4: Clear Accumulator. The STORE operation (Step 3) did not affect the contents of the accumulator. This necessitates another CLEAR operation. The CLR instruction in storage location 04 performs the operation as described in Step 1.

Step 5: Add 22 to Accumulator. With the next clock pulse, instruction ADD 22 is transferred via transfer gates 2 from storage location 05 to the instruction register. The OP code is decoded as before, and the resulting output, in conjunction with a pulse on the ADD line, causes the data in storage location 22 to be added to the accumulator. The accumulator now contains the value VI which appears in the second FORTRAN statement, Table 2.5.

Step 6: Add 23 to Accumulator. In the same manner the value $-V_o$ at storage location 23 is added to the accumulator so that it now contains the quantity $V_i - V_o$. This quantity is equivalent to $VI + VO$ in the FORTRAN statement. Assuming $-V_o$ to be equivalent to VO avoids a subtraction operation.

Step 7: Shift Right. To obtain the value of the FORTRAN variable *DEL* ($= \Delta I_o$), the contents of the accumulator must be multiplied by 1/2. Since the limited instruction set of this hypothetical CPU does not include MULTIPLY or DIVIDE, the multiplication is accomplished by shifting the contents of the accumulator to the right by one bit.

The procedure for transfer of the SHR (SHIFT RIGHT) instruction from storage location 07 for decoding, resulting in shifting of the accumulator contents, is similar to earlier steps. The accumulator now contains the FORTRAN quantity $DEL = (1/2) * (VI + VO)$. The asterisk denotes multiplication.

Step 10: Store Accumulator Value in Location 24. The next clock pulse advances the step counter from octal 7 to octal 10 (since the radix 8 provides for a numerical sequence from 0 through 7). In a manner similar to Step 3, contents of the accumulator are transferred to storage location 24.

Step 11: Initiate ADC Reading. Because of the finite time required to convert an analog reading into digital form, the ADC must now be activated so that the ADC register will contain a new value for the next calculation of the algorithm. This is done by the INA (INITIATE ADC READING) instruction, transferred and decoded in the usual manner.

Steps 12 through 17. These steps consist of ADD, CLEAR, and STORE operation similar to those described. These instructions cause the accumulator content to be $IOI = IOI + DEL$ which is the equivalent of the algorithm $I_{oi} = I_{oi-1} + \Delta I_o$. This new value of IOI is stored in location 26 while the accumulator is cleared, then brought back to the accumulator for transfer to the output.

Step 20: Load DAC. The step counter advances from octal 17 to octal 20 to initiate the LDD (LOAD DAC) instruction. This implements the fifth FORTRAN statement, OUTPUT DAC, *IOI*. The instruction is transferred from storage location 20 to the instruction register where its OP code is decoded. The output of the decode network activates transfer gates 4 via the LDD line, causing the value of *IOI* in the accumulator to be transferred to the DAC register. The output of the DAC, changed to a pneumatic signal by the I-P transducer, positions the process valve.

Step 21: Branch to Beginning of Program. The last statement, GO TO 23, resets the step counter so that the program may be repeated. The instruction BRA 1 in location 21 accomplishes this operation. A pulse from the OP code decoder on the BRA line activates the gates and transfers the address into the step counter. This address is 000 (Table 2.5) in order that the next clock pulse will properly advance the step counter to 001.

The power of programmed computer control is exemplified by the fact that at Step 21 (above) the branch instruction could have been used to go to any other sequence in an overall program, deferring the instruction GO TO 23 to some later point in the program. Or provision could be made for calculating a new branch address at the end of the example program based on a condition in the process.

In a modern operating system, program control at the end of the example program would be transferred to a "supervisory" program which controls the sequence in which programs are run. The supervisory program would initiate the next program to be executed and, after a certain period of time, might again pass control to the example program. Such cycles could be repeated indefinitely.

The data flow of an actual industrial computer control system is more complex than the hypothetical system described above. Most systems, for example, are capable of controlling multiple ADC's and DAC's. In addition, a large number of process variables are measured by connecting them to one of the ADC's through a multiplexing network controlled by the CPU. Hundreds of input data points can be individually addressed. In this way industrial computers are capable of handling a variety of digital input and output functions such as process interrupt, voltage and contact sense, contact operate, and pulse output. With an industrial control computer goes all the peripheral equipment such as typewriters and display units that make up a man-machine interface. This is the subject of Chapter 3.

THE MODERN MINICOMPUTER*

The modern minicomputer, although much smaller and less complex than the bigger computers, is more complicated than the hypothetical computer considered in the previous section. Conceptually, however, the minicomputer is similar in construction and operation to the ideas presented above. In the remaining portion of this chapter, the minicomputer is considered in terms of its characteristics and performance parameters.

---

*There exists no generally accepted definition of the term "minicomputer." (See the discussion in the Preface.) Since the principles involved in the construction of a computer are essentially the same for "big" and "little" computers, a rigorous definition really is not necessary for the purpose of this chapter. Suffice it to say that the majority of industrial computer control systems utilize computers which their manufacturer calls a "minicomputer" or which are recognized by knowledgeable users as being "minicomputers." In this and subsequent chapters, the term "small general-purpose computer," with or without the additional adjectives of "real-time" or "industrial," is used interchangeably with the term "minicomputer."

Today there are more than 100 manufacturers of computers which fall into the class of minicomputers and some of these manufacturers offer several models or lines of equipment. Each manufacturer has his own design with its own unique characteristics, advantages, and disadvantages. For this reason, it is impossible to discuss minicomputers in terms of a single design. The approach here is to consider general characteristics that apply to most minicomputers. Specific details of a particular design can be obtained from the manufacturer.

Conceptually, most minicomputers can be divided into four subsystems as shown in Fig. 2.9. The Arithmetic and Control Unit is the portion of the computer in which the instructions are executed and the data are manipulated. The Storage is the unit in which instructions and data are stored until accessed by the Arithmetic and Control Unit. This storage is often called main storage to differentiate it from auxiliary or bulk storage, which provides large quantities of storage at, generally, lower access speeds and lower cost. For our purposes, bulk storage devices such as disk and magnetic tape are considered as input/output (I/O) devices and are discussed in Chapter 3. The channel is a subsystem in the minicomputer which controls the communication with, and the operation of, the I/O devices. The channel, depending on its design, may be capable of executing a limited set of instructions. Its primary purpose is to relieve the arithmetic and control unit

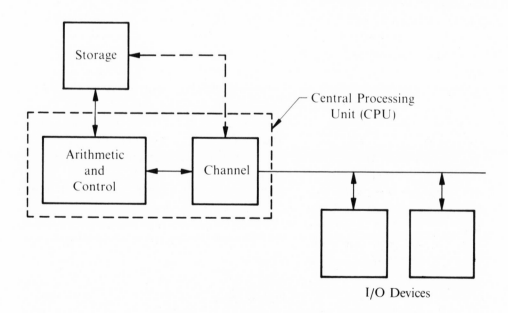

FIG. 2.9
Industrial Computer Subsystems

of the burden of direct control of I/O devices. The channel and the arithmetic and control unit, taken together, are often called the Central Processing Unit or CPU. In some designs it is not possible to separate the CPU into channel and arithmetic and control unit subsystems. Conceptually, however, it is convenient to think of them as individual units. The I/O devices are the equipment used by the CPU to communicate with the operator and the outside world. Typical I/O devices, in addition to the bulk storage devices mentioned above, are card readers/punches, printers, graphic display units, analog input subsystems, and communication devices. These devices are connected to the I/O channel in most designs, although in some cases they may be "natively attached"; that is, attached directly to the CPU without an intervening channel subsystem.

CPU CHARACTERISTICS

There are a number of parameters which characterize the CPU of most minicomputers. These include word size, instruction set repertoire, and instruction execution times. Of these, the instruction set is perhaps the most distinctive and important, since it represents the means by which the programmer communicates with the machine. The internal arrangement of registers, accumulators, and other hardware is important to the hardware designer and affects the performance of the machine. Generally, however, the exact details of this hardware are not so important to the user of the machine.

The "word" is a fundamental unit of information in a computer and is described in terms of its length. From a hardware point of view, the word length generally determines the size of registers (i.e., the number of flipflops or storage elements that they contain) and the width of the data paths that interconnect the various parts of the machine. The word length imposes a number of significant constraints on the hardware designer. It affects, for example, the format of single word instructions and the number of storage words that can be directly addressed in a single word instruction. It also has an affect on the cost of the hardware, since it is an indication of the degree of parallelism that exists in the machine. From a user's point of view, it determines the precision with which calculations may be performed without resorting to special techniques.

In most modern minicomputers, the word length is 16 bits. Machines are available, however, with word lengths of 12, 18, and 24 bits. Large machines, not considered as minicomputers, generally use word lengths of 32 or more bits.

Although a word is the fundamental unit of information in the minicomputer, other units are also used. Technically, the "byte" is a unit of information which is anything less than a word. Through popular usage, however, the byte has come to be defined as an 8-bit unit of information or, in the case of a 16-bit machine, a half-word. The byte is convenient for many operations in a computer since, for example, 8-bit coding of alphanumeric data is common. When instructions which operate on single bytes are provided, this greatly simplifies the manipulation of alphanumeric characters since each character can be handled individually.

For certain operations and data, the single word does not provide enough precision. For example, the largest integer that can be expressed in 16 bits is 65,535 or less than five decimal digits. If a calculation requires greater precision (for example, keeping track of the national debt to within $1.00), other methods must be used. One such method is to allow calculations involving more than one word. In the case of double precision, for example, the higher-order bits are stored in one word and the lower-order bits are stored in a subsequent word. In some computers, instructions such as "Double Precision Add" are provided which automatically manipulate both words to provide a double precision result. If not provided in the instruction set, such calculations must be done with programming.

Two other situations also require more than one word in typical minicomputers. In order to control some operations, the information required by the computer from the instruction may require more than 16 bits. This is common, for example, in the control of I/O devices where a function, I/O address, and other information must be provided to the device in order for it to perform its job. In many cases, all of this information cannot be coded into a single-word instruction. It is common, therefore, to provide for double-word instructions which are stored in sequential locations in main storage. The CPU accesses the first word and, recognizing it as a double-word instruction, automatically accesses the second word in the process of executing the instruction. Except for the additional time required, this is transparent to the programmer.

A second case which often requires multiple-word instructions is for storage addressing. An instruction which requires access to main storage must specify the address in storage and the function to be performed. The number of bits available for the address, therefore, is less than the number of bits in the word. For example, in a 16-bit computer it is not unusual for the number of address bits to be as small as seven bits. This only allows for direct addressing of 128 storage locations, whereas storage may have 65,536 or 131,072 locations. There are several ways to solve this problem, some of which are discussed in subsequent sections. However, one way is to provide a double-word instruction in which the storage address is located in the second word. This allows for direct addressing of up to 65,536 storage locations in a 16-bit machine.

Instruction Set

The instruction set is the vocabulary of the computer. It defines the primitive operations that the computer is able to perform and it is the fundamental language through which a user may communicate with the machine. As indicated in the hypothetical machine discussed above, the instruction specifies the operation to be performed and provides the necessary information such as addresses for its execution. Although it is possible to build a computer with as few as 10 or 12 instructions, the typical minicomputer has on the order of 50 to 100 instructions in its instruction set. Although all instruction sets contain certain basic instructions such as ADD, there is no uniformity between the instructions sets used by different manufacturers. There may be a uniformity or compatibility between computers which belong to the same family, but this rarely extends between manufacturers. The reason for this is that the instruction set is significantly affected by the exact arrangement of hardware elements in the CPU and each designer attempts to select an arrangement to satisfy the goals of performance that he wants to achieve. Although this lack of uniformity can be a problem for the user in that he must sometimes learn a new instruction set, selecting a single instruction set for all computers would stifle the creativity and advances in performance that have characterized the computer industry.

Despite the lack of uniformity, most instruction sets can be separated into categories of instructions which contain functions found in most minicomputers. For the purposes of this discussion, five such categories have been selected: Arithmetic and Logical, Load and Store, Branch and Test, Machine Status and Control, and Input/Output. Each of these categories is briefly discussed after first considering the problem of addressing.

Addressing Modes

In general, instructions can be divided into those that require access to storage, and hence a storage address, and those that do not. As indicated above, the short word length of most minicomputers prevents the direct addressing of all available main storage locations. This, and other considerations related to the convenience of programming, have given rise to a number of different methods of generating the actual address used in accessing storage. This address, known as the "effective address," is automatically generated by the CPU based on information provided in the instruction. The address generation procedure may involve one or more accesses to storage or to internal registers and algebraic calculations. The procedure, however, is done automatically and is transparent to the user of the machine.

Index Addressing. Index addressing enhances the capability of the computer to do repetitive calculations on different sets of data. For the indexing function, the address portion of the instruction is automatically added (or subtracted) to another quantity, known as the index, to form the effective address used for accessing storage. The index is often stored in one of several special registers known as index registers. Instructions are provided for loading the index registers and otherwise manipulating their content. For example, instructions are often provided which automatically add 1 (or subtract 1) to the content of the index register following execution of the indexed instruction. This provides a convenient programming tool for manipulating files of data which are stored sequentially in main storage. An instruction which utilizes indexed addressing provides, in addition to the operation code which specifies the function to be performed, the quantity to be added to the index and the address of the particular index register which is to be used.

Base Addressing. Base addressing is virtually the same as indexing with the difference being primarily in the intent of use. The content of a "base register" is automatically added to the address portion of the instruction to form the effective address. Instructions are provided for loading the base address into the base register.

Base addressing is used to solve two problems in computer use. The first is the problem of limited addressing range which was discussed above. The range of the base is sufficient to provide access to all of the directly-addressable storage and the displacement address in the instruction is used to select the exact address to be used.

The second problem has to do with the relocation of programs. In today's programming systems, the actual location of programs and data in storage may change from time to time depending on the requirements of the application. They may, in fact, change dynamically under the control of the operating system. Under these conditions, it is impossible for the programmer to assign exact addresses for his data and instructions. With base addressing, programs are written as though the first address in the program was the first address in storage, namely, 000...000. When the program is executed, a base value is provided by the operating system which relocates or displaces the program and/or data to their actual location in storage. The base value when added to the address in each instruction results in an effective address representing the true storage address.

A variation of base addressing which avoids the time-consuming necessity of adding two numbers to obtain each effective address is "page" or "block" addressing. In this scheme, the address portion of each instruction is concatenated with the quantity stored in the base address register. The quantity in the base register provides the higher-order bits of the effective address and the address in the instruction provides the lower-order bits. The effect of this is to divide storage into blocks or pages whose addresses are represented by the higher-order bits stored in the base register. The quantity in the base register remains constant unless reference is made to a location on another page. In this case, an instruction which modifies the contents of the base register must be executed.

Indirect Addressing. In indirect addressing, the address portion of the instruction being executed refers not to the address of the data but to the storage location which contains the address of the data. Thus, for example, the instruction may contain the address 25. The computer fetches the contents of storage address 25 which may be 1256 and uses this quantity as the address of the actual data required in the execution of the instruction. Due to the multiple storage accesses, indirect addressing increases the execution time but it does provide flexibility at a lower cost than, for example, indexing. It can be used to overcome the limitation of short word length since the effective address can occupy a full word in storage. Indirect addressing can also be used for the purpose of relocation by providing a table of relocation addresses, which are addressed by the instructions being executed.

Relative Addressing. Relative addressing is similar to indexing in that the effective address is the sum of the address in the instruction and another quantity. In this case, the quantity to which the address in the instruction is added is the address of the instruction itself. The address of the instruction being executed is available in the "program counter" or "instruction address register" which keeps track of which instruction is being executed. The effect of relative addressing is that the effective address is always related to the absolute location of the instruction itself by the amount in the address field of the instruction.

Arithmetic and Logical Instructions

The category of arithmetic and logical instructions contains those instructions necessary to manipulate the value of data. Almost all minicomputers provide the functions of algebraic ADD and SUBTRACT. Multiply and divide are sometimes available only as optional features. When multiply and divide are provided or installed as optional features, double precision add and subtract are usually included in the instruction set since the additional registers required are already provided for the multiply and divide function.

There may be several different variations of the basic arithmetic operations provided. One variation has to do with the location of the operands. For example, a simple ADD instruction may assume that the addend is located in the accumulator and the augend is located in main storage. In this case, the ADD instruction contains the main storage address or the information necessary to automatically calculate the effective address. Another possibility is to perform the addition of two numbers which are stored in internal registers in the CPU. If there are multiple internal registers, the ADD instruction contains the addresses of the two particular registers to be involved in the operation.

A second variation has to do with the data structure that is assumed. In most minicomputers, arithmetic operations are assumed to take place in fixed-point format; that is, the location of the binary point (analogous to the decimal point in decimal arithmetic) is assumed to be fixed. The problem of keeping track of the decimal point during a calculation is left to the programmer. This mode of arithmetic limits the range of numbers that can be used in a calculation because of the word length of the machine (unless double precision instructions are available).

A second mode of arithmetic is known as floating-point. In this representation the number is represented as a mantissa and an exponent similar to that used in the scientific notation. For example, the number 0.23456×10^3 is completely specified by the mantissa 0.23456 and the exponent 3. In the computer, the mantissa might be stored as one word and the exponent as another. This can provide for a tremendous range of numeric values. For example, if the exponent is stored as a 7-bit value, all the numbers from 10^{-128} to 10^{+128} can be represented to a precision determined by the precision of the mantissa. Although not always provided as a standard feature, floating point hardware and the corresponding floating point instructions are available on most minicomputers.

The logical instructions are those that perform the logical functions of AND, OR, and Exclusive OR in a manner analogous to that described for the logic blocks discussed earlier. These operations are performed in parallel on a bit-by-bit basis; that is, the first bit of one operand is compared to the first bit of the second operand, the second bits of each operand are compared, etc. As in the case of the arithmetic operations, the operands may be located in registers or in main storage. Similarly, any of the addressing modes discussed above may be provided.

A third set of instructions commonly found in this category of instructions are those for shifting the position of the contents of a register. In the shifting operation, the content of one register position is replaced by the content of the adjacent register position. For example, in SHIFT LEFT, the content of each position in the register is replaced by the content of the position on the right. The content of the highest-order position is lost in the SHIFT LEFT operation and the content of the lowest-order portion is replaced by a 0. This type of shift operation is called a "logical shift." The shifting instruction may result in a fixed number of shifts per instruction execution or the number of shifts may be specified in the instruction. Shifting instructions are useful in the manipulation of bit-significant data. In addition, they provide an easy method of multiplying or dividing by factors of 2.

A variation of the shift instruction is a circular shift wherein the content of the end position of the register is shifted to the other end of the register. For example, in a left shift the content of the highest-order position is shifted into the lowest-order position.

Another variation, distinguished from the logical shift, is the arithmetic shift. This distinction is necessary because of the manner in which positive and negative numbers are represented in the computer. Although simplified, the idea is that for a positive number, the highest-order bit is a 0 and for a negative number it is a 1. This high-order bit is called the sign bit. In a logical shift, the shift is performed without regard to sign and the sign bit is shifted along with the other bits. In an arithmetic right shift, the sign bit is retained and repeated in vacated positions to return the correct sign of the result. In an arithmetic left shift, an error is flagged by setting an appropriate flipflop when the sign of the number changes as a result of the shift operation.

Load and Store Instructions

Although the names load and store may not be explicitly used, all computers have a category of instructions which are used to control the movement of data between storage and the various registers of the CPU. These are necessary for the manipulation of both data and instructions. A typical instruction is a simple STORE instruction which transfers the contents of the accumulator to a specified storage location. Similarly, a LOAD ACCUMULATOR instruction may be provided to transfer the contents of a storage location to the accumulator. If the CPU has general purpose or index registers, instructions are provided for loading them or transferring their contents to storage or another register.

The load and store functions may be combined with other functions such as clearing or incrementing a register. Similarly, a single instruction may provide functions that require several different instructions in another computer design. As an example, several minicomputers treat I/O devices and all internal registers as an extension of storage and assigns them storage addresses. The single instruction MOVE with a source and destination address provides all of the functions necessary to load and store data in any register, storage location, or I/O device.

Branch and Test Instructions

A common requirement in programming is to jump or skip to a new instruction sequence which does not immediately follow the instruction currently being executed. This capability is called "branching." Almost all computers have the equivalent of an unconditional branch, in which the program execution sequence is directed to start at a new address independent of any conditions that may exist in the CPU or data. The GO TO 23 statement in the FORTRAN program discussed earlier is an example of an unconditional branch as implemented in a high level computer language.

In other cases, the branch must take place only if some condition is satisfied. One or more conditional branching instructions are usually included in the instruction set. Typical conditions that are included are to branch when the data are positive, negative, even, or odd. In some computers, the conditional branch instructions apply to only a single condition at a time; for example, BRANCH ON ACCUMULATOR ZERO. In others, provision is made to specify multiple conditions such as branch when the accumulator is negative and odd.

In the typical computer, if the conditions for the branch are not satisfied, the program continues with the next sequential instruction. If they are satisfied, program execution continues with the instruction specified by the address in the branch instruction. A variation on this type of branching instruction is the skip instruction. In this case, the program skips only the next sequential instruction when the conditions are satisfied. If not satisfied, the next instruction is executed.

Testing instructions are related in the sense that they are used in conjunction with branching instructions. A testing instruction normally examines the content of a specified register and sets condition codes (status flags) that can be used by subsequent instructions as conditions for skipping or branching. Thus, testing instructions allow the programmer to check the status of certain portions of the machine or to test for characteristics of data. For example, an instruction may test as to whether a number in a register is positive or negative. This involves determining whether the most significant bit is 0 or 1. Similarly, testing for even or odd involves determining if the least significant bit is 0 or 1. Other conditions may also be available for testing.

Machine Status and Control Instructions

Most computers have a certain amount of error checking built into them. For example, hardware may be provided to indicate that an invalid instruction has been detected or that a storage address that does not exist has been addressed. In many cases an action such as this results in an interrupt, whereby the normal processing is suspended and the operator or executive program is notified that an error has taken place. The exact cause of the error may be summarized in status bits or a status word located in a register in the CPU. Instructions are normally provided to read this status word so that the operator or executive program can determine the exact cause of the error and initiate corrective action, if possible.

Input/Output Instructions

In most computers the input/output (I/O) equipment is connected through a channel subsystem. An instruction is generally provided to instruct the channel what functions it is to perform. In addition to the operation code specifying that it is an I/O instruction, the instruction generally contains the address of the I/O device to be actuated and the function the I/O device is to perform. In most cases, this function is a **READ** or **WRITE** depending on whether data is being accepted from the device or sent to the device. The I/O instruction may also contain the address of the storage location or register in which the data to be transferred out is stored or to which the input data from the device is to be stored. In some cases, this address is not required since it is specified that all I/O transfers take place between the channel and a predetermined register such as the accumulator. Due to the amount of information that must be provided to the channel, the I/O instruction is often a two-word instruction in 16-bit machines.

MICROCODED IMPLEMENTATIONS

In the hypothetical computer developed earlier in this chapter, the interpretation of the instructions (decoding) and the subsequent actions which were invoked were provided by digital logic circuits. This type of implementation is known as "hardwired control." A second form of implementation, although known for many years, has recently become popular in minicomputers. This is known as a microcoded implementation of an architecture.

The basic concept of the microcoded implementation is that the decoding of a machine level instruction does not result directly in the generation of the sequence of signals necessary to perform the function specified in the OP code of the instruction. Instead, control is passed to a Microcode Control Unit which executes a series of primitive instructions, known as microinstructions, which, when completed, will have implemented the function called for by the OP code of the machine level instruction. (One can argue that the microinstructions are the "machine level instructions" in this case but doing so causes semantic difficulties so the previous meaning of "machine level instruction" will continue to be used in this description.) In essence, the OP code function is implemented by a subroutine of microinstructions.

Figure 2.10 illustrates a general microcoded implementation which corresponds approximately to Fig. 2.8. The CPU data flow contains the various registers necessary to store parts of the machine level instruction,

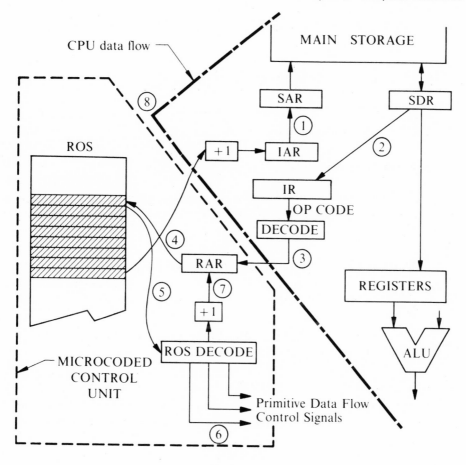

FIG. 2.10
Typical Microcoded Implementation

addresses, and intermediate results. It also contains the Arithmetic and Logic Unit (ALU) which approximately corresponds to the accumulator in Fig. 2.8. The ALU is that portion of the data flow in which the various arithmetic and logical operations are performed.

The Microcoded Control Unit consists of a Read-Only-Store Address Register (RAR) which contains the address of the location in the Read-Only-Store currently being accessed. The Read-Only-Store (ROS) is similar in function to a main storage unit in that it contains the instructions to be executed. In this case, however, the instructions it contains are the microinstructions. The ROS also is designed such that it can only be read; that is, it is not possible for the CPU to store information in the ROS. The information in the ROS is permanently fixed at the time of manufacture. The ROS Decode network performs a function similar to the instruction decode in

Fig. 2.8; that is, it decodes the microinstruction and generates unique signals for each microinstruction OP code.

The operation of the microcoded implementation can be understood by tracing through the eight steps indicated in Fig. 2.10.

1. The Instruction Address Register (IAR) contains the address of the next machine level instruction to be executed by the CPU. This address is placed in the Storage Address Register (SAR) and results in the addressed instruction being placed in the Storage Data Register (SDR).

2. If the accessed location is an instruction, it is transferred from the SDR to the Instruction Register (IR) which is exactly equivalent to the instruction register of Fig. 2.8.

3. The OP code of the instruction is transferred to the ROS Address Register (RAR) where it (or a transformed version of it) is used as an address to access (4) the ROS.

5. The contents of the RAR causes the word at the addressed location in the ROS to be placed in the ROS Decode network register.

6. The result of decoding the ROS word is a series of primitive control and sequencing signals which control the transfer of data and operations within the CPU Data Flow. These control signals are similar to the LDD, CLR, etc., signals discussed in connection with Fig. 2.8 but they are usually much simpler. For example, a single control signal might only cause data in one register to be presented as an input to the ALU as only one of many steps necessary to perform an addition using the ALU.

7. Following completion of the primitive action caused by the accessed ROS word, the RAR is incremented by one and the next ROS word is accessed, decoded, and signals are sent to the CPU Data Flow.

8. When the sequence of microinstructions necessary to perform the function specified by the OP code of the machine level instruction have been executed, the IAR is incremented. This causes the accessing of the next machine level instruction in the program being executed and the sequence begins again.

Microcoded implementations have two primary advantages. The first is that they can be used to provide a very flexible computer utilizing a relatively simple CPU Data Flow. It is possible, for example, by using the correct microcode, to use the same data flow to implement several different instructions sets. In a similar way, it can be used to implement very complex instructions which would not be attractive economically if implemented directly in hardware. One could have an instruction, for example, which would continue to subtract a sequence of numbers from a starting number until the sum became less than zero; this would all be done by a single machine level instruction.

In some minicomputers, the user of the computer has access to the ROS and can essentially design a unique instruction set for a particular application. This approach is not recommended for the novice computer user as the design of instruction sets is extremely complicated and costly. In general, the use of customized microcode is counter to the trend of the user using higher level languages and, in this author's opinion, should be reserved for the sophisticated user and very special cases.

The second advantage of microcoded implementations is economy. The cost of a single ROS word is very low due to the advances made in large scale integration (LSI). On the other hand, the design of sequential control circuits is expensive and prone to errors which are difficult to correct in an LSI environment. The use of the microcoded implementation makes it easier to correct design errors since only the ROS words must be changed (during the design phase, a read-and-write memory (RAM) typically is substituted for the ROS). In addition, since the amount of ROS which is equivalent to a single logic function costs less than the corresponding logic circuit (gate), the microcoded implementation provides a tradeoff leading to a less expensive implementation. The same computer architecture can be implemented using thousands of words of ROS and few regular logic circuits or more circuits and less ROS can be used. The tradeoff is that machine level instructions implemented through microcode are slower since each instruction involves executing a number of microinstructions. Thus, the tradeoff is a cost (price)/performance tradeoff. As a specific example, two models of a minicomputer were designed. In one, there were about 6K of ROS bytes and 5000 logic circuits. In the second, there were about 2000 circuits and about 16K bytes of ROS. Both implementations executed exactly the same instruction set but the first executed machine level programs about three times faster than the second. The first was also more costly by approximately the same factor.

CHANNEL CHARACTERISTICS

The channel is the subsystem that controls the operation of the I/O devices. It is, in a sense, a specialized computer capable of executing a limited set of instructions concerned with the control of I/O devices. In some designs, there is no specific piece of hardware designated as the channel but its function is provided in all minicomputers.

In the general case, the channel takes the information provided in the I/O instruction and controls the operation of the devices attached to the channel and the transfer of data to and from such devices. In doing so, the channel must know the particular device being addressed, the source or destination of the data, and the exact function that the I/O device is to perform. The channel then takes care of the detailed timing, formating of data, and other details necessary in controlling the I/O device. Once the channel has initiated its operation, the arithmetic and control unit may proceed to the next instruction even though the channel operation has not been completed. This is known as overlapping.

There are two basic methods of controlling the channel. For lack of better terminology, these will be called direct control and indirect control. In the direct control channel, each channel operation must be initiated by the execution of an I/O instruction. For example, if 20 characters of data are to be read from a card reader, the CPU must execute an I/O instruction to read the first character. When the read operation is complete, the CPU must execute a second I/O instruction to read the second word, and so on. Obviously, this type of operation places a significant computing burden on the CPU, particularly in the case where high speed I/O devices such as disk storage are being controlled. This type of channel control, however, requires the simplest hardware and, as a result, the least cost.

The indirect method of channel control is known by a number of different names such as cycle steal and direct storage access (DSA or DMA). It is characterized by the fact that once the I/O operation is initiated, repetitive channel operations can occur without the intervention of the arithmetic and control unit. In the case above, for example, the channel is given a single I/O instruction which, in effect, says "transfer 20 characters from the card reader and store the data in main storage starting at location 3000." The channel initiates all of the actions necessary to complete the entire operation. In the meantime, the arithmetic and control unit continues with the concurrent execution of subsequent instructions in an overlapped mode. The operation of the channel does not involve the use of any registers of the arithmetic and control unit in this case so that the concurrent operation is possible. Whenever the channel requires access to main storage, it "steals" a cycle from the arithmetic and control unit. The instruction execution taking place in the arithmetic and control unit is periodically interrupted by this cycle stealing, but the degree of interference is much less than in the case of the direct control channel.

The advantage of cycle stealing is that the operation can proceed at a much higher rate of speed since multiple executions of the I/O instruction and the constant interruption of the arithmetic and control unit are avoided. The disadvantage is that the indirect controlled channel is much more complicated and, hence, results in more hardware and cost.

Interrupt

The interrupt function is closely related to the operation of the channel and the arithmetic and control unit. The necessity for having a means to interrupt or temporarily suspend the execution of instructions in the arithmetic and control unit comes from two causes. The first is the relatively slow speed of many of the I/O devices. For example, card readers operate at electromechanical speeds that are measured in milliseconds, whereas the electronic circuits of the arithmetic and control unit operate at speeds measured in fractions of microseconds. If the arithmetic and control unit is forced to stop and wait for the completion of the relatively slow I/O operation, a significant portion of the computing power is being wasted. Interrupt provides a means whereby the I/O operation can continue concurrently and, at its completion, the arithmetic and control unit can be interrupted to provide the next information required by the I/O unit.

The second requirement arises from the real-time nature of many of the applications in which minicomputers are used. Asynchronous and unexpected events can occur in the process which require the attention of the computer for servicing. For example, a vat of liquid may be close to overflowing and the computer must react to this unexpected event by closing the proper valve in the process. The interrupt mechanism provides the means whereby this notification of the CPU and the temporary suspension of the current program can be effected.

On the occurrence of an interrupt and either under hardware or software control, the content of the registers in the CPU are saved in predetermined locations. The program then branches to a subroutine that services the interrupting event. Once the service is complete, the program or hardware restores the information that was saved and branches back to the original program which then continues from the point at which it was interrupted.

In the simplest interrupt schemes, only a single interrupt signal is provided. This signal can be initiated by any of the I/O devices having a need to do so. When an interrupt occurs and after the status of the CPU has been saved, the hardware or software must determine exactly which device caused the interrupt so that the proper servicing routine can be initiated. It must also provide some means of selecting one of the several devices which may be requesting service simultaneously. This is generally done through a polling scheme. For example, each device may be interrogated (polled) in a defined sequence. The first of the polled devices that has generated an interrupt request responds by presenting its address on the channel to be read by the arithmetic and control unit. Having analyzed the address, the program then branches to the appropriate routine. Other requests are ignored until the first request has been serviced. The polling operation and the determination of which software servicing routine to initiate can be implemented in software or hardware. In the simpler and less expensive machines, it is usually done in software.

In the interrupt scheme described above, the CPU is interrupted for every interrupt request even though it may be servicing a very important event, unless it disables all interrupts by an operation called "masking." In order to avoid this and to enhance the efficiency of the interrupt servicing process, some minicomputers provide a system of priority interrupts. In this case, there are multiple (usually 4 or 8) interrupt lines to which devices can be assigned by hardware or software. As an example, suppose that there are four interrupt levels numbered 0 through 3 with the 0 level having the highest priority. Further suppose that the CPU is servicing an interrupt on level 2. If another interrupting source activates the level 3 interrupt, the processor does not suspend its servicing of the level 2 program. Instead, it completes the servicing of the level 2 routine before accepting and servicing the level 3 interrupt. If, however, the CPU is on level 2 and a level 0 interrupt occurs, the processor suspends its current activity to immediately service the level 0 interrupt. When it finishes this service, it returns and services the lower order pending interrupts in their order of precedence.

STORAGE

The main storage of the computer is characterized by its size (number of storage locations), its speed, and its technology. Storage is usually made available from the manufacturer in increments up to some maximum available number of locations. Typically, the increments are at least 4096 words, although some manufacturers offer storage in increments of 2048 or 8192 words. (In the computer industry terminology, the quantity $1024 = 2^{10}$ is designated by the symbol K. Thus, 4096 words of storage is called a 4K storage.) The maximum number of words available on many minicomputers is 64K ($= 64 \times 1024 = 65536$ words), although some machines are restricted to 32K and others offer 128K or more. In the 16-bit machine, 64K is the maximum number of words (or bytes in a byte-addressed machine) that can be directly addressed due to the limitation of the word length. Special techniques are used to address larger storage spaces.

The speed of the storage is measured in terms of the total time it takes for each repetitive access of a single word from the storage unit. This is called the "cycle time." In today's technology, the cycle time ranges from about 300 nanoseconds to about 2 microseconds for most computers. To a certain extent, the cycle time is dependent on the technology used in the storage with semiconductor storage offering the faster cycle times. The fastest cycle time available for a particular computer generally determines the minimum instruction execution time. The execution time of other instructions may be a multiple of the storage cycle time if multiple references to storage are required as, for example, when indirect addressing is used.

Two primary technologies are used in current storage systems. The first, and the oldest, is magnetic core storage. In this type of storage each bit is stored magnetically in tiny doughnut-shaped pieces of ferrite material as shown in Fig. 2.11. Very fine wires pass through the center of the core. By controlling the amount and direction of the current flow through these wires, it is possible to magnetize the core in one direction or the other. Each direction of magnetization represents one of the binary states 1 or 0. By

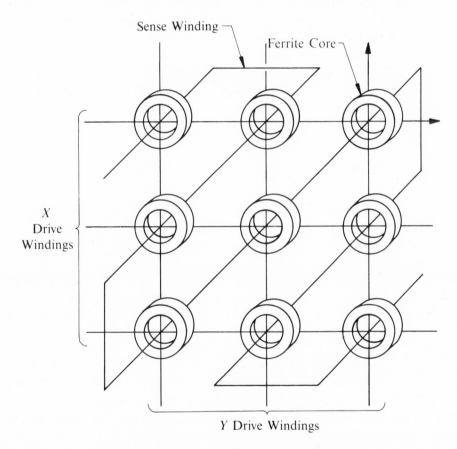

FIG. 2.11
Magnetic Core Storage Circuit

causing the direction of magnetization to switch from one direction to the other, it is possible to induce a signal into a sense winding which, when amplified and shaped, corresponds to a 1 or 0. The act of reading the state of the core resets it to the 0 state. However, associated circuits automatically rewrite the contents of the core following reading.

Core storage tends to be slower than semiconductor storage and typically requires one or two microseconds to access the information. It has the advantage that it is non-volatile. That is, the information stored in a core storage is not lost when electrical power is removed.

Semiconductor storage consists of registers made up of flipflops or similar transistor circuits that store information in the form of 1's and 0's. Development of Large Scale Integration (LSI) has allowed the construction of devices which store thousands of bits of information on a piece of silicon that is less than 0.20 inch square.

The access time of semiconductor storage tends to be faster than that of core storage with sub-microsecond speeds being common. Semiconductor storage has the disadvantage that information is lost if power is removed from the unit. A number of minicomputers feature a battery backup system which maintains power to the storage unit for some period of time if the main power source is lost. Semiconductor storage, in addition to its speed advantage, is attractive since the continuing development of Large Scale Integration has resulted in continuing declines in cost.

COSTS AND COMPARISONS

The costs of minicomputers are changing on almost a daily basis. In addition, the inclusion of other services or software in the base price of the hardware makes comparison difficult. Generally speaking, a minicomputer is considered to be a computer in which the minimum useful configuration (usually the CPU, 4K of storage, and a simple I/O device) costs less than $25,000. However, within this range there is a tremendous variation in what you receive for the price. Stripped down minicomputers which essentially consist of only the base CPU can be obtained in quantity for less than $1000. To this must be added the cost of storage, sometimes the cost of I/O interfaces, and the cost of I/O devices before the computer can be useful. Such stripped down minicomputers are attractive to OEM manufacturers who incorporate them into custom equipment. They are rarely of direct interest to the ultimate user of the machine.

The actual cost of the computer for a particular application can exceed the minimum configuration cost by many times. The cost of I/O equipment and additional storage almost always far outshadows the base cost of the CPU. In addition, differences in service and software can have a significant effect on the total application cost and a meaningful tabulation of typical costs is almost impossible to provide. A caution is given, however, that the user should consider the total cost of the application including programming, and not be unduly influenced by the hardware cost of the CPU alone.

The question of comparing computer designs is equally complex. Almost any computer will do any application if cost and performance are not factors; that is, a minicomputer usually can do the job of a large computer if enough time is provided. In real-time applications, however, the time factor is an important consideration.

There is no simple means of comparing minicomputers. Each computer has advantages and disadvantages when compared to another. The problem is not a question of determining which computer is best, but rather of determining which computer system best satisfies a particular application. Thus, the user must evaluate the available machines in the context of his application. The number of considerations is tremendous: speeds, instruction sets, physical packaging, service requirements and aids, reliability, available software, power consumption, characteristics of I/O devices, and tolerance of physical environment, to name a few. A single guideline for comparison is not possible. A methodology in which the most important factors for the particular application are enumerated and assigned priorities is suggested as being the only practical way of approaching this problem. Certainly a key point in the selection process is an understanding of computers and an understanding of the application.

BIBLIOGRAPHY

Bartie, T. C., *Digital Computer Fundamentals*, 3rd Ed., McGraw-Hill Book Co., New York, 1972.

Bell, C. G. and Newell, A., *Computer Structures: Readings and Examples*, McGraw-Hill Book Co., New York, 1971.

Chu, Y., *Computer Organization and Microprogramming*, Prentice-Hall, Inc., Englewood Cliffs, 1972.

Considine, D. M., *Encyclopedia of Instrumentation and Control*, McGraw-Hill Book Co., 1971.

Flores, I., *Computer Organization*, Prentice-Hall Inc., Englewood Cliffs, 1969.

Harrison, T. J., *Handbook of Industrial Control Computers*, John Wiley & Sons, New York, 1972.

Harrison, T. J., "Hardware: A Matter of Logic, Memory, and Timing," Control Engineering, November 1967, pp. 74–79.

Harrison, T. J., "How Hardware Responds to Software," Control Engineering, December 1967, pp. 65–70.

Korn, G. A., *Minicomputers for Engineers and Scientists*, McGraw-Hill Book Co., New York, 1973.

Lewin, D., *Theory and Design of Digital Computers*, John Wiley & Sons, New York, 1972.

Peatman, J. B., *Microcomputer-Based Design*, McGraw-Hill Book Co., New York, 1977.

Salisbury, A. B., *Microprogrammable Computer Architectures*, American Elsevier, New York, 1976.

3 PERIPHERAL (INPUT/OUTPUT) DEVICES

Thomas J. Harrison, Ph.D.
INTERNATIONAL BUSINESS MACHINES CORPORATION,
BOCA RATON, FLORIDA

Chapter 2 was concerned with concepts, ideas, and implementations of the central processor unit (CPU) of the computer system. The basic concept was that the computer is an information processor which, internally, manipulates only numbers or numerically-coded information. It was demonstrated how this manipulation could be done using the binary number system and relatively simple electronic circuits. No indication, however, was given as to how the information is entered into the computer or how the computer presents information to the operator. These are the functions of the input and output devices which are the subject of this chapter.

INPUT/OUTPUT CONCEPTS

The information used by the computer exists in a number of different forms external to the computer system. The best known, and most obvious, is information in the form of decimal numbers and alphanumeric information. Examples of these include names and numerical values which represent setpoints or measurements. A related form of information is data which are stored in the computer on mass storage devices, such as disk or drum storage. This information is coded in binary form although, with the appropriate

97

programming, it may be addressed using either a numeric or alphanumeric address.

In the previous two cases, the information exists in discrete form; that is, it can be expressed using a finite number of symbols, such as the ten digits and the twenty-six alphabetic characters. Some information from the process, however, does not exist naturally in a discrete form. For example, temperature is an analog quantity; that is, it can take on any value between two limits and is not restricted to certain discrete values. When one speaks or writes about temperature, it is expressed as a discrete quantity, such as 23 degrees Celsius. However, this is a discrete approximation to the analog quantity which actually may be more closely approximated as 23.000245... degrees Celsius. For convenience and in order to use it in numerical form, the analog quantity is converted into a discrete or digital quantity. This is done, for example, by using a thermometer in which the height of a mercury column (an analog quantity since the height can be of any value) is compared to a scale. In reading the thermometer, the operator performs an analog-to-digital conversion.

There are other examples of analog quantities that typically are found in processes. Most common are flow rate and pressures. Other analog quantities include position, depth, and angle of rotation.

An industrial computer system must be able to accept analog information and convert it into the digital or discrete form which is required for the internal operation of the computer. The equipment which provides this capability is generally known as an analog-to-digital converter (ADC) and is provided as a part of the analog-input subsystem.

In addition to being able to accept information in analog form, it is sometimes required that the computer system provide an output in the form of an analog voltage. This might be used, for example, to position a valve. The analog-output subsystem of the computer includes a digital-to-analog converter (DAC), which takes binary-coded numerical information provided by the CPU and converts it into a continuous analog voltage or current. The analog-input and analog-output subsystems of the industrial computer system are often called the "analog front-end" of the system.

There is also information concerning the process which is not analog in nature but which must be gathered by the computer system in an industrial application. This information already exists in binary form as, for example, in the case of a switch being on or off, or a bin being full or not full. In most cases, this type of information is represented by the on or off state of a switch or relay so the industrial computer system must have the ability to sense the state of the switch. Another example of a digital quantity is when the computer merely must sense that a quantity has exceeded a particular value or threshold. This might be represented, for example, by a voltage which exceeds a preset limit such as 2.5 volts or a current exceeding 10 milliamperes. The ability to sense switch states and thresholds is provided in the industrial computer system by the digital-input (DI) subsystem. This subsystem generally provides both "contact sense" and "voltage sense" options.

Analogous to the digital-input function, the computer system often needs to control a binary device in the process. A common example is when the computer must actuate a switch, turn on a pump, or illuminate an alarm light. This capability is provided by the digital-output (DO) subsystem of the industrial computer. It provides, in essence, computer-controlled switches which may be connected to process equipment.

Classes of Input/Output Subsystems

The various computer input/output subsystems which are provided to handle the forms of information discussed above are generally divided into two classes: Data Processing Input/Output (DP I/O) and Process Input/Output (PI/O). Data processing I/O devices or subsystems are those which generally are available on any general-purpose computer system. They include card and tape readers/punches, graphic display terminals, printers, teletypewriters, and data entry consoles of various types. In all of these cases, the conversion of the information into the appropriate form for use by the computer or the human is performed by the device and it is discrete alphanumeric information. Mass storage devices such as magnetic tape, disk, and drum units are, for the purposes of this chapter, considered to be DP I/O devices.

Process I/O, the second class of input/output devices, includes the analog-input (AI) subsystem, the analog-output (AO) subsystem, the digital-input (DI) subsystem, and the digital-output (DO) subsystem. As noted previously, these are the subsystems used to connect the industrial computer system to the process.

General Subsystem Organization

The general organization of the DP I/O and Process I/O subsystems is similar and is shown in Fig. 3.1. The devices are generally attached to the I/O channel of the CPU although, in some systems, one or more of the I/O devices may be attached to the CPU hardware directly without an intervening channel. The hardware between the actual channel attachment and the I/O device itself may be divided into several functional blocks, some of which may be combined with other blocks or some of which may be entirely missing in particular system designs.

With reference to Fig. 3.1, the channel attachment hardware is the electronics which are physically attached to the channel bus and which are primarily concerned with the detailed operation of the channel. The exact

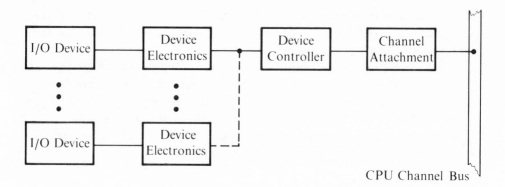

FIG. 3.1
I/O Subsystem Organization

design of the channel attachment and the functions that it provides are highly dependent on the design of the channel itself and the overall system architecture. The channel attachment generally includes high-power driver circuits and special receiver circuits, since the normal computer logic circuits are not suitable for driving signals over the long distances required on the channel. It may, in addition, provide detection features for certain types of errors. For example, if parity checking is provided on the channel, the parity checking circuits for incoming signals and the parity generation circuits for outgoing data typically are provided in the channel attachment. The channel attachment includes the circuits for the timing of demand and response signals that are used to control communication over the channel. If the channel is serial (that is, if information is transmitted a bit at a time) and if the I/O device is parallel (that is, handles information a byte or a word at a time), the channel attachment provides the necessary serializing and deserializing circuits.

The device controller is concerned with the detailed operation of the I/O device. Common functions provided by the device controller are the interpretation and execution of commands that it receives over the channel. For example, in an I/O device which has the capability of either writing or reading data such as a disk file, the controller determines which of these actions is desired and provides the necessary detailed control of the device. It may also provide address decoding when, for example, the I/O device consists of many inputs or outputs. An example is digital-input where the input device may consist of many words of DI, each of which has a unique address. The device controller also provides the timing circuits that are necessary in controlling the I/O device.

The controller design is highly dependent on the characteristics of the I/O device and each device has unique requirements. With the advent of large scale integration (LSI) and the microcomputer, many device controllers are being designed using the microcomputer. This has the advantage that a single generalized hardware design can be utilized for a variety of I/O devices. The particular requirements of each I/O device, known as its personality, is provided by the program that is stored in the microcomputer. When only a single hardware design is required, the development and manufacturing costs are reduced. Due to the fact that it can be programmed, a microcomputer can often provide functions that would be too expensive or too complex to be incorporated into a specialized hardware design. For example, with the microcomputer's inherent computational capability, functions such as complex error correcting procedures or limit checking can be included with essentially no extra hardware.

Depending on the particular device being controlled, the device controller may be very simple or very complex. In the case of more complex devices, such as disk files, the controller may be used to control more than one I/O device on a time-shared basis to amortize the cost of the complex attachment.

The device electronics shown in Fig. 3.1 are those circuits necessary for the detailed control of the I/O device. Examples of functions which are unique to a device include the servo system that is used to position the heads on a moving-head disk file or the electromechanical equipment to control the movement of paper in a printer. These electronics are often provided as part of the I/O device and may not be easily recognized as a separate function.

The I/O device itself is the equipment which establishes contact with the outside world. In the case of DP I/O, this is very often an electromechanical device such as a printer or card reader. Other forms of DP I/O such as graphic outputs utilizing TV displays, have very little electromechanical equipment associated with them. The process I/O devices generally are mostly electronic in nature. They interface directly into instruments and other process equipment such as analog controllers and valves.

In the following sections, the characteristics of specific I/O equipment are discussed. In general, the discussion provides the purpose of the equipment, its physical characteristics and how it works, and the performance parameters which characterize its operation.

ANALOG-INPUT SUBSYSTEMS

The purpose of the analog-input subsystem is to provide the industrial computer system with the capability of accepting analog data from the process to which it is connected. Since the digital computer deals only with discrete numerical values, the analog-input subsystem must convert the analog quantity into a coded digital representation suitable for use by the computer. This process is known as analog-to-digital conversion.

The analog-input subsystem is connected to the instrumentation or sensor that is measuring the quantities of interest in the process. In most cases, this instrumentation or sensor converts the physical quantity being measured (the measurand) into an electrical signal. For example, a thermocouple converts a temperature measurand into an analog voltage proportional to the temperature; a pressure transducer often converts the pressure into an electrical current in the range of 4 to 20 milliamperes, which is easily converted into a voltage signal. The vast majority of analog-input subsystems are designed to convert a voltage input signal into a coded numerical quantity representing the value of the input voltage, and, hence, the value of the measurand.

The general organization of the analog-input subsystem is shown in Fig. 3.2. Input signals from the process are passed through signal conditioning circuits which may modify them to be compatible with the remaining equipment used in the conversion process. Since the amplifiers and ADCs are relatively expensive, they are time-shared between many input signals. The multiplexer is a device that selects a particular signal to be converted into computer-compatible form at any particular time. It is, in essence, a selector switch which is under the control of the I/O device controller and, indirectly, the CPU. An amplifier is necessary in many cases to adjust the magnitude of the input signal so that it can be properly converted by the ADC. For example, many thermocouples provide a voltage output on the order of 50 mV and most ADCs are designed with a full scale range of 5 V. In order to obtain maximum resolution in the conversion process, an amplifier with a gain or amplification factor of 100 is used. The gain of the amplifier may be fixed or it may be under the control of the device controller. The ADC is the device which

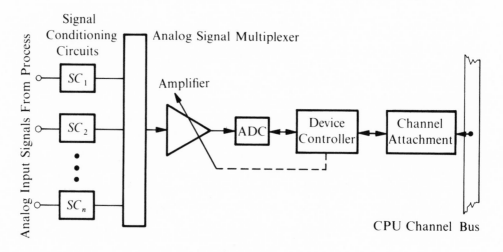

FIG. 3.2
General Analog Input Subsystem

converts the value of the analog-input voltage into its digital equivalent. Its ouput is a binary word representing the magnitude of the input voltage, usually as a fraction of the maximum voltage which can be accepted by the ADC. The general functions of the device controller and the channel attachment have been discussed above. The detailed operation of the other parts of the analog-input subsystem are discussed in subsequent sections.

Differential and Single-Ended Subsystems.

Before discussing the detailed function and design of the various parts of the analog-input subsystem, it is necessary to understand the difference between differential and single-ended measurement devices. In Fig. 3.3a a voltage is being measured with a single-ended instrument. A single-ended instrument measures the voltage or potential difference between its input terminal A and its ground terminal G. In Fig. 3.3b a differential instrument is being used to measure a voltage. It has two input terminals in addition to a ground terminal and the voltage which is measured is the difference in potential between the two terminals A and B. Note that there may also be a

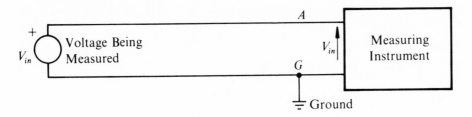

(a) Single-Ended Measurement

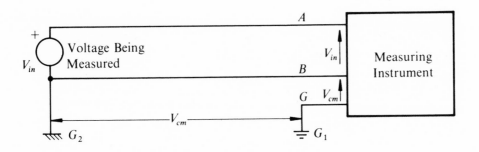

(b) Differential Measurement

FIG. 3.3
Single-Ended and Differential Measurements

voltage difference between terminal B and the ground terminal G. This voltage theoretically does not affect the value of the measurement. As illustrated in Fig. 3.3b, the voltage source being measured may also be connected to a ground potential G_2 which differs from the ground potential G_1 found at the instrument. The voltage between terminal B and the instrument ground G_1 is:

$$V_B = V_{cm}$$

The voltage between terminal A and the instrument ground G_1 is:

$$V_A = V_{cm} + V_{in}$$

Thus, the voltage V_{cm} is common to both input terminals of the measuring instrument and is called the "common-mode voltage." The voltage V_{in} is called the "normal-mode voltage."

Using a single-ended instrument when a common-mode voltage is present as in Fig. 3.3b results in an error, since V_{cm} appears in series with the input signal V_{in}. The measurement error is equal to V_{cm}, which may be much larger than the signal voltage V_{in}.

Theoretically, the use of a differential instrument allows accurate voltage measurements to be taken when a common-mode potential is present. In practice, there always is an error due to the common-mode potential. This error is called the common-mode error and its magnitude is a performance measure of a differential instrument. The performance parameter most frequently used is the common-mode rejection ratio (CMRR) which is defined by the equation:

$$\text{CMRR} = \frac{\text{Common-mode voltage in volts}}{\text{Error in volts due to common-mode voltage}}$$

The CMRR commonly is expressed as a ratio such as 1,000,000 to 1, which means that for every volt of common-mode voltage applied, there is an error of one microvolt.

The CMRR also is expressed in decibels using the definition:

$$\text{CMRR(dB)} = 20 \log_{10} (\text{CMRR})$$

Thus, a CMRR of 1,000,000:1 is equivalent to a rejection ratio of 120 dB.

In general, common-mode errors are most serious in instruments used to measure low-level (less than 1 volt) signals. It is common, therefore, to find high-level (usually 5 volt full scale) analog-input subsystems that are single-ended, whereas low-level subsystems are usually differential.

Signal Conditioning

The signals produced by process instrumentation may not be entirely compatible with the characteristics of the analog-input subsystem and may require some modification. Common signal conditioning requirements are attenuation, current-to-voltage conversion, and noise filtering. If the magnitude of the input signal exceeds the capability of the analog-input subsystem, the signal conditioning element is typically a resistive voltage divider which attenuates the input signal. If the subsystem is differential, the attenuator is electrically balanced with respect to ground, since common-mode error is directly proportional to unbalance in the input circuit of the subsystem.

A second common signal conditioning requirement is a circuit to convert a current signal to a voltage signal, since current signals are quite common in process applications. Generally, this merely involves using a series resistor to convert the current signal into a voltage signal. A current range of 4–20 mA is the preferred value in the United States.

Many process signals are noisy; that is, they are subject to fluctuations that are due to influences other than variations in the measurand. A simple filter composed of passive electrical elements (usually resistors and capacitors) can attenuate rapidly changing electrical signals while not affecting slowly changing process signals. In general, most manufacturers of industrial computer systems provide a selection of filters as signal conditioning elements. In addition, they may provide cards that can be altered by the user for the design of custom filter networks.

Multiplexers

The multiplexer is essentially a selector switch which is used to select a particular input signal for connection to the ADC. The relatively high cost of ADC's and precision amplifiers, coupled with the fact that the value of any particular input is required only periodically, make it practical and economical to time-share the amplifier and ADC among a number of input signals. The multiplexer and its associated controls provide the means of time sharing.

The multiplexer basically consists of a switch placed in series with each input signal that is to be converted by the ADC. If the subsystem is single-ended, the switch is a single-pole, single-throw (SPST) switch as shown in Fig. 3.4a. Each of the n input signal paths is called an input channel. When it is required to convert one of the input signals into a digital word, the CPU provides the address of the particular channel to the device controller. The controller decodes the address and closes the switch associated with that particular channel, so that the input signal is applied to the amplifier and

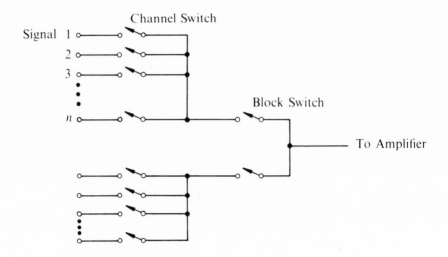

(a) Single-Ended Multiplexer

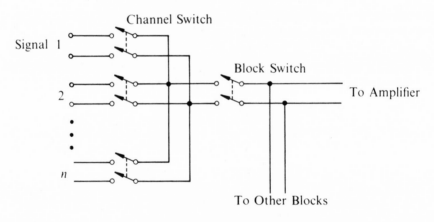

(b) Differential Multiplexer

FIG. 3.4
Basic Multiplexer Configurations

ADC. When the conversion is completed, the controller opens the switch and transfers the ADC reading to the CPU through the CPU channel.

Some applications require only a few analog-inputs, whereas others may require thousands. The number which can be connected to a single analog-input subsystem depends, in part, on the design tradeoffs made by the manufacturer. In general, the larger the number of inputs, the more difficult it is to control sources of errors including, in particular, noise and crosstalk (one signal affecting another) errors.

One means of increasing the number of input channels that can be connected to a single amplifier and ADC is illustrated in Fig. 3.4a. Each group of n input points is connected to a second level multiplexing switch called a block switch. This has the effect of isolating parallel leakage paths and capacitances which are major sources of errors in multiplexers. The number of switches in each group depends on the characteristics of the switches used in the multiplexer and certain other physical factors, but n is on the order of 16 or 32 in most designs.

If the analog-input subsystem is designed for differential measurements, the multiplexer must also be differential. As shown in Fig. 3.4b, this means that a switch is provided in each of the two input lines for each input channel. In some cases, a third switch is provided to switch the shield associated with the use of shielded twisted-pair signal wiring. Block switching is used as in the previous case and for the same reasons. In designing a differential multiplexer, care must be taken to maintain electrical balance (i.e., equal capacitances and leakage resistances) in both input lines to avoid degrading the common mode performance of the subsystem. This, as well as the cost of the extra switches, means that the differential multiplexer has a higher initial cost than a single-ended multiplexer. The noise immunity is far superior, however, and often results in fewer installation and maintenance problems.

A common differential multiplexer which differs from that shown in Fig. 3.4b is the "flying capacitor" multiplexer. Two channels of a flying capacitor multiplexer are shown in Fig. 3.5. When a channel is not selected, the input

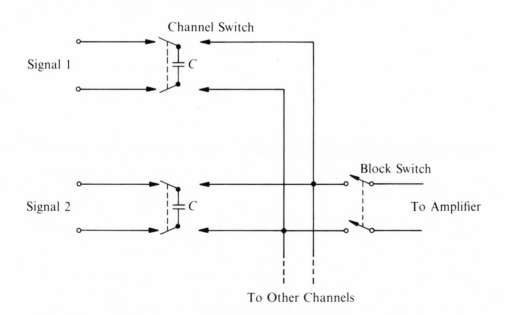

FIG. 3.5
Flying Capacitor Multiplexer

signal is applied directly across the flying capacitor C. The capacitor accumulates charge, such that the voltage across the capacitor is equal to the input signal voltage. When a signal is to be read, the switches transfer to the output contacts and the voltage stored on the capacitor is applied to the amplifier input. Since the input impedance of the amplifier is very high (typically greater than 10 megohms) and the capacitor is quite large (typically 100 microfarads or more), the voltage across the capacitor remains essentially constant during the conversion interval.

Due to the switching and holding action, the input signal is never directly connected to the amplifier and, therefore, the amplifier theoretically never is subjected to common-mode voltage. In actual fact, however, some common-mode voltage is transferred on stray capacitances between the switch armature and ground. The common-mode rejection ratio is equal to the ratio of the value of the flying capacitor to those of the stray capacitances. Since the stray capacitances are on the order of picofarads and the flying capacitor is on the order of microfarads, a CMRR of greater than 120 dB is obtainable.

In the differential multiplexer, the common-mode voltage is limited by the breakdown voltage of the multiplexer switches and the breakdown voltage of the input transistors of the amplifier. If relays are used as switching devices, the switch breakdown voltage is not a problem, since relays can easily sustain several hundred volts of common-mode voltage. In the flying capacitor multiplexer, the amplifier is effectively disconnected from the common-mode voltage, so that amplifier breakdown is not a significant problem. Due to the isolation provided by the multiplexer switches, a single-ended amplifier can be used and this results in a simpler and less expensive amplifier design.

Another advantage of the flying capacitor multiplexer is that the signal is disconnected from the amplifier and ADC during conversion. Thus, if a noise spike occurs on the signal line during the conversion interval, it does not affect the reading.

A disadvantage of the flying capacitor multiplexer is that it is limited to rather low speed operation, on the order of 100 to 200 samples per second, and the effective signal bandwidth is usually quite small, on the order of 10 Hz or less. The speed limitation is due to the fact that relays are used for the multiplexer switches. It is possible to build a flying capacitor multiplexer using transistor switches, but most of the advantages are lost since transistor switches can only sustain 20 or 30 volts of common-mode voltage. The bandwidth limitation is a consequence of the large size of the flying capacitor. Coupled with the line resistance and any resistance in the signal conditioning elements, the capacitor forms a low-pass RC filter, with, typically, a bandwidth of less than 10 Hz.

The flying capacitor multiplexer is relatively expensive compared to simpler all-transistor multiplexers. Its advantages, however, far outweigh its disadvantages for many applications that require immunity to noise and high common-mode voltages. For this reason, it commonly is used in process control applications where sampling rate requirements are not high and where severe electrical environments demand high noise immunity and the ability to withstand large common-mode voltages.

As indicated above, relays are often used as the switching devices in signal multiplexers. In general, the relay usually is either a mercury-wetted contact relay or a dry-reed contact relay. Although the cost and reliability of the dry contact relay is less than that of the mercury-wetted relay, both are satisfactory for industrial use and give years of reliable operation if the sampling rates are not too high.

The other device commonly used for multiplexing switches is the field-effect transistor (FET). The FET is capable of switching operations in excess of 100,000 samples per second and has very high reliability. It also has the advantage of small size and arrays of multiplexer switches can be fabricated on a single chip of silicon using integrated circuit techniques. In general, the breakdown voltage of the FET is on the order of 30 volts, so that common-mode potentials must be limited to on the order of 10 volts.

Amplifiers

An amplifier is almost always included in the analog-input subsystem. In the case of a high-level subsystem, its function is to provide a high impedance load to the signal source to minimize loading errors and a low impedance source to the ADC. In low-level systems, it provides the additional function of increasing the magnitude of the input signal so that it is compatible with the range of the ADC.

If the subsystem is differential and a flying capacitor multiplexer is not being used, the amplifier must also have a differential input. In general, the ADC input is single-ended so the amplifier output is typically single-ended. The other important characteristics of the amplifier are its gain and offset stability and its temperature characteristics. The amplifier is in series with the input signal, so that any changes in amplifier gain or offset translate into subsystem errors. Similarly, changes in offset with time or temperature result in drift or temperature errors. In addition, noise generated by the amplifier affects the repeatability of the subsystem.

The amplifiers typically used in modern industrial computer systems may employ either fixed gain or variable gain. In the case of a fixed-gain amplifier, all signals connected to the amplifier by the multiplexer are amplified by the same factor. This type of amplifier, less expensive than the variable-gain amplifier, can effectively be used when the input signals all fall into the same general range of values or when they can be grouped into several ranges with one amplifier provided for each group.

In the variable-gain amplifier case, a single amplifier provides several gains under control of the computer or the analog-input subsystem. In a typical case, the command issued by the computer includes the address of the input to be read and the value of the gain to be used. During the time that the multiplexer switches are being selected, the gain switches are set to the desired range for the subsequent conversion.

An alternative is that the analog subsystem automatically selects the optimum gain without intervention from the computer. One method makes an initial conversion on the highest range (or the second highest) and, on the basis of the numerical result obtained from the ADC, adjusts the amplifier gain for a subsequent conversion. Since this requires two ADC operations, it results in lower overall subsystem speed. In an automatic gain system, the selected value of gain must be sent back to the computer for use in subsequent scaling calculations.

Analog-to-Digital Converters

The analog-to-digital converter (ADC) converts the analog-input signal into a numerical value for use by the computer. There are a large number of different methods that can be used for analog-to-digital conversion. The names of some of these techniques are multiple comparator, successive approximation, voltage-to-frequency, ramp, and dual ramp integration. Each technique has its advantages and disadvantages in terms of cost and performance. In this brief introduction, it is not possible to consider all types of converters and the reader is referred to the literature for a complete survey. (See, for example, the references by Harrison, Hoeschele, or Schmid.)

In many cases, the technique for converting an unknown input voltage into its digital representation involves converting the magnitude of the input signal into another parameter, which can be more easily measured by electronic means. For example, the signal magnitude may be used to control an oscillator whose frequency can be measured by electronic means. Another popular method involves using the input signal to control the time duration of a digital pulse. The length of the pulse is measured using a constant frequency clock signal and a counter.

The dual ramp ADC shown in Fig. 3.6. This ADC, in essence, converts the input signal magnitude into a time duration which is measured using a constant frequency clock and counter. The switches S_1 and S_2 are electronic switches, typically FET's, which connect either the input signal or a constant reference signal $-V_{ref}$ to the integrator. The integrator is an electronic circuit whose output voltage is the mathematical integral of the input voltage. The comparator is a circuit whose output is a binary 1, if its input is greater than zero volts, and a binary 0, if the input is a negative voltage. The AND gate is identical to that described in Chapter 2 and produces a binary one output if, and only if, both inputs are binary 1. The clock produces pulses representing

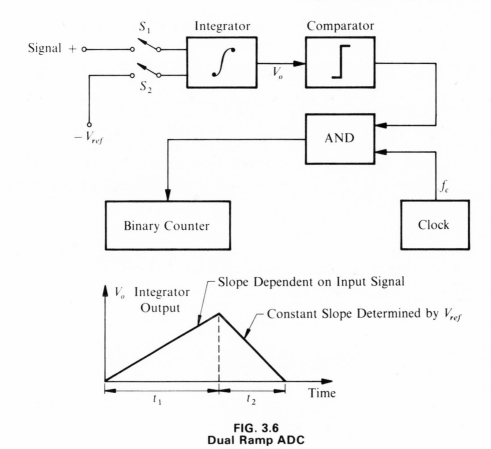

FIG. 3.6
Dual Ramp ADC

binary 1's at a constant frequency f_c. The binary counter is similar to that described in Chapter 2 and records the number of binary 1's which pass through the AND gate.

At the beginning of the conversion cycle, control circuits reset the binary counter to zero. When the "start convert" command is given, control circuits close switch S_1 to apply the unknown signal voltage to the input of the integrator. Since the signal voltage is assumed to be essentially constant, the output of the integrator increases at a constant rate as shown in the timing diagram. The slope of the integrator output voltage is directly proportional to the magnitude of the input signal. Since the output of the integrator is positive, the output of the comparator is a binary 1 and pulses from the clock enter the counter. The integration continues for a fixed period of time t_1; typically, this time is the time required to fill the counter to its full capacity and provide an overflow pulse. The overflow pulse actuates the control circuits and switch S_1 is opened, disconnecting the input signal. The output of the integrator now is equal to the average magnitude of the input signal times t_1. Switch S_2 is then closed by the control circuits and reference voltage $-V_{ref}$ is applied to the integrator. Since this voltage is negative and constant, the integrator output decreases at a constant rate determined by the value of the reference. At the time switch S_2 is closed, the counter is reset to zero. Since the output of the integrator is still positive, clock pulses are gated into the counter. When the output of the integrator reaches zero after a time interval of t_2, the comparator output switches to binary 0 and counting stops. This is the end of the conversion cycle and the control circuits open S_2 and transfer the counter contents to the computer. The number in the counter is directly proportional to the magnitude of the input signal; that is, if the input signal is one-half of the maximum allowable signal, the number in the counter is a binary number representing 0.5.

This example of the operation of the dual ramp ADC is simplified and does not represent the actual complexity of a real ADC. The ADC is a precision measuring device and its design requires specialized knowledge of analog and digital circuits. Although ADC's were expensive devices due to their precision nature and complexity, great strides have been made in using integrated circuits. This has led to dramatic cost decrease in the past several years. If the trend continues, it may eventually be possible to eliminate the multiplexer and provide a single ADC for each input point. This is already being done in some specialized applications where the number of input points is small or the requirements are very stringent.

Subsystem Performance Parameters

As compared to digital I/O features, the number of parameters which characterizes the analog-input subsystem is quite large. Some of the more important parameters are range, resolution, accuracy, repeatability, and stability.

The range of the analog-input subsystem is the parameter which indicates the magnitude of the voltage inputs that can be accepted. The range may be unipolar (that is, accept voltages of only one polarity) or it may be bipolar (provide for voltages of both polarities). In general, analog subsystems can be divided into high-level and low-level range categories. High-level systems usually provide a single range of 0 to $+5$ volts for unipolar systems and -5 to $+5$ volts for bipolar subsystems. Low-level systems often provide several ranges in the range of 0 to 0.5 or 1 volt. A typical subsystem, for example, provides ranges with full scale values of 10 mV, 20 mV, 40 mV, 80 mV, 320 mV, and 512 mV.

The accuracy of the subsystem is a measure of the degree to which the digitized readings represent the true value of the input. Accuracy is typically expressed in terms of the error or inaccuracy, such as 0.1% of full scale. This means that all (or a statistically significant number, depending on how the particular vendor defines accuracy) readings will be within (0.001 × full scale volts) of their true value. One problem with stated accuracy specification is that there are a number of ways to define the term. The term "mean accuracy" may be defined as the accuracy of the mean of a large number of readings so that, effectively, the effects of noise are eliminated. "Typical accuracy" may refer to the results that are usually achieved under reference conditions but are not guaranteed by the manufacturer. "Total accuracy" may refer to the error from all causes at constant temperature for any particular reading. Until national or international standards are widely accepted for the definition of accuracy, the user is cautioned to fully understand the definition being used by a particular manufacturer.

It is important to recognize the difference between accuracy and resolution. Resolution is a measure of the precision of a reading (that is, the number of significant digits in the reading) and is independent of the accuracy. The resolution of the subsystem is the increment of input change that can be detected. Since the output of the subsystem is digital, it can only take on particular values and the difference between two adjacent values is the resolution of the system. For example, if the output of the system is a 10-bit binary number, it can resolve 1024 distinct values. If the maximum input voltage is 5 volts, the minimum detectable change that can be detected reliably is 5/1024 or approximately 0.005 volts. Resolution typically is specified in terms of the number of bits in the output word, the percentage that one-bit represents compared to the full word, or as an absolute number of volts. Taking the example of a 5-volt subsystem with a 10-bit binary output word, the resolution may be specified as being 10-bit resolution, 0.1% of full scale, or 0.005 volts.

Resolution is a limit on the accuracy which can be attained. For example, in a 10-bit subsystem, the answer is known to no better than 0.05% or one-half the least significant bit. For this reason, it is common to specify accuracy in terms of the error plus or minus one-half the resolution as, for example, in the specification that accuracy is equal to 0.6% of full scale plus or minus 1/2 LSB (least significant bit).

Repeatability is a measure of the consistency of a number of readings taken from the same input over a short period of time, typically less than 10 minutes. Due to electrical noise in the subsystem and surrounding environment, multiple readings taken from a single point will not be precisely the same. Repeatability is often specified as one-half the maximum spread or "scatter" of a specified number of readings and is expressed as a percentage of the full scale input. Since the manufacturer has no control over the physical environment in which the subsystem is installed by the user, it is typical to specify repeatability under reference conditions. This gives an indication of the internal noise of the subsystem. External noise degrades the repeatability to some degree. For this reason, in the user environment careful attention to noise sources, grounding, and other factors is required during the installation and use of an analog-input subsystem in an industrial environment.

The above paragraphs give only a brief introduction to the performance parameters of the analog-input subsystem. A comprehensive treatment is available in references such as the one by Harrison and in standards such as ANSI MC8.1-1975.

ANALOG-OUTPUT SUBSYSTEMS

The analog-output subsystem generates analog signals that can be used by external devices. Examples of such devices include graphic displays, setpoint controllers, and valve actuators. In reality, the analog-output subsystem cannot provide a true analog signal in terms of either amplitude or time. The computer has a finite word length so the output signal can only be specified with a finite precision. Similarly, due to the time-shared use of the computer, the analog-output signals are updated only at programmer-defined intervals. Thus, the subsystem provides an approximation to a continuously varying signal which is discrete in both time and amplitude.

The organization of the analog-output subsystem, shown in Fig. 3.7, is similar to that of the other I/O subsystems. The subsystem typically is attached to the I/O channel of the CPU through a channel attachment. A device controller is used to provide the detailed control of the analog-output points. The actual hardware which converts the digital number provided by the CPU into an equivalent analog signal is the digital-to-analog converter

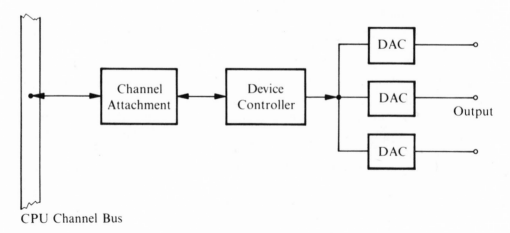

FIG. 3.7
Analog Output Subsystem

(DAC). Depending on the particular design, the subsystem controller may control a number of DACs. In general, the output of the DACs is not multiplexed; that is, a DAC is dedicated to each output point and no attempt is made to share a single DAC among many output points. Economics is the primary reason for this, in that individual DACs are less expensive than a multiplexer and the required analog storage units.

Digital-to-Analog Converters

There are a number of ways to build a circuit which converts a binary word into a corresponding analog voltage or current. In general, most of the methods involve the use of a resistor network, in which branches of the network are switched into the circuit or isolated from the circuit, depending on whether the corresponding bit in the digital input word is a 1 or 0.

Figure 3.8 shows a popular circuit for converting a binary number into the equivalent analog voltage. It is, in essence, a voltage divider which has the characteristics that the voltage division is proportional to the binary weights attributed to each bit of the input word. This network is known as an R-2R ladder network since it is composed of resistors having the values R and 2R. The fact that the resistors take on only two values is an advantage in fabricating the network. Other networks require resistors having a maximum to minimum ratio of 2^n:1, where n is the number of bits in the input word. For $n = 10$, this means that the ratio of the largest resistor in the network to the smallest is 1024:1. For practical reasons, it is difficult to manufacture precision resistors having this range of values. This is particularly true in thin-film and

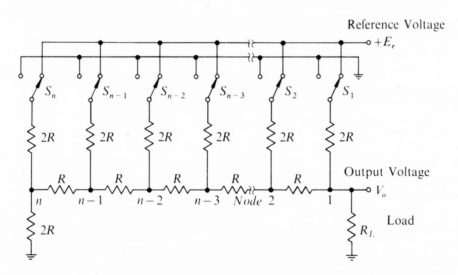

FIG. 3.8
Voltage Controlled Ladder Network

monolithic technologies where resistor values are related to the physical area of the device. In the case of thin-films, the total dependence on area can be avoided by using pastes or depositions of different resistivity, but this often leads to problems in temperature tracking. The disadvantage of the R-2R ladder network is that it takes approximately twice as many resistors as some other configurations.

In Fig. 3.8, the voltage E_r is a precision reference voltage. If the load resistance is very high compared to the value of the resistors in the network (i.e., R_L is much greater than R), the full scale output voltage is approximately equal to the reference voltage E_r. The switches S_1 through S_n are controlled by the bits in the input binary word. If the corresponding bit is a 1, the switch is connected to the reference source E_r as shown in the figure; if the bit is a zero, the switch is connected to ground.

The output voltage depends on the load. In order to maintain accuracy, therefore, the load must be known or it must be constant. In order to insure this, it is customary to connect a buffer amplifier between the ladder network and the output. The output impedance of the buffer amplifier typically is very low. Thus, it presents a low source impedance to any load and approximates an ideal voltage source.

Subsystem Performance Parameters

The performance parameters which characterize the analog-output subsystem are similar to those used for the analog-input subsystem. In addition to the usual parameters concerning timing and address and command formats, the important analog parameters are range, accuracy, resolution, noise, temperature coefficient, and stability.

The range of the analog-output subsystem is equal to the full scale value of the output. In most cases, this is either 0 to 5 volts or 0 to 10 volts. Some DACs provide bipolar output; that is, they have the capability of providing voltage of both polarities. The term span is sometimes applied to the algebraic difference between the minimum and maximum output values. In addition to the range or span, a specification is provided indicating the driving capability of the output. This is given either in the form of a maximum current (typically, 10 mA) or a minimum load resistance. In some cases, the specifications also indicate if short-circuit protection is provided and the maximum short-circuit current that flows in such a case.

A 10-bit resolution (0.1%) is typical in present analog-output subsystems. This is sufficient for most applications that are common in process control. In many cases, an 8-bit resolution (0.4%) is sufficient and such systems are also available. Laboratory applications, some graphics applications, and precision testing may require higher resolution. DACs with resolutions of up to 14-bits are commercially available for such applications. It is important to note that the cost of the DAC increases significantly as the resolution is increased from

10-bits to 12-bits and from 12-bits to 14-bits. Thus, the user should not overspecify the requirements.

The accuracy specification indicates how closely the actual output of the DAC approaches the true or intended value. Typically, the accuracy is specified under steady-state reference conditions; that is, it does not include variations due to temperature or other environmental influences. At the lower resolutions of 8 or 10 bits, the error in present analog-output subsystems usually is limited by the resolution. Therefore, accuracy specifications of 0.4% for 8-bit units and 0.1% for 10-bit subsystems are common. At the higher resolution of 14-bits, accuracy is determined by the accuracy of the reference supply and other components in the DAC. A specification of 0.01% of full scale is typical for a 14-bit DAC.

The output of the DAC typically is high level and noise is usually not a significant problem if good installation practices are followed. Typically, the noise is either a steady state ripple, usually at the line frequency, or a transient associated with the switching action of the DAC switches. If the analog-output is being used to drive a relatively slow device, switching transients, which typically last less than a microsecond, have no effect on the driven device. On the other hand, if the output device is electronic and can respond to the transient spikes, the switching noise may be objectionable. As an example, the transient spikes may cause streaking of the display in a CRT graphic display.

DIGITAL-INPUT/PROCESS INTERRUPT SUBSYSTEMS

In addition to the analog variables in a process, there are typically variables that are binary in nature; that is, they only take on one of two values such as off or on, full or not full, opened or closed. In many practical cases, these signals take the form of electrical switch contacts that are either open or closed. The switch may be actuated by a variety of means depending on the application. For example, it may be connected to a float in a vat of liquid, which indicates when the vat is full or it might be a limit switch, which indicates that a mechanism has reached the end of its travel. A second type of signal found in processes is a threshold signal. In this case, the signal is analog and indicates the magnitude of an analog variable. For control purposes, however, it is only necessary to know that the variable has exceeded a certain value. For example, the signal might be derived from a slidewire or potentiometer and have a total range of 0 to 5 volts. In the particular application, it might be necessary to notify the computer when the signal exceeds a fixed value such as 3 volts. The exact value of the variable is not required, only the indication that it has exceeded a predefined limit.

The digital-input subsystem provides a means to monitor such binary events. The input signal typically must be electrical in nature, either a voltage or current or, as in the case of a contact closure, a change in resistance. In the latter case, the switch closure can be changed into a voltage signal using a power supply and load resistor. As a result, the digital-input circuits generally are designed to be sensitive to voltage level. Basically, they are threshold circuits whose outputs switch to the binary 1 state if the input voltage exceeds a predefined level.

Subsystem Configuration

The basic configuration of the digital-input (DI) subsystem is shown in Fig. 3.9. As in the previous subsystems, the DI subsystem is attached to the CPU I/O channel through the channel attachment hardware. This hardware takes care of the necessary decoding and timing associated with the operation of the I/O channel. The device controller provides the functions unique to the digital-input subsystem such as decoding of addresses, transferring data from input registers to the channel, and the necessary timing of the internal operations in the subsystem.

The input path for the signals from the process generally consists of signal conditioning circuits followed by a sensing circuit, which senses the binary

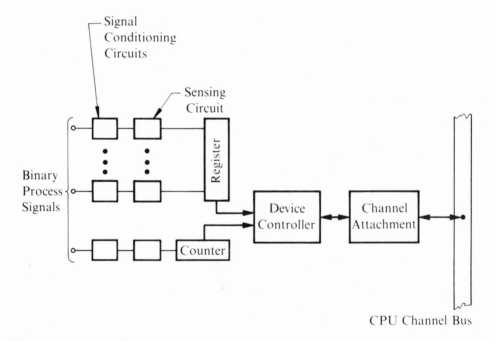

FIG. 3.9
Digital Input Subsystem Configuration

state of the input signal. The output of the sensing circuit is used to set a single bit in a register. The output of this register then is available to be read into the system under control of the CPU.

As indicated in the figure, the digital-input points generally are arranged in groups, with the number of inputs per group equal to the number of bits in the computer word. This is primarily a matter of convenience and addressing efficiency. A single digital-input subsystem may consist of many groups of digital inputs. Even though the digital inputs are manipulated on a group or word basis, it is important to note that the input data itself may be bit-significant. That is, each bit in the input group may convey information that is independent of every other bit. As a result, the word of data read into the CPU may not have meaning when considered as a word. This is to be contrasted to the case of the analog-input subsystem (and most other subsystems, for that matter) in which the word delivered to the CPU represents a value or a coded character. As a specific example, suppose that four inputs representing the overflow limits on four tanks are connected to a particular digital-input group. At some given time, the state of the inputs may result in the binary word 1001 being transferred to the CPU. In this case, the value of the word 1001 (= 9 in decimal) is not significant. What is significant is the individual states of the four-bits which show that tanks 1 and 4 are full. This bit-significance has major implications in terms of system design and programming. It means that the programmer, either through hardware or software aids, must have the facility to manipulate individual bits in a word. Although this facility is generally available on any computer, it is used much more extensively in a control computer and specific hardware and instructions which facilitate bit manipulation sometimes are provided in industrial control computers.

There are cases where the input word does have word significance. This is the case, for example, when the digital-input subsystem is used to interface to another digital device, such as a digital voltmeter, whose output is a parallel digital value.

A second type of digital input is also indicated in Fig. 3.9. This is the counting function. The sensing circuit is connected to a counting register, which accumulates the number of times the input circuit has been actuated. Counters are often used in process applications to accumulate events such as the pulses coming from a turbine flowmeter. By recording the number of pulses received in a fixed-time period, the flow through the meter can be determined.

Signal Conditioning and Sensing Circuits

A variety of signal conditioning and sensing circuits may be provided in the digital-input subsystem, depending on the intended use. In the simplest case, the signal conditioning circuits and special sensing circuits are omitted;

the digital-input signals are connected directly to the register inputs. This type of digital-input arrangement generally is meant to be used in connecting the computer system to other nearby devices that use circuits similar to those used in computers. Examples include the output from digital voltmeters, pulse counters, or frequency meters. In almost all cases, the input specifications are compatible with TTL (transistor-transistor logic) signal levels. This means that input signals of less than approximately 0.2 volts (including negative signals) are detected as binary 0 states and signals in excess of approximately 2 volts are detected as binary 1 states. The maximum allowable voltage is on the order of 6 volts and the normal operating range generally is restricted to 5 volts. A signal in the range of 0.2 volts to 2.0 volts is in the indeterminent range and, depending on the design of the TTL register circuits and other factors, may be detected as either a 1 or 0. The response characteristics are determined by the characteristics of the TTL logic. Typically, this means a switching speed of less than 20 nanoseconds.

The input circuit typically is single-ended; that is, one side of the input is connected to ground in common with all of the input circuits. Differential input circuits are available and have the advantage of better noise immunity. They also provide the user with the capability of reversing the input leads to interchange the significance of the binary 1 and binary 0 output states. Their disadvantage is that they are more expensive than single-ended inputs.

The input register may be designed to be either latching or non-latching. In the latter case, the output of the register always reflects the instantaneous binary state of the input signal. For a latching input, the register is initially set to 0 binary state. When a binary 1 state occurs on the input, the output state changes to the 1 state and this 1 state is maintained even if the input state changes back to a 0 at some later time. In a sense, the register saves the information that the input was temporarily in the 1 state. When the register is read by the CPU or as the result of a specific reset command, the register is reset to the 0 state. In some cases, the latching function is provided through the software and priority interrupt system, although here the performance is significantly affected by the characteristics of the software. The advantage of latching is that it provides the ability to capture events that are fast compared to the response time of the total system.

In addition to the TTL inputs provided on the digital-input subsystem, input circuits having special characteristics are sometimes provided. In general, these fall into the two categories of voltage sensing circuits and contact sensing circuits. In voltage sensing, the function provided is identical to that described previously for the TTL inputs. The primary difference usually is in the range of input voltages that can be accommodated and in the provision for signal conditioning. A typical circuit provides for sensing voltages in the range of -50 to $+50$ volts. The point at which the output switches from the binary 1 to binary 0 state may be adjustable, but usually is the same point as in the TTL case. Signal conditioning typically consists of a simple RC filter that slows the response of the circuit to eliminate sporadic responses to noise. The circuit may be single-ended or differential and latching or non-latching.

The second major category of input circuits is intended to sense the state of a switch contact. These are essentially resistance sensing circuits, whose output is in the 1 state if the input resistance is below a certain value and in the 0 state if the resistance is high. Resistance sensing typically is accomplished indirectly using a voltage sensing circuit. The contact to be sensed is placed in series with a power supply and a load resistance. When the contact closes, a voltage is applied to the input of the voltage sensing circuit to cause it to change to the binary 1 state. If the power supply is provided as part of the computer, it usually is a separate supply so that switching transients created by the input contacts can be isolated from the computer circuits. In general, the supply used for sensing contact states should be at least 24 volts to break down the contaminant film that develops on open relay contacts.

The signal conditioning for contact sensing usually consists of arc suppression networks and contact bounce filters. The function of the electrical arc suppression network is to minimize burning of the contacts due to the electrical arc which is produced when the contact opens. The contact bounce filter slows the response of the sensing circuit to eliminate multiple indications of a single contact closure event.

In both voltage sense and contact sense, the simpler, less expensive circuits are generally single-ended and direct-coupled; that is, one side of the input is grounded and there is a direct electrical connection between the input and the output register. A relatively recent development, however, has been the optically-coupled input circuit. The input signal is used to actuate a light source, usually a light-emitting diode (LED). The optical output of the LED is coupled to a phototransistor which is connected to the register input. This arrangement provides electrical isolation between the digital-input and the computer system. Common-mode voltages up to the breakdown voltage of the LED-phototransistor combination can be accommodated. The input is differential but the proper input polarity must be maintained to actuate the LED. Effective electrical isolation can also be provided by using transformer coupling in the input circuit. This is somewhat more complicated, however, since a transformer only passes AC signals.

The use of isolated input circuits is extremely useful in noise control and greatly simplifies grounding problems. Although generally more expensive than direct-coupled circuits, they often result in a lower total system cost when the cost of solving difficult installation problems is considered.

Priority Interrupt Subsystem

The concept of priority interrupt was introduced in Chapter 2. The input circuits used for the priority interrupt system are usually identical to those provided for the digital-input subsystem. The difference lies in the control of the subsystem. In the case of the priority interrupt subsystem, changes in the input signal state result in a signal to the processor.

The interrupt feature is simply a hardware subsystem which automatically checks for interrupt events between program steps. The use of the interrupt feature eliminates the need for frequent program controlled scanning of input signals. As such, it reduces programming and provides better time responsiveness to external events.

Priority interrupt subsystems differ widely among industrial computers in the amount of function provided in the hardware. In general, the design tradeoff is between the amount of hardware function provided and the time it takes the system to respond to an external interrupt.

In the simplest systems, a single interrupt line is provided. When an interrupt event occurs in the process, the CPU is signalled on the interrupt line. The processor, either under hardware or software control, then stores the contents of pertinent registers and indicators in preparation for servicing the interrupt. This action is necessary so that the processor can restart its original task after the interrupt has been serviced. The processor then commands that the interrupting device address be put on the address or channel input data bus. This procedure is known as polling. Based on the interrupting device address, the software interrupt servicing routine determines what is to be done. If the requesting device has a lower priority than the currently executing task, the software records the interrupting request and returns control to the higher priority task. If, however, the interrupting source is of higher priority, the servicing routine determines what must be done to respond to the interrupt. This may involve requesting further identification information from the interrupting subsystem, such as a sub-address, and a more specific determination of the source of the interrupt. Based on this information, control is passed to the subroutine which is associated with the interrupting event. After the interrupt has been serviced, the contents of registers and indicators that had previously been saved are restored and execution of the interrupted program resumes.

In more complex interrupt systems, all or part of the above procedure is done automatically by the hardware. The first level of sophistication is usually hardware comparison of the interrupting event priority to the present executing task priority. If the interrupting event is of lower priority, it is recorded by the hardware but the processor is not interrupted until it has completed all higher priority tasks. On the other hand, if the interrupting task is of higher priority, the interrupt is passed to the processor and the servicing sequence described above is followed.

Further levels of sophistication might involve the automatic storing of registers and indicators without any intervention through the software. Rather than having to go through a polling process to determine the exact cause of the interrupt, hardware can be provided to automatically load a branching address which transfers control to a specific interrupt handling routine. The effect of implementing these additional functions in hardware is to reduce the software overhead associated with responding to the interrupt. This results in a faster time response for the system. The disadvantage, of course, is that the additional hardware results in a higher system price.

The assignment of particular devices, events, or subsystems to each of the priority interrupt levels is a complex problem because it can significantly affect the performance of the system in a particular application. A simplistic approach is to assign priorities on the basis of the importance of the event. For example, events which could result in catastrophic failures in the process would be assigned the highest priority to ensure that they would be promptly corrected if they occur. A more sophisticated approach is to assign priorities on the basis of the importance of the event *and* the overall efficiency of using the computer resources. In this case, relatively unimportant devices might be assigned high priority to maintain high efficiency. As a specific example, a character printer used for printing periodic logs might be assigned a high priority, even though the log is merely for historical records. The printer might interrupt the processor for each character (about every 100 milliseconds) and require 1 millisecond to service. This degrades the processor performance by 1 millisecond out of 100 milliseconds or 1%. However, it keeps the printer operating at top efficiency. If the printer were assigned to the lowest priority, the processor might have slightly higher efficiency, but the efficiency of using the printer would be degraded severely.

The assignment of devices to interrupt levels usually is done by hardware means. Several methods are used. In some cases, interrupt priority is determined by the physical position that the attachment card has in the chassis. In other cases, the attachment card is altered by wire jumpers or switches to determine its priority level. A few systems provide software control of priority. In this case, commands are issued to the subsystems, assigning them to particular priority levels. This priority assignment is stored in the subsystem. Although this method requires more hardware, it results in a very flexible system in which priority can be dynamically altered to account for changing conditions in the process.

Subsystem Performance Parameters

The performance parameters of the digital-input subsystem generally relate to two major areas: the characteristics of the input circuit in terms of its electrical specifications and the functional and time performance of the entire subsystem.

Most of the parameters associated with the input circuits have been mentioned in the previous descriptions. They include such factors as the range of input signals, the switching point, the availability of signal conditioning and its characteristics, and functional capabilities such as latching or non-latching inputs. Time response characteristics such as the rise time of the input circuit are also important in some cases. When signal conditioning is provided, for example, to eliminate the effects of contact bounce, the characteristics of the signal conditioning circuits are important parameters. In the case of high speed inputs, such as those which would normally use the TTL-type of input circuit, the input characteristics are often not the determining factor in the subsystem performance. Since the input circuits in this case are very fast, in the 20–30 nanosecond range, the determining factor is more often associated with the logical design of the subsystem. In this case, subsystem performance parameters such as the maximum data transfer rate are more indicative of actual performance.

DIGITAL-OUTPUT SUBSYSTEM

The digital-output subsystem is the complement of the digital-input subsystem. It provides the system with the capability of providing binary control of devices in the process. Fundamentally, the digital-output circuit is a switch which can be turned on or off under computer control. By using the switch to control a voltage or current source, electrical devices in the process can be turned on and off. Examples include controlling lights on a console or annunciator panel, opening and closing solenoid valves, and starting and stopping electrical motors.

The subsystem configuration shown in Fig. 3.10 is similar to that used for the other process I/O subsystems. Digital-output points typically are addressed as groups of outputs, with the number of outputs in each group equal to the number of bits in the computer word. The state of the output is controlled by a corresponding bit in an output register in the subsystem. Using the group address, the CPU transfers a word of data to the appropriate register in the subsystem. The data are stored in the register and the output of the register controls the state of the output switch. By convention, a 1 stored in the register usually means that the output switch is closed or on.

As in the case of the digital-input subsystem, the output data may be bit-significant; that is, each bit in the output word may control a separate device which is independent of any other device. In this case, the value of the digital-output word does not have alphanumeric significance. The digital-output subsystem, however, also can be used for the parallel transfer of digital data to external digital devices and, in this case, the output data may have word significance.

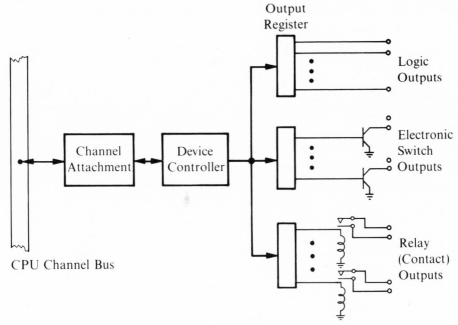

FIG. 3.10
Digital Output Subsystem Configuration

Figure 3.10 shows three possible output switches. In the first case, the output of the digital-output register is directly connected to the output terminals. The output signal is a logic-level voltage; in present machines, this usually means that the levels are compatible with TTL logic, with a down level of approximately 0 volts and an active level of about 5 volts. The switching speed of this type of logic level output is dependent on the characteristics of the logic which is used, but is typically on the order of 20-30 nanoseconds. The data transfer rate is largely determined by the subsystem control electronics and the characteristics of the I/O channel. For example, if it takes 2 microseconds to transfer a word of data from the CPU to the subsystem, the transfer rate has an upper bound of 500,000 words per second.

The primary use of this type of digital-output is to couple the computer system to other digital devices. The output circuits themselves have limited driving capability and signal conditioning usually is not provided. For long distance high speed data transfer, the characteristics of the output wiring should match those of the driver.

The second type of output switch shown in Fig. 3.10 is the electronic switch. This is typically a semiconductor switch, usually a transistor, intended for switching low to medium power DC loads. A typical specification is a maximum voltage of 50 volts and a maximum current of 0.5 amps. This is sufficient for controlling many small electrical loads and for driving interposing relays for the control of high power devices. Since this type of output is often intended for controlling relays and other inductive loads, provisions are usually made for the installation of clamping diodes to protect the output transistor from inductive transients.

Although shown as a direct-coupled connection in the figure, the output transistor may be electrically-isolated from the system. One means for doing this is by using a transformer. Electrical isolation allows separate grounding of the computer system and the process. This tends to minimize ground currents from the process equipment flowing through the computer grounding networks and creating noise in the system.

The third type of output switch shown in Fig. 3.10 is the electro-mechanical relay. In general, the use of a relay provides an isolated switch for use in the process and usually allows relatively high power loads to be switched. The relay has the advantage that its characteristics approach those of the ideal switch, so that it does not exhibit the offset and leakage errors inherent in the semiconductor switch. It is also insensitive to the polarity of the load and can be used to control AC devices. The switching speed of the relay is considerably slower than that of electronic switches due to its elec-tromechanical nature. Typical switching times are on the order of 1 or 2 milli-seconds for small relays and up to 10 milliseconds for larger relays. The data transfer rate of the subsystem is limited by the switching speed of the relay, rather than by the subsystem control logic as in the case of logic output.

The functions of the subsystem control logic and the channel attachment are similar to those described for the other subsystems. The channel attachment logic handles the communication and data manipulation requirements of the channel, including address identification, handshaking, error detection, and channel timing. In the simplest case, the subsystem control logic provides for decoding the group address and transferring the incoming data to the proper output register. Additional hardware functions can be provided, however. One of these functions is momentary output. In this case, the output switch is closed for a predetermined length of time and then opened. In more sophisticated subsystems, pulse trains of varying durations and with various length pulses can be produced under hardware control. The provision for functions such as this can significantly reduce the burden on the processor and channel and simplify programming. An example of where such a feature is useful is in the control of stepping motors, in which pulse trains are used to position the motor shaft.

DATA PROCESSING I/O SUBSYSTEMS

"Data processing input/output" (DP I/O) is a generic term applied to a large class of I/O devices that are commonly found on a computer. In contrast to process I/O or sensor I/O, which is primarily concerned with data transfers to and from the process instrumentation and control devices, DP I/O devices are concerned primarily with the collection and display of data derived from the system operator or from sources internal to the computer itself. These data are alphanumeric in nature and, in many cases, can be read directly and interpreted by the human operator. Specific devices included in the DP I/O category include printers, punched card units, punched tape units, and graphic displays. Mass storage devices such as magnetic tape, drum, and disk storage also are considered DP I/O devices, although they are primarily concerned with the storage of data generated by the system itself.

Although the different kinds of DP I/O devices found on today's computers are about the same as they were ten years ago, great advances have been made in device performance and function. There are today literally hundreds of DP I/O devices available for attachment to computers. While all devices may not be attached to any particular computer because of differences in the individual design, most computer vendors and independent manufacturers of peripheral devices offer a variety of devices for use with each particular computer.

Subsystem Configuration

As in the case of the other I/O subsystems, the DP I/O devices attach to the I/O channel of the computer. Figure 3.1 shows the general subsystem configuration which is common in current machines. The basic functions provided by the various parts of the subsystem were described early in the chapter and apply to the DP I/O subsystems as well.

Depending on the nature of the particular I/O device and the design selected by the manufacturer, the attachment hardware may be dedicated to the support of a single I/O device, a group of similar devices, or a group of dissimilar devices. In general, the complexity of the attachment increases as the number of devices or the number of different kinds of devices is increased. It is common to use a shared controller with relatively slow speed, and low function devices such as character printers. Other devices, such as disk storage, often have dedicated controllers due to their specialized nature and their performance characteristics.

In the following sections, each of the general categories of DP I/O devices briefly are discussed in terms of their operation, performance, and use. An exhaustive description of every technique presently in use today for each device is not possible, due to the large number of devices that are available. However, an attempt is made to introduce the more common techniques used in each class of device. Graphic display I/O devices are described in conjunction with the section of the chapter on operator communications.

Mass Storage Devices

Mass storage devices are designed to store large quantities of data, typically millions of computer words. Their use in computer systems is primarily a matter of economics. Compared to semiconductor and magnetic core storage, mass storage devices provide storage which is up to 100 times less expensive. As a secondary benefit in comparison to semiconductor storage, most mass storage devices are non-volatile; that is, the stored information is not lost if the system power is removed. Furthermore, some types of mass storage devices are such that the storage medium physically can be removed from the machine. This provides the capability of virtually unlimited storage of data and programs. Their disadvantage is that they are thousands of times slower than main storage.

The quantity of data and programs associated with an industrial control machine can be significant. Programs exceeding 100,000 instructions are not uncommon and data bases consisting of millions of words of data can easily be compiled. For example, if summary data are collected from 1000 input points on an hourly basis for a month, over 700,000 values are accumulated. Not only would it be relatively expensive to preserve this data in main storage, but most minicomputers do not have addressing structures which allow direct access to this quantity of data. Thus, for economic and other reasons, the use of mass storage devices on computers is common. Programs not currently being used by the processor and data tables typically are stored on the mass storage devices. When required by the processor, the programs and data are read into main storage for execution and use.

The most popular forms of mass storage in use today on minicomputers are magnetic disks and diskettes, and magnetic tape. In each of these devices, the storage medium consists of a thin layer of magnetic oxide deposited on a surface. Information is stored by magnetizing the surface in accordance with the pattern of binary 1's and 0's to be stored. Although more complex forms of coding typically are used, one can think of a 1-bit being stored as a magnetic spot on the surface and a 0 as the absence of a spot. The information is read by passing the surface near a pickup coil or "head." As the magnetized surface moves past the head, it induces an electrical current in the coil which, when amplified, is interpreted as a pattern of 1's and 0's. The recording and playback techniques are similar to those used to record and playback music or voice using an audio tape recorder.

Magnetic Disk Storage. The principles involved in magnetic disk storage conform to those described in the previous paragraph. The surface used for the magnetic recording is the flat surface of a disk, as shown in Fig. 3.11. The disk is driven by an electric motor, typically at about 3000 rpm. Recording and playback of information on the disk is accomplished by the use of a read/write

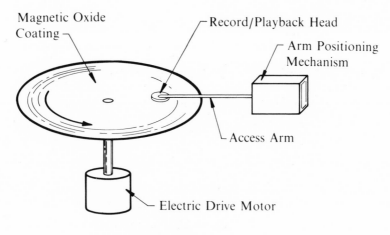

Magnetic Oxide Coating

Record/Playback Head

Arm Positioning Mechanism

Access Arm

Electric Drive Motor

FIG. 3.11
Magnetic Disk Storage

head. One or more heads may be used for each disk and the position of the heads may be fixed or movable.

In the case of a movable head disk, the head is mounted on an access arm parallel to the surface of the disk. The access arm moves in the lateral direction in discrete steps. The recording surface under the head at each of its discrete positions forms a recording track. A typical disk may have more than 200 tracks. In some cases, multiple disks are mounted on the same drive spindle, forming a stack of disks, each with its own access arm. Corresponding tracks on the multiple disks form what is called a cylinder. For ease of addressing, each track is typically subdivided into sectors. A combination of the track or cylinder address and the sector address provides random access to the data. The position of the disk at any instant of time is known to the controller electronics by means of a timing track having a prerecorded pattern, or by a mechanical device such as a slot in the disk coupled with an internal timer.

The time required to access data in a movable head disk file is the sum of the time it takes to position the head over the proper track plus the time it takes for the data to appear under the head. The positioning time of the head is not a linear function since, due to acceleration and deceleration time, the time it takes to move a short distance is proportionately longer than a longer movement. In addition, once the head has reached its final position, a short delay is required to allow for settling of mechanical vibrations before data can be read reliably. The number often quoted for settling time is one-half the time it takes to completely traverse the disk. The settling time of available disks varies considerably depending on the mechanism used to control the access arm. Figures from 10 to 90 milliseconds are common.

In addition to the arm settling time, there is an average rotational delay or latency, which is the average delay time before the desired data passes below the read head. This delay is dependent on the speed of rotation and typical times range from 8.7 milliseconds to 20 milliseconds. Some cautions in comparing specifications are in order. Some manufacturers separately quote the average settling time and the average latency, whereas others combine the two numbers into a single average access time figure.

Disk storage units also are available in which multiple fixed heads are provided for each disk. Units with up to 256 heads per disk are available. Their primary advantage is that they are faster than movable head units, because there is no positioning time. The disk on a fixed-head disk unit typically is not removable.

One of the features of disk storage units which makes them attractive is that, in many cases, the disk storage media can be removed for off-line storage. This makes the possibility of virtually unlimited storage of data economical. In some units, each disk is contained in a cartridge. The cartridge is inserted in the drive mechanism which connects the drive spindle to the disk. Another common arrangement is to have several disks stacked on a common spindle. This forms a disk pack which can be removed for off-line storage. In addition to off-line storage, the removable disk concept provides the means to transfer data between different computers in a convenient and high density format.

Due to the variety of arrangements of drives, disks, and controllers, it is difficult to provide typical specifications for disk storage units. Units that typically are used with small computers have a storage capacity of up to 5 and 10 million bytes per disk. Drives having up to 20 recording surfaces (10 disks, top and bottom surfaces) are available. The number of words or bytes that can be stored is dependent upon formatting requirements, the manner in which sectoring is accomplished, and the overhead due to error checking words.

The life of the recording media essentially is infinite and reliability of a disk storage unit usually is related to the characteristics of the drive mechanism. The recording heads do not touch the surface of the disk in normal operation. The spacing between the disk and the head is determined by the aerodynamic properties of the head; the head literally flies about 100 microinches over the surface in the airstream created by the moving disk. Most units are equipped with a mechanism which automatically retracts the heads if the speed of the disk drops below a certain point, as in the case of a power failure. This prevents the heads from contacting the disk and scarring the surface. Particles of contaminant matter on the surface of the disk or on the head can also result in head contact ("head-crash"). For this reason, disk storage units often are sealed and provided with a filtered air flow. With proper preventive maintenance, the surface of the disk rarely is damaged and has almost infinite life.

Magnetic Diskette Storage. A relatively recent development in disk storage which is popular for small computers is the so-called "diskette" or "floppy disk." The diskette consists of a 5 to 8-inch diameter disk of flexible plastic which is coated with magnetic oxide to form a recording surface. The disk in enclosed in a paper envelope to form a cartridge. The cartridge is inserted into the drive mechanism and the disk is spun inside the stationary envelope. A radial slot in the envelope provides access to the disk surface for the read/write head. Diskettes use the moving head technique with the access arm driven either by a stepping motor or by a lead screw.

Diskettes presently available have a capacity of between 2 and 8 million-bits. They are typically organized with either 64 or 77 tracks. Track-to-track positioning times are on the order of 6 to 10 milliseconds and the rotational delay is typically 83 milliseconds, corresponding to a rotational speed of 360 rpm. Data transfer rates are on the order of 250,000-bits per second.

Diskettes provide moderate amounts of storage at very low cost. They are well suited as a load/dump device and provide a convenient data and program interchange media. The diskettes are easy to handle and can be mailed without special packing. Although also used for program residency in some cases, their slow speed dictates careful planning to avoid excessive swapping of programs between the diskette and storage, since this significantly affects performance. The read/write head is often in contact with the recording surface so wear of the diskette results in a finite life.

Magnetic Tape Storage. Another popular form of mass storage and one of the earliest available on computers is magnetic tape. The recording and reading principles are identical to those involved in disk storage, except that the recording medium is a flexible plastic tape which has been coated with a magnetic oxide material.

There are three common forms of magnetic tape used in the computer industry. The oldest and most used magnetic tape is 0.5-inch wide. Data are recorded on 7 or 9 tracks across the width of the tape at a linear density of either 800-bits per inch (bpi) or 1600 bpi in most cases. A 10.5-inch reel contains 2400 feet of tape and provides storage for approximately 46 million 7 or 9-bit characters at a density of 1600 bpi. In actual use, the useful capacity of the reel is less since blank spaces (interrecord gaps) are left between records for purposes of addressing. It is also typical to include header information and error checking characters at the beginning and/or end of each record which also reduces effective data storage capacity.

In recent years, another form of magnetic tape storage has become popular, particularly for small computers. This is the tape cassette or tape cartridge. The tape cassette or cartridge is a self-contained unit housing both the feed and take-up reels. The unit is inserted in the drive mechanism which engages the hubs of the reels, positions the head against the tape, and, if a capstan is used, engages the capstan.

The earliest popular form of cassette is the Philips cassette, which is well known from the audio recording industry. American National Standard X3.48–1975 is based on the Philips cassette unit. This cassette holds up to 600 feet of 0.15-inch tape, although most units intended for computer use are about 300 feet in length. At a recording density of 800 bpi, this provides a total capacity of almost 3 million bits. Due to formatting and interrecord gaps, the usable capacity is less.

Tape storage is inherently a serial storage medium and does not possess the random access properties of disk storage. Access time depends on the present position of the tape in relation to the position of the desired data. If the data are at the far end of the tape, the access time can be tens of seconds, even for a high performance drive. In the case of a cassette running at a tape velocity of 20 inches per second, it takes three minutes to travel the length of the tape.

Other Mass Storage Devices. Although the magnetic disk and tape storage devices are by far the most popular mass storage units used on small computers, other mass storage techniques are used in the computer industry and new techniques are being developed.

One of these new techniques involves the magnetic bubble memory. In this technique, a magnetic material a few microns thick is deposited on a substrate. By applying an appropriate magnetic bias field, it is possible to create small cylindrical "bubbles" a few microns in diameter, which have a magnetic orientation opposite to that of the surrounding area. By the use of various arrangements of conductors to create magnetic fields, these bubbles can be created, destroyed, and moved from place to place. If the presence of a bubble at a particular point is interpreted as a 1-bit and the absence as a 0-bit, the stream of bubbles can be used to represent binary data.

The magnetic bubble technology has the potential of providing non-volatile mass storage at very low cost and very high density. It appears that a million-bit storage element can be built in volume of less than 2 cubic inches. The unit would be entirely electronic and eliminate the mechanical complexities and power consumption associated with disks and tapes. Access times of about 1 millisecond appear feasible.

Other mass storage techniques which appear likely, at least for moderate amounts of storage, are based on semiconductor technology. One technique which is in the development stage is the charge-coupled-device (CCD). In essence, this is a long shift register, in which bits are represented by small electrical charges stored on the inherent capacitances associated with the semiconductor device. Very high densities appear possible since the semiconductor devices can be very small. As in the case of bubbles, CCD storage devices are available but have not yet been used commercially in minicomputers. The CCD storage, along with other semiconductor storage units, have the disadvantage that they are inherently volatile, although their low power makes battery backup quite feasible.

Printers

Printers are the primary means by which data stored or generated by the computer are displayed in a permanent, human-readable form. A printer of some sort is included in almost every computer installation, although graphic display units using the cathode ray tube (CRT) are displacing some printers where a permanent record of the data is not required.

Printers generally are categorized by the manner in which the line of print is formed (character by character or a line at a time) and by the technique used to form the printed image (impact printing or non-impact printing). In character printers, the characters are formed individually as the writing head moves across the paper, generally from left to right. The typewriter or teletypewriter are the best-known forms of character printer. In the line printer, a full line of printing is produced essentially simultaneously. Line printers operate at much higher speeds than character printers and are more expensive.

The printing element in a character printer typically takes one of two forms. In the one case, the letters and symbols of the character set are engraved on a ball, cylinder, or disk. The element is positioned by rotation and/or tilting to select the particular character to be printed. In the second case, the print element provides a column of wires. Typically, there are 7 or 8 wires, each of which can be individually controlled. By selectively controlling the wires, a column of dots can be printed. As the printing head is moved laterally, the column of dots form the character. Thus, the character is formed as a matrix, usually 5×7. Figure 3.12 shows a sample of the images that are formed and an enlargement of one of the characters to show the dot pattern used to form the character. The printer used to obtain this sample uses a 7×8 printing matrix. The eighth wire is used for special purposes, such as underlining or forming the descender on lower-case letters such as p or q. This printer can be used for printing upper- and lower-case letters. Many wire printers using the 5×7 matrix are restricted to upper-case printing.

Non-impact character printers also are available for use with computers. Several techniques are used to form the characters. In some cases, a specially treated paper is used and the characters are formed by electrical, thermal, or optical techniques. In electrostatic printing, for example, the paper is electrically conductive. The printing element is a series of vertically positioned wires similar to those used in wire matrix impact printing. An electrical potential between the printing wire and the paper results in an electrical discharge or arc, which results in the darkening of the paper surface. Untreated paper is used in non-impact printers utilizing ink-jet printing or electrophotographic techniques similar to those used in some office copiers.

The most common character printer used today in conjunction with minicomputers is the teletypewriter. This device was originally designed for

```
Special character sets
can be formed using the
wire matrix printer.
Consider the APL character
set:

1234567890+×
¨¯<≤=≥>≠∨∧‾÷

QWERTYUIOP←
?ωερ~↑↓ιο⋆→

ASDFGHJKL[]
⍺⌈⌊_∇∆∘'⎕()

ZXCVBNM,./
⊂⊃∩∪⊥|;:\
```

FIG. 3.12
Wire Matrix Printing

use in the communications industry and was adopted by the minicomputer manufacturers as an inexpensive I/O device. It operates at a speed of 10 characters per second and uses a cylindrical engraved printing element. Other forms of impact printing using a cylinder or spherical engraved printing element provide speeds of up to about 30 characters per second. Wire matrix printers typically are much faster with speeds of about 165 characters per second being common and speeds up to 300 characters per second being available.

Line printers are distinguished from character printers in that the total line is printed essentially simultaneously. Both impact and non-impact techniques can be used, with the impact methods being much more common. The performance of line printers is measured in terms of the number of lines per minute that can be printed. Units are available with printing speeds ranging from about 200 lines per minute (lpm) to 13,000 lpm. The very high speed units typically use non-impact printing methods. The units most commonly found in conjunction with industrial computers are in the range of 200 to 600 lpm.

Punched Card Units

The computer punched card is familiar to everyone in modern society and it was the first I/O media used with computers. Its use actually predates the invention of the computer and it was used extensively in conjunction with mechanical sorting machines and various tabulators. Its origin can be traced back to the use of cards with holes punched in them for control of the Jacquard loom, invented around 1800. Even earlier, musical instruments had been built which were controlled by rolls of punched paper. In his design of the "analytical engine" in about 1833, Charles Babbage planned to use punched cards for the entry of both data and instructions. Its first widespread use for computing was the result of Herman Hollerith's design of an electric tabulating machine for use in the 1890 census. With the invention and development of the electronic computer in the 1940's, the punched card became the primary I/O media of early computers.

The best-known punched card is the 80-column card illustrated in Fig. 3.13. Information is recorded as a series of small rectangular punches in each of the 80 columns of the card. Each column can contain up to 12 punches and a number of different codes are used. American National Standard X3.26-1970 describes a card code for 256 characters, including the 128 ASCII characters. The picture on the left-hand page, Fig. 3.13a, shows a card punched with alphanumeric data. Each character is represented as a combination of up to three punches in a column. The interpretations of the punches are printed along the top edge of the card. The picture on the right-hand page Fig. 3.13b, shows a card into which binary data have been punched. Each binary word is represented as a series of punches in a single column of the card. The presence of a punch is interpreted as a binary 1 and the absence of a punch represents a binary 0. Up to 960-bits of information can be stored on the card.

A variety of card-handling equipment is available for use on small computers. Units provided for punching cards, reading cards, and a combination of reading and punching are available.

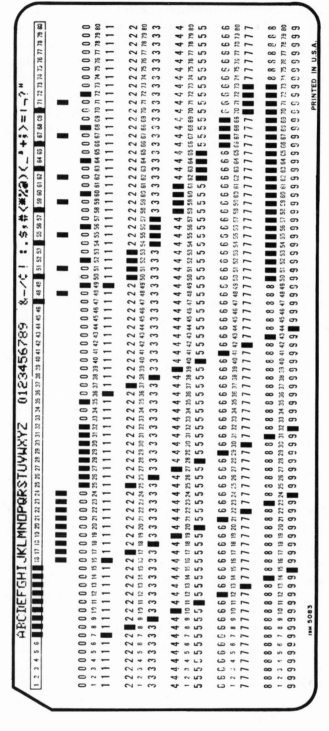

(a) Alphanumeric Data

136

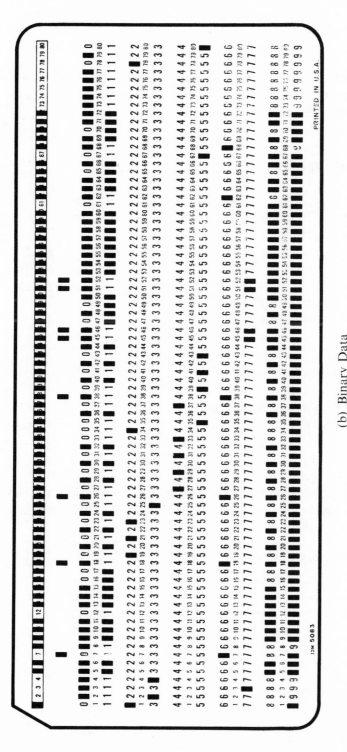

(b) Binary Data

FIG. 3.13

80-Column Punched Card

137

The primary performance parameter of card reader/punches is the number of cards that can be read/punched per minute. In general, the punching speed is considerably slower than the reading speed. Card readers are available with speeds over 2000 cards per minute. A speed of 200 to 300 cards per minute is typical of most units. Punching speeds of 60 to 250 cards per minute are typical.

Punched Tape Units

Punched tape is a popular input/output media for use with small computers. The popular teletypewriter usually includes a paper tape punch and reader as an integral part of the unit. Punched tape is similar to punched cards in that data are represented as punched holes. The difference is that, instead of punching data into separate cards, they are punched into a continuous strip of paper or plastic tape. It does not have the advantage of providing easily-handled unit records, as do cards. It is essentially a serial media and has found widespread use in loading of programs and data. Its primary attraction is its low cost, due to its relatively simple mechanical requirements and simple computer interface.

The tape commonly used in the computer industry is one-inch wide paper or plastic tape. A standard 8-inch roll of tape contains 800 feet. Fan-folded paper tape is also used.

Characters are represented in coded form along the tape, with the bits of each character being punched in a row perpendicular to the edge of the tape. Each bit-position is called a channel. Tape having 8-channels most commonly is used with computers. Figure 3.14 illustrates the commonly used paper tape code. The row of small holes between the third and fourth channel are feed holes. A toothed sprocket engages these holes and pulls the tape through the reading or punching mechanism.

The primary performance parameter is the speed at which tape can be read or punched. As in the case of cards, punching is a significantly slower operation. Reading speeds of up to 1000 characters per second are available, with many units being available in the 600 character per second range. Punching is in the range of 75 to 100 characters per second although 600 character per second units are available. The common teletypewriter units read and punch at 10 characters per second.

Keyboards

Keyboards for the entry of data are provided in conjunction with a number of the output devices discussed in previous sections. Most commonly,

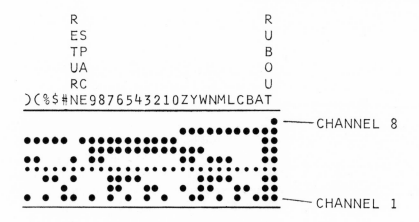

FIG. 3.14
Example Paper Tape Coding

they are combined with character printers or CRT displays as an entry device. They also are used off-line in conjunction with card punches and tape punches to provide for the off-line preparation of computer input.

Typically, the keyboard is similar to the standard typewriter keyboard, with the addition of special function keys to provide for the control of the medium or for communication with the computer. Typical functions include an interrupt key, control of a cursor or position indicator in the case of CRT displays, delete or erase keys, and skipping or line feed functions. Special characters to satisfy non-English language requirements may be provided.

OPERATOR INTERFACE

A key part of any process control computer installation is the means provided for the process operator to communicate with the computer. The operator must be able to extract data from the system and to give commands to the system. The design of the operator-machine communication system is a complex but extremely important task. It is often a major factor in the psychological acceptance of the system by the operator.

Operator communication devices range from the very simple to the very complex and elaborate. In the simplest case, a teletypewriter is used for both input and output. Messages to the operator are typed out; the operator responds or enters commands through the keyboard.

At the other end of the spectrum are custom consoles tailored for a particular application. These may include one or more keyboards for the entry of commands and data. Also included are function switches which activate particular computer routines. An example is a single button which, when actuated, causes a printout of all of the alarm conditions in the plant. Similarly, a variety of lights or other indicators may be provided to indicate the status of certain variables or other conditions in the plant. In most cases, these consoles are custom designed to satisfy the particular needs of the application. In some cases, they cost at least as much as the computer and represent a sizable investment.

The graphic display unit is very popular as an operator communication device. This unit combines a cathode ray tube (CRT) similar to those used in ordinary TV sets with a keyboard and, perhaps, special function keys. In the simplest case, the display is limited to alphanumeric characters. Messages to the operator are displayed on the CRT and responses are made through the keyboard or with a light pen.

Some graphic displays provide the capability of displaying graphical figures on the CRT. With this capability, process diagrams can be made available to the operator by giving a simple command or through the actuation of a single function switch. Indicated on the diagram can be the values of key variables and the various control options which can be exercised by the operator. Color displays also are used to highlight certain variables or other conditions of importance. The variety of options virtually is limited only by the imagination of the programmer.

COMMUNICATIONS

It often is desirable to transmit information to or from a computer over long distances. For example, I/O devices may be located at a remote location, or it may be desired to have one computer directly communicate with another located some distance away. This situation is becoming increasingly common as users interconnect computers and I/O equipment to form networks of computers. Providing the multiwire cable normally required for this type of communication over significant distances is often economically unattractive and may be legally impossible. When going more than a few hundred feet or across public thoroughfares, a two or four-wire system is much more desirable than having to lay a 65-pair cable! For distances of a mile or more, the use of common carrier communications facilities is almost always more desirable.

Communication links between computer equipment generally take one of three forms. The first is point-to-point connection between two stations. With more than two stations, point-to-point communications may be established between every station and every other station, or between every station and a single central station.

A second form of communication network is the multidrop or multipoint arrangement in which several stations are connected to a single line, similar to the telephone party line. In computer networks, control of the line usually is vested in a single master station, although the master control may be passed among stations on a first-come, first-served basis.

The third arrangement is the loop communication system. In this case, the stations are connected to a single line which starts and ends at the master computer. Messages for the various stations are placed on the loop and are intercepted by the addressed station. Messages back to the master from the remote stations are inserted in the data stream in empty "frames" or by delaying incoming data. One advantage of the loop is that data transmitted by the master station can be checked when they return to verify that errors have not been created during transmission.

The communications line is interfaced to the computer through a communications adapter which, typically, is connected to the I/O channel and functions as an I/O device. The communication adapter may connect directly to the communication line for low-speed DC signaling, or it may provide a modulator-demodulator (modem or data set) function. The modem translates the transmitted signal into a high frequency signal suitable for high speed, long distance communication. At the receiving end, the modem demodulates the signal to recreate the original digital data. Various modulation techniques are used including frequency shift keying (FSK), pulse-coded modulation (PCM), and phase modulation (PM).

Another distinguishing characteristic of communication lines is the direction in which data can flow. In the simplest case, data can flow in only one direction; this is called a simplex circuit. This technique might be used, for example, to connect a remote printer where no return communication is necessary. Half-duplex lines provide for communication in both directions, but in only one direction at a time. This system is used for many interactive demand-response applications where the remote station responds to commands issued by the master station. Duplex operation allows for simultaneous transmissions in both directions.

Data rates which can be sustained on a particular communication network are a function of the bandwidth of the communication channel and the modulation technique employed. In general, the cost of the communication channel increases as its bandwidth increases. Low speed lines are those which are capable of providing communications up to about 100 Baud. (A Baud is the reciprocal of the length of the shortest signal element measured in seconds. For the modulation techniques generally employed in the computer industry, one Baud equals a one-bit per second signal rate.) Medium-speed lines are those generally used for voice communications in the telephone industry. A high quality voice-grade line can accommodate data rates up to about 5000 Baud. Over 5000 Baud is considered high speed transmission. This type of service is relatively expensive and does not find extensive use in industrial control applications.

The characterization and design of communication networks for use with computers is a complex subject that has been the subject of several books. The reader is referred to the literature and to the installation manuals provided by the various manufacturers for more detailed information.

INDUSTRY STANDARD INTERFACES

Although not strictly an I/O device, the subject of industry standard interfaces deserves a few paragraphs in this book. In recent years, there has been growing national and international activity directed toward the development and acceptance of one or more standard I/O interfaces. The adoption of such a standard(s) would mean that the equipment of a single peripheral manufacturer could be attached to a variety of CPUs or vice versa. The objective is to ease system design and to provide the user with increased flexibility, since one could choose from a broad array of equipment offerings. The availability of an interface standard covering the electrical and mechanical characteristics of an interface would not, however, result in complete interchangeability of equipment, due to differences in the required programming support.

There is some feeling, however, that the standardization of interfaces could have some potential disadvantages. It is argued that if the standard is applied at the I/O channel of the CPU, it could be restrictive in that the design of the channel and the architecture of the CPU are closely intertwined. Thus, the standard interface could restrict the implementation of new features and inventions in CPU design. In addition, the channel designs offered by each vendor have their own unique characteristics, which are optimized toward the peripheral equipment which that vendor offers. As a result of this optimization, the system usually achieves a performance level that could not be achieved within the contraints of a generalized standard interface.

One attractive approach is to assume that the standard interface is to be implemented as a derivative of the I/O channel. This approach allows the designer freedom in his selection of achitecture and channel design. The vendor can design channel attachments for his own peripherals, which provide optimum performance by taking advantage of the unique characteristics of the channel design. The standardized interface can be provided, in essence, as an interface translator that translates the unique I/O channel interface into the standardized interface. This provides the user the choice of using a standardized interface to obtain interchangeability, or the vendor's unique interface to obtain performance optimized to the vendor's peripherals.

At the time of this writing (August, 1977), there are several standard interface efforts in national and international standardization bodies that may be of interest for industrial control. The first, popularly known as the General Purpose Interface Bus (GPIB), has been adopted by the Institute of Electrical and Electronic Engineers as a standard (IEEE 488-1975) and by American National Standards Institute (ANSI) as American National Standard MC1.1-1975. Simultaneously, essentially the same document has been approved by the International Electrotechnical Commission (IEC) as an international standard.

The GPIB is a relatively simple interface originally designed for connecting laboratory instrumentation to a computer. It contains 16 lines of which 8 are used for data transmission and 8 are used for various control functions. It is intended for use over relatively short distances (less than 20 meters). Data transmission is parallel by byte (8-bits) at rates up to about one megabyte per second.

The second well-known interface standard activity is known as CAMAC. This work originally grew out of the ESONE Committee in Europe, which is composed of a number of nuclear and high-energy physics laboratories. In recent years, the U.S. Atomic Energy Commission (AEC), now the Environmental Resource Development Administration (ERDA), has collaborated with the ESONE Committee. The standards have been widely used in physics and nuclear laboratories and are beginning to find use in industry.

In reality, there are three CAMAC interface documents which have been adopted as standards by the IEEE and the IEC. They are currently being considered for adoption as American National Standards. One of these standards relates to a physical package called a crate, into which various I/O and measurement devices, housed in modules, can be plugged. Also included in this standard is a detailed description of the bus, called the Dataway, which interconnects the modules in a single crate (IEEE 583-1975).

A second standard is related to a parallel interface bus called the Branch Highway (IEEE 596-1976). The Branch Highway is designed to connect up to seven crates to a computer fitted with a suitable Branch Driver. At the present time, Branch Drivers are available for a number of minicomputers. In addition, several hundred types of modules have been made available by a variety of manufacturers. Most of these modules are intended for use in the laboratory and are not well-suited for use in process control. Recently, however, interest in CAMAC among process control users has increased and modules suitable for industrial use are being made available.

The third interface included in the CAMAC standards is a high-speed serial loop interface for bit-serial communication which, in another form, can be used for byte-serial communications (IEEE 595-1976). Data rates of up to 5 megabits or 5 megabytes per second are considered in the standard. This serial interface, of the three interfaces, appears to be the one that is of most interest to the process control user. It is general-purpose in nature, has good data integrity, and a high level of function.

Other organizations are considering interface standardization. The IEC Technical Committee 65 (IEC/TC65) on process control has a working group (WG6) which has developed a functional requirements document for a serial interface. A working group of the International Organization for Standardization (ISO), ISO/TC97/SC13/WG1, presently is working on a standard related to the uniform specification of the process I/O interface. In the United States, subcommittees X3T9.2 and X3T9.3 of the ANSI committee X3T9 are developing interface standards proposals relating to minicomputers.

Standards activity in the United States in this area is supervised by the Measurement and Control Standards Management Board (MACSMB) and the Information Systems Standards Management Board (ISSMB) of ANSI. MACSMB has assigned the national responsibility for interface work in the area of process control to the Instrument Society of America (ISA). The ISA manages the work through its standards committee SP72, which is a working group of the Interface and Data Transmission Committee of the International Purdue Workshop on Industrial Computer Systems. The Purdue Workshop is sponsored by the Instrument Society of America (ISA), Purdue University, and several other organizations. Branches of the Purdue Workshop are active in Europe and Japan. It meets semi-annually at Purdue University and, in addition to the interface activity, is active in the standardization of computer languages for industrial control and is studying a number of related subjects, such as man-machine communications and system reliability.

BIBLIOGRAPHY
(Also see Bibliography for Chapter 2)

Anon., "Hardware Testing of Digital Process Computers, ISA Recommended Practice RP55.1." Instrument Society of America, Pittsburgh, 1975 (Also American National Standard MC8.1-1975).

CAMAC Instrumentation and Interface Standards, Institute of Electrical and Electronic Engineers, Inc., New York, 1976.

Carroll, R. F., "Guidelines for the Design of Man/Machine Interfaces for Process Control." International Purdue Workshop, Purdue University, W. Lafayette, IN, 1976 (Revised).

Harrison, T. J., *Handbook of Industrial Control Computers*, John Wiley & Sons, New York, 1972.

Hoeschele, D. F., Jr., *Analog-to-Digital/Digital-to-Analog Techniques*, John Wiley & Sons, New York, 1968.

"IEEE Standard Digital Interface for Programmable Instrumentation," IEEE Std. 488-1975, American National Standard MC1.1-1975, Institute of Electrical and Electronic Engineers, Inc., New York, 1975.

Martin, J., *Design of Man-Computer Dialogues*, Prentice Hall, Englewood Cliffs, 1973.

Martin, J., *Future Developments in Telecommunications*, Revised, Prentice-Hall, Englewood Cliffs, 1977.

Schmid, H., *Electronic Analog/Digital Conversion*, Van Nostrand Reinhold, New York, 1970.

4 INTRODUCTION TO SOFTWARE

Thomas J. Harrison, Ph.D.

INTERNATIONAL BUSINESS MACHINES CORPORATION.
BOCA RATON, FLORIDA

The word "software" is a generic term which describes the total set of programs which are used with a computer, including the programs which are unique to a particular application. Also included are the operating system program which controls the computer resources and a variety of support programs, such as language processors and diagnostics.

"Programming" is the activity through which software is created. The term "programming" often is interpreted to mean only the process of coding an application into the computer instructions for a specific computer. In reality, programming has a much broader meaning and includes defining and analyzing the problem, designing a suitable algorithm, coding and debugging the algorithm, installing the program in the application, and maintaining it over the life of the application.

In this chapter, attention is directed to the design of the algorithm, its transformation into machine usable form, and its interaction with other programs within the system. The various types of languages and language processors through which the algorithm is described and converted to computer-usable form are presented in a tutorial fashion. The operating system, its purpose, and some of its features are discussed similarly. The final section of the chapter considers programming methodology and concentrates on the concepts of structured coding, top-down design, and the chief programmer team organization.

147

THE PROGRAMMING PROCESS

The general purpose of programming is to make the computer system do useful work. The hardware described in the previous chapters is insufficient, in and of itself, to satisfy the needs of an application. What is required is a sequence of specific instructions which the machine must execute in order to solve the problem or to direct computer resources in satisfying the particular needs of the application.

As noted in the introduction, "programming" often is restricted to mean only the creation of the sequence of the computer instructions. In reality, programming involves at least seven different phases as shown in Fig. 4.1. The first phase is the definition of the problem. In defining the problem, one must determine what inputs are required, what outputs are desired, and what is the relationship between the inputs and the outputs. In control system terminology, this latter step is equivalent to finding a transfer function.

By analyzing the inputs available and the desired results, the programmer must design an algorithm which solves the particular problem. An algorithm is a systematic procedure which leads to the answer of the problem in a finite

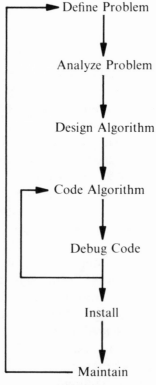

FIG. 4.1
Elements of Programming

number of steps. It is not necessarily a mathematical formula. For example, an algorithm can be defined which allows a traveler to find his way from the airport to the motel. Such an algorithm could consist of a sequence of instructions indicating which turns the traveler should take and the distance between the turns. In general, many of the algorithms involved in the use of a computer are non-mathematical in nature. Rather, they consist of procedures for manipulating data in prescribed sequences in order to obtain a desired result.

Once the algorithm is designed, it must be expressed in a form which is acceptable to the computer. This generally is done through the use of one of several different types of computer languages. The various levels and types of languages are discussed in more detail in a later section. The actual coding procedure involves writing down a sequence of instructions, somewhat like abstract English sentences, and then having this sequence of instructions converted into a form which can be used for input to a computer. This might consist, for example, of punching the instructions into cards or typing them directly into the computer storage by means of a typewriter-like terminal device. The electronic circuits in the terminal convert the input key strokes into coded sequences of binary digits which can be stored in the main storage of the computer.

For most languages, a translation program is required to convert the actual input produced by the programmer into the machine instructions necessary to control the computer. Depending on its design and the type of language, this translator may be called an assembler, a compiler, or an interpreter. Although varying in details, conceptually all three of these types of processing programs convert the alphanumeric-coded input language into sequences of binary-coded machine instructions.

Most translation programs include error detection features which alert the programmer to possible coding errors. Since the translation program does not know the purpose of the user's program or the problem that is being solved, the error detection typically is limited to verifying that the rules for the use of the language (i.e., the syntax) have been observed. Computer languages are defined very precisely and the syntax rules must be followed exactly if they are to result in useful programs. For example, if a semicolon is to be used as a delimiter in a programming statement and the programmer erroneously uses a colon, this results in an error. Errors which appear trivial to the human and which can be easily recognized and ignored in understanding what the programmer wants to do, are not tolerated by the computer and result in a machine malfunction.

Once the algorithm has been translated into a sequence of machine instructions, the programmer tests the program by running it on the computer. Except in rare circumstances, one finds that there is at least one error in the program. The error may arise from a number of sources. There might be an error, for example, in the algorithm; that is, the programmer may have used the wrong sequence of actions in solving the problems and the program will not operate properly.

A second possibility for error is failing to recognize the result of a particular disallowed combination of input data. For example, if the algorithm is a mathematical routine involving the square root of a number, a particular combination of data might result in a negative operand. Most computers are designed so that they will not take the square root of a negative number; rather, the machine stops and indicates an error condition.

These and the numerous other errors which are possible are called "bugs" in a program. The process of finding the bugs and correcting them is called "debugging" the program. This is generally an iterative process with the programmer finding and correcting an error, retrying the program, and discovering that yet another error exists. Although the number and types of errors which are possible using the various types of programming languages are, to a certain degree, a function of the language being used and the ability of the translator program to detect such errors, errors are almost inevitable and a certain amount of debugging activity always is required.

Once the program has been debugged and tested to the satisfaction of the programmer, it must then be installed on the computer. The exact activity involved in installing a program depends upon the characteristics of the computer and its operating system. In general, however, it involves verifying that the necessary inputs are available, that they are being accepted properly by the computer, and that the program results in the proper output. Secondly, links between the particular program and the operating system must be verified and tested.

Once the installation phase is complete and the program is operating to the satisfaction of the programmer and user, it enters a maintenance phase. One of the characteristics of programs is that it is very difficult to anticipate all errors that can result from interactions between programs or various combinations of data. As a result, there is a common saying in programming that a program never is debugged completely. Throughout the life of an installation, therefore, one expects that bugs may arise. When errors are identified, their cause must be found and the necessary corrections made. The processes for finding and correcting such errors are very similar to the programming process itself; that is, it starts with finding and analyzing the problem, designing the correction, coding it, debugging it, and installing it. The maintenance phase lasts for the total useful life of the program. The failure mechanism in software is different than it is in hardware, in that software does not wear out or drift out of adjustment. Nevertheless, the failure characteristics are similar in that most errors are found immediately after installation and as the application matures, the number of malfunctions becomes very small.

ALGORITHMS

As noted previously, an algorithm is a systematic procedure designed to lead to the solution of a problem in a finite number of steps. Figure 4.2 illustrates a mathematical algorithm which is familiar from elementary algebra. The specific problem is to find the roots of a second order equation by using the quadratic formula. A graphical description of the algorithm which provides the solution is shown in Fig. 4.2 and is called a flowchart. In the flowchart, each step in the solution of the problem is shown as a separate and distinct procedure. The shapes of the blocks in the diagram have specific meanings as defined in American National Standard X3.5-1970: A circle represents a starting or ending point; a rectangular block indicates some action which must be taken; a diamond shaped block indicates that a decision must be made at that point. Flowcharts have been used in programming for many years. In recent years, other methods of describing algorithms have become more common, but the flowchart is used here since it requires little explanation and is easy to use.

In examining the flowchart of the quadradic equation algorithm, note that there are three parameters A, B, and C. The first step in the computer solution is to read the parameters A, B, and C. In actually coding a computer, the computer must be told where to find the parameters; for example, the parameters may be stored in main storage or on a mass storage device, or, perhaps, they must be read in as input from the analog-input subsystem.

The next step in the algorithm is to calculate the radical (RAD) term. At this point in analyzing the program, the programmer has recognized that the value of the radical may be either positive or negative, depending upon the relative magnitudes of A, B, and C. Since a computer will not take the square root of a negative number, the programmer must account for this possibility. Therefore, the next step in the algorithm is to test whether or not the radical is greater than or equal to zero. If the radical is greater than or equal to zero, the algorithm proceeds to calculate the two roots $X1$ and $X2$ directly. Following their calculation, the values are printed on an appropriate output device.

On the other hand, if the radical is less than zero, the programmer must deal with the imaginary roots which are produced. This is done by taking the absolute value of the radical before calculating the square root. Once this has been done, the real and imaginary parts are calculated separately and can be printed as two separate numbers. This completes the other possible path through the algorithm.

In this particular example, the algorithm is mathematical in nature. This very often is not true in actual programming situations. For example, a common problem in data processing is to alphabetize a list of names or to find a particular name in a list. Here the procedures are not mathematical, but

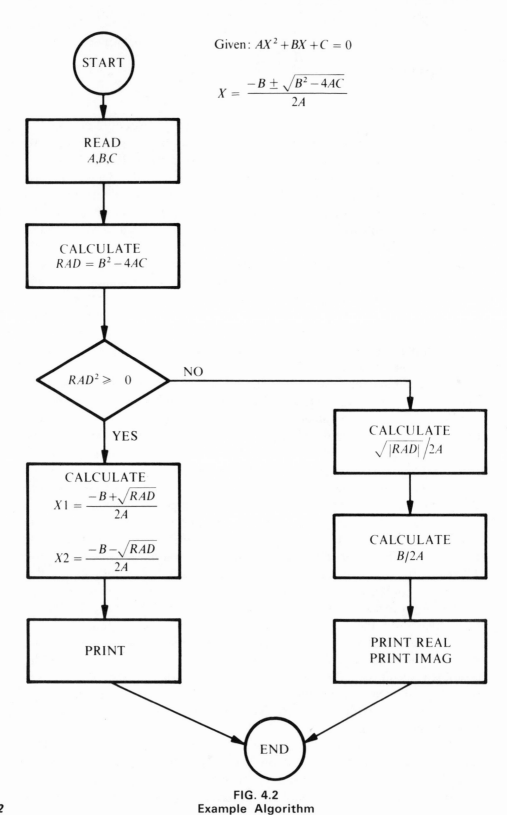

Given: $AX^2 + BX + C = 0$

$$X = \frac{-B \pm \sqrt{B^2 - 4AC}}{2A}$$

START

READ
A,B,C

CALCULATE
$RAD = B^2 - 4AC$

$RAD^2 \geqslant 0$

NO

YES

CALCULATE
$\sqrt{|RAD|}\big/2A$

CALCULATE
$X1 = \dfrac{-B + \sqrt{RAD}}{2A}$

$X2 = \dfrac{-B - \sqrt{RAD}}{2A}$

CALCULATE
$B/2A$

PRINT

PRINT REAL
PRINT IMAG

END

FIG. 4.2
Example Algorithm

rather are logical in nature. Computers, although often thought of as numerical calculating machines, really are symbol manipulators and non-mathematical algorithms are very common.

COMPUTER LANGUAGES

The programming step called coding consists of expressing the algorithm in a form which is useful to the machine. This usually is done by means of an artificial language which provides control over the various functions which the computer can perform. A computer language is very similar conceptually to a natural language used by humans for communicating. In general, a written natural language consists of an alphabet, which is a set of allowable symbols which can be used within the context of the language. The second element of a language is the vocabulary consisting of allowable words, which are strings of the allowable symbols. In a computer language, a certain set of words in the vocabulary are predefined by the language designer; other words, commonly used to identify constants and variables in the problem being coded, can be defined arbitrarily by the programmer. The third element of a language is its syntax. The syntax of a language consists of the rules which must be followed in using the language; these commonly define the grammer for the language. For example, in many natural languages there is a relatively small set of allowed constructions. One such construction in the English language is that the subject of the sentence is followed by the verb which, in turn, is followed by the direct object. The fourth language element is the semantics or the meanings of the particular set of vocabulary words and constructions used in the language. In a computer language, the semantics are the basis for the design of the language translator program.

Although computer languages conceptually are similar to languages used by humans, there are some significant differences. A primary difference relates to the precision with which the syntax and semantics of the language must be used. Although a human often can determine the meaning of a sentence which is enunciated poorly or which contains words that are spelled incorrectly, the computer is not as flexible.

The precision of definition and the rigidity of interpretation are both a practical necessity and a consequence of how computers work. Precision is needed to eliminate ambiguity in the language. Each word or construction can have one, and only one, meaning if the programmer is to be ensured that the program will run in the intended manner. It is important to realize that the computer does not *understand* the words that are being used; to the computer, the words are merely strings of symbols separated by blanks. The computer compares each character in the word with the corresponding character in its dictionary of known words. If it finds a match for every character in the string, it executes a predefined sequence of instructions corresponding to that word. If a match is not found, the character string is assumed to be a programmer-defined word or an error.

There usually are several different languages available for use with any given computer. One or more of these languages may be unique to the particular model of the machine being used. Other languages provided for the computer, however, may be the same as those provided for a computer of another model. In general, languages can be categorized by their level. Although the concept of a programming language level is not defined precisely, in general the higher the level of the language, the more it resembles the language of a human. A consequence of this definition is that the higher level languages progressively are easier for the human to use in expressing an algorithm. For the purpose of this chapter, languages have been categorized into six levels, starting with the basic machine language and progressing upward through the turn-key package.

Machine-Level Languages

An example of a machine-level language representation of a program fragment is shown in Fig. 4.3. In the machine-level language, each instruction is represented as a string of binary 1's and 0's. As described in the previous chapter, this single machine instruction typically consists of an operation code (OP) defining the function to be performed, a modifier (MOD) specifying a modification to the basic function, and either an address (ADDR) or an operand. All three portions of the instructions are coded in a binary code which is usable immediately by the computer; that is, a machine-level language instruction can be loaded into the computer storage and executed directly.

Each line in the machine language program is a single instruction which can be executed by the particular computer. In this sense, it is a one-for-one

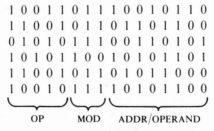

FIG. 4.3
Example Machine-Level Language Program

language, meaning that one line of input code results in one machine instruction. When using machine-level coding, the programmer must assign the actual addresses at which data or instructions are found in main storage. These addresses and operands must be provided in binary representation for each instruction.

As can be seen easily by reference to Fig. 4.3, machine-level language is totally unnatural to the human user. Remembering the many binary codes for the various operations that a typical minicomputer can execute is almost impossible for most programmers. Similarly, converting all addresses and operands into their binary codes is a significant task which is very prone to human error. Therefore, it is very difficult to program in machine-level language and equally difficult to debug a program with any effectiveness. In addition, the requirement that absolute addresses be provided at the time of coding the algorithm means that the programmer must do considerable recordkeeping to avoid errors.

In contrast to its difficulty of being used, machine-level programming is one of the most flexible forms of programming in terms of access to the machine functions. Any function which the machine is capable of doing can be described through its machine language.

Because of the difficulty of using machine-level programming, it is used only rarely in programming a computer. The only notable exception is in the early stages of machine design when translator programs for higher level languages have not yet been developed. There is virtually no reason to ever use machine-level programming in an application environment.

Assembler Languages

Assembler language is the next higher level language commonly provided with computers. It shares many of the characteristics of machine-level languages but is considerably easier to use. It is a one-for-one language, in that each line of code corresponds to a single machine instruction. A significant

```
        L D X ,  1 ,  2 ,  A D R O T
        L D X ,       ,  1 ,  5 3
        L D   ,  L ,       ,  P A C K D + 5 3
        B S C ,       ,       ,  C
        N O P
CKSUM A        ,  L ,  2 ,  P A C K D - 1
        B S C ,       ,       ,  C
        A                  D 0 0 0 1
        M D X ,       ,  2 ,  - 1
```

FIG. 4.4
Example Assembly-Level Language Program

difference is that the various portions of the instructions are represented as alphanumeric mnemonics rather than as binary codes. This is shown in Fig. 4.4 which is a fragment of an assembler language program. Considering the first line of the program in Fig. 4.4, for example, the mnemonic LDX represents the binary string which is the operations code for this particular instruction. In general, mnemonic OP codes are chosen by the computer designer such that they have some meaning to the programmer. In this case, for example, LDX is the abbreviation for the command "load index." Following the mnemonic OP code, the two numerals one and two represent modifiers to the basic OP code. Finally, the alphanumeric string ADROT is a programmer-defined symbolic representation of the address. The use of symbolic addresses in assembler language is a distinct advantage over the requirement for absolute addresses in machine-level language. Symbolic address names can be chosen to be meaningful to the programmer without reference to their actual location in storage. The assignment of the absolute address is done by the translation program which processes the assembler-level code.

Although still unnatural, assembler-level language is more natural than machine-level language. This naturalness is due primarily to the selection of meanginful abbreviations or mnemonics for the operation code, modifiers, and addresses.

Assembler-level language is as flexible as machine-level language, since each line of code corresponds on a one-to-one basis to a machine instruction. Thus, any function which can be performed by the computer can be expressed in the assembler language.

Since the assembler language is expressed in terms of alphanumeric symbols and the basic machine instruction is a binary-coded sequence of bits, the assembler language program, called the "source program," must be processed by another program to translate or convert it into the machine-level representation which is called the "object program." The translator program is called an assembler and may run either on the same computer for which the program is being prepared or on another machine. In the latter case, the assembler program is called a cross-assembler or a host assembler.

The primary function of the assembler is to substitute the correct binary-coded representation for the mnemonics used in the assembler program and to assign absolute addresses in place of the symbolic addresses. However, most assembler programs do considerably more than this simple substitution. Most assembler programs test each source statement to ensure that it is correct in terms of its syntax. It also detects if a variable used by the programmer has been defined previously so that it is known to the program. In addition, it provides many of the recordkeeping functions which are necessary in writing, documenting, and debugging the program.

Essentially all computers have a defined assembly language and, with the exception of computers designed to be programmed only in a high level language, manufacturers usually provide an assembler program. Since there is a one-to-one correspondence between the assembler instructions and the actual machine instructions, the assembler-level language is unique to each particular computer. In many cases, several models of a manufacturer's computer line use the same assembler-level language or various super- and subsets of it.

Macro-Assembler Languages

Macro-assembler languages were prompted by the observation that the programmer frequently requires the same identical sequence of assembler instructions to perform a routine function which is more complex than that provided in a single assembler instruction. For example, a common requirement is to read cards from a card reader. Most computers do not have a single instruction which performs this function; rather, it is accomplished by a sequence of machine-level instructions. However, it is possible to write a short segment of code which provides this function whenever it is required by the programmer. This short sequence of code is assigned a name and is called a "macro-instruction." In Fig. 4.5, the third line is an example of such a macro-instruction. When processed by the macro-assembler translator program, a predefined sequence of assembler-level instructions is substituted for the line which contains the macro name "READ." Thus, this single line of source code creates multiple lines of object code.

As can be seen from the figure, the appearance of a macro-assembler language is very similar to that of assembler language. The facilities provided through the language are also very similar, in that mnemonic operation codes and symbolic addressing are provided. The ability to use a macro-instruction, however, eases the programmer's task when a particular high level function must be used repeatedly throughout the program. If a macro-assembler is provided, the computer manufacturer generally provides a set of commonly used macro-instructions as part of the assembler. In addition, the user usually can define other macros which are useful in the particular application.

```
L D X , 1 , 2 , A D R O T
L D X ,   , 1 , 5 3

R E A D   A , B

B S C       C
N O P
```

FIG. 4.5
Example Macro-Assembler-Level Language Program

The processing of macro-level language statements is similar to the processing of assembler-level statements. The translator program, called a "macro-assembler," substitutes the sequences of instructions which represent each of the macros whenever they appear.

Macro-assembler languages are easier to use than assembler languages, primarily because the precoded macro routines ease the repetitive tasks which the programmer must perform. In general, macro-assembler programs are as flexible as assembler programs. In some cases, however, some flexibility is sacrificed, since the macro provided by the language may be somewhat less efficient than what is possible on the assembler-level language level because it must be written for general use. Except for subsetting or supersetting between models of a computer provided by a single manufacturer, macro-assembler languages are unique to each particular computer design.

High Level Procedural Languages

High level procedural languages are designed specifically for coding procedures or algorithms without concern for the details of the structure or configuration of the computer. Some of these languages are oriented to a particular use, such as scientific programming or commercial programming. High level procedural languages are characterized by using a vocabulary largely consisting of standard English words and mathematical symbols. They also utilize a sentence structure similar to that of a natural language. A program fragment written in a high level procedural language is shown in Fig. 4.6.

In most high level procedural languages, a vocabulary of key words is defined by the language designer for use within the language. This vocabulary consists of verbs such as GET and PUT, various mathematical operations such as addition, subtraction and multiplication (usually denoted with conventional mathematical symbols), and some other words used for control such as THEN and ELSE. In addition to this predefined set of words, the user can assign symbolic names for variables and addresses, as in the case of the lower level languages.

$$\text{GET LIST } (XMIN)$$
$$XMAX = XMIN$$
$$\text{LOOP: GET LIST } (X)$$
$$\text{IF } X > XMAX$$
$$\text{THEN } XMAX = X$$
$$\text{IF } (X - XMIN) > 0 \text{ THEN}$$
$$\text{GO TO LABEL 4}$$
$$\text{ELSE GO TO LOOP}$$

FIG. 4.6
Example High Level Procedural Language Program

Although somewhat constrained in style, most procedural level languages are almost natural in their expression. For example in Fig. 4.6, the intent of the program following the word LOOP is understandable even to an inexperienced programmer.

Another common feature of high level procedural languages is the facility to incorporate an independently-written program into another program. This is similar in concept to the macro-instruction in that the program, called a subroutine, provides a common function that may be needed in several algorithms. The subroutine is a program which is assigned a name by the programmer and which can be referenced in another program. A typical means of invoking the subroutine is through a statement such as CALL NAME (A, B, C), where NAME is the assigned name of the subroutine and A, B, and C are parameters needed during the execution of the subroutine. A, B, and C must be calculated or assigned by the calling program prior to invoking the subroutine.

Libraries of subroutines for common functions usually are provided by the computer vendor in association with the language processor programs with which they are used. Examples of subroutines commonly found in these libraries are programs to calculate trigonometric functions, floating point arithmetic (if not provided in the language itself), and specialized algorithms, such as plotting and curve fitting. In most cases, the using programmer can define additional subroutines and add them to the library.

Although clearly easier to use, high level languages usually are less flexible than assembler languages. This results because the program which processes the high level language must have standardized procedures for each language function and structure. These standardized procedures must be very general so that they are applicable in all cases. As a result, they often cannot take advantage of special characteristics of the problem or data which might be available to the programmer coding in assembler-level language. The loss of flexibility, however, is generally a very good trade for the considerable increase in the ease-of-use and productivity of the language.

High level procedural language source programs must be processed by a translator program which converts them into the machine language object program required by the computer. There are two common approaches to translator programs available for high level procedural languages. The first is called a compiler. In a compiler, the source program is converted into a sequence of machine-level instructions and absolute addresses or their equivalents are substituted for the various mnemonic names assigned by the programmer. A compiler produces the entire sequence of machine instructions before any are executed; that is, the compiler does all of the language processing before the program itself is executed.

The second type of translator program is known as an interpreter. In this program, each line of source code is executed at the time it is processed by the interpreter. For example, if the line of source code reads $A = B + C$, the interpreter actually executes the addition operation rather than merely creating the necessary sequence of machine operation for later execution. In contrast to the compiler, the interpreter must analyze each line of source code every time the program is executed.

Both the compiler and interpreter modes of translation have their advantages and disadvantages and, in fact, are sometimes both used in the same translator program. Interpreters often are used in interactive programming applications, where the user is interacting with a computer through a terminal or similar input/output device. Interpreters result in a longer execution time for any given program, due to the requirement for analyzing every statement prior to each execution. This is generally of little consequence in an interactive environment, however. Compilers, on the other hand, generally produce faster code and, very often, more efficient code in terms of storage requirements. A disadvantage is that the application program must be compiled as a separate procedure before it can be executed. Compilers are less convenient, therefore, for an interactive environment.

High level procedural languages theoretically are hardware independent; that is, the language itself does not depend on the existence of unique features in the particular computer on which it is to be run. A program written to run on one computer design should run on any other computer which accepts the language. In actual implementations, however, there often is some hardware dependence, in that certain functions available in the language may or may not be provided in a particular computer.

A number of high level procedural languages are available for most computers. Some of the best known are COBOL, FORTRAN, BASIC, and PL/I. In addition, many manufacturers provide proprietary high level procedural languages oriented toward their product or toward particular applications, such as real-time industrial control.

Application Languages

Application languages are a special case of high level procedural languages. Typically, the language is designed for use in a particular industry

> READ ANALOG $A1$
> CLOSE VALVE $V1$ AT 60 MIN
> TURN ON ALARM
>
> .
> .
> .

FIG. 4.7
Example Application Language Program

or application and uses the vocabulary of that particular industry. Figure 4.7 illustrates several lines from an application language program. An application language generally includes a series of verbs such as READ or WRITE, similar to those found in a high level procedural language. In addition, however, it uses a specialized vocabulary related to the particular application area. For the example shown, VALVE and ALARM are words associated with the process control industry. In addition to a specialized vocabulary, the language may provide built-in algorithms which are characteristic of the particular industry, such as the three-mode control equations used in the process control industry.

The characteristics and processing of an application language essentially are identical to those of a high level procedural language. In general, they are very easy to use and are familiar to users in the particular application. In one sense, they are less efficient for the same reason that high level procedural languages may be less efficient than assembler languages. On the other hand, if looked at in a broader context, they are generally more efficient since they allow a programmer to accomplish more in a shorter period of time and with less training.

Although relatively machine independent, application languages often are written by manufacturers for their particular machines. Examples of this type of language offered by manufacturers include PROSPRO and AUTRAN. Some application languages such as ATLAS have found relatively broad usage and are available for a number of computers. ATLAS, in particular, has been approved recently as an IEEE Standard (IEEE 416–1976).

Turn-Key Packages

The term "Turn-Key Package" implies that the only thing the user must do to use the computer is to "turn on the key and press the start button." In a sense, therefore, a turn-key package really is not a language, although it may have a language associated with it for communication between the operator and the machine. In general, turn-key packages are very easy to use and require a minimum of training for the user. They are very inflexible compared to the other languages, in that they are designed to provide a certain set of functions or to solve a particular problem. If the requirements of the application differ, the turn-key package will not be suitable without modification. Due to the differences between applications and the particular process hardware with which the computer interfaces, most turn-key packages require some tailoring at the time they are installed.

Turn-key packages are designed for a particular application and, therefore, have limited applicability. Due to this limited application, relatively few programs of this type have been made available by computer manufacturers for industrial computers because of economic reasons. Very often, turn-key packages are produced by the user using one of the procedural or assembler languages, or by companies which specialize in producing software for a variety of computers in a limited application area.

The High Versus The Low Question

In the previous sections describing the various languages, it was pointed out that the higher level languages tend to be less flexible than lower level languages. At the present time, a large percentage of the programming for industrial computers is done with assembler-level languages. This is motivated by the contention that assembler-level programs run faster, are more efficient in their use of storage, and provide better control of the machine.

Although this contention is sometimes true, the question of what language to use in programming an industrial application must be examined carefully. This examination should be a very broad view which recognizes that the primary goal of a computer user is to solve a particular application problem. In today's environment of increasing wages and inflation, the question of programmer productivity is often far more important than the question of execution time (assuming the program runs fast enough) and the efficient use of storage (assuming storage requirements do not exceed the machine capability). Thus, if the use of a high level language results in a program which is adequate, but perhaps not optimal, the use of such a language may be preferred by the fact that the user can solve his problem faster as a result of significantly improved programmer productivity.

Programmer productivity is a difficult quantity to measure. A commonly-used criterion is the number of lines of code that the programmer produces, tests, and documents in a given period of time. One rule of thumb is that a programmer can code, test, and document five to ten lines of code per day in any given language for a particular type of program. This means, for example, that the programmer can code five to ten lines of assembler code or five to ten lines of code in a high level language, such as FORTRAN or PL/I. The difference, of course, is that one line of code in a high level language such as PL/I can be equivalent to hundreds of lines of assembler code. Furthermore, high level languages tend to be self-documenting, in that very little explanation of the code is required other than the code itself. Thus, if productivity is measured in terms of the time it takes to finish a given programming job, it generally is agreed that high level languages provide about a four to one increase over assembler code in productivity.

It is generally true, however, that a highly-skilled assembler-level programmer can produce a program that runs faster than a program produced by a compiler from a high level language and, furthermore, that the storage requirements for a skillfully-coded assembler program may be less than those required for the corresponding compiler-generated program. The use of the adjectives "highly-skilled" and "skillfully-coded" in the previous sentence was intentional and significant. Experience has shown that a well-designed compiler, utilizing presently available optimization techniques can produce excellent code, both in terms of execution time and storage efficiency. In fact, most assembler-level programmers cannot produce code which is better than that produced by a well-designed optimizing compiler, even though a highly-skilled assembler-level language programmer might be able to do so. Despite one's best recruiting efforts, a realistic manager must admit that only a few of his or her programmers are "highly-skilled."

A second consideration is the fact that the cost of storage for computers has been decreasing dramatically over the past several years. This has been due largely to the advent of large-scale integration (LSI) and the widespread use of semiconductor main storage. On the other hand, the salaries of programmers have been increasing. One must consider carefully, therefore, the tradeoff between lower programmer cost through greater productivity and the cost of the additional storage which may be required as a result of not realizing the highest storage efficiency.

The question as to whether to use a high level or lower level language basically reduces to an economic consideration. The benefits of improved programmer productivity, self-documentation, and the other advantages of high level languages must be compared with the cost of possibly increased storage requirements and possibly slower execution time. A method increasingly being adopted by many users is to use high level languages as the usual method of coding. Once a program has been written and debugged, it is tested in the application environment. As a result of testing, inadequacies due to slow execution or to the use of excessive storage can be identified. In general, it has been found that these problems only affect a small portion of the total set of application programs. These programs, or portions of them, can be recoded in assembler-level code in order to provide the necessary execution speed or improved storage efficiency. Thus, assembler-level coding is used only on an exception basis. Although this procedure may involve recoding certain modules within the application program set, the initial use of a high level programming language still may have benefit, in that it allows the programmer to test the logic of the solution without being conerned with the language detail. The ease of debugging the program in a high level language as compared to assembler-level language is an obvious advantage in testing the logical flow and mathematical correctness of the program. Recoding the selected module in assembler-level coding then becomes a much easier task and the risk of error is reduced greatly. Experience has shown that the net result is better code at a lower total development and maintenance cost.

OPERATING SYSTEMS

The use of the programming languages described in the previous sections allows the user to satisfy the requirements of the applications by controlling the various actions available from the computer. Much of this control, however, is concerned with the computer system itself and is relatively independent of the application program. As examples, a programmer may desire that a program be run at a particular time of the day, or might want a summary status report to be produced at the end of every work shift in an industrial plant. In order to do this, the computer must keep track of the time of day. These are only two examples of relatively routine services which a programmer requires in satisfying the requirements of any application. It is customary to provide these types of services by means of a program which has overall control of the computer resources.

This program is known variously as the operating system, the executive, the monitor, or the supervisor. It is, in essence, a program which controls the execution of other programs needed in a particular application. Although the details of operating systems vary considerably from one computer system to the other, they generally provide facilities for the following functions:

(1) Scheduling of tasks;

(2) Handling internal and external interrupts;

(3) Switching of tasks;

(4) Management and allocation of main storage;

(5) Detection of errors and, if possible, recovery from errors;

(6) Control of standard input/output devices;

(7) Utility functions which are useful in many applications.

In the following sections, each of these functions is described in more detail.

The main purpose for the operating system is to provide for the efficient use of the computer resources through optimum scheduling, sharing, and overlapped use. The operating system is also largely responsible for providing time-responsiveness to events in the industrial process by means of its interrupt handling service. As an aid to the programmer, the operating system provides many functions which ease the programming task by providing routine operations and coordination functions which otherwise would have to be written by the application programmer. And lastly, the operating system typically provides a measure of safety for the application, in that it includes various checks and safeguards which prevent the inadvertent destruction of a program, or other catastrophic events, as the result of an error or other occurrence.

The operating system may provide the programmer with a machine whose appearance differs greatly from that of the basic hardware. For example, the basic hardware may not include a multiply instruction. By providing the appropriate services through the operating system and its support programs, this function can be provided as a built-in software subroutine. Thus, the programmer sees a machine which has a multiply instruction, even though the basic hardware does not provide this capability. In a sense, the combination of machine hardware and the operating system software create a virtual machine which has its own language, its own capability, and a distinct personality. To a very large extent, the ease of using a particular computer is dependent upon the interface between the programmer and the operating system, rather than on any direct interface between the programmer and machine hardware.

Although different in detail, most operating systems provided for minicomputers are similar in the services they implement. One possible categorization of these services is into resource management functions, functions related to man-machine communications, various functions provided by subroutine libraries, and utilities and diagnostics.

Resource Management

The resources of a computer system are those functions of the computer system which are available to the programmer. These include, certainly, time to use the central processing unit itself. In addition, however, the programmer requires access to main and mass storage so that storage is also a resource. Most computers have a variety of input/output devices and these devices are resources for the programmer. Finally, the software itself is a resource, in that the programmer may call upon precoded subroutines or other software functions for use in application programs.

CPU Management

The central processing unit of the computer represents the resource which provides the computer system with its logical and arithmetic capability. Typically in today's system, there is only a single central processing unit and this CPU executes only one task at a time. There are, in most typical industrial applications, however, a number of tasks contending for the use of the single central processing unit. For example, there may be a need to produce a status log at a certain time of day and, simultaneously, there may be a request from an external device for service by the CPU. Thus, the allocation of CPU time becomes an important function for the operating system.

There are a number of criteria under which the time of the CPU may be allocated to the various contending tasks. CPU time may be allocated on the basis of priority or the importance of the contending task, on the basis of the time of day, on the expiration of a defined time interval, or simply on the availability of the CPU.

A common factor in all methods of CPU management is the idea that at any given time there may be a series of tasks awaiting execution within the computer; that is, there is a waiting list or queue of tasks which require CPU time. Physically, the queue consists of a table in main storage containing the addresses of the programs which are to be executed. When a program is due to be executed, either as the result of a particular time of day occurring or an elapsed time interval or some other event, the starting address of that program is placed in the queue and, depending on the particular task scheduling algorithm, the program will be executed in turn according to one or more predefined criteria.

Figure 4.8 illustrates one task scheduling algorithm which is used. In "Round Robin" scheduling, the queue of waiting programs is known as a "first-in-first-out" (FIFO) or a "first-come-first-served" (FCFS) queue. This type of queue is such that the first program request placed in the queue is the first program which is executed. When the CPU is available, the starting address of the first program is accessed by the operating system and the CPU begins executing the program. Program execution continues until one or more criteria are satisfied. Typically, there are three such criteria: The first is that a fixed-time period elapses; that is, the CPU is allowed to execute the particular task for a predefined period of time, usually only a fraction of a second. If the task has not been completed by the end of this time interval, execution is suspended and the request is placed at the bottom of the ready queue. This method of allocation often is called "time-slicing," since each task is allocated a fixed "slice" of time in which to execute. Time-slicing algorithms are

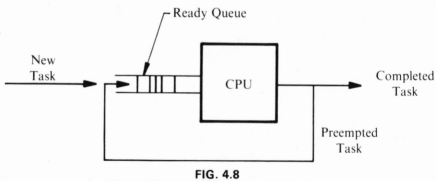

FIG. 4.8
"Round Robin" Scheduling Technique

common in interactive programming applications and, in slightly modified form, have been used in industrial control computers.

A second reason for suspending the execution of a task is that a needed resource is unavailable. For example, a program may require data which are stored on a disk file and, at the particular instant that they are needed, the disk file is servicing a prior request. In this case, the executing task is prempted and is placed at the bottom of the queue.

The third reason for suspending the execution of a task is that it has been completed. In this case, the operating system is notified that the task is complete and the next task waiting in the queue is activated. New tasks to be executed are added to the bottom of the queue at the time they are scheduled by the operating system.

The "round robin" technique is implemented by means of programs in the operating system. It may, however, be assisted by special hardware built into the computer. For example, if a time-slicing algorithm is in use, the hardware may provide an automatic signal at the completion of the predefined time interval. This relieves the operating system of keeping track of the time intervals.

A priority task scheduling procedure is illustrated in Fig. 4.9. The general philosophy in this type of scheduling is that more important tasks are given precedence in their request for CPU time. Multiple ready queues are maintained, one for each defined degree of priority. Within a given priority level, the queue acts as a FIFO queue. CPU time is allocated first to the task at the top of the highest priority queue. After all tasks in the highest priority queue have been executed, CPU time then is allocated to the next highest priority queue.

When operating on a queue which has less than the highest priority, a

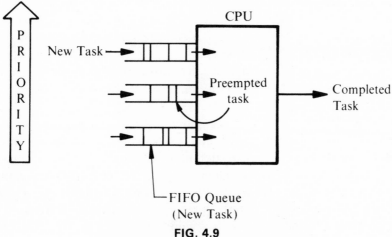

FIG. 4.9
Priority Scheduling Technique

task is preempted by the assignment of a task to a higher priority queue. For example, if priority 1 is the highest priority and the CPU is currently executing a task from the priority 2 queue, an external event or other occurrence may cause the operating system to assign a new task to the priority 1 queue. In this case, the execution of the priority 2 task is suspended, the priority 2 task is returned to the top of the queue, and the CPU is assigned to the higher priority 1 task. Upon completion of the higher priority 1 task, or subsequent higher priority tasks which have been scheduled in the interim period, the CPU is assigned to the priority 2 task which was suspended previously. Within each queue at a given level of priority, secondary scheduling of algorithms according to an algorithm such as time-slicing or sub-priority is also possible. As in the case of the "round robin" algorithm, the priority scheduling algorithm may be implemented totally in software, or hardware may be provided to assist in its implementation.

Although the term "priority" is used in describing this method of operation, it is important to realize that the priority of a task and its importance within the application may or may not be related. A very important process event, such as a critical alarm, may suggest that the program associated with this event be given the highest priority. On the other hand, there are other criteria for assigning priorities. For example, it may be preferable to assign a very slow speed non-critical input/output device to the highest priority level to allow it to operate at its maximum efficiency. Specifically, a character printer operating at the rate of 10 characters per second requires a new input every 100 milliseconds. Providing the new character to the printer may only require 10 microseconds of CPU time. It may be desirable, therefore, to place the printer requests at the highest priority level so that, even though the CPU is interrupted every 100 milliseconds for about 10 microseconds, the character printer can operate at maximum speed; the occasional 10 microsecond interruptions caused by the printer do not affect significantly the speed at which other tasks are executed.

The assignment of priority to a particular task may be defined by the user or by hardware means. It is common, for example, to fix the priority of certain input/output devices by means of physical wiring within the computer hardware. On the other hand, programmers often can assign priority to their programs through the software.

In a real-time industrial computer, a very important source of information related to the scheduling of tasks is the external interrupt subsystem. The concept of an external interrupt is a key factor in a real-time computer system. In essence, when an external event in the process occurs, the computer must respond and service the request within some time constraint. The servicing of an external interrupt requires a sequence of steps, some of which may be controlled by the software and others of which may involve the assistance of specialized hardware.

Chapter 3 includes a description of the hardware which is used in conjunction with the external interrupt system. This hardware must be supported by the appropriate programming routines. Assuming that the current executing task is to be interrupted, the software and/or hardware must provide for the following functions: First, the currently executing task must be suspended in such a way that it can be restarted at a later time. This generally involves saving the contents of various registers and the address of the next instruction. Secondly, the source of the interrupting event must be identified. If immediate servicing is required, the operating system must service the interrupt by calling the appropriate software routine or by placing it in the appropriate queue. After servicing, a test for additional pending interrupts must be made and, if none are present, a switch back to the original task must be done with the appropriate restoration of register contents and other information.

In most industrial control computer applications, a system of preemptive priority interrupts is implemented. In this technique, the currently executing task is suspended only if the interrupting task is of higher priority. If it is of equal or lower priority, the request is queued for later execution. Such systems may be implemented entirely in software or they may be assisted by hardware.

In a software implementation of a preemptive priority system, the occurrence of an external interrupt causes a task switch to the interrupt handling routine in the operating system. If the interrupting task has higher priority than the currently executing task, the operating system saves the necessary status of the currently executing task and switches control to the new higher priority task. When all higher priority tasks have been serviced, the lower priority task processing is resumed with the assistance of the operating system interrupt handling routine.

In a system having hardware-assisted premptive priority interrupt, the hardware determines if the interrupting task is of higher priority. If it is not, the currently executing task continues with no interruption. The hardware automatically queues the request for the lower priority interrupt. The essential sequencing of events for servicing a higher priority interrupt are shown diagramatically in Fig. 4.10.

Even though a preemptive priority system may be in use, there are certain tasks within a typical computer system which cannot be interrupted, no matter how high a priority external event may occur during their execution. This feature often is crucial in maintaining the integrity of the operating system and its associated application programs. An example of a non-interruptible task are the instructions which store the next address upon the receipt of an external interrupt signal. If an interrupt were allowed during the execution of these instructions, the next address might be lost and it would be impossible to resume the interrupted task. A similar situation occurs when the software is updating a data file. If this operation were allowed to be interrupted, the data file would exist for some period of time with a combination of new data and old data within the file. The result of mixing new and old data in a subsequent calculation could have disastrous effects. As a result of these types of

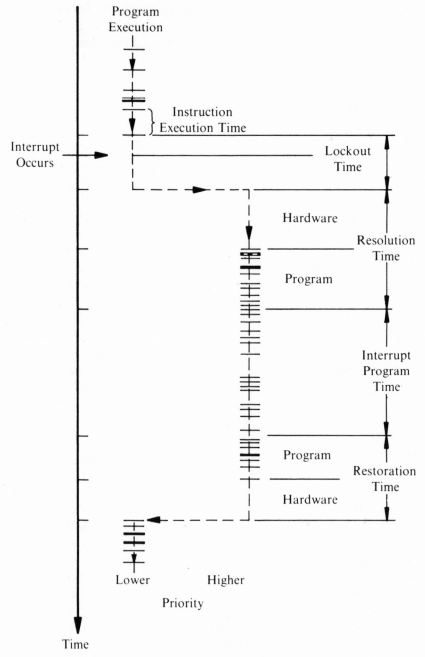

FIG. 4.10
Interrupt Servicing Procedure

situations, most hardware implementations provide a facility which allows the programmer to force a short program to be non-interruptible. This technique is referred to as "masking interrupts."

Task scheduling and the servicing of interrupts are two very important operating system functions. The allocation techniques and the interrupt handling techniques discussed in the previous paragraphs are only a few of the methods currently available. Some methods are combinations of those discussed above. The methods presented, however, are in use today and illustrate the basic ideas behind the management of the CPU time resource.

Storage Management

The purpose of the storage management functions within an operating system is to allocate storage space to the various programs and data residing in the system at any given time. The particular method used can affect both the time response of the system and the efficiency with which the storage is utilized. To a certain extent, time response and storage efficiency are competing factors in the management of the storage resource. Fast time response can be obtained by maintaining all programs in the main storage of the computer. In this case, the access to any given program is limited by the operating system overhead and the access time of the main storage medium. However, such an approach usually requires an excessive amount of main storage. Although the cost of main storage has been steadily dropping, the price differential between main storage and mass storage devices, such as disk storage, still is significant. It is common in most applications, therefore, that the system includes both main storage with its fast access time and mass storage with its much lower price but longer access time.

In the following paragraphs, the emphasis is on the management of the main storage space. All of the allocation methods described, however, assume the existence of a mass storage device, such as a disk, for backup storage. Allocation and management methods for the mass storage device are not considered here in detail.

Four storage allocation approaches are considered in this brief description. The first, and by far the simplest, is the single allocation method in which the main storage and, for all practical purposes, the total system are dedicated to a single task. The other allocation methods relate to the shared use of main storage between several concurrently executing programs. These methods, called partitioned allocation and virtual storage, all imply multiprogramming, a concept described later.

Inherent in the basic idea that storage management is required are two basic assumptions: The first assumption is that the total number of lines of executable code exceeds the capacity of the main storage unit. This assumption implies, therefore, that the main storage unit must be shared between various programs that are required in the application. The second assumption is that only a portion of the main storage unit is available for the sharing of these programs. A certain portion of the main storage must be dedicated to parts of the operating system and, perhaps, other routines which must be permanently resident in main storage. In general, the concept of storage management refers to the storage available for sharing programs; that is, that portion of main storage which is not used for permanently resident program storage.

Single Allocation. The simplest storage management philosophy is that of single allocation. In this case, that portion of storage which is available for shared programs is allocated to a single task at any given time; that is, only one program or portion of the program is resident in main storage at any particular instant. As a specific example, suppose that a system has a main store of 64KB. A portion of this, say 16KB, is required for the operating system nucleus and other resident routines. The remaining 48KB is available, therefore, for other programs. In the single allocation approach, the total 48KB is assigned to the current executing task. If the task requires less than the available 48KB, the excess storage is unused. On the other hand, if the current program requires more than the available space, the program must be partitioned (usually by the programmer) such that a portion of it may reside temporarily on a mass storage device when not in use. If access is required to this portion of the program during the execution, the current segment must be rolled out to the disk and the required segment rolled into the main storage. In doing this, an appropriate linkage mechanism must be established so that the parameters of the initial portion needed by the second portion of the program are available to it when it is rolled into main storage.

The outstanding advantage of single allocation is its simplicity. This is best understood when it is compared to the methods described in later paragraphs. Basically, however, the advantage lies in the fact that the operating system need only make a minimum number of decisions in allocating space to a using program. Since the available space is known to the operating system and is always the same, the determination or calculation of effective addresses is simplified, since the program always occupies precisely the same contiguous address space whenever it is executed.

Although it greatly simplifies the storage management algorithm, single allocation has several significant disadvantages. The main storage is a relatively expensive resource and it generally is not used as efficiently as possible with the minimal sharing implied by single allocation. As a practical matter, on the average there must always be unused main storage in the system, since the system must be designed with the idea that the main storage can contain the largest anticipated program segment.

The second major disadvantage relates to the interrupt-driven environment in which many minicomputers are used. When single allocation methods are utilized, the occurrence of an external interrupt of higher priority than the currently executing task requires that the entire main storage space be reloaded with the disk resident interrupt servicing routine associated with the external interrupt. This results in two disadvantages, the first of which is that the interrupt servicing time is lengthened, since every interrupt servicing requires a roll-in from the disk. The relatively slow access time of the typical disk, as well as the operating system overhead, reduces the time responsiveness of the system to external interrupts. A second and related disadvantage is that the interrupt service overhead can be quite high. The repetitive roll-in/roll-out disk operations mean that the CPU spends a considerable amount of its total capability doing only this operation. Since the CPU is not executing a user program during this period of time, this operating system overhead is non-productive from a user point of view.

Multiprogramming. The other storage allocation methods described in this chapter assume what is known as a multiprogramming philosophy of resource management. The term "multiprogramming" implies that several tasks are resident in main storage at the same time. These tasks may be part of a single program or they may be portions of totally unrelated programs. The particular task which is being executed by the CPU is determined by factors such as the availability of resources and the priority of the task or the interrupt which invokes the task.

In contrast to the previous method of storage allocation, the typical storage map in a multiprogrammed system consists of a resident portion, which is always in main storage, and a number of partitions dedicated to various tasks. In the single allocation case, the total remaining storage beyond that required for the resident operating system was dedicated to a single task. In the multiprogramming case, the available space is used for a number of concurrently resident tasks.

Conceptually, the total storage space of the computer in a multiprogrammed system can be thought of as consisting of two types of areas. The first is for those routines which are permanently resident in main storage; that is, a portion of main storage is dedicated to the storage of these tasks, whether or not they are currently executing or have been invoked. Typically, the tasks which are permanently resident are certain portions of the operating system which are necessary for the control of the computer system, the interrupt handler (due to its frequent use and time response requirement), and other frequently used routines which are part of the operating system or part of the application programs. The primary reason for permanent residency is to minimize the overhead which would otherwise be associated with frequent transfers of these programs into main storage from disk, and the resulting deterioration of time responsiveness for these routines.

The second major type of storage area can be termed a transient area. This area is available for one or more application or operating system routines. The transient area is shared between programs and any particular program is maintained in main storage only for the period of time during which it is required. Once it has been executed, the space which it has occupied is available to be overlayed by another program.

It is important to realize that in a multiprogramming system, the particular space which a program occupies may not be the same each time the program is executed. Rather, the program is loaded into the space which happens to be available at the time it is invoked. This implies, therefore, that the operating system or another mechanism must be used to provide address translation. This generally is provided by making the program or program segments relocatable. The program, as written by the programmer and compiled or assembled by the language translator, assumes that the program is operating in an address space which starts from zero and extends to some upper bound. Address references within the program are relative to the zero address lower boundary. At the time the program is transferred into main storage for execution, the operating system provides a displacement for each address, based on the physical location of the program in main storage. The assignment and implementation of displacement address translation is dependent on the hardware architecture of the computer. The availability of displacement addressing and relative addressing modes within the architecture greatly facilitate this required address translation.

Since the particular complement of programs resident in main storage is not the same at all times in a multiprogrammed system, the operating system must maintain a catalog of which routines are present in main storage and their physical location. At the time a particular program or routine is invoked, the operating system first determines whether or not the required routine is resident in main storage. If it is resident, control is transferred to the program and it immediately begins execution. If the required routine is not resident in main storage, the operating system determines its location on the mass storage device and transfers it into main storage. If space is available in main storage, the required program is loaded into that space. If, however, all available space in main storage currently is in use, the operating system must delete a currently resident program to make room for the new program being loaded from mass storage. This requires that the operating system update its catalogs of information relating to the use of main storage.

Partitioned Allocation. Partitioned allocation is another method of allocation utilized in multiprogrammed systems. In this method, each task is allocated a contiguous space within the transient area of main storage. The size of the allocated partition is determined by the user in either an explicit or implicit way. If the space required by the user exceeds the defined partition size, the user physically must partition his program in such a way that only segments of it need be in main storage at any given time. Once a segment has completed execution, the next segment is brought in from mass storage. This technique is called overlaying. To use overlayed partitions, the user programmer must establish a means for communication between the overlayed segments; that is, parameters and intermediate results determined in the execution of the first program segment must be saved in such a way that they are available to the second overlay.

In using partitioned allocation, the user typically must request and release the storage space necessary for a particular program. In some cases, this is done explicitly through request or release statements to the operating system; in other cases, the allocation is provided implicitly as, for example, by defining the size of an array. The request may or may not extend beyond the particular task being executed; that is, a space request may only apply for a particular task and, as soon as the task has completed execution, the space is released automatically by the operating system. It then is available for other tasks. This generally is called local allocation. On the other hand, if the same space is required by two different tasks, it must be allocated on a global basis. This is the case, for example, in establishing a communications area between two tasks. Various operating systems and high level languages have different means for differentiating between local and global definition of space requirements.

One characteristic of partitioned allocation is that, after a certain amount of time, fragmentation of storage may result; that is, there may be many small fragments of available space scattered throughout main storage. In order to understand this, it is useful to consider how the operating system allocates space in response to a user request. At all times, the operating system maintains a catalog of the unused space in main storage. The catalog contains information as to the starting address and size of the unused space. When a using task requests space, the operating system searches through the catalog and finds the first space which is large enough to satisfy the request. It then allocates the necessary space to the user and modifies the catalog entry by replacing the original available space description by a description of the remaining space. As a specific example, suppose that the first available space in the catalog consisted of an area of 1500 bytes. If the request is for 1300 bytes, the operating system modifies its catalog to show that 200 bytes now are available to subsequent users.

Considering this method of allocating space, one can see that after a certain period of time the available space in main storage may consist of many small segments scattered throughout storage. This is referred to as fragmentation. A point is reached where a request for space cannot be honored because a large enough contiguous space does not exist, even though the total unused space within the storage may be sufficient to satisfy the request. In order to prevent this phenomenon from happening too often, partitioned allocation methods normally provide for periodic consolidation of small available areas of storage. This is sometimes referred to as "garbage collection." The operating system invokes a utility program which rearranges the programs in storage so that the small unused areas of storage are collected together to form larger available spaces. In doing so, of course, the various catalogs and displacement information maintained by the operating system for each of the resident tasks must be updated.

The advantage of the variable partition allocation method is that the address translation problem is relatively simple, due to the fact that each program or task occupies a contiguous space. As a result, program references throughout the program can all be calculated from the same base address. A second advantage is that the storage space is used in a relatively efficient manner. This follows from the fact that each program is allocated exactly the space which it requires for execution. Fragmentation detracts from the efficiency, but with periodic garbage collection or other strategies this inefficiency can be minimized.

A disadvantage of the variable partition allocation method is that the allocation method itself is somewhat complicated. For each request from a user program, the operating system must search through its catalog of available space and assign space to the requesting program. It is possible at the particular time of a user request that there may not be space available in the main storage. In this case, the operating system must have a means of either displacing a program currently in storage or delaying the execution of the requesting program.

Paged Allocation. The primary difference between paged allocation and the partitioned allocation method discussed previously is that in paged allocation, tasks or data are assigned to fixed length storage segments called pages. The length of the page (that is, the number of words or bytes contained within the page) differs between systems and often depends on the architecture of the particular system or operating system. In many cases, the length of the page for minicomputers is determined by the direct addressing span allowable within the addressing structure of the CPU architecture.

When space is requested by a using program, the operating system assigns a sufficient number of fixed length pages to satisfy the request. As opposed to the partition allocation method, the pages may not be contiguous; that is, they may be scattered throughout storage. Rather than having a single displacement as in the previous case, the operating system must now provide a starting address for each of the pages involved in a particular task.

Figure 4.11 indicates a mapping technique which might be used in a paged addressing allocation method. The programmer, the language translator program, or the operating system considers the actual program address to consist of two portions, a page address and a word address. The word address is given relative to the beginning page boundary. When a particular program is executed, the page portion of its program address is compared to a page table, which maps the program page into the physical page in the main storage. The physical page address is concatenated with the displacement provided by the word address from the program address and the result is the physical storage address. Although it is possible to implement a paging scheme totally in software, it is common to provide hardware assistance, primarily in terms of registers which store the page address.

The advantage of paged allocation is that it is a somewhat simpler allocation algorithm. In addition, the maximum length of the tables associated with allocation is now fixed, since the physical storage consists of a known number of pages. The use of a paged allocation method relieves the problem of fragmentation since only total pages are assigned. Whether or not paged allocation results in the efficient use of main storage depends primarily upon the nature of the programs being executed. If they naturally fill full pages or almost full pages, the storage utilization can be quite high. If, on the other hand, the typical program occupies only a small part of a single page, considerable unused storage space exists in main storage.

The degree of operating system overhead incurred as a result of paging depends primarily on the locality characteristics of the particular program. If most program references are within a page, the operating system overhead is relatively low, but if the program lacks locality such that addressing frequently is beyond a page boundary, the operating system must be invoked quite frequently.

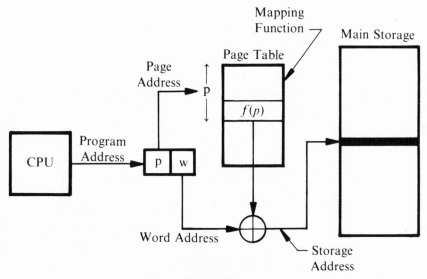

FIG. 4.11
Paged Address Mapping Technique

Virtual Storage

The virtual storage space allocation method is typically a paged allocation scheme. The difference is that all of the pages assigned to a particular task may not be resident in main storage. A page directory is maintained to keep track of the physical location of each page in the system. If the executing program addresses a page which is not resident in main storage, it is said that a "page fault" has occurred. The "page fault" invokes an operating system routine which causes the required page to be brought into main storage from the mass storage device. Since the disk access represents a relatively long time compared to the instruction execution time of the CPU, the occurrence of a "page fault" results in a significant delay in the program execution. As a result, locality is an important consideration in determining the efficiency of the virtual memory system.

When a "page fault" occurs and the operating system must bring a new page into main storage, it typically must displace a page already in main storage. A suitable algorithm for determining which page to replace must be provided in the operating system. The selection of the algorithm can affect the amount of operating system overhead incurred by page faults. One possible algorithm is called the least-recently-used (LRU) technique. In this technique, the operating system records each access to a particular resident page. When a "page fault" occurs, it replaces the page in main storage which was least recently used. A natural consequence of this technique is that frequently used pages, such as those associated with commonly used operating systems functions, tend to be in storage most of the time.

The outstanding advantage of virtual storage is that the storage management is totally automatic and the user need not be concerned about the physical configuration or allocation of space between main and secondary storage units. The user sees a total contiguous storage space which theoretically extends from 0 to the maximum number of bytes or words allowed by the system architecture. The ability to deal with a single contiguous space without concern for detailed paging and storage allocation greatly simplifies the programmer's task.

While simplifying the user's task, virtual storage tends to result in a more complex operating system. This generally means a larger operating system and greater overhead. These penalties, however, are often justified by the increased ease of use for the programmer.

Virtual storage systems are not used commonly in industrial computer systems. There essentially are two reasons for this: The first is that virtual storage has been found most useful on very large systems and these typically are not used in industrial control situations. The second consideration is one of performance since, in an industrial situation, the response time of the program may be critical and, in general, must be predictable. In a virtual storage system, the execution time of a program depends on the particular tasks currently resident in main storage. If main storage is occupied totally by high priority programs, a lower priority program may respond quite slowly, due to the very large number of times that it is moved out to disk in order to make room for higher priority pages. This results in a variable execution time which often is not acceptable in a real-time application.

I/O Management

The I/O (input/output) management portion of the operating system provides a single overseer for the I/O operations within the system. One of its primary purposes is to allow for the overlap or concurrent use of the CPU and input/output equipment. By allowing concurrent use, the CPU is not forced to wait until the completion of an I/O operation; rather, it can continue with another task while the I/O device completes its operation. Since many I/O devices such as printers and disk files are slow, compared to the electronic speeds at which the CPU operates, system performance would be significantly degraded if the CPU had to wait for these long input/output operations.

I/O management also provides for the exclusive use of a particular device by a task. For example, it does not allow a particular task to use a printer until the printer has completed its current task. This prevents the intermixing of messages in the middle of a management report being produced by a previous task, for example. In providing this exclusivity of use, the operating system must contain algorithms which prevent deadlocks. A deadlock is a situation where a device becomes totally inactivated because of conditions relating to tasks contending for its use. For example, if Device A requires the services of Device B before proceeding but, through a different task, Device B requires Device A in order to proceed, a deadlock could occur which prevents either A or B from proceeding.

In computer systems oriented primarily towards data processing, the computer user quite often is not given direct access to input/output devices. All input/output requirements must be satisfied by making a request to the operating system. In many cases, the instructions which invoke input/output operations are privileged and are not available to the user. Should a programmer attempt to use them directly in his program, an error condition is declared and the user program likely would be aborted by the operating system.

In industrial computer systems, however, users often have the desire to deal directly with input/output. This is particularly true in the case of sensor I/O. In order to insure fast time responsiveness, it often is unacceptable to be forced to go through the operating system with its resultant delay and overhead. Thus, the operating system for an industrial computer application must either allow direct user access to the input/output, or provide for low overhead, fast time response use of input/output equipment through the operating system.

Another significant difference between the management of input/output operations for industrial computer systems and those in conventional data processing applications, is that industrial computer systems often involve a large number of input/output addresses. Whereas the number of input/output addresses required to address standard DP I/O devices may be 10 or 15, a real-time system having sensor I/O may have several thousand analog-input points or digital-input groups, each having a distinct I/O address. This large number of addresses affects both the hardware architecture of the input/output channel design and the design of the operating system. In addition, the time dependence requirements of a real-time situation often dictate that data be collected at precisely timed intervals. This dynamic time dependent requirement of the real-time system must be considered in the design of the I/O management portion of the operating system.

Software Management

The software management routines included in the operating system control access to the various software resources available to the system. A software resource is any program available to the users of the system. They include, for example, disk utilities, shared subroutine libraries, and common tables for use by several tasks.

An important aspect of software management relates to providing access to reentrant and serially-reusable subroutines. A reentrant subroutine is a program which is written in such a way that it can be used concurrently by several tasks. For example, suppose that a particular subroutine is entered by a task and during its execution it is interrupted by a higher priority event. Further suppose that the interrupting event invokes a routine which uses the same subroutine. If the subroutine is reentrant, the interrupting source servicing program can utilize exactly the same code without modification. Clearly, in order for a routine to be reentrant, the execution of the routine must not modify the code. This generally is accomplished by maintaining all parameters relative to a specific execution of the routine in separate tables. In controlling the use of reentrant routines, the operating system provides the displacement or pointers to the appropriate tables for the particular task which is using the reentrant routines.

In serially-reusable subroutine, once a task begins to use the subroutine, the subroutine must be completed before another task can use it. The requirement is that at the end of its use, the serially-reusable routine must be restored to its initial condition if it has been modified during execution.

The operating system must also provide access to non-shared routines through its software management algorithms. These are private routines which may be accessible only to a particular program or to a particular set of tasks.

A closely related concept is the idea of protection or security in the programming system. The operating system must be designed in such a way that a programmer cannot access areas in main storage to which access privileges have not been granted. There are many reasons that a system designer might want to restrict access. For example, if a programmer were to make an error in writing a routine and cause a branch into a data area, the subsequent accesses to storage would bring data into the instruction register. These data would be interpreted as instructions and the reaction of the CPU would be totally unpredictable. Security often is accomplished by requiring that the user use protection keys or other code words prior to an access to a particular area or data file. This insures that the requesting routine is authorized access prior to the routine being given access to a particular data file or storage area.

The software management responsibilities and algorithms are similar in many ways to those required for the management of hardware resources. For example, the printer is a serially-reuseable hardware resource; that is, once a printer is assigned to a particular task, the task must be completed before the printer is available to any other task. To fail to do this can result in the mixing of output messages on the printer. Similarly, access and control of data files on the disk is similar to the access and control of the subroutine library.

Man-Machine Communications

The purpose of the man-machine communications portion of the operating system is to assist in the communications between the operator or programmer and the operating system. In a sense, these are the features of the operating system which allow a man to "talk" to the machine.

In considering man-machine communications, there are a number of different people who must have access to the machine. Their purpose in communicating with the computer differs and their need to access particular data may differ. For example, a process engineer requires access to the tuning constants in the various control loops. In general, the process operator is not given access to such tuning constants. Just as the needs of the various people differ, so does the acceptable language. In the case of a programmer, for example, a rather abstract programming language may be entirely satisfactory. In the case of a process operator, satisfactory communications may only be possible if the interactive interchange through a keyboard/printer or a keyboard/CRT resembles a normal conversation in his native language.

Figure 4.12 indicates the various people who might require access to the computer system. Also indicated are the requirements that they may have relative to effective communications. Other chapters in this book emphasize the necessity for involving all concerned personnel in the design of the system. This is particularly true in designing the features which make up the man-machine interface. In this relatively brief treatment, it is not possible to cover all aspects of the design of the man-machine interface. It is, however, an extremely important interface, whose design can greatly effect the effectiveness which with the machine can be used by the various people involved in an application. Typically, the programming system provided by a computer vendor provides the interface for the programmer and the computer operator. Interfaces to the process engineer, the process operator, and other users of application programs usually must be provided by the application programmer. The design of the man-machine interface, particularly in the case

---

● **PROGRAMMER**
   *Suitable languages, processors and text handlers to express algorithm and control processing

● **COMPUTER OPERATOR**
   *Ability to initiate, terminate, control operation of computer, determine existence of error conditions, recover and restart

● **PROCESS ENGINEER**
   *Process-oriented languages, simple job control to solve particular application problem

● **PROCESS OPERATOR**
   *Ability to change set points, request data and/or logs, display trends, etc., with switches or simple commands

   *Alert operator to alarms, out-of-limit conditions, etc. and provide means for corrective action

Note: One person may function in several of these roles.

FIG. 4.12
Industrial Computer Users

of the process engineer and process operator, requires detailed knowledge of the application and the methods which are utilized in the specific plant. The International Purdue Workshop recently has published extensive guidelines on this subject which are useful to both system and application designers.

Subroutine Libraries and Utilities

Although not concerned directly with the control or allocation of the computer resources or the process to which it is connected, programs typically are included in the operating system which are of general usefulness for any application. For example, there often is a requirement for certain mathematical routines, such as the evaluation of trigonometric functions. These functions can be provided by a common library of subroutines which are available to all users. A similar situation applies to certain procedures which are required in the operation of the computer system. For example, the ability to print out the contents of a certain segment of storage is a common need. A subroutine available to all users, which provides this "dump" of main storage is often included in the subroutine library. Similarly, language processors for the various high level languages in use usually are provided.

Although the exact complement available for various machines varies, the general categories of subroutine libraries and utilities can be divided into language processor programs, mathematical function programs, data processing I/O routines, and application subroutines.

As indicated in the early part of this chapter, computers are programmed with one or more languages. These languages range from assembler to one or more high level languages or programming packages. The language processors necessary to convert the programming language source program into machine code usually are provided in the programming system. In a typical industrial computer system, this includes an assembler and one or more compilers for high level languages. In addition, other programs related to the use of the language processors often are included; for example, a link editor which is used to assist in integrating program modules and a loader which loads the object code from an external device into the appropriate storage locations typically are available.

Mathematical function subroutines typically are provided within the programming system, so that each user need not duplicate the writing of these commonly used routines. The complement of mathematical function subroutines provided depends upon the particular offerings of the vendor and the intended use of the machine. In most cases, the evaluation of trigonometric functions is a common member of the mathematical function subroutine library. In addition, however, programs may be provided for curve fitting, the solution of differential equations, complex arithmetic, and various multiple precision mathematical operations.

The data processing I/O routines found in the subroutine libraries are provided by the vendor of the programming system to assist the user in often-used functions relating to the DP I/O equipment. A typical example is a subroutine which provides for loading a program from a paper tape reader to a disk file. Similarly, a routine for copying one disk file onto another and for printing the contents of certain portions of storage are provided. In general, these routines are intended to be run as low priority tasks in a multi-programmed system, or as a separate task using the dedicated resources of the machine.

The subroutine library also may contain programs specifically oriented to a particular application. For example, programs might be provided for converting raw input data into engineering units. Another example would be a standard three-mode controller algorithm calculation. The application subroutines may be provided by the vendor, but most often are added to the library by the application programmer.

Although the computer vendor provides a set of subroutines and utility programs for use with his machines, the programming system usually is designed such that the user can expand the library with programs for his particular application. These user programs provide functions not available in the standard subroutine library or special versions of functions tailored to the particular requirements of the application.

Error Routines And Diagnostics

Although there is a popular myth that computers never make errors, errors occasionally do occur. Most programming systems provide facilities for detecting such errors and, if possible, recovering from them. In general, errors can be classified as being either transient, also known as soft, or permanent, also known as hard. A hard error often is caused by some type of equipment failure, such as the burn-out of an electronic component or a slippage in a mechanical adjustment. Errors resulting from these types of phenomena generally are consistent and reproducible. The solution requires that a service person be called to replace or readjust the malfunctioning component.

A soft error may occur due to a variety of reasons. In general, the error does not repeat itself and its correction does not require the intervention of a service person. Examples of sources of soft errors include an electrical transient caused by a lightning strike or a piece of dust temporarily lodged between a disk head and the disk surface.

The purpose of the error routine diagnostics is to provide the computer user with assistance in detecting the occurrence of an error and identifying its source. In an on-line, real-time computer system, automatic recovery from the error often is attempted. Although not always possible, the goal is that the error be corrected without the intervention of the operator, so that the machine can continue to run the application.

The actions provided in the programming system for the detection and recovery of errors depends upon the design of the particular programming system and the particular device to which they apply. In some devices there is no opportunity to automatically retry the operation as a recovery technique. An example is a card reader in which an error is detected during a read operation. Since the card usually has moved past the reading station by the time the error is detected, it rarely is possible to reread the card automatically in an attempt to recover from a soft read error. Other devices, however, such as disk.files, have the capability to repeat an operation to determine if the error can be eliminated. In a device where a retry operation is possible, the operating system automatically attempts to repeat the operation until the error is cleared. For example, if an error is detected in reading a disk, the programming system or the disk controller retries the operation a specified number of times. If this is unsuccessful and the error persists, the programming system initiates a specific recovery activity, or notifies the operator that manual intervention is required.

Because the recovery technique to be used often depends on the particular application characteristics, the recovery procedures provided by the vendor programming system may be relatively elementary. Knowing the characteristics of the application, however, the user can often supplement these with procedures useful in his specific application. The usual recovery procedures are to attempt an automatic retry if the defective device allows this action. If the error persists and the use of an alternate device is possible, this may be automatically provided. This would be the case, for example, where a system has several printout devices and the malfunction of one can cause the operating system to assign all subsequent printouts to another printing device. If automatic recovery is not possible, the programming system typically provides a message to the operator indicating that intervention is required and providing whatever information is available to assist the operator in clearing the fault.

In a real-time industrial situation, the philosophy of error recovery very often is different than it is in a commercial data processing application. Because of the dependence of the industrial process on the computer, the usual goal is to keep the computer system operating, if at all possible. Equally important, however, is that the computer not lose control of the process or take any action which could jeopardize the safety or security of the process or personnel. A typical action when an error is detected, therefore, is to reduce the functions performed by the computer to the minimum level necessary to keep the process running. Only as a last resort is the computer system shut down or disconnected from the process. The idea of continuing at a lesser functional level often is referred to as "fail soft" or "limp-along" operation. It is important to recognize that these procedures must be designed carefully by the user to insure that the integrity of the process being controlled is not jeopardized.

Diagnostic routines are provided as a part of the programming system to help identify the source of a hard error. Various levels of diagnostic capability may be provided by the vendor in the form of diagnostic programs. In small computers, the diagnostics often consist of a series of programs which are exercisers. These programs cause the machine to execute each of its possible actions and then, by using an alternate approach, check to insure that the action has been executed properly. If it has not, the machine notifies the operator that an error has occurred in a particular routine. For example, an exerciser which checks the multiplication function first might multiply together two random numbers, using the multiply instruction in the computer. In order to check this calculation, the program then can execute a routine which performs the same mathematical operation by repeated additions. The result of the multiply operation and the repeated additions is compared to determine that the same mathematical result has been obtained.

In some cases, more sophisticated diagnostics are provided for use by the user or by service personnel. These can consist of a series of programs which, in addition to identifying an error, provide assistance in identifying the exact cause of the error. Such programs are called "fault-locating diagnostics." Rather than merely notifying the operator that a storage error has taken place, through a sequence of tests the programming system diagnostic routines may be able to tell the operator that the error is occurring at a particular location in storage and that a particular storage card should be replaced. The development of "fault-locating" diagnostics is extremely complex and relatively expensive. In addition, they generally require more storage space than a simple exerciser diagnostic program. The results of using a "fault-locating" diagnostic, however, are often worth the additional cost and storage space, since the time required to repair the machine often can be shortened significantly. This means that the computer can be repaired more quickly and placed back in operation on the process. The loss of the benefits of computer control, therefore, are minimized and this often is a significant economic advantage to the user.

Despite the availability of error routines and diagnostics, a serious error may occur which is not recoverable. In this case, the only recourse is to shut down the computer system. Whether or not this also requires shutting down the process to which it is connected, depends upon the particular application. In any case, however, it is important that the shut down be done in an orderly fashion. Merely disconnecting the computer from the process conceivably could result in the process going out of control. Although the requirement of shutting down the computer occurs infrequently in a typical application, the user is well advised to carefully design procedures whereby the computer and, if necessary, the process are shut down in a manner which minimizes danger to personnel and equipment and the loss of production.

System Generation

The previous sections of this chapter indicate that the programming system consists of many different pieces. Furthermore, it was indicated that the use of some of the features in the programming system depends upon the particular application or the particular hardware configuration. The programming system typically is provided by the computer vendor and is designed to be a general-purpose system applicable to many different processes and to all of the machine configurations provided by the vendor. For any given application and system configuration, therefore, the programming system must be tailored to the requirements of the process and installation. This tailoring procedure often is called "system generation."

The "system generation" procedure is done only at the initial installation of the computing system, or following changes made in either the computing system or the process. Physically, the procedure consists of running a series of programs which tailor the programming system modules provided by the vendor. The details of "system generation" vary, depending upon the characteristics of each vendor's programming system and machine. Typically, however, the user must specify to the "system generation" program the particular hardware configuration which is to be supported by the programming system. For example, the user must specify the number of disk files in the system, the size of the main storage, the number of analog-input points, and other similar parameters. Based on this information, the "system generation" program does the necessary assignment of storage table sizes and other allocations that depend on the physical configuration.

A second major activity during the "system generation" procedure is to select those program components which are required for a particular application. Since the programming system provided by the vendor must provide for the support of all of the devices available to the system, in any particular application some of this software may not be needed. For example, although the vendor provides routines for the control of the analog-output subsystem, a particular application may not have an analog-output subsystem and, therefore, the associated programming support is not needed. During the "system generation" procedure, the program components associated with analog-output would be deleted, resulting in a saving of storage space.

The "system generation" procedure often allows for the fine tuning of the programming system for optimum performance. This is done by specifying parameters which allow the "system generation" program to optimize the operating characteristics of the programming system. Examples include specifying table sizes so that only the minimum necessary space is allocated, specifying the degree of multiprogramming which is required in the application, and assigning task and device priority.

Although the "system generation" procedure ideally must only be done the first time the machine is put on-line, typically it is a procedure which is done several times during the initial phases of installing the machine. The repeated "system generation" tends to be due to two factors: The first is that, since it is an unfamiliar procedure, errors are made during the procedure, requiring that it be redone. Secondly, it is often very difficult to predict what particular set of parameters provided to the programming system will result in optimum performance. As a result, during the early phases of the installation a certain amount of experimentation is required to find the best possible programming system configuration. In selecting a particular computer, the user should examine the "system generation" procedure to arrive at a judgement as to its ease of use and its flexibility in obtaining an optimum programming system for the particular application.

PROGRAMMING METHODOLOGY

Programming often is described as an art rather than a science. Within limits, this view probably is correct, in that programming requires the seemingly intuitive ability to organize a program into a logical sequence which always guarantees a solution. The concept of programming as an art form also was propagated by the lack of specific study of the techniques of programming. The earliest programmers tended to be the engineers who designed the early machines. Many of these engineers eventually became full-time programmers, who were largely self-taught in the skills of programming. Due to the fact that computer science curricula in the universities are a relatively recent phenomenon, the early programming ranks were filled by people who did not have specific college level training in computers and programming.

In recent years, however, several changes have occurred which have focused attention on the growth of a more ordered approach to programming. First, universities have developed computer science courses specifically oriented toward programming, and this has resulted in significant research into preferred techniques for developing programs.

Secondly, with the decreasing cost of hardware and the growing complexity of programming systems, the investment in programming is becoming a greater part of the expenditures necessary to install and maintain a computer system. It generally is agreed that software cost is equal to or greater than the cost of the hardware in today's systems. Since the cost of hardware is likely to continue to decrease and programming, because it is labor intensive, is likely to increase in cost, there has been considerable attention on increasing the productivity of programmers. Simultaneously, it has been recognized that, although there is an element of art in programming, it is a discipline which can be organized into a coherent body of knowledge and that specific techniques can be developed to enhance productivity and quality.

In this section, recent developments relating to programming methods are discussed. Although other programming methods and disciplines are available, current emphasis is being placed on a technique called "structured programming," which has demonstrated significant increases in the productivity of individual programmers and in the quality of the resulting programs.

"Structured programming" in its current usage is a generic term whose definition varies with individual speakers and authors. In this generic sense, "structured programming" can be considered to consist of three main topics: Structured coding, top-down design, and the chief programmer team organization.

Structured Coding

Structured coding is a discipline used in constructing the logical flow of a programming algorithm. This discipline is constrained by two basic guidelines: The first is that each programming module shall have only a single entry and a single exit point. The second guideline is that the flow of control structures used within the program, and within any particular module of the program, are limited to three specific structures. It has been shown that these three structures are sufficient for the expression of any algorithm.

The first allowable flow of control structure is shown in Fig. 4.13. This structure, called sequential execution, implies that there is a single path from the entry point to the exit point; that is, no decision points or alternate paths between the entry and exit are necessary. An example of such a structure is the evaluation of a mathematical formula, such as a second-order polynomial.

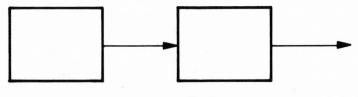

Sequential Execution
FIG. 4.13
First Flow of Control Structure

Given the parameters for the polynomial, no additional decisions or alternate paths are required. The program merely does the necessary multiplications and additions to obtain the final result, which is the exit point.

In many situations, however, it is necessary that decisions be made between one or more alternate courses of action, depending upon the value of a parameter or other conditions. The basic flow of control structure which allows the selection of alternatives is shown in Fig. 4.14. This is called an "If, Then, Else" structure. Fundamentally, it allows a decision to be made according to the following logical construction: IF a parameter satisfies a specified condition, THEN execute the following lines of code; ELSE (otherwise) execute a different sequence of instructions. Note that in accordance with the stated guidelines, this structure has a single entry point and a single exit point. In some situations, it is necessary to make a decision involving multiple alternatives. This is the case in, for example: If a parameter equals 1, do a particular action; if it equals 2, do a different action; if it equals 3, do yet a third action. This multiple choice structure can be constructed using the "If, Then, Else" structure. Although this structure can be realized in any programming language, recent high level languages specifically provide the syntax to program the "If, Then, Else" structure directly.

A common logical requirement in a computing system is to continue doing a particular operation or sequence of operations until some condition is satisfied. For example, in filling a box with bottles, the control action is to continue adding bottles until the box contains 24 bottles. This type of logical control structure is provided by the "Do-While" structure shown in Fig. 4.15. Basically, it tells the computer to DO the following sequence of instructions WHILE a particular condition remains true. This type of structure also is known as "looping." As in the previous cases, this structure has a single entry

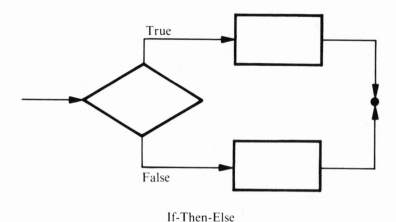

True

False

If-Then-Else
FIG. 4.14
Second Flow of Control Structure

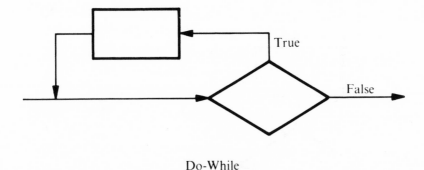

Do-While

FIG. 4.15
Third Flow of Control Structure

point and a single exit point. In recent high level languages, syntax is supplied
to provide this structure directly through the language.

An important feature of structured programs is that they are reducible;
that is, since each of the structures has a single entry and exit point, they can
be represented by a single block similar to the individual blocks used in the
sequential execution structure. An example of reducing a program flow is
shown in the sequence of Fig. 4.16 through 4.18. In Fig. 4.16, the "Do-While"
structure consisting of Q and D can be replaced by a single block E. This
results in the structure shown in Fig. 4.17. However, the two sequential
execution blocks C and E can be combined into a single block F. The reduced
diagram shown in Fig. 4.18 is now of the form "If, Then, Else." Thus, the
blocks B, P, and F can be replaced by a single block. This procedure of
reduction can be continued until the program is represented by one block
having a single entry and a single exit.

The reducible nature of a structured program with a single entry and exit
for each block significantly reduces the number of interfaces in a problem
solution. Given that the operation of a single block can be proved correct by
showing that all the possible input states provide the proper output states,
subsequent testing of the program need not be concerned with the internal
structure of the block. Thus, by tracing through a program in the same
manner in which the above example was reduced, a program can be verified for
any given set of inputs and desired outputs.

Top-Down Design

Top-down design is really a mechanization of a problem-solving
technique. The fundamental idea is to take a large problem and to break it
down into smaller individual problems. It is, in essence, the opposite of the
reduction example given in the previous section.

The beginning of a top-down design is a definition of the total problem to

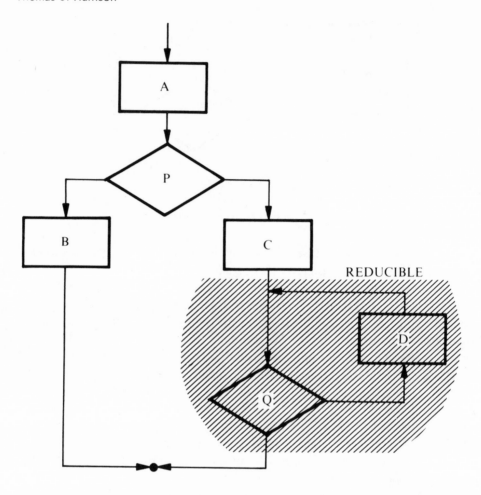

FIG. 4.16
Program Reduction: Step 1

be solved. The problem is defined as though it were a single block in a flow diagram. The inputs to the block consist of all of the parameters necessary to solve the problem. The output is the desired result. As the design proceeds from the top down, the total problem is subdivided into levels of smaller problems, each of which have carefully defined interfaces. Thus, for example, the overall problem may be broken into three subproblems at the first level. The next step is to take each of the subproblems and further subdivide them into smaller lower level problems. This procedure of sequentially breaking down each level of problems into lower levels is referred to as "top-down decomposition."

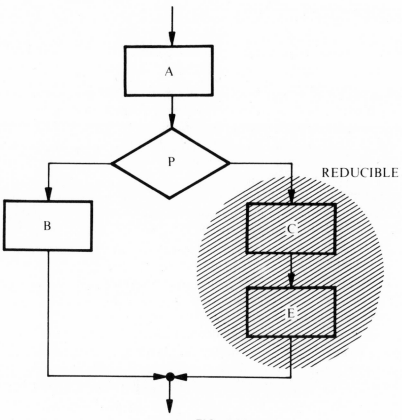

FIG. 4.17
Program Reduction: Step 2

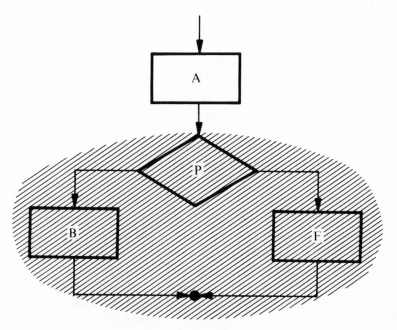

193

FIG. 4.18
Program Reduction: Step 3

The "top-down decomposition" is continued until the total problem consists of a series of modules which satisfy given criteria. The general criterion is that each subproblem must be intellectually manageable. Although some definitions of "intellectually manageable" have been given in terms of the number of variables with which the subproblem is concerned, intellectual manageability generally is a matter of judgement. It essentially means that a single person can understand the total subproblem and can provide a solution in a short period of time.

At the lowest level of the subdivision, as at all other levels, each subproblem has a carefully defined interface which specifies the interaction of that module with modules on the next higher level. In addition, the individual subproblems may need to satisfy a specific criterion as to their physical size as an aid to intellectual manageability. For example, it is common to require that the code associated with any given subproblem must be limited to less than one page of printout in the particular programming lanaguage being used. A second criterion may be that the subproblem must be capable of being coded and tested within a specific period of time such as one week.

Although the restrictions on length and time are arbitrary, there are some benefits which provide the rationale for this approach. Restricting the code associated with a given subproblem to one page eases the task of the programmer. With a single page of code, the programmer does not have to make repeated references to other pages in the program listing. This greatly reduces the chance of an error and tends to contribute to a level of complexity which is within the capability of a single programmer to understand thoroughly. Limiting a module size in terms of the length of time required to code and test the module is valuable as a management tool to maintain progress tracking.

It should be noted, that since each subproblem has a defined input and a defined output, the programming segments associated with each problem can be tested independently. This allows virtually complete testing of the individual modules as they are developed without waiting for the total system to be developed.

Once the problem has been decomposed logically from the top down, a series of programs can be written which correspond on a one-to-one basis with the various levels of the decomposed problem. Thus, for example, a main program can be written representing the top level of the design. This program can be written immediately, assuming that subsequent programs at the lower levels will provide the necessary parameters. This is illustrated in Fig. 4.19. Here the overall program consists of a routine called MAIN, which involves an initialization procedure, a print procedure, and a move procedure. Having defined interfaces for the three subprocedures, it is possible to write the overall program MAIN with appropriate calls to the subprocedures. The procedure MAIN can be tested by simulating the actions of the later-to-be-developed subprocedures with temporary programs, called stubs, which provide a simulated interface. Thus, at a very early stage in the development of the total programming solution, a functioning system is provided.

Following the writing and testing of the procedure MAIN, the subprocedures can be developed and tested independently in a similar manner. When these subprocedures are tested thoroughly, they can be substituted for the stubs used in developing the MAIN program. If a third level of decomposition exists, the programs for this level are written independently, tested, and then integrated into the next higher level. In the example of Fig. 4.19, the two subprocedures PRINT and MOVE require a common subroutine. With the defined interfaces, the program modules PRINT and MOVE are written and tested, using a stub prior to the actual

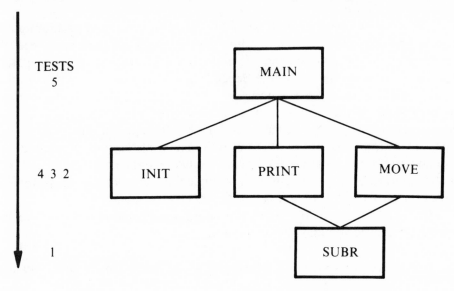

Top Down

1 Write main	8 Write print
2 Write init stub	9 Write subr stub
3 Write print stub	10 Test (main, init, print)
4 Write move stub	
5 Test (main)	11 Write move
	12 Test (main, init, print, move)
6 Write init	13 Write subr
7 Test (main, init)	14 Test (main, init, print, move, subr)

FIG. 4.19
Example Top-Down Program Implementation

writing of the common subroutine. When the common subroutine has been written, it is integrated into the system.

It is instructive to observe that the most important programs in a top-down approach are the ones which are tested most often. In the example of Fig. 4.19, the top program MAIN initially is tested as a standalone module. However, it is subsequently tested again when each of the modules INIT, PRINT, and MOVE are integrated into the system; it is tested again when the common subroutine SUBR is integrated into the system. In tracing through the figure, it is found that the main program is tested five times. The programs on the second level of the decomposition are tested less often and the subroutine is tested only once. Thus, the most important overall program has been the most frequently tested and has been well-used by the time the total system is developed.

The top-down design also is helpful in the identification of programming errors. Errors within a given module are localized to that module and generally are discovered during the independent testing of the particular module. If an error in a module depends upon its interaction with other modules, this is discovered at the time it is integrated into the next higher level of the system. If the overall system at any stage of the design has been successfully tested and if a new module has functioned properly in its independent tests, the failure of the overall system at the time of integration probably can be attributed to the interaction between the new module and the existing system. Thus, the integration of single modules localizes the probable causes for errors and results in a shorter debugging time.

In summary, the advantages of a top-down design and implementation of a program can be summarized as follows:

1. An executable system is provided at an early stage in the development.

2. Each newly-developed module adds function to the total system.

3. The integration process is continuous.

4. The most important code is the most exercised.

5. New errors are localized.

6. The small modules improve the readability of the code and make them easier to check.

7. The well-defined interfaces between the various submodules are beneficial in organizing the documentation and in debugging the system.

8. Restricting each submodule development to a fixed period of time improves project control.

Chief Programmer Team Organization

Although sometimes considered as part of the generic definition of structured programming, the Chief Programmer Team concept is really a management and organizational factor in the development of programs. Inherent in the organization is the idea that structured coding and top-down design procedures are to be used. In addition, the chief programmer team organization provides for the assignment of tasks within the programming organization.

The chief programmer team organization typically consists of four or five programmers per team. The chief programmer (CP) is the technical leader responsible for a certain segment of the programming project. The CP personally designs, codes, and integrates the critical portions of the program for which he or she is responsible. The CP also oversees the integration of other modules within his/her part of the system. In terms of the top-down decomposition method described earlier, this means that the chief programmer is responsible for writing the highest level module in the system.

Since the chief programmer typically is a skilled programmer, these responsibilities take advantage of the CP's skill and experience in the critical portions of the design procedure. Less critical tasks, not requiring this high level of skill, are assigned to other programmers on the team by the CP.

The second most important person on the chief programmer team is the backup programmer. The backup programmer provides support for the chief programmer at a detailed level. He or she is totally familiar with the design and the activities of the chief programmer and can take control of the project if the chief programmer becomes unavailable. In addition to providing support for the chief programmer, the backup programmer often is assigned the responsibility of investigating alternate designs or testing methods which, if proved successful, can be integrated into the system.

The remainder of the programmers, typically three or four, are responsible for the individual modules involved in the lower levels of the program design. The programmers take their technical direction from the chief programmer and assist in the overall integration and testing of the system.

The last member of the team is the librarian, who maintains the programming production library. The purpose of the programming production library is basically two fold: The first is to separate the clerical and intellectual tasks associated with developing a program. As any programmer knows, a great deal of activity associated with programming is clerical in nature. During the development of a particular program, many versions of the program exist, with each subsequent version an improvement on the last. It is necessary, therefore, to keep careful track of which particular version is the latest program. An additional problem is that in a large programming project, an individual programmer may require, or be dependent on, other program segments being written independently by other programmers. Thus, not only must the individual programmers keep track of the various versions of their program, they must also provide this information to all other affected programmers.

In the programming production library concept, a single individual is assigned as the librarian. The librarian is responsible for maintaining the latest level of each subprogram in both its internal machine readable form and in the external human-legible form. When an individual programmer updates a program segment to a new level, it is the librarian's responsibility to update the program listings and the computer data files. A programmer requiring a subprogram from another programmer obtains a copy only from the librarian. In this manner, it is guaranteed that there is only one "official" version of the program available at any given time. The existence of only one version of the program greatly reduces errors caused by programmers using down-level versions of another programmer's module. The librarian also frees the individual programmer from many of the cataloging and other clerical tasks associated with the development of a program by keeping records and providing such services as copying program listings.

Two other techniques often are associated with the chief programmer team organization. The first is called code reading. In this technique, a segment of code written by a particular programmer is given to another programmer to read and verify based only on the listing. The technique provides several advantages: By having an independent programmer look at a segment of code, errors that are not obvious to the coder often are detected at an early stage. The code reading technique also tests whether or not the segment of code is documented to the degree where a programmer unfamiliar with the code can follow the coding. This is an important test in terms of future maintenance, wherein a different programmer may be called upon to fix a problem. A less quantifiable advantage of the code reading technique is that it provides clear visibility of the programmer's work. Thus, an individual programmer knows that his or her code will be read by another member of the group. As a matter of personal pride and reputation, the programmer is likely to use his or her best skills to insure that the code is correct.

Another technique sometimes associated with the chief programmer team organization is the code walk-through or review. In this procedure, a group meeting is held in which the programmer responsible for a particular segment of code "walks the group through" the code. The responsible programmer explains in detail what parameters are available and describes the logic flow to the group. This technique has a similar advantage to code reading in that it provides peer visibility. It also provides "the fresh look" from other uninvolved programmers, which often uncovers errors that have escaped the original coder. A third advantage, not provided by the code reading technique, is that the code walk-through generally involves all of the programmers who are dependent upon the individual programmer's work. By explaining the program segment to the total group, the interfaces between the module and the other modules being written by other programmers often are clarified. This is important in promoting a common understanding and adequate communication of the interfaces between the various modules of the system.

Structured programming, taken in the generic sense, currently is gaining considerable favor in large programming projects. Although programming productivity is difficult to measure, there is general agreement that the chief programmer team concept results in greater productivity, fewer errors, and a resultant program which is better documented. Compared to the often quoted rule of thumb, which predicts a productivity of 1000 to 2500 lines of documented and tested code per programmer year, documented cases of structured programming have resulted in 10,000 lines per programmer year of effort. In addition, the number of errors has been shown to be reduced dramatically. In one example, only 46 errors were found in over 83,000 lines of code during the first year of use. Of these, 21 were found in the first five weeks and each was fixed in less than a day.

CONCLUSION

This chapter is a tutorial introduction to software. Since a skilled programmer requires several years of specialized college training or its equivalent, the chapter cannot be considered as adequate to provide the reader with the skills and knowledge necessary to design and write computer programs. As intended, however, it should serve as an introduction and provide the base of understanding which is required to read many of the books which currently are available on programming and the design of programming systems.

BIBLIOGRAPHY

Carroll, R. F., "Guidelines for the Design of Man/Machine Interfaces for Process Control." International Purdue Workshop. Purdue University. W. Lafayette. IN, 1976 (Revised).

Dahl, O. J., Dijkstra, E. W., Hoare, C. A. R., *Structured Programming*, Academic Press, London, 1972.

Denning, P. J., "Third Generation Computer Systems," ACM Computing Surveys, December, 1971.

Donovan, J. J., *Systems Programming*, McGraw-Hill Book Company, New York, NY, 1972.

Elson, M., *Concepts of Programming Languages*, Science Research Associates, Chicago, IL, 1973.

Freeman, P., *Software Systems Principles—A Survey*, Science Research Associates, Chicago, IL, 1975.

Gear, C. W., *Computer Organization and Programming*, 2nd Edition, McGraw-Hill Book Company, New York, NY, 1974.

Gear, C. W., *Introduction to Computer Science*, Science Research Associates, Chicago, IL, 1973.

Gries, D., *Compiler Construction for Digital Computers*, John Wiley & Sons, New York, NY, 1971.

Hansen, B., *Operating System Principles*, Prentice-Hall, Englewood Cliffs, NJ, 1973.

Kirnighan, B., and Plauger, P. J., *Software Tools*, Addison-Wesley, Reading, MA., 1976.

Knuth, D., *Fundamental Algorithms*, Addison-Wesley, Reading, MA., 1968.

Martin, J., *Design of Man-Computer Dialogues*, Prentice-Hall, Englewood Cliffs, NJ, 1973.

McGowan, C. L., and Kelly, J. R., *Top-Down Structured Programming Techniques*, Petrocoll/Charter, New York, NY, 1975.

Nicholls, J. E., *The Structure and Design of Programming Languages*, Addison-Wesley, Reading, MA., 1975.

Pratt, T. W., *Programming Languages: Design and Implementation*, Prentice-Hall, Englewood Cliffs, NJ, 1975.

Sammet, J. E., *Programming Languages: History and Fundamentals*, Prentice-Hall, Englewood Cliffs, NJ, 1969.

Shaw, A. C., *The Logical Design of Operating Systems*, Prentice-Hall, Englewood Cliffs, NJ, 1974.

Wirth, N., *Algorithms + Data Structures = Programs*, Prentice-Hall, Englewood Cliffs, NJ, 1975.

Wirth, N., *Systematic Programming: An Introduction*, Prentice-Hall, Englewood Cliffs, NJ, 1973.

Yourdon, E., *Techniques of Program Structure and Design*, Prentice-Hall, Englewood Cliffs, NJ, 1975.

5 JUSTIFYING COMPUTER CONTROL

Thomas M. Stout, Ph.D.
PROFIMATICS, INC., WOODLAND HILLS, CALIFORNIA

Process control engineers know that their organizations have many ways to spend money: new facilities or research programs, increased advertising, added staff, expanded employee benefits, acquisitions, and so on. In their own area of responsibility, they know that process performance can be improved by expenditures for:

1. New process equipment
2. Improved maintenance
3. More analytical instruments
4. Better alarm systems
5. Better operator selection and training
6. Modernization of control equipment, including the use of analog and digital computing devices

Investment in a control system including a digital computer is, therefore, only one of many ways of expending the organization's resources in the hope of enhancing its performance.

Benefit/cost comparisons obviously call for separate estimates of benefits and costs, followed by their evaluation against a payback or return-on-investment criterion. Obtaining reliable benefit estimates is the most difficult part of the analysis. This chapter attacks the problem of estimating benefits in several ways: by listing possible sources of benefits, by describing characteristics of processes that are likely to offer attractive applications for process computers, by identifying potential benefits with individual computer functions, and by suggesting general methods for estimating benefits. Where possible, illustrative examples are included.

The chapter concludes with a checklist of cost items to be evaluated, a discussion of several payback and return-on-investment criteria, and some cautions concerning application of the ideas and methods presented here.

SOURCES OF BENEFITS

Process computers can be beneficial in many different ways. Some of the benefits are tangible, meaning that they are directly identifiable with increased profits or reduced costs. Others are intangible, a term used to indicate that the benefits are real but their profit-and-loss impact is indirect or fuzzy. In other words, tangible benefits are relatively easy to evaluate; intangible benefits are difficult to evaluate and, to save effort, are often merely listed as additional arguments for the proposed investment. These distinctions can be clarified by examples.

Tangible benefits can be found in:

Increased production (by operating closer to capacity limits, reducing downtime, and converting rejects or losses into usable products).

More profitable product mix (by increasing yield of more-valuable products at the expense of less-valuable products).

Improved control of product quality (resulting in lower operating costs, less "quality giveaway," or a better market position).

Better use of raw materials (by increasing yields; reducing waste, rejects, or losses; reducing consumption of fuel, steam, catalysts, etc.).

Reduced maintenance (by reducing wear-and-tear and catastrophic failures, increasing time between shutdowns, and reducing repair costs).

Reduced operating manpower (primarily from logging or reporting functions, but sometimes—as in batch processes—from control functions; must be balanced against manpower associated with the computer system).

Savings in capital investment for new units (from reductions in indicators, recorders, panel space, or other control system elements, or from reduced intermediate storage facilities made possible by closer coordination between units).

Intangible benefits can be found in:

Improved engineering and accounting data (by on-line instrument calibration, converting volume flow-rates to mass flows, accurately integrating and averaging frequent measurements, and adjusting flows to satisfy material balances; partly a result of closer control and smoother operation).

Increased process knowledge (partly from intensive study of the process during system design, and partly from the data collected during system operation).

Smoother operation with fewer major upsets (from frequent, small adjustments of process conditions; allows operators to devote attention to other duties).

Greater safety for personnel and equipment (from process monitoring and alarm functions).

Faster startup of new plants (from earlier discovery of design or construction errors).

FUNCTIONS

Process computers should be used for functions which are performed less effectively, at greater expense, or not at all, by alternative methods. For purposes of this discussion, process computer functions can be classified as:

(a) *Non-Control.* Related to data acquisition, processing, and communication with operators and others.

(b) *Control.* Related to the direct manipulation of valves, drives, and other actuators.

"Operator guide" systems, in which an operator takes control actions based on information supplied by the computer, could be placed in either category.

Non-Control Functions

The non-control functions of a process computer include data acquisition; conversion of values to engineering units; integrating, averaging, or smoothing the input signals; and limit checking to detect instrument failures or undesirable process conditions. These functions provide a basis for other, more important, non-control functions:

Alarming	Providing signals or messages to inform the operator of abnormal conditions.
Indicating	Communicating the instantaneous value of a process variable by means of a pointer-and-scale or equivalent mechanism.
Recording	Writing values of a process variable in permanent form using such media as strip and circular charts.
Display	Communicating the instantaneous digital value of a process variable by means of a row of alphanumeric characters or a CRT.
Logging	Printing a tabulation of values of process variables and computed quantities, either periodically or on demand.
Reporting	Producing a set of data related to a unique event, such as a summary of data for a particular heat of steel or a day's operation of a continuous process.
Performance Evaluation	Calculating yields, efficiencies, heat rates, heat and material balances, variables not directly measurable such as heat transfer coefficients, catalyst activities, reflux rates, etc.

In addition, the computer can perform non-control functions concerned with inventory control, plant accounting, and maintenance, as well as running diagnostic programs to check its own performance.

Many of the non-control functions have been and still can be performed without a computer. Nevertheless, a computer may offer advantages in versatility, flexibility, improved performance, and lower investment relative to alternative devices, especially where many of these functions are required. For general-purpose performance evaluation and reporting, as well as more advanced data processing functions, the digital computer has no effective substitute.

The basic non-control functions listed above are a necessary foundation for operation of a computer control system and, in such cases, require no justification. However, for a computer system performing no control functions, justification depends heavily on intangible benefits. This avenue to·

justification demands a recognition that information, as such, has no value until it is acted upon; e.g., log sheets gathering dust in a corner do not improve process operation until an operator or engineer does something with them. Despite the difficulties of evaluating intangible benefits, however, many computer users have found significant benefits from non-control functions.

Examples: Several companies have reported that they can obtain material balances with greater accuracy using an on-line process computer. One company found it could obtain far more accurate measurements of catalyst performance and, therefore, used its computer-equipped plant as a catalyst testing facility. A computer installed in a crude oil distillation unit revealed excessive vapor rates and, therefore, heat input to a large fractionating column. Other computers have been credited with finding a leaking relief valve and a bad valve spring in a gas compressor.

Process monitoring and alarm functions are difficult to evaluate quantitatively, because they involve reducing the likelihood of rare events, such as catastrophes causing severe equipment damage, injuries to personnel, or both. Systems for large, modern, boiler-turbine-generator combinations have been justified on this basis, however. These evaluations deal in probabilities, not in reasonable certainties.

Control Functions

Control functions of a process computer can be classified as:

Sequencing   Carrying out a series of actions such as opening or closing valves and starting or stopping pumps in a prescribed order.

Regulation   Keeping process variables close to their specified target values or set points.

Optimization   Operating a process to achieve maximum profit, minimum cost, or some similar objective.

Sequencing is appropriate for the startup and shutdown of continuous processes, shifting operations from one product to another in a continuous process (an action referred to as grade change), and the operation of batch processes. Benefits may be found in operating efficiencies (such as faster startups or grade changes, or shorter batch times) or in prevention of occasional catastrophes caused by operator mistakes when following a complicated series of control actions.

Regulation is most significant for continuous processes in which the target values or set points are relatively constant. In such cases, process variables can be characterized by their average values and a measure of the dispersion about the average. Improved control is manifested by a smaller dispersion. A digital system can perform the basic regulation functions, acting either on the setpoints of analog controllers or directly on the final actuators. The digital approach can give better control as a result of providing more stable, precise, and drift-free parameter settings; more complex control relationships for difficult control problems, such as processes with large dead times; and easier means for keeping variables under closed-loop control. The greatest advantage of the computer is its convenience in implementing advanced control techniques—feedforward, multivariable, adaptive and optimizing—which can be cumbersome and expensive to implement with analog devices.

Optimization is applicable to all types of processes. For a continuous process, it can mean periodic determination of the best setpoints for individual control loops; for a semi-continuous process, the best times for equipment cleaning or catalyst replacement; for a batch process, the best pattern of variation with time for temperature, pressure, or material addition, with the immediate objective of completing the batch cycle in a minimum time or in a fixed-time at minimum cost. In all cases, optimization results in a higher average profit or a lower average operating cost. While optimization can be performed in some situations by special-purpose analog devices, no real alternative to the digital computer is available for optimization problems of any complexity.

PROCESS CHARACTERISTICS

Attributes of processes likely to offer attractive applications for process computers are well known. These characteristics can be classified as technical, economic and personnel.

Technical Characteristics

Operating or control problems arise from frequent disturbances and process complexity. Disturbances are produced by unit startup or shutdown, changes in product rates or specifications, changes in raw material characteristics or availability, changes in ambient conditions, and equipment wear or breakdown. The term "frequent" in this context generally means at intervals of minutes or hours. Disturbances at intervals of seconds or less probably should be counteracted by analog controls or process changes, while very infrequent changes can be compensated by off-line calculation.

Complexity is determined by the number of variables needed to describe the process, the degree of interaction between the variables, the number of product specifications that must be met, and the number of constraints or restrictions on process operation that must be observed. Complexity may also come from a need to carry out a large number of control actions in the correct sequence and at the proper times, as in a power plant startup or in control of a batch process. It may also arise from the need to remember process history over a long time period to control very slow processes effectively.

Process computers are most useful where the best process conditions are not easy for an operator to determine or maintain. Because an operator's ability to control a process depends on the time available to think or to consult tables and graphs, complexity and frequency of disturbances must be considered together.

Prospects for a successful installation hinge on the availability of process knowledge and adequate instrumentation. For many processes, a surprising amount is known which is not applied routinely for process control and can be exploited by a computer. System designers may need to assemble information from many sources such as research reports, published papers, and theses.

Process computer investigations are sometimes stalled by a real or apparent lack of suitable instruments. Some seemingly essential measuring devices may not exist, others may be lacking in dependability, stability, accuracy, and other important characteristics. Without investigation, however, it is not always easy to state what variables must be measured. A computer can help to solve some measurement problems by calculating variables that cannot be measured directly.

Economic Characteristics

Process size, measured in dollars of annual product value or operating cost, is a critical factor in justifying a process computer. Other things being equal, the bigger the process, the bigger the benefits. Since the computer system cost does not depend greatly on the size of the process, the ratio of benefits to costs is more favorable for larger process units.

The market environment of a particular plant must also be considered. Three distinct situations can be identified:

Market-Limited. Production is limited by the ability of downstream units to utilize additional material or by inability to sell more product.

Capacity-Limited. Production is limited by physical constraints within the process.

Supply-Limited. Production is limited by the inability to buy more raw material or by the capacity of upstream units.

Example: The incremental profit available to a pulp mill varies with the operation of its batch digesters. As shown in Fig. 5.1, the independent variable in this case is the permanganate number of the pulp, which is a measure of its lignin content and, therefore, a measure of the extent of the pulping reactions. For the market-limited and supply-limited cases, the curves show an optimum because wood costs decrease (yield increases) and bleaching chemical costs increase as the permanganate number increases. The capacity-limited case arises from limited capabilities for processing and recovering the spent pulping liquor; profit increases with throughput for operating conditions satisfying this constraint.

As the above example and other examples indicate, the profit potential is greatest in capacity-limited situations where more product can be sold if it can be made. Justification is more difficult in the other cases which depend on cost reductions.

The future outlook for the process is also important. If the process is about to be replaced by a newer and more efficient process (e.g., a group of batch digesters by a continuous digester), a substantial investment in a process computer is difficult to justify. Expansion of a process unit can increase the

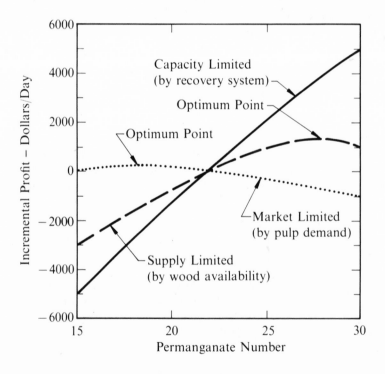

FIG. 5.1
Profit for a Bleached Kraft Pulp Mill for Three Different Process Environments

benefits by adding to the process complexity or can decrease the benefits by converting a capacity-limited plant to a market-limited situation.

Personnel Characteristics

A computer control system can function only in a positive atmosphere, so employee attitudes should be considered. If the process supervisor is indifferent or openly hostile, chances for success are dim. Similarly, operator cooperation is vital because a computer system generally requires manual input of some essential data.

Availability of qualified technical people is a factor in the decision to install a process computer. People with the necessary qualifications are, in fact, in short supply. If a small or medium-sized company does not have a continuing need for such people, help can be obtained from a computer vendor or a consultant. The ability to supply this type of assistance is a factor in vendor selection in some cases.

BENEFIT ESTIMATES

Possible sources of benefits from using a process computer have been discussed in previous sections and characteristics of suitable processes have been listed. Now methods are described for estimating benefits likely to be realized from a process computer installation.

At least six methods are available for estimating benefits. The following sections treat these methods in order of increasing cost, reliability, and credibility.

Experience in Similar Applications. The easiest, cheapest, and least reliable method for estimating benefits is to apply guidelines derived from published data or personal investigations of existing installations, such as a two-percent to five-percent gain in production or a 50-percent decrease in rejects. Although it is useful and comforting to know that a computer system has been successful elsewhere for the same process, the guidelines may be unreliable because of crucial differences in local technical or economic factors.

Example: In 1962, an oil refinery reported that a computer had increased the product value from its fluid catalytic cracking unit by better than two percent. This result is suggestive and not atypical, but it could change radically with different feed and product prices.

Comparison with Previous Best Performance. Another relatively simple method for estimating benefits is to compare average or instantaneous plant performance with the best previously-observed performance. Corrections should be made for recognized effects influencing performance and abnormal periods should be disregarded. A potential difficulty is deciding what fraction of the difference between average and best performance will be realized, and a convincing technical explanation must be offered to show how the computer system will accomplish the resulting gain. The estimate probably will be conservative, however, because the best past performance does not necessarily match the best attainable.

Example: Data for a furnace, burning fuel oil to make steam, are plotted in Fig. 5.2 and tabulated in Table 5.1. A line through the points of minimum fuel consumption corresponds to an efficiency of 75 percent. As shown in the table, if furnace control was improved so that all points fell on the dashed line, a saving of 2.9 gallons/minute would be realized. If the average saving is only 1.5 gallons/minute and fuel oil costs $12 per barrel, the daily saving would be about $600. This example is simplified but illustrates (*a*) correcting the data for a major variable (the effect of steam demand on fuel oil requirements) and (*b*) the conservatism of the result (because 75 percent may not be the best efficiency attainable).

Comparison with Theoretical Best Performance. In some cases, the best possible or optimum performance can be computed from theoretical considerations. This method and the previous method are perhaps most useful for rejecting unattractive computer applications.

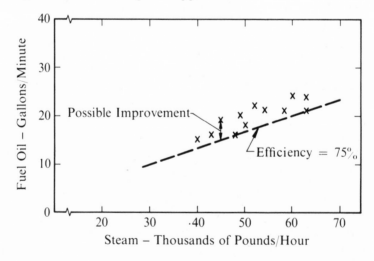

FIG. 5.2
Fuel Oil Consumption vs. Steam Demand for an Industrial Furnace

TABLE 5.1
Estimation of Possible Fuel Oil Savings
for an Industrial Furnace

STEAM—10^3 LB/HR	FUEL OIL—GALLONS/MINUTE		
	Observed	At 75% Efficiency	Difference
40	15	13.3	1.7
48	16	16.0	0
58	21	19.3	1.7
60	24	20.0	4.0
63	24	21.0	3.0
63	21	21.0	0
54	21	18.0	3.0
52	22	17.3	4.7
50	18	16.7	1.3
45	19	15.0	4.0
42	16	14.0	2.0
49	20	16.3	3.7
		Average =	2.9

Example: A computer application to a 200 tons/day sulfuric acid plant is being considered. Since sulfuric acid is 32.7 percent sulfur, 654 pounds of sulfur are required to produce a ton of sulfuric acid. Typical plants use 680–690 pounds, so the maximum potential saving is 25–35 pounds of sulfur per ton of acid. For the plant under consideration, the maximum saving is about 3 tons/day or $150/day at a sulfur price of $50/ton; the attainable saving, considering unavoidable losses, is less. A computer installation costing over $40,000 would probably not be justified for this plant.

Simulation Using Historical Data. This technique requires developing a mathematical model of the process, devising a control scheme, and simulating their combined performance on a digital, analog, or hybrid computer. Simplified models can be used for preliminary benefit estimates. A major difficulty with this technique is obtaining good data on process disturbances. This method gives more reliable results than the previous methods, but requires appreciably more time and effort. It has the advantage that, if the results are favorable, much of the system design work is already completed.

Example: In a feasibility study for a complicated chemical process, hourly data for one week of operation were collected and used as the basis for evaluation. Three computer runs were made:

1. To test the accuracy of the simulation, the model was adjusted to match process conditions at the beginning of the week and production rates

were calculated for the process conditions actually observed. The difference was a few tenths of one percent.

2. To determine the possible improvement, a run was made using the proposed control relationships. The gain was about 2.5 percent.

3. To explore the possible benefit from once-a-week optimization, the best operating conditions were calculated at the start of the week and the model was used to calculate the effects of control adjustments suggested by an experienced operator for the disturbances that later occurred. The resulting gain was slightly better than one percent.

Following this evaluation, a computer was installed and the increased production was about as predicted.

Plant Tests by Manual Methods. A computer control scheme can sometimes be tested by putting experienced engineers into the plant with calculators, charts, or a terminal connected to a remote computer. The performance achieved in this way gives an indication of the benefits to be expected from a closed-loop computer control system.

Example: One company tried this method for a synthetic rubber process. The proposed control techniques were tested using two engineers per shift, around the clock, for a week. Although the engineers used simplified relationships and sometimes had difficulty keeping up with the process, the test showed the soundness of the proposed control techniques and their potential benefits. After the plant trial, a computer control system was installed.

Plant Tests with a Temporary System. Several companies have used computer systems mounted in trailers or vans for data collection and short tests of computer control schemes. This method provides the most realistic and reliable results but it is clearly expensive.

COST ESTIMATES

Computer equipment costs have been decreasing steadily. Engineering and programming costs also have decreased with the accumulation of experience, standard programs, and various tools for simplifying these tasks. All of the costs, however, are subject to long-term inflationary trends and short-term perturbations from a variety of sources. For these reasons, any detailed cost data supplied here would soon be obsolete. This section, therefore, offers only a checklist of costs to be evaluated and some general comments about project costs.

Checklist

The following cost items should be estimated as accurately as possible in any study of a possible process computer installation:

Computer and associated peripheral devices (central processor, storage, input multiplexer, analog-to-digital converter, logging and alarm typewriters, tape or card readers and punches, etc).

Required new sensors and analytical instruments.

Transducers required for connecting new and existing instruments to the computer.

Equipment such as computer-manual or setpoint stations for connecting the computer to controllers, valves, or other actuators.

Wiring, conduit, and instrument air lines.

Special consoles and other devices for operator-computer communication.

Site preparations such as air conditioning or control room expansion to house the computer.

Engineering effort and other labor directly associated with equipment planning, design, selection, testing, and installation.

Technical effort for developing process equations and control schemes.

Programming effort for the preparation and maintenance of programs not provided by the computer vendor.

Project administration for coordinating schedules, costs, and documentation.

Training.

Maintenance.

Comments on Costs

Minicomputers available in the mid-1970's offer remarkable computing capability at relatively low prices. Prospective users should not be misled by the low cost of the central processor, however, because the total system includes the other elements listed in the above checklist.

Hardware costs can be predicted with some precision after a complete system design and specification is prepared. Costs of engineering, programming, and other services might equal the hardware costs at a minimum, but can easily escalate to much higher multiples. Suggestions for effective project management given elsewhere in this book help to minimize service costs.

The cost and quality of system maintenance can vary greatly depending on the location and expected response time of the serviceman: on-site (minutes), a nearby field service base (hours), or the supplier's main headquarters (days).

Packaged and Custom Systems

Two different routes to process computer control are now available; they can be called, for brevity, the *packaged system* and the *custom system*. Because their costs differ, the choice between them affects system justification.

Packaged systems are assemblies of computer hardware and software with suitable sensing, actuating, and display devices to perform some well-defined but limited functions. These functions may be control of a specific process unit, such as a paper machine or a compressor, or a general-purpose combination of non-control and basic control functions applicable to a variety of processes.

Packaged systems for specific processes have some built-in flexibility for adapting to the process variations which are inevitably encountered and they have a limited capability for expansion. The supplier usually furnishes a "User's Manual," but no program documentation to avoid divided responsibility for system performance and to maintain its proprietary nature. Programming by the user is prohibited or strongly discouraged. In some cases, the computer itself is essentially "invisible," being merely an inexpensive source of arithmetic, logic, and storage capability, and the user is scarcely aware that he is involved in the world of computer control.

As products developed for a mass market, packaged systems offer the usual mass-production economies at the expense of flexibility and generality. By definition, the packages have been carefully designed and installed in many locations, so uncertainties of program development cost are removed for the user. Packaged systems carry a clearly-stated price and are ideal for users who want the functions which they perform. They are not as good for users with a serious desire to develop a staff capable of installing general-purpose computer control systems.

Custom systems are intended for users who have unique problems or other reasons for not using a packaged system. As the name implies, the custom system is a unique assembly of equipment and programs which meets the special requirements of a single user. In general, the various pieces of equipment are standard items and the computer programs— especially the routines for non-control functions—may also be standard routines taken from other installations. While the individual system components may not be new, the total system is unique. Because of its unique design, the custom system can be expected to cost more than a packaged system of comparable scope.

FINANCIAL ANALYSIS OF A PROPOSAL

To allocate organizational resources between many competing demands, managers generally attempt to rank possible investments in order of attractiveness. Starting at the top of the list, investments are approved until the available resources are exhausted. Some proposals concern actions necessary for continuing operation of the process, such as repair or replacement of broken equipment, or addition of waste treatment facilities or safety devices required by law; these expenditures have very high benefits (which may or may not be explicitly calculated) and are placed at the top of the list. Others are desirable but not essential.

Process computers are, generally, in the nonessential category. As a result, they must compete with other possible investments for the remaining corporate resources. The last proposed investment to be approved sets a minimum standard (which will vary from time to time, depending on the general business environment, an organization's own cash situation, or its investment objectives) against which future proposals can be measured. With knowledge of these minimum standards, system engineers and others can avoid wasting effort on projects with no chance for approval.

After computer system costs and expected benefits have been estimated, several criteria may be applied to judge the attractiveness of this investment. Exact procedures differ from one company to another, so it is impossible to examine all of the possible methods in detail. In the following paragraphs, three criteria are discussed: payback period ignoring taxes and depreciation, payback period considering taxes and depreciation, and return on investment (ROI). For concreteness, these criteria are illustrated by a common example.

Data for Example

For purposes of illustration, the following data are assumed for use in subsequent examples:

Initial Costs:

Computer hardware	$120,000
Instrumentation	50,000
Process modifications	30,000
Engineering and programming	150,000
Total	$350,000

On-going Expenses:

Equipment maintenance	$ 20,000/yr
Program maintenance	30,000/yr
Total	$ 50,000/yr

Income:

Improved process operation	$250,000/yr

Payback Period (Before Taxes and Depreciation)

The payback period before taxes and depreciation is used by some managers for quickly assessing the attractiveness of a particular investment. Use of the method is simple and direct: The total initial cost is divided by the expected net annual benefits to arrive at a calculated payback period in years. For the present example:

$$\text{Initial Cost} = \$350,000$$
$$\text{Annual Benefits (Net)} = \$250,000 - 50,000$$
$$= \$200,000$$
$$\text{Payback Period} = 350,000/200,000 = 1.75 \text{ years}$$

Most companies in the process industries expect a payback period of two years or less. Very stable industries, such as electric power generation, will accept a longer payback period. More changeable industries, such as drug manufacture, may demand shorter payback periods. This simple criterion is not really adequate, however, because it ignores the effects of taxes, depreciation, and the time relationships of incomes and expenses.

Payback Period (After Taxes and Depreciation)

A somewhat more elaborate calculation, considering both taxes and depreciation, is illustrated in the following table:

	First Year	Succeeding Years
Income	$250,000	$250,000
Expense:		
Engineering and Programming	150,000	————
Equipment Maintenance	20,000	20,000
Program Maintenance	30,000	30,000
Depreciation (8-year basis)	25,000	25,000
(1/8 of $200,000 capital investment)		
Total Expenses	$225,000	$ 75,000
Net Income (before taxes)	$ 25,000	$175,000
(Income less total expense)		
Taxes (at 50%)	12,500	87,500
Net Income (after taxes)	$ 12,500	$ 87,500
Cash Flow		
(net income + depreciation)	$ 37,500	$112,500

To obtain the payback period, the total capital investment is equated to the cash flow for the first T years of system use and the resulting equation is solved for T. In this example, the capital investment is $200,000 for the computer, instrumentation, and process modifications.

$$\begin{bmatrix} \text{Total} \\ \text{Capital} \\ \text{Cost} \end{bmatrix} = \begin{bmatrix} \text{Cash Flow} \\ \text{First Year} \end{bmatrix} + (T-1) \times \begin{bmatrix} \text{Cash Flow} \\ \text{Succeeding} \\ \text{Years} \end{bmatrix}$$

$$200,000 = 37,500 + (T-1)\,(112,500)$$
$$T-1 = (200,000 - 37,500)/112,500$$
$$T = 162,500/112,500 + 1$$
$$= 1.45 + 1 = 2.45 \text{ years}$$

In this example, the engineering and programming cost is considered an expense and is written off during the first year. In some cases, these costs must be capitalized; the appropriate IRS guidelines should be consulted. The remainder of the initial cost is then depreciated over an 8-year period. In an actual situation, the period of depreciation depends on the accounting practice of the organization and other factors. Equipment and program maintenance are annual expenses. Taxes subtract from income, while depreciation adds to income in computing the cash flow.

Return on Investment (ROI)

Perhaps the best criterion for judging the attractiveness of competing investment opportunities is the expected rate of return on the investment. This criterion is based on the reasonable notion that, if a dollar will be worth $(1+i)^n$ after n years at an interest rate i, a dollar at the end of n years is worth $1/(1+i)^n$ today. The $1/(1+i)^n$ discount or present-value factor is tabulated in books on engineering economics or it can be calculated as needed. (See, for example, the reference by H. G. Thuesen listed in the Bibliography.)

The ROI method requires estimates of future income and expenses over the entire life of the project. The present values of these series of payments are then calculated using an assumed interest rate. The rate of return is defined as the interest rate that results in a zero net present value of the difference between income and expense. The actual rate of return is determined by cut-and-try calculations using assumed interest rates, until a zero net present value is obtained or, at least, the rate of return is bracketed between two rates.

A typical calculation is shown in Table 5.2. Several trials were necessary to establish that the rate of return is between 40 and 44 percent. Linear interpolation using the net present values for these two interest rates shows that the expected rate of return on investment is 42.2 per cent. This rate may seem high in relation to standard bank interest rates or overall business rates of return. However, the higher rate represents a measure of protection for the risks and uncertainties involved in projects of this kind.

The calculated rate of return can be compared with the rates for other proposed investments, the ROI objectives of the organization, and the cost of money. Unless the calculated rate of return exceeds the rates for alternative process improvements or other rate criteria of the organization, an organization with money on hand should pass up the investment in a process computer. In principle, a cash-short organization could borrow money to finance a process computer if the rate of return was larger than the interest charged for the loan. More accurately, the attractiveness of this approach could be judged by including the interest charges as one of the expenses; the corresponding tax relief results in an approximate 50 percent reduction in the cost of borrowing money.

Aside from the computational effort involved, the ROI method has the drawback that future events cannot be predicted with any certainty. Assumptions have to be made regarding revenues, expenses, taxes, and depreciation over the life of the project. Fortunately, because of the discount factors, events in the remote future have less influence on the rate of return than events in the near future.

Despite its drawbacks, the ROI method presents a realistic picture of the attractiveness of an investment opportunity. It allows consideration of the effects of the timing of income and expense items, as well as their magnitudes.

TABLE 5.2
Calculation of Return on Investment
(Dollars in Thousands)

Year	Gross Income	Total Expenses	Taxable Income	Tax 50%	Net Income	Deprec 8-years	Net Cash Flow	Present Value Factors 40%	Present Value Factors 44%	Discounted Cash Flow 40%	Discounted Cash Flow 44%
0		200					−200	1.000	1.000	−200	−200
1	250	225	25	12.5	12.5	25	37.5	0.714	0.695	26.8	26.1
2	250	75	175	87.5	87.5	25	112.5	0.510	0.483	57.4	54.3
3	250	75	175	87.5	87.5	25	112.5	0.364	0.335	41.0	37.7
4	250	75	175	87.5	87.5	25	112.5	0.260	0.233	29.2	26.2
5	250	75	175	87.5	87.5	25	112.5	0.186	0.163	20.9	18.3
6	250	75	175	87.5	87.5	25	112.5	0.133	0.113	15.0	12.7
7	250	75	175	87.5	87.5	25	112.5	0.095	0.079	10.7	8.9
8	250	75	175	87.5	87.5	25	112.5	0.068	0.054	7.6	6.1
				Salvage Value			25.0	0.068	0.054	1.7	1.7
				Net Present Value						10.3	−8.3

The ROI method offers the best approach for evaluation of lease arrangements, since it permits proper consideration of varying lease rates and also purchase options after a period of years. In comparing purchase of a process computer system with a lease, the initial equipment outlay is reduced (but not eliminated) by leasing, depreciation is reduced or disappears (if small or special equipment items are expensed when they are acquired), and lease payments become a periodic monthly or annual expense. (Hardware maintenance may or may not be included in the lease, but is a periodic expense in either case.) The net effect of these changes must be evaluated in order to make sound buy-or-lease decisions.

The ROI method can also be used to show the effect of different system installation schedules on the actual rate of return and to dramatize thereby the importance of aggressive project management. This is illustrated by the following example:

Example: A process computer installation offers potential benefits of $25,000/month when fully operative, derived from five distinct control functions each earning $5,000/month. The system cost includes three components:

(1) A continuing manpower cost of $5,000/month for a project team of $2\frac{1}{2}$ men (equivalent), each assumed to cost $24,000/year with overhead;

(2) A one-time cost of $60,000 for new sensors, transducers, control room changes, wiring, etc., taken as $10,000/month for six months;

(3) The computer system itself, leased for $5,000/month, with payments starting in the fifteenth month.

Timing of these expenditures is shown in Fig. 5.3, as well as two possible schedules for control function implementation:

(A) All control functions become operative simultaneously at the fifteenth month.

(B) Control functions become operative one at a time at intervals of three months, starting at the fifteenth month.

Case A represents an optimistic schedule for the operation of control functions. Figure 5.3 indicates that $120,000 has been spent at the end of one year and $135,000 by the time the computer system lease payments begin. Since the system nets $15,000/month, it earns $135,000 during the nine months remaining in the second year of the project and starts the third year even. At $180,000/year in net earnings, the total earnings (without discounting) are $540,000 for a five-year period.

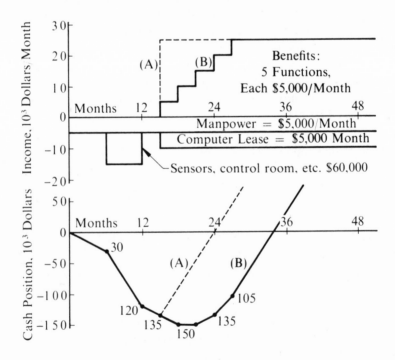

FIG. 5.3
Income and Cash Position with Time for Typical Process Control Computer Project

Step-wise implementation of control functions at three-month intervals is assumed in Case B. This is probably a more realistic schedule in view of normal technical difficulties and manpower limitations. In this case, the cash position reaches − $150,000 at the end of 18 months. At this time, with two control functions operating, the system pays its own way on a month-by-month basis and the cash position holds unchanged at − $150,000. With three or more control functions operating, the system starts to earn money. At the end of the second year, the cash position is improved to − $135,000. The project "moves into the black" at 34 months. Because of the slower implementation of control functions, the difference between Cases A and B thereafter is an irretrievable $150,000 not earned or "lost" between the 15th and 27th months.

The calculated rates of return, assuming that the income and expense items continue for five years, are approximately 65 and 50 percent for Cases A and B, respectively. The payback period is 34 months for Case B compared to 24 months for Case A.

The above example indicates that any delays in the operation of control functions have a detrimental effect. In fact, a schedule assuming step-wise implementation of control functions as in Case B but one year later, with no other changes, has a return on investment of only 11 percent and a payback period of 54 months. This outcome is so unattractive that, if the schedule could be anticipated at the start, the project would not be undertaken.

CAUTIONS

A few cautions are appropriate concerning justification of process computers and the application of ideas presented in this chapter.

Preliminary or detailed justifications take place months before a process computer system goes into operation. Profits realized from its use depend on factors such as product prices and raw material characteristics a year and more after the justification date. These future conditions cannot be predicted with great accuracy.

Post-installation evaluations are inherently difficult because it is impossible to run the process under identical conditions with and without the computer system. Furthermore, they are inevitably complicated by other process changes, such as addition of new reactors, use of a new catalyst, or installation of new analytical instruments. Some of the observed improvement actually may be caused by the intensive study of the process during the system design phase, or simply the phenomenon of greater managerial and technical attention to operator performance. It is not easy to isolate these effects and give proper credit to the computer system itself.

Small improvements in process performance are obscured by measurement errors. Because the standard deviation of an average decreases as the square root of the number of observations, a 1 percent improvement can be found with 3-percent instruments. However, it takes time.

Finally, as return-on-investment calculations in the previous section demonstrated, the quality of project management has a crucial bearing on the ultimate payback of a process computer system. For reasons listed above, benefits cannot be predicted or measured with great precision. Therefore, where preliminary checks show that a reasonable return can be expected, managers should demand more attention to project planning and less effort on super-precise benefit or cost estimates.

BIBLIOGRAPHY

Brewster, D. B., "Economic Gains from Improved Quality Control," *P. & P. Mag. Canada*, Vol. 71, 1970, pp. 55–58. (Analysis of paper machine considering process dynamics and spectral characteristics of disturbances.)

Eliot, T. Q., and Longmire, D. R., "Dollar Incentives for Computer Control," *Chem. Engineering*, Vol. 69, January 8, 1962, pp. 99–104.

Hall, C. R., "Is It Worth the Cost?," *CEP*, Vol. 56, February, 1960, pp. 62–66.

Harrison, T. J., *Handbook Of Industrial Computer Systems*, John Wiley & Sons, New York, 1972.

Shinskey, F. G., "The Values of Process Control," *Oil and Gas Journal*, Vol. 72, February 18, 1974, pp. 80–83.

Stout, T. M., "Economics of Computers in Process Control," *Automation*, Vol. 13, October, 1966, pp. 82–90; December, pp. 91–97. (Justification procedure and difficulties; summary of results from actual installations.)

Stout, T. M., "Estimating Plant Profits for Process Computer Control," *Instrumentation Technology*, Vol. 16, June, 1969, pp. 56–61. (Example showing profit variations for recycle process under market, capacity, and supply-limited conditions.)

Stout, T. M., "Economic Justification of Computer Control Systems," *Automatica*, Vol. 9, 1973, pp. 9–19. (Survey paper covering general considerations; example illustrating shift of average value with a reduction in standard deviation; additional results from actual installations.)

Stout, T. M., and Cline, R. P., "Control System Justification," *Instrumentation Technology*, Vol. 23, September, 1976, pp. 51–58. (Develops general relationships for calculating benefits from shifting average operating point and reducing dispersion around the average for quadratic and cubic performance functions; three examples.)

Thuesen, H. G., *Engineering Economy* (*2nd Edition*), Prentice-Hall, Inc. Englewood
    Cliffs, N.J., 1957. (Investment criteria; various tables.)
Williams, T. J., "Studying the Economics of Process Computer Control," *ISA Journal*,
    Vol. 8, 1961, pp. 50–59.

6 PLANNING AND DESIGNING THE SYSTEM

Richard L. Curtis, B.S.E.E.*
ALUMINUM COMPANY OF AMERICA, PITTSBURGH, PENNSYLVANIA

T he approach discussed in this chapter is that of dividing a problem into several levels of definition. As each level is defined in terms of its objectives, constraints, operations, and resources, a pattern emerges that lends itself to further definition at the next lower level. This process, called "top-down decomposition," is continued until a group of individually-manageable activities is described fully.

In this approach, the project leader personally is responsible for both the definition and the design of the uppermost level of activity in the project. Other people, including suppliers, assume responsibility for lower-level units of work. Work on the design of these lower-level modules begins only when they are fully defined in terms of their support of the next-higher-level module.

Planning the overall system involves defining the performance specifications of the highest-level module, which is the system itself. Factors to be considered include a description of how the system is to support its environment, how it is to be integrated into this environment, and what constraints apply to its implementation.

Designing the overall system then involves decomposing each layer in the hierarchy of modules into the next lower layer as illustrated in Fig. 6.1. A plan for each module in that layer is then produced.

The planning and design process is continued, down through the system

225

---

*Deceased.

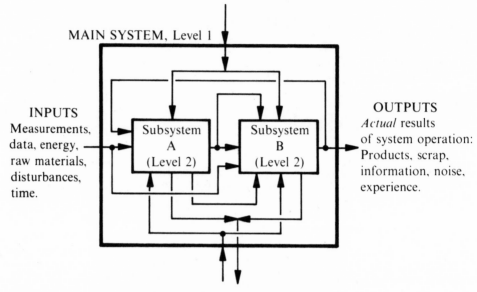

OBJECTIVES AND CONTRAINTS
What the system *should* do, limits on behavior.

MAIN SYSTEM, Level 1

INPUTS
Measurements,
data, energy,
raw materials,
disturbances,
time.

Subsystem A (Level 2)

Subsystem B (Level 2)

OUTPUTS
Actual results
of system operation:
Products, scrap,
information, noise,
experience.

TEMPORARY RESOURCES
People (system design team, operating crew),
system generation facilities, maintenance
tools, catalysts, plant machines and processes, methods, technology, training and
skills.

FIG. 6.1
A Project Manager's View of a System

structure, until it is found that all planned modules are either already available
or can be produced by means of a brief (i.e., a few days) individual effort. If this
strategy is followed strictly, with formal written specifications for all modules,
it can be said that one has an "intellectually-manageable" project with a high
probability of success.

The results of the planning and design activities are almost entirely
paperwork. (If a need for new technology is uncovered, some hardware
development may be done at an early stage of a project.) The project is seldom
a single straight-through sequence of orderly planning and design steps, but
usually involves backing up and modifying plans when a reasonable design
cannot be achieved at a particular level or for a particular module. For this
reason, modularity in the system design is a key factor in preventing problems
from rippling through the entire structure of a project, tumbling it like a house
of cards.

System implementation involves translating the lowest level design modules into hardware and software modules. These are then integrated to form the next-higher-level modules which, in turn, are integrated to form the next level. This process continues until the entire system is built and integrated with its operating environment.

PROJECT MANAGEMENT

A project is a well-defined effort to produce specified results at a specified time. Projects are conducted within predetermined constraints on the resources that may be used. The job of the project manager is to achieve the specified results without violating the stated constraints.

Projects are always unique, by definition, as contrasted to normal on-going departmental activities. A project organization usually is used to develop a specific product or a specific system (even though the project team might be part of an on-going engineering or research department) in order to bring the necessary skills to bear directly on the problem at hand and to provide a quick-reacting communications system.

Project management is different from the management of a functional department. Most often, the project manager is supervising people under the administrative control of other managers, including both department managers and other project managers. It is difficult to achieve a balance between the tasks at hand, the conflicts between projects, and the interests and loyalties of project team members. The project manager's problems are further complicated by the necessity to deal with outside suppliers, consultants, research and production organizations, corporate management, and (usually) a few sources of unwanted advice.

Project management is not the easiest way to break into the management ranks and the possibly unfamiliar technology of industrial computers further complicates matters. Nevertheless, management techniques that have proven successful in other areas do apply to the engineering of industrial computer systems. Higher management's recognition of the project manager's role and his problems and their efforts to support the project manager by resolving conflicts and providing the necessary resources are key factors in the success of the project organization concept.

The project manager's problems are proportional to the size and complexity of the project. Therefore, the simpler the project is, the better. It is prudent for both organizations and individuals to establish experience and a record for success on low-risk projects of limited scope before embarking on earth-shaking jobs.

Since project organizations are formed to get people "next to the problem," the project management function is highly technical. Technical people are often described as having 80–20 jobs, meaning 80% of their activities are technical and 20% are related to organizational matters. Departmental management jobs are then said to be 20–80. The typical project manager probably has an 80–80 job and can reasonably expect to work hard. As the techniques of project management and the unfamiliar technologies are mastered by the manager, or if a surplus of assistance is available, project management theoretically could be reduced to a 50–50 job. This has yet to be done, of course.

The project manager is, most of all, a manager. Other people may help design and implement the system, but no one else can manage the project if any semblance of an organization is to be maintained. Given a choice, emphasis must be on good management. But a manager must know enough about the tasks to be managed to allocate the proper resources to those tasks and to monitor the conduct of the project intelligently.

This section is intended to provide an introduction to the management skills typically required in the role of the project manager, to describe some of the problem areas for which these skills apply, and to suggest some approaches that might be used. This material is valid even though the project manager actually might hold a title such as project leader, senior engineer, or group leader. The job at hand is to manage the project and it almost always involves getting some of the work done by other people.

Management Skills

Promotion to a management job does not automatically make a person into an effective manager. New skills must be learned and many of them are quite abstract. Non-managers do things, but managers get things done. Workers use resources, managers allocate them. Resource allocation would be a trivial problem if resources were plentiful, but they rarely are. As a result, the manager's job involves resolving conflicting requirements for scarce resources.

The guidance of human activities is remarkably similar to the regulation of physical systems, but there is one very important distinction: physical systems may be goal-seeking but they are not goal-setting. Engineers moving into management jobs are probably as well equipped for these assignments as anyone if they can recognize the significance of human volition. Our volition is what causes us to constantly create goals for ourselves. One of the manager's jobs is to achieve organizational goals while adequately satisfying the personal goals of all the people concerned with the project.

The manager's job is divided into two areas: (1) the management of people and (2) the management of other resources. A manager must be part psychologist and part technician. Management jobs are inherently less structured than non-management jobs because managers provide the structure required for others to do their work. There is no magic formula that produces a good manager and management styles vary considerably from one manager to another. The only common factor that identifies successful managers, from the organization's viewpoint, is the successful accomplishment of desired results.

Still, many skills are recognized as being desirable for a manager to have, even though their individual perfection does not guarantee success. Certainly, some knowledge of what makes people tick and familiarity with general business methods is valuable. The project manager must be familiar with the technology on which the project is based and with project planning, organization, and control methods. Most important, the manager must have a sincere desire to be responsible for the success of other people.

The four basic management functions are to plan, organize, direct, and control the work of others. Management is the art of bringing ends and means together; it is the art of purposeful direction. On the psychological side, this involves both leadership and supervision. Leadership involves helping others reach goal-oriented achievements by motivating people to adopt common goals and work toward them. Supervision, on the other hand, involves helping others to avoid penalties for misdirected actions, those that are contrary to the pursuit of accepted organizational objectives.

Since managers accomplish things through other people, it is natural that managers spend most of their time communicating—reading, writing, talking, listening, and observing. As a result, essential management skills include reasonable mastery of the language(s) used, including technical and organizational jargon, and the ability to organize one's thoughts. Many new managers find they are immediately swamped with reports, proposals, and other literature and correspondence to read. The ability to skim or to speed-read makes it possible to sort out masses of printed material so that concentrated study can be applied as appropriate.

The new manager also finds that some writing ability is needed in order to efficiently handle the newly-assigned reporting responsibilities. Projects also seem to go more smoothly if team members (including outside suppliers) can work from clear, concise written specifications, policy statements, and instructions. There are few formal opportunities for learning to write well so each individual should take advantage of those that are available, such as by presenting papers at technical conferences or by writing articles for trade magazines. These occasions offer a chance for feedback via peer review, which is probably the best measurement of comprehension available.

Surveys indicate that managers spend over half their time in verbal communications. There is an obvious need to be able to make presentations, to educate and train other people, and to help sell the project. The manager also is required to conduct a great deal of business in interview situations where only two or three people exchange information, and through conference situations where three or more people carry on a somewhat more formal exchange. When two or more people exchange information, various psychological factors are at work. Differences in organizational rank can be a barrier to communications and a manager must learn to lower these barriers to bring out other people's viewpoints. This is often referred to as "being a good listener." On other occasions, as often happens in conference situations, the manager must sometimes erect barriers as a means of asserting authority, controlling the conduct of meetings, and keeping them on the track. The ability to manage the exchange of information without bruising the egos of other people is delicate but invaluable.

Technical management relies heavily on teaching as a means to multiply the skills of the manager. Project managers, in particular, must be able to teach subordinates what must be done and to pass along the methods to be followed. Experts in education stress two fundamentals of teaching— repetition and reinforcement, the two "R's." A third "R," for "relevance," might well be added.

The objective of the teaching process is to develop insight into the subject through a series of sensory perceptions. Relevance provides the motivation to learn. An effective teacher establishes this motivation very quickly, by showing how the student will benefit by mastering the material.

The subject of human motivation is a complex one. A manager's ability to accomplish things through other people depends not only on rank and authority, but also on the manager's ability to gain the support of others through informal means. Studies of human behavior have produced few hard and fast conclusions, such as those implied by the laws of physics. Some apparent correlations are worth noting, however. In people, all actions (except reflex actions) seem to be motivated toward some self-serving individual need. These needs vary both with the individual and with the circumstances at a given time. Individual needs range from the survival level up through biological needs, social needs, and ego satisfaction needs. Studies indicate that the individual tends to be entirely self-serving at the survival and biological levels, but becomes more willing to participate in group-oriented pursuits in order to satisfy social and egotistical needs. The satisfaction that comes from peer approval is considered to be one of the most powerful motivational influences if lower-level needs are maintained above some minimum level of satisfaction. Any action taken by a given individual at a given moment is designed by the individual to maximize his overall satisfaction.

Repetition involves going over material several times, usually from slightly different points of view. Reinforcement involves the simultaneous use of several senses, as in the use of audio-visual teaching aids. Notetaking, chalktalks, examinations, and homework all provide both repetition and reinforcement. Examinations and dialogue with the students provide feedback to the instructor, which enables him to measure the progress of the overall effort from the student's viewpoint.

Many new managers have trouble learning to delegate effectively. Yet delegation is merely the assignment of the responsibilities and authority needed by others to accomplish management's objectives through application of resources. Delegation is management's support of its goals.

There is a tendency to use at least one level less delegation than is appropriate for the scope of a project. This probably is due to a reluctance to delegate and the notion that a good manager can always contrive some way to accomplish the objectives. Reliance on the good humor and innate charisma of the project manager when the project gets into trouble and positive leadership is needed most, is a risky business.

The skills of business management should also be a part of the project manager's arsenal. Many digital system projects are larger than some entire businesses and their effective management is not trivial. Proper accounting procedures, safety precautions, and work rules have legal implications, some of which are even more important than the contracts with system suppliers.

Assessment of risks is one of the more difficult areas for which to prepare management skills. Ideally, the project manager should be familiar not only with corporate objectives but with the company's tendency either to take or to avoid risks. A digital system offers a tremendous opportunity either to put too many eggs in one basket or to pay for too many baskets (via excessive backup provisions). Decisions in this area tend to become quite emotional, but analysis methods are available to help evaluate the costs and benefits of various contingency provisions.

Technical personnel are frequently appointed as project leaders or project managers with little or no formal management training. If you suddenly find this has happened to you: (1) Congratulations! You will find this is probably the most interesting work experience of your career, so far. (2) Go see your manager of training for new supervisors and have a frank discussion about how to learn your new job. Training managers have a wealth of both formal and do-it-yourself material available. You might, for example, consider taking a two or three-week foreman's course even though your role will differ in many ways from that of a foreman. This can have a secondary benefit, in that it probably will lead you to work closely with the plant operating people who will be using the system you are about to build. Investigate nearby universities to see if their evening programs can be of help. Visit libraries and book stores and read a few books on management and business. Make a special point to try to learn the differences between project and other types of management. Above all, ask questions of other managers you respect and whose style you would like to emulate. Finally, make sure you understand the expectations of your manager.

Project Definition

A project is defined somewhat roughly at first and then expanded in detail as plans are developed. This process begins in the conceptual phase to establish the overall scope, objectives, policies, and rough estimates of schedules and costs. These "ballpark" budget estimates are compared with initial estimates of benefits to establish preliminary justification. It must be realized that these are only rough estimates and that refinement will be needed later.

The initial budget estimates typically are used to select investment alternatives. Each alternative or option is listed with its estimated cost, return, and probable risk level, along with subjective weighting factors. Options which do not meet organizational criteria then may be discarded early before much work is done on them. Dependencies between options are also evaluated to make sure that all work necessary for the success of the overall project is included and properly evaluated.

This first project definition may require anywhere from a few days to several weeks and should include preliminary discussions with potential vendors. If this is an initial experience with digital systems, some time should be allowed for familiarization with similar applications or to find vendors with related experience.

Throughout the early stages of project definition, a special effort is needed to record questions that arise. These questions and their answers provide information for the development of the formal written scope of the overall project. The nature of vendors' questions, for example, indicates what the vendor needs to know about the project. Process operators' comments and answers to their questions also should be faithfully recorded. Although much of this information will change as the project develops, a great deal of confusion can be prevented by good notetaking. Besides, if the project lasts over a year, several of the people initially involved may be assigned to other work before the project is complete and their notes are valuable to replacement personnel.

The conception of a project often takes place without benefit of a project organization. The project formally is born when management recognizes it and assigns people to work on it. Thus, one of the earliest project definition tasks is to define a nucleus for the emerging project organization and to assign responsibilities for continuing the development of the project. Most organizations formalize a project organization before funds are authorized for the full project, pending a more complete definition of the project.

A formally-designated project leader must be selected when management requests a formal project definition. This is the most important phase of the project because the overall project plan must be developed. A lack of positive leadership in this early phase of a project is almost a guarantee of later trouble.

The project definition consists of the detailed plan for the uppermost functional level of the system. This includes specifications for the performance of the system, the means by which this performance is to be achieved and verified, the physical characteristics of the system, the operating, cost and scheduling constraints, the standards for the conduct of the project, the estimates of technical and economic feasibility, and other resource requirements for the project.

Detailed justification studies (see Chapter 5), the formal authorization to proceed on the project, and the actual conduct of the project are all based on the formal definition of the project. Failures of projects to meet expectations are almost always traceable to incomplete project definitions or to weak project organizations used during the definition phase.

Definition of a project involving an industrial computer system can be relatively straightforward if not many capabilities of computers are to be used. For example, if a control system involving only isolated single-loop controllers with a small amount of sequencing is involved, the system is very similar to a continuous analog control system with a few relay interlocks or alarms. Functional specifications for these systems would have little concern for the differences in technologies involved.

On the other hand, computers are often used because of their economical ability to handle more complicated functional requirements. As a result, computer projects typically require more involved project definition phases. Even so, the computer should not confuse the issue or cause emphasis to be shifted away from the true functional requirements of the system.

Project definition is an iterative process. The engineer begins with some idea of a need to be met. After some thought about these requirements, a preliminary mental design begins to be synthesized. The preliminary design usually suggests the need for additional information, either about the original requirements or to support the evolving approach. Additional information may suggest alternate approaches. As various options are explored, some problems with the original specifications or assumptions may be recognized. The iterative nature of the design process is illustrated in Fig. 6.2.

Several iterations of the above sequence usually result in a tentative design that can be investigated in more detail. Perhaps feasibility now can be tested by contacting potential system suppliers. These contacts may result in further revisions to the starting assumptions, and so on. At some point, it may be decided to defer high-risk ideas for a later project. Other acceptable ideas may be added to the project.

An obvious requirement of a project definition is specifying just what the project is to accomplish in terms of organizational objectives, such as increasing product volume or quality, reducing scrap or costs, improving operational continuity, reducing personnel or equipment hazards, or improving delivery performance. It is also wise to take a broader look at the

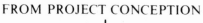

FROM PROJECT CONCEPTION

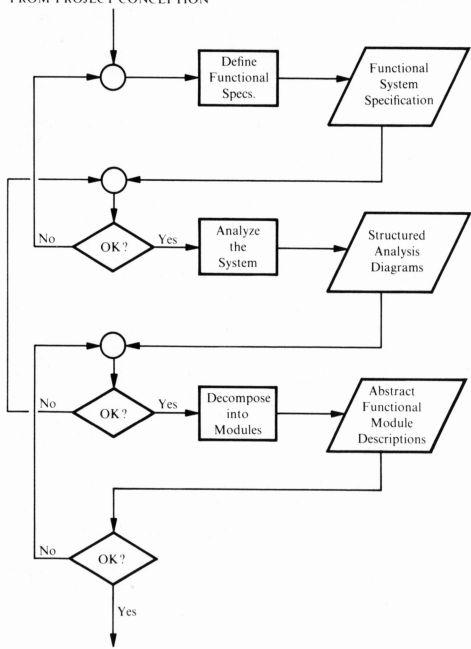

TO DETAILED DESIGN

FIG. 6.2
Illustration of Iterative Project Definition

environment in which the proposed system is to be built and consider the commercial and organizational factors involved. Of particular interest should be the identification of potential problem areas so the project plan can properly allocate effort to them.

The project definition forms the foundation for the project organization and the more detailed project design tasks. In addition to the project evaluation methods already mentioned, a formal communications and control system is needed as the project staff grows. Plans must be made for the staff itself: what skills are needed when, and what training is required. The project manager must plan for these factors in advance of the phase where they are needed.

Project Organization

Organizing a project involves assigning the tasks to the people available and providing for the individual and overall project management tools needed to reach a stated objective. The nature of a given project organization depends on the project involved, the organization within which it is conducted, and the skills and personalities of the project leader and team members.

Project organization is the development of an overall action plan for that project. The first-level plan must reflect the needs of the project and the project manager, since this is the manager's personal plan. The basic strategy of the project manager is no different than that for other engineering projects: (1) Establish detailed action plans to achieve the project goals within the approved financial, time, and other resource constraints. (2) Develop means to measure progress against the plan. (3) Direct the overall activity of the project by making necessary progress measurements and judgements and by taking action to make corrections in performance or objectives. (4) Repeat the above sequence until the objectives are met.

The project team is created for a special, relatively short-duration task. It can borrow people from existing company organizations, or it can be part of an on-going functional department that specializes in building digital systems. The formality of the project organization is usually greater in the former case but depends quite a bit on the authority delegated to the project manager. If the project manager is actually a team leader with little authority to delegate to project team members, the project organization may be quite informal.

The size of the project also is a factor that determines the size of the project team and the degree of organizational formality involved. One of the project manager's jobs is to acquaint corporate management with the magnitude of the project and its skill requirements, so that a proper organization can be formed. This requires considerable effort on the part of the project manager to educate and cultivate other managers who may lose people, priorities, or funds to the project.

With these constraints, most initial users of digital systems should consider forming a modest in-house project team and then relying on the help of experienced vendors and consultants for specialized expertise. This tends to reduce the magnitude of the immediate technical problems and the administrative and logistic burdens. Of course, this is accomplished at the expense of having to locate suitable sources of outside help. This topic is discussed later.

The following subsections describe some of the factors to be considered in the establishment of an organization for a project. Because of the relative unfamiliarity that might be expected in software planning, this subject is considered separately and in more detail in the last section of this chapter.

Task Breakdown and Assignments. Once the overall project is defined and the manager has an initial action plan, various major tasks can be identified. Several possible groupings of task breakdown are:

(1) Functional breakdown, usually done in terms of easily-identified major subsystems in a project, such as support systems, operators' console-related functions, process models, or management information systems.

(2) The obvious hardware/software divisions.

(3) Capability breakdowns such as process research studies, training, programming, or installation.

(4) Vendor/user division of responsibilities.

(5) Sequential structuring of any other task breakdown.

Projects are usually organized via some combination of these breakdowns because the capabilities of people available often do not match exactly the functional needs of the project schedule. Some overlap of these divisions is also desirable, particularly in the hardware/software tradeoff area.

The ultimate aim of the task breakdown as shown in Fig. 6.3 is to provide action plans for small, individually-manageable units of work and to identify all work required to complete the project. This, in turn, leads to a definition of required resources and often suggests an organizational structure.

As each task is broken down, estimates of the resources needed to accomplish it are made. If the time required for one person is more than one week, a further breakdown is in order. Unique training requirements can be identified readily by this method. Even if the project manager understands

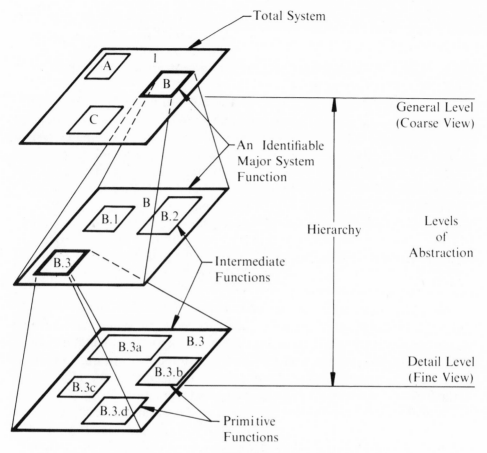

FIG. 6.3
Top-Down Decomposition of a Complex Project

absolutely nothing about some of the tasks structured in this manner, management control is still possible (after one week, see if the task is done!).

Staffing. Staffing involves providing the organization with the required human capabilities. These capabilities must be related to the job to be done so staffing actually involves a combination of skills, time, and needs.

A staff for a project must provide the required skills and it must have time available to work on the job to be done. A staff cannot be stockpiled, since time passes whether the available skills are used profitably or not. A staff that is highly trained, but in skills that are not relevant, really is not bringing the proper capabilities to the job. A proper staff only can be prepared if needs are recognized in time to develop and organize the required skills.

Staffing involves resource allocation and, therefore, is a management function. The project manager must consider the requirements of the project and evaluate organizational capabilities before personnel selection and training can begin. This often is difficult to accomplish early in the project, when objectives have not been well defined and the problems to be faced are largely unknown. One of the first things to do, then, is to get help defining objectives and identifying problems.

A great deal has been said about the ways in which people go about designing computer systems and about the kinds of people who seem to gravitate to that kind of work. Much of it is inaccurate. A computer system design project requires a great deal of close coordination and cooperation. "Inventive geniuses" tend to invent themselves into a lot of trouble and "loners" find that the results of their work do not integrate properly with the work of others. System design and programming involves keeping track of too many inter-related details to be done successfully in ivory towers or closets.

The project staff should be selected from people who can work extremely well in teams, who show an aptitude and an interest in learning the technology, and take satisfaction in getting results. If they have experience with computers, that can be considered a bonus.

Special attention should be paid to providing labor-saving aids and applying good engineering methods as a way of reducing staffing requirements for the project. The structured system design approach, computer-aided design techniques, the extensive use of support software, high-level programming languages, and good project management are all effective methods for reducing system engineering efforts and costs.

It is difficult to suggest what personal qualifications are required by the project staff, other than those already mentioned. People of average abilities and with a wide range of experiences have successfully built industrial computer systems. Knowledge of the application, the theory behind it, or of the process, can be helpful. The project manager may end up with a staff consisting of people with college degrees in any of several fields and some people who have not finished high school. The only apparent significance to such a mixture is that the manager's role as a leader, trainer, and motivator, is more critical than it would be in a functional department where backgrounds are apt to be more homogeneous.

The project staff members' most necessary characteristic might best be explained backwards with reference to Fig. 6.4. The team members must be motivated to achieve the objectives of the project. Such motivation can best be developed if the team is enthusiastic about the project. Enthusiasm is best founded on a belief in the project, its goals, its methods, its participants, and many other factors. Belief, in turn, is based on either faith or knowledge. Knowledge is somewhat manageable and can be developed from a sincere interest in the project if the person has the ability to learn. Interest in the project can come from curiosity. Pick your people from those who show insatiable curiosity.

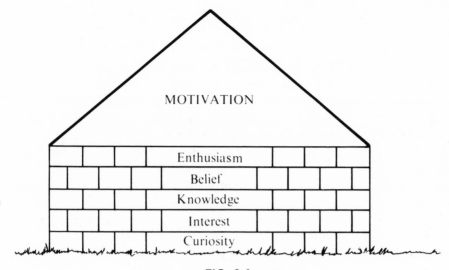

FIG. 6.4
The Foundation of Motivation

Scheduling. Scheduling of a project is approached in either of two ways, depending on whether or not the system start-up time is an important constraint. If it is, the project generally is scheduled backwards from the assigned start-up date and task assignments and staffing are adjusted to fit within the time constraint. Some leeway must be allowed in budgeting time to provide for contingency actions that usually are required in such projects. These contingency actions generally require additional personnel or overtime work to handle unforeseen problems without upsetting the existing project completion deadline.

Most projects are scheduled from start to finish with an allowance for some slack time. This provides for the possibility that the system start-up may need to be delayed if major problems arise. This approach is usually less costly in terms of project implementation, but the project manager must realize that a long-delayed startup can effectively nullify the economic value of the project.

Many activities comprise a computer system implementation project. Some activities must be completed before others can be started because they provide information, facilities, or other resources for the subsequent activities, or because staff limitations preclude working on all activities in parallel.

Although long-duration projects are not recommended for initial ventures into digital systems, these projects can often be broken into several phases or even several projects and scheduled so the phases with the greatest potential returns are accomplished first.

Detailed scheduling cannot be done until the system is broken down to determine the nature of all the tasks to be performed. The integrated planning and design sequence of a structured project has an apparent disadvantage in that it seems that firm schedules cannot be developed early in the project. Actually, this problem exists with non-structured methods too, and early scheduling estimates are apt to be quite rough in either case. However, the structured approach allows estimates to be refined in an orderly way, as specifications for each function and each task are developed.

As the project breakdown and definition progresses, it becomes possible to identify different functional modules and their inter-relationships, the system resources needed to accomplish each function, the project resources needed to accomplish each task, and clues about organizing the work. A schedule is derived from this information, and is refined in greater detail as the system itself is defined in ever-increasing detail.

The project schedule is a management tool but its use is not restricted to the project manager. It is used by all project team members to organize and control their own work and to prepare for known future events. It is used to maintain liaison with the eventual end users, the plant operating staff, and other organizations concerned with the project. This broad usage requires the use of graphical techniques to depict project status in a clear manner. PERT (Project Evaluation and Review Technique), CPM (Critical Path Method), Gantt (a man's name), or GASP (Graphical procedure for Analytical and Synthetical evaluation and review of construction Programs) charts are the most commonly used graphical techniques.

PERTing was popular in aerospace projects and many attempts have been made to use the computer-aided project planning tools that are available. Generally, only the network diagrams are now used. The PERT chart suffers from apparent complexity and it is difficult to depict the current project status.

A GASP chart is simply the familiar bar chart extended to show relationships between activities as shown in Fig. 6.5. Dependent activities are joined by vertical bars, while slack times are indicated by dashed horizontal lines. Currently, the GASP chart is gaining acceptance as the favorite graphical scheduling and control method.

Budgeting. Budgeting involves the development of a schedule of expenditures of the financial and other resources needed to get the job done. Some early estimates are needed for purposes of project evaluation, but these estimates are usually very approximate unless it is known that the project is likely to be approved. When it is not known in advance that the project is likely to be approved, there is no justification for the significant effort needed to develop accurate estimates.

Detailed estimates are developed as the design of the system progresses. The top-down design approach emphasizes major system functions early in the project, so that large deviations from early budget estimates are apt to be identified early. Design teams with little or no experience in digital systems typically need to lay out plans for most of the system's functional modules,

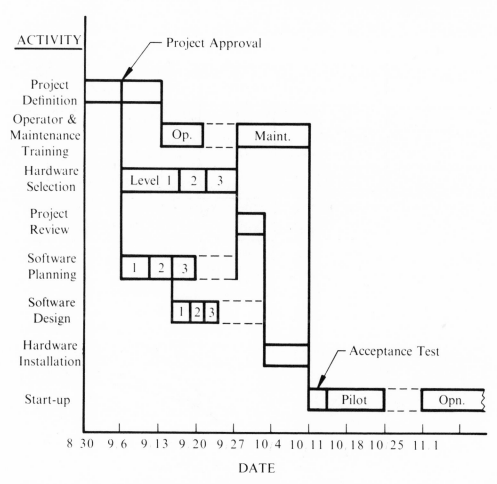

FIG. 6.5
A GASP Chart of Related Activities

and get formal bids from outside suppliers of hardware and software before accurate estimates can be made.

It is important to include in the budget all of the resources needed to perform each function to be accomplished, including in-house design and software efforts, construction and installation costs, all training expenses, and reasonable allowances for mistakes and contingencies.

When all the required resources are known, it is usually helpful to plot graphic "activity profile" and "expenditure profile" charts similar to those shown in Fig. 6.6. The activity profile is packed together to show the overall staff commitment. An alternative form has each activity arranged according to the person responsible for it. Such charts help reveal where personnel shortages or surpluses are apt to occur, and they identify the major financial events of the project. Staffing problems might be reduced by rescheduling

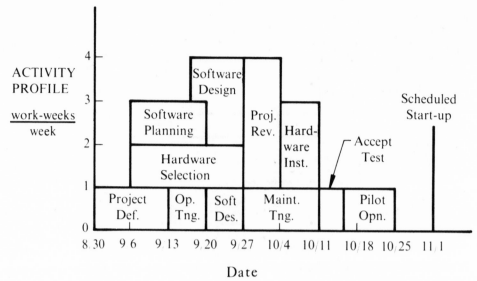

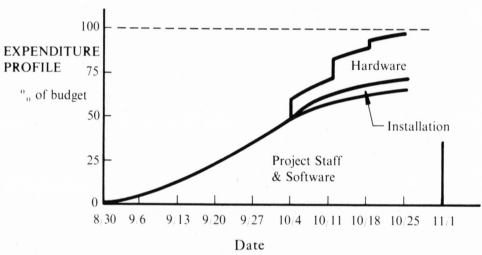

FIG. 6.6
Activity and Expenditure Profiles

some of the activities to help level the workload. The major financial events are often used as project review points to make sure the project is on the right track before the expenditures actually are made.

The project budget, like the activity schedule, is a control tool. It often is tempting to try to scrounge, bury charges in overhead, or otherwise defeat these tools (especially the budget) for the sake of appearances, but the project team itself stands to gain the most from the use of accurate schedules and budgets. On the other hand, if budgets are used by the parent organization as a bureaucratic dampener to inhibit the proper response of the project team to legitimate problems, loss of control is inevitable.

Project Control

Control of the project is essential if the objectives are to be met. The project plan is never perfect so it must be adjusted from time to time during the project. This must be done in an orderly way or a great deal of confusion can result.

Other than when the project plan itself is being altered, the plan is used as the standard against which progress is measured, so that corrective action can be taken when deviations are found. The project plan should be designed with control in mind, just as a production process is designed with control in mind. The goals that people set for themselves seldom are achieved by accident.

All the techniques described previously for organization of the project, and those described later in the section on software design, are designed to aid in control of the project. These techniques attempt to provide the earliest possible identification of problems, allow time to react to them, and reduce the impact of incorrect decisions. The structured breakdown of a project provides many checkpoints for monitoring progress and the consumption of resources. It also helps identify areas in which technological gaps may occur—areas in which the project team does not have the technical capability required—in time to look for help.

The control of the project is always the responsibility of the end user of the system even when outside help is used. The outside supplier is faced with a different set of problems and priorities than the end user and may have to adjust schedules to the detriment of some customers in order to optimize the conduct of his business. The user must be alert to such possibilities since, after the user has committed to the supplier, it is difficult to change suppliers.

There is a school of thought that de-emphasizes deadlines, stressing motivation and the inherent noble spirit of people as being all that should be required to accomplish the world's work. Unless you have personally mastered these techniques, a series of well-publicized target dates should be used for all phases of the project.

Continuous documentation of all work, as the work progresses, can also be used as a control tool. Digital systems projects involve some software to replace formerly-used and more tangible hardware and the documentation is the only evidence of the work being done. This documentation should be produced as part of the design effort so that it can aid in the design itself, as well as serving as a project control tool and later as a training and maintenance tool.

Documentation of the project manager's job is also required. Besides the project objectives, schedules, and budgets already discussed, the project manager should document each individual assignment, its objectives, constraints, person responsible, and the reporting and communications relationships involved. Each project team member has a right to know the expectations of the project manager.

HARDWARE AND SOFTWARE REQUIREMENTS

Two levels of hardware and software are needed. The top level ends up as the final system and is needed solely to meet the functional objectives of the system. The lower level is the set of hardware and software "tools" needed to build, test, and maintain the top level. This lower level is the support system and usually is given little direct attention or deliberate planning, despite its crucial importance to project success.

The support system has a great influence on engineering productivity, system reliability and maintainability, and the all-around smooth conduct of the project. Management is well advised to pay particular attention to the support system, so that the project team is able to design and implement the main system in a business-like manner.

Viewing the system as a two-level structure aids in designing a "clean" system at the upper (functional) level because issues at this level are not clouded by support problems. Also, under current technology, the support system may be a physically different system, perhaps remote from the final installation site. A cleanly-designed functional system, built via an adequate support system, also is fairly easy to integrate, test, and get running.

After start-up, the entire system still should be adequate for maintenance requirements. This may mean that part of the support system is no longer required (as in extremely small projects) but, even so, the support level should be designed deliberately for whatever work remains to be done. Many functional systems have been operated successfully, albeit briefly, and then were abandoned because they could not be kept in operation or changed to meet new requirements.

Even though an outside supplier with considerable expertise in the application area may provide a system that appears to meet exactly the objectives of the project, it is still very common for the users of these systems to discover new, more profitable applications or features to add. It is only a matter of time before any system must be repaired, replaced, or otherwise modified to meet changing business conditions.

An industrial computer system is essentially a data processing system equipped with the means to pass information to and from an operating manufacturing process quickly enough to beneficially affect the operation of the process. The various hardware and software components of such a system are determined entirely by the functions (including support functions) to be performed.

An obvious need is for some sort of computer to process the data and for the necessary equipment to interface it to the plant and its operators. Many systems in the past have been designed from the inside-out, beginning with the computer and adding hardware and software until eventually the system reached the plant. The approach used here, however, is to concentrate on defining functional objectives and breaking them down into ever finer detail until the objectives reach the computer. At a fine level of detail, both the hardware and software functional units are quite simple and easy to define. Even if the required modules are not available, they can probably be developed in a short time at low cost and risk.

This top-down approach, considering both the plant functions to be performed and the project functions necessary to build the system, tends to keep the system design on the track, including all required features, but inhibiting the inclusion of needless complexity.

What Is Needed?

The top-down structured analysis results in a detailed description of all data-processing transactions the system is to perform. Some are performed by hardware, as in simple filters to remove spurious switching transients, and others are performed by the operation of software within the computer.

It is necessary to go through the structured analysis activity and data diagrams to analyze each transaction and data operation, and to determine in detail how to accomplish each function. Such an analysis, if carried down to a proper level of primitive detail, may produce many activities to be analyzed, but each activity should then be fairly simple and straightforward.

Some experience with this analysis method results in a collection of commonly-used primitive operations, such as scan packages for inputting and outputting plant data, that can be reused and that simplify future projects considerably. The hierarchical analysis structure also provides convenient groupings of functions, as in the scan package, where input functions are grouped together. The input functions may be further subdivided into analog (continuously-variable, multi-valued) inputs and digital (logical event, two-state) inputs.

Suppose the system is to monitor and control a material handling system, such as a railroad classification yard where cars of incoming trains are sorted into new combinations to compose the outgoing trains. It is required to physically control the movement of each car through the yard from several incoming tracks, through a single "humping" track, and into several outgoing tracks. The identification of each car must be acquired and maintained throughout the sorting process. The makeup of each incoming and outgoing train is assumed to be known at least an hour in advance of the sorting. It is necessary to schedule all the incoming trains for sorting and to schedule the departure of each outgoing train as their sorting is completed.

Each car must be physically controlled for speed and routing through the hump yard to ensure that the makeup of new trains is correct and to prevent damage to cargoes. The cars are pushed to the top of a small hill, where they are uncoupled and allowed to roll down onto the classification tracks. Two retarder (or braking) stations are provided to control the speed of the cars as they roll off the hump. The acceleration of each car is measured as it rolls down the hump and a distance-to-go figure is maintained for each car. The first retarder station is used to adjust all cars to a standard speed. The second retarder adjusts each car to the proper speed for coupling at 3-4 mph when considering the rolling characteristics of the car, the distance-to-go, and other weather factors.

A structured analysis of such a system shows that the system performs a basic material handling function plus an associated information processing function. The information processing requirements require some means to input the composition of incoming trains, the desired make-up of outgoing trains, and sensor signals to track the actual car movements. Output requirements include provision for outgoing train makeup reports and deviation reports. Some output information might be provided to an operator on an on-line basis, in which case some operator inputs are probably also required.

The physical form of each input and output transaction must be determined, such as whether CRTs or hard copy devices are to be used. Then the path of each input/output (I/O) communication channel back to the computer must be described. Finally, specifications for the computer software to receive or generate each I/O transaction can be written.

A similar procedure is followed for the second major system function, the physical control of the cars. In this case, retarder and switch actuation signals are the main outputs from the system. Inputs come from car position and speed sensors such as wheel detectors, scales, radar, and weather sensors. Each device must be selected to be appropriate for the application, and suitable interface equipment must be provided to convey these signals to or from the computer. Again, specifications for the computer software to handle each I/O transaction are required.

After each function is reduced to a group of simple primitive functions and the small hardware and software modules needed for each primitive function are identified, it is a good idea to examine the support functions that might be needed to aid in implementing and maintaining the system. The added cost for such items as maintenance displays and disk storage for program maintenance is usually quite low, considering the labor savings, improved documentation, or possible reductions of outages that can result.

What Is Available?

Few vendors are in precisely the business of providing railroad classification yard control systems, but an initial step would be to locate any potential supplier of systems or components to determine what is readily available. The example of the rail classification yard is basically a material handling system, so it may be possible to build such a system from components of other types of material handling systems.

The user's problems are compounded by the need to adapt the methods of one business to the needs of another, but this is often the only available solution to pioneering applications. The ability to look at one solution and see another is certainly one valid definition of creativity.

Contacting other users of systems similar to the proposed application can be helpful if the competitive (or legal) environment allows it. Actual viewing of similar systems in operation can aid considerably in risk assessment.

Whether contacting potential vendors or experienced users, it is important to distinguish between existing systems and components and those that are proposed for future development.

Tradeoffs

Initial attempts to locate suppliers of systems and components for a specific project usually result in the inability to find an implementation exactly as visualized. Perhaps it is not possible to detect rail cars via light beams directed across the car body (an open door might look like two cars): the answer may be to count the wheels and divide by four. Car lengths vary so maybe weights should be derived from the sum of two truck weights, saving the cost of a large scale platform and eliminating the possibility of two short cars being on the scale at once. The expense of a proportional retarder might be eliminated by timing the action of a simpler on-off retarder. System support hardware might be shared with the yard operator by putting the computer in the operator's tower.

As indicated by this discussion, it seems that almost anything can be done at least two ways, but judgments of relative merits are difficult without experience. Cost trends should be kept in mind—hardware keeps getting less expensive if it is produced in volume, but software remains expensive since it is seldom produced in volume.

The reliability of a system suffers from complexity so some trade-offs might be made for these reasons alone. For example, if the system hardware is quite simple but the software is getting very complicated, the next trade-off might be made in favor of hardware implementation even at a slight penalty in cost.

The proper organization of hardware/software trade-offs is important.

Figure 6.7 shows how various levels of hardware and software in a system are related to each other. Maintaining clearly-defined interfaces between modules and levels of modules reduces unwanted interactions. Trade-offs should be made between related levels of hardware and software and, in general, not between two adjacent levels.

The cost to acquire a unit of hardware or software is also different from the cost to use it, so the end-user must continually compare prices with estimates of total costs of various approaches. End-use costs should include provision for any required training, spare parts, maintenance services, software updating, and probable expansion or revision costs. These factors may be very difficult to quantize but at least should be considered in a qualitative manner.

Planning for Integration

By the time a project is broken down into fine detail in preparation for

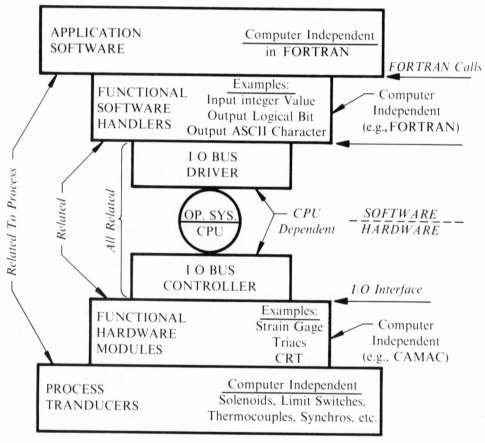

FIG. 6.7
Hardware—Software Relationships

the writing of detailed specifications, it is necessary to make a special effort to preserve the structure of the project and the system. Careful attention to structure prevents the necessary tradeoff process from producing unwanted side effects. A check for system integration side effects should be made as each tradeoff or specification parameter is decided upon. The prevention of unwanted side effects is one of the keys to achieving an orderly, relatively error-free system integration.

Specifications for each lower-level module should also be reviewed to make sure that low-level modules do not interact and that each module as specified does indeed accomplish its intended functions in support of a higher module. A check should also be made to ensure that low-level modules do not do anything extra that does not directly support the next-higher module. Finally, another top-down analysis should be made to ensure that all desired functions are completely provided for by the system and that nothing has been omitted.

The original structured analysis diagrams, descriptions, and other notes aid in making these checks. Notes on the nature of design trade-offs and the reasons behind them also should be preserved. It is reasonable to expect some errors in the system design which will require correction later, so all the earlier documentation should be retained for use in system integration and, later, for maintenance and expansion.

This is a good stage in the project, when the team members' minds are most attuned to module interface considerations, to make early plans for testing of system modules. Complete ground work for a project prevents a lot of confusion later by providing a basis for any required changes and by providing almost automatic documentation for any changes that need to be made.

ACQUIRING AND EVALUATING BIDS

Very few end-users of industrial computer systems attempt in-house production of all the hardware and software needed to build a system, so one or more outside vendors are required. These suppliers always attempt to make a profit. Almost everyone has read humorous horror stories of fiascos in the computer business; stories which sometimes end with everyone involved supporting hordes of lawyers. While making good copy, very few adventures of this sort ever result in good systems.

The first section of this chapter outlined various strategies for breaking a project down into manageable chunks, specifying functional requirements and constraints, and providing tools for project control. When outside suppliers are involved, these same management tools are used to develop a contract between the customer and the supplier. The contract is a legally binding statement of the performance each party expects of the other and is always a two-way arrangement. Vendors and customers share the success of a project; they are partners in a business venture.

Other than the fact that society has an interest via the contract, there is little difference in the conduct of a project due to the presence of an outside supplier. In fact, some experienced project managers advocate the use of interdepartmental contracts for the added discipline they offer in specifying organizational relationships. The idea is that, if a good contract can be written, the relationship probably is described adequately for the project.

A great deal of labor specialization has developed in the digital systems business. The resulting economies of specialization frequently are plotted graphically to show (particularly in the hardware area) how dramatically purchasing power has increased over the years. Mass-produced, general-purpose digital systems do indeed offer a lot of capability for their cost, but they still must be customized to each application. The task is to find the right combination of suppliers, so that when their work is integrated with that of the end-user into a system, the project objectives are met.

Vendors generally take exception to certain items of a specification, and propose alternative methods based on their experience, capabilities, or standard products. Direct comparisons of such alternatives offered by different vendors are difficult, but they must be made because it is the total system that solves the application problem.

Locating Potential Suppliers

Most people in either the control engineering field or the data-processing field have little trouble locating at least a few potential suppliers of industrial computer systems. However, many thousands of small businesses having potential applications of small systems might have neither a control engineering department nor a data-processing department. The problem is even more difficult if the potential user does not want to deal with a system supplier, but decides to purchase components and build the system in-house.

Trade magazines, such as the Instrument Society of America's "Instrumentation Technology," are readily available. Most system and component suppliers advertise widely in these and other general business publications. A half-day at a public or university library should result in a list of at least two dozen system suppliers. A library is also a source of large-city telephone books (look in the yellow pages, under such topics as automation, computers, controls, data processing, engineering, consultant, industrial equipment, management consultants, material handling equipment, operations research, and many others).

Professional and trade conferences are also a good place to meet and talk informally with both suppliers and users of industrial computer systems. Most professional groups, such as the Instrument Society of America (ISA), the Society of Manufacturing Engineers (SME), or the Institute of Electrical and Electronics Engineers (IEEE), have local monthly meetings in medium and large cities. Most users of industrial computer systems, even if they are competitors, will refer you to potential suppliers. Engineering faculty members of nearby colleges can also be helpful.

As a list of potential suppliers is developed, initial talks with sales representatives quickly eliminates those who actually are oriented toward other businesses or other application areas. It is important not to waste your time, and theirs, if there is little possibility of doing business.

A potential user who is totally unable to locate at least three or four potential suppliers in a couple of days had best engage a consultant to help get things started, or to show that the application is not feasible.

The application should be discussed with potential suppliers to determine which suppliers really have capabilities in that area. Ask sales representatives to bring in their technical specialists to suggest ways to solve various problems. Do not assume, however, that these specialists will be available later to help with your project unless they are named in writing in a contract. Even then, the contract is with the supplier, not the specialist.

Bid Specifications—First Round

Initial contacts with potential vendors usually produce an abundance of ideas on how to get started. Most suppliers genuinely are interested in having their systems result in successful applications. Careful notetaking and asking the same questions to several suppliers helps sift the sales talk and buoyant marketing optimism for the more subtle hints of technical capability.

Notes from vendor contacts, added to the original (but probably revised) project specifications, form the basis for the first round of bidding to get firm prices. Unless it has been shown clearly by all potential suppliers that something is wrong with the early specifications, the user should specify exactly what is initially needed.

Do not rely on anything promised verbally, but specify all requirements in writing and expect all responses, item by item, in writing. Request that alternative approaches be offered by vendors who cannot comply exactly with the specifications and that these also be identified by item.

The system and its original specification generally are confusing enough; a consistent format for bids greatly reduces the time required by the user in evaluating the bids and the time required by the vendors to explain the bids. An orderly format also aids in checking for missing items and in considering composite systems made up from components from more than one vendor.

Item-by-item pricing also helps identify ways to trim the system in the event that prices come in above justifiable expectations.

The buyer should specify all relevant commercial matters or request descriptions of the vendors' commercial practices whenever formal quotations are requested. It might turn out that only one bidding round is required and shipping and payment schedules, legal rights, acceptance tests, and other such matters can then be clearly understood. Again, the users' preferences in these matters should be stated explicitly and agreed to by the vendors before any actual orders are placed. Your company purchasing department really can help here.

What Happened?

It is rare that a user with little experience can produce an adequate specification on the first try. Vendors usually can offer alternative proposals using lowest-cost standard components or software packages, or can advise on areas of the project where risks or technical feasibility might be poor.

The user must examine all returned bids to determine what the next step should be. Any tactic which simplifies the job at this stage helps. Any disqualifying features of a bid should be examined, such as prices well out of line with other vendors (either high or low), an apparent lack of interest or understanding of the project, or failure to come close to required delivery dates. Obvious disqualifying factors eliminate the need to expend time and effort evaluating other factors.

Item-by-item comparisons of bids, perhaps via a side-by-side arrangement on large conference tables, provides an overview of the situation. Obvious advantages and weaknesses of different approaches might be circled with large marking pens of different colors. Ranking by ability to meet the most important requirement might be attempted. Many people have tried to apply weighting functions and other scientific methods, but these methods are difficult to use in all situations. So-called scientific evaluation methods also tend to omit such important factors as user familiarity with the vendors' products and methods, or the vendor's simple willingness to help.

Unless a vendor just happens to quote exactly what the user needs, the idea of this initial bid evaluation is to adjust the project requirements or the system specifications in order to produce a viable design. Special note should be made of all remaining areas of confusion to make sure that such items are clarified in the next specification. If any areas of required research or development are revealed by a lack of vendor response to urgent requirements, this R&D work should be planned promptly and the project schedule adjusted accordingly.

The system should be re-bid after the necessary adjustments are made to the specifications, valid vendor ideas incorporated, and disqualified vendors removed from consideration. Two rounds of bids should be sufficient for modest initial projects. Even large projects can be conducted with two rounds of bids when the user acquires some experience. Smaller projects can then be handled with a single formal proposal phase.

Most experienced users evolve to the use of old bids, vendor price lists, and informal budget estimates to reduce the work involved in soliciting formal bids and evaluating them.

Total Cost vs. Lowest Bid

Many organizations evaluate proposals based on original costs or those costs which can be defined precisely at some point. Others attempt to weigh total costs over the entire system life cycle. Either approach can be highly misleading if the wrong assumptions are made. Most commercial users of industrial computer systems should at least attempt to define intangible and long-range cost factors, since these costs can easily be greater than the hardware costs for the initial system. Procurement policies of many institutional users, unfortunately, preclude such judgment factors.

Specific bids should be added to the user's internal design, installation, operating and maintenance costs (including consideration for spare parts, training, and any other identifiable costs) to arrive at the total costs of system ownership and operation. The different approaches used by the various vendors have a different effect on each of these factors.

Availability of vendor support and service coupled with the required response can be traded off against the user's need for spare parts and maintenance training, or the system availability and possible production losses.

The user pays in terms of engineering efficiency, training costs, and probable design errors if emphasis is placed on pushing the state of the art, or if each new system uses a new line of hardware, software, or design methods. Progress is good if tempered with the stability needed by a given commercial enterprise and weighed against its true costs.

Vendor assistance can reduce the users' design costs if the vendor has competence in the application area. Conversely, the user can sometimes expend a great deal of effort in educating vendors.

Recent studies have indicated that system maintenance costs over the life of the system can be two or three times the original system implementation cost. Vendor documentation practices, design simplicity, adherence to industry standards, quality control, software support, and general business stability and reliability, are all factors that influence the system maintenance costs.

If the design team is relatively inexperienced, but has been assigned to provide a new system for a plant in which other industrial computer systems have already been installed by other project teams, support and maintenance costs depend on local precedents that have been set in the earlier projects. The team on the new project then should consider such factors as existing parts inventories, maintenance experience or agreements with vendors, or other support features that could be used to advantage in the new system.

A large plant may eventually contain several industrial computer systems. Even on the first project, some thought should be given to a long-range plan for future systems to provide for local capabilities and to prevent taking an independent approach to each project. This does not mean that all projects need be conducted with the same vendor; in fact, some thought should be given to the possibility that other vendors certainly will be involved in the future. The user should try to provide a consistent design and implementation environment but should not become overly vendor-dependent. The costs of providing for the future must be added to the costs of the projects in which the provisions are made.

CONTRACTING AND PURCHASING

Formal purchasing contracts should be just that, formal! Complete agreement should be reached between the user and vendor(s) as to exactly what is needed in the system in terms of functional capability, what constraints are involved, all system inputs and outputs, and what environmental considerations are of importance. Responsibility for each item should be specified clearly in writing as part of the contract. This prevents misunderstandings, omissions, and duplications, and aids in system documentation.

The contract also should specify commercial factors such as delivery date(s), titles and revision dates of all attachments, shipping instructions, design review procedures, acceptance testing procedures, maintenance and warranty agreements, start-up assistance, the provision of any included assistance or software upon which the agreement is based, user and vendor contact people (by name with addresses and phone numbers), provisions for progress reporting and project control, names of people authorized to conduct further negotiations (as for specification or price and delivery revisions), provisions for contract termination, handling of confidential or proprietary information, patents or rights, handling of events beyond the control of the vendor or the user, or restriction on personnel assignments or solicitation of employment.

Technical factors should be covered thoroughly in the contract, but only to the point of assuring that user objectives are met. The contract should not otherwise restrict the vendor's performance or methods and should not contain provisions of no real interest.

Users are advised to centralize the purchasing of industrial computer systems, at least until methods are well developed. Purchasing specialists can be a great help in expediting and administering contractual matters. Technical matters, including eventual selection of the vendor, should be handled by the project team. Corporate officers generally should not select computer suppliers unless they are the project managers.

Most of the material of this section applies to systems involving over $25,000 in hardware costs. Procedures can be simplified for programmable controllers, programmable instruments, and most microcomputer applications, because the impact of any mistakes made on a small system is probably small also. In fact, on some occasions a user can visit a vendor's sales office, purchase demonstration equipment right off the shelf, and take delivery then and there. One service call by the vendor's maintenance representative usually gets the equipment up and running after the user delivers it by personal auto.

The user-vendor relationship is that of a joint business venture and should be based on mutual trust and support backed up by a clear specification of what is to be provided by each party. On-time deliveries are of the same importance as on-time payments. The user's responsibility for a clear specification equals the vendor's responsibility for adequate documentation. Industrial computer users often are interested in systems with a long life, of the order of 10–30 years, so the user-vendor relationship should be built and maintained carefully.

INSTALLATION AND INTERFACING CONSIDERATIONS

Each company or department that is the eventual end-user of an industrial computer system has unique requirements, problems, operating methods, and capabilities. No two manufacturing processes are completely identical and no two project teams use identical methods to solve a problem. Stored-program computers lend themselves well to applications in such environments, since at least the computer part of a system can be tailored to a given environment fairly easily.

This flexibility of stored-program devices has led to their broad application and has allowed mass production to lower computer mainframe hardware costs by significant amounts every year. The situation is that now a large part of the system hardware cost goes into providing special-purpose equipment to interface the mass-produced general-purpose computers to their application environments. Users invest a great deal of engineering effort in the specification and acquisition of a large variety of process input/output interfaces to enable the computers to be connected to a variety of sensors and actuators. Even though various vendors provide pre-engineered process interface equipment for commonly-used applications, time and cost overruns frequently result from the difficulty of anticipating the unique requirements of each application.

The user may be able to meet a broader range of requirements by dealing with several vendors, each of which may specialize in different process measurement technologies. This approach may give access to more sensing technology but, since all vendors do not presently work to industry-wide interface standards, the user is still left with many system integration problems.

Another problem area arises because process operators have different mental pictures of the operation of various processes and even different operators on the same process have different viewpoints. An engineer's mental image of a process is still another matter. Design of adequate operator's consoles and other man/machine interfaces is largely undisciplined, due to a lack of familiarity with uniform design methods.

There is a tendency to believe that in plant automation systems the need for operator interaction with the process is decreased and to pay only minimal engineering attention to human interfaces. Even if the process does require less human attention, someone still has the full-time job of operating the system. The interface to this operator, illustrated in Fig. 6.8, has a great influence on the effectiveness, utility, and success of the system. Even though the lack of straightforward methods for the design of man/machine interfaces leads to a lot of cutting and trying, head-scratching and rework, most engineers find this part of a project to be the most interesting and educational.

While the system is being designed to meet its functional requirements and to fit into a human organization, the realities of many physical problems also must be considered. For example, a large industrial plant typically requires long wiring runs to the many signal sources to be used. These low-energy signals must not be contaminated by electrical influences generated by large machines. Temperature extremes are a problem for most electronic equipment. An industrial computer system must be designed so it can be maintained adequately in a plant environment.

Physical Considerations

Physical considerations involve the conventional environmental problems of providing energy and physical protection for the system and the physical forms of the information passing through the system processor.

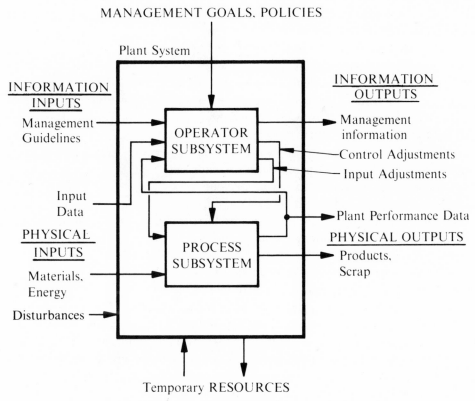

FIG. 6.8
The Operator Subsystem and Information Interfaces

Industrial sensors and actuators, process operators' devices, and communications channels between computer system devices use practically all known technologies. Limit switches produce information in one physical form, tachometers in another. Fluid process control valves use information in one physical form, CRTs in another. The computer industry is still so young that completely standardized physical forms have not yet been developed for information transfer between most devices of interest. Some progress is being made, as in the Electronic Industry Association (EIA) Standard RS-232C for data communication equipment and the American National Standards Institute (ANSI) Standard X3.4-1968, Code for Information Interchange. Other standards exist to provide ready-made solutions to the problem of providing campatibility between information sources and destinations. Some standards exist both industry-wide, to provide compatiblity between the equipment of different vendors, and within single companies, to provide compatibility within a product line. From the user standpoint, the broader the compatibility, the better.

The physical interface equipment must provide compatibility in several mutually-independent areas before a complete communication channel is established. The physical arrangement, such as mechanical dimensions, must be considered. Signal levels must be high enough to achieve successful propogation in an electrically noisy environment, but not so high as to damage the channel or other channels. Pin assignments must be compatible so that channel alignment can be preserved. Signal coding and protocols must be defined and data rates must be compatible.

The process interface of an industrial computer system is usually somewhat unique to that process and extends over a large area of the plant. On the other hand, data processing peripheral devices are fairly common to many applications and usually are located in close proximity to the computer. Standards, for the most part, help to solve the simpler problem of handling the peripheral interfaces, but leave vendors and users to solve the process interface problems.

The way in which interface problems are solved has an effect on the future expansion and maintenance capabilities of a system. Most application requirements vary with time as business circumstances vary. It is also common for users to rapidly generate ideas for additional application features for digital systems, since the strength of programmable computers is flexibility and the strength of most people who work on such systems is creativity. An interface system that is the result of an ad-hoc design approach literally can obsolete the entire system in as little as a few months.

The nature of the process interface requirements and the design used to meet them largely determines the nature of the system installation problems. The bulk of the effort on most systems is in the installation of field wiring, termination panels, and signal conditioning equipment. The trend toward use of remote multiplexing of plant signals and the attendant use of serial communications schemes is helping to reduce this effort.

Even though a simple loop of coaxial cable or a twisted pair of wires may eliminate the bulk of the plant wiring, it is still necessary to provide common-mode voltage isolation of many signals, to amplify, attenuate, or filter them, or drive sensing devices. Remote multiplexers also must be protected from damage when they are located near the process equipment. This protection might include features for control of corrosive atmospheres, vibration, heat, electrical noise, process fluids, or physical access to the equipment. Provisions for power and maintenance also must be provided.

It is impossible to present a comprehensive checklist or set of recommended installation practices in this limited space for all the interface problems that are likely to be encountered over the wide range of industrial computer applications that exist. The best advice available is to request the vendor of every piece of hardware to provide proven detailed installation instructions or recommendations and follow them to the last detail.

Personnel Considerations

Organizational considerations relate to how the system fits into the human side of the plant environment. The system interfaces to people in many ways. People are involved in analyzing the system, designing and building it, installing and testing it, operating and maintaining it. People must train each other to fulfill all these roles. Each stage of the system design has an effect on the manner in which all future work is conducted.

The programmable feature of digital computers provides the flexibility to handle a wide range of complex problems in dynamic business environments. Digital systems can have, as a result, a great effect on the operation of a commercial enterprise. On the other hand, the flexibility of a digital computer system allows the impact of human errors in its design to be relatively low, because this flexibility allows changes to be made so easily.

It is important to consider the interface between the process and the human operator very carefully, no matter what level the operator's job involves in the human hierarchy, because the information bandwidth easily can go beyond human capabilities. The time-constant boundaries of human jobs as shown in Fig. 6.9 are very real and must be considered in system designs. Operators cannot be responsible for resources over which authority is not provided in the form of control mechanisms, time, or information.

If people are too busy (or uncomfortable) at a task that is quite dynamic, they tend to ignore some requirements until a comfortable operation is achieved that can be handled to their own satisfaction. This sort of operation may not result in ranking priorities in the same way these priorities might be ranked by the person's supervisor. The result may be organizational conflict.

On the other hand, if a given job is too routine, people tend to make work of their own choosing. Some of this made-work can be of benefit but the yield in this respect, as far as the overall organization is concerned, is apt to be low if such activities are without purposeful direction.

A new control system presents an upsetting situation to an operator, unless the operator is involved in its development and is trained in the proper use of the system. The system also must perform useful functions for the operator, personally. The operator must not be a slave to the system, but must always be in command.

Provision of some convenience features, solely for the comfort of the operator, is a good idea. These can take the form of an enclosed workplace (Fig. 6.10) to reduce heat, noise or other distractions, or improved communication with the people with whom the operator most frequently interacts. These conveniences frequently justify themselves in terms of improved operator performance.

The ease with which a digital system can acquire data and produce reports presents a very real danger in terms of operator acceptance. The

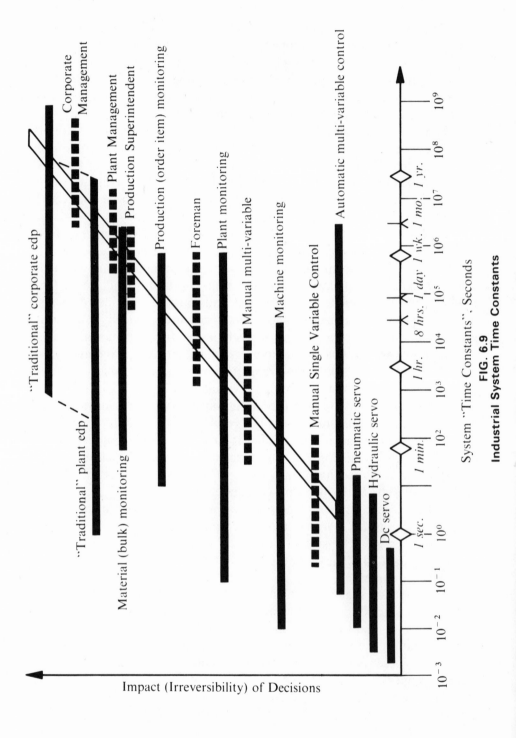

FIG. 6.9
Industrial System Time Constants

Impact (Irreversibility) of Decisions

System "Time Constants", Seconds

Corporate Management

Plant Management

Production Superintendent

Production (order item) monitoring

Foreman

Plant monitoring

Manual multi-variable

Machine monitoring

Automatic multi-variable control

"Traditional" corporate edp

"Traditional" plant edp

Material (bulk) monitoring

Manual Single Variable Control

Pneumatic servo

Hydraulic servo

Dc servo

1 sec.

1 min

1 hr.

8 hrs. 1 day 1 wk. 1 mo. 1 yr.

10^{-3} 10^{-2} 10^{-1} 10^{0} 10^{1} 10^{2} 10^{3} 10^{4} 10^{5} 10^{6} 10^{7} 10^{8} 10^{9}

FIG. 6.10
A Typical Process Operator's Console. (Courtesy of ALCOA)

system should not advertise publicly the normal but harmless mistakes made by the operator, such as entries of improper data. Notification of such things to the operator is proper, but notification to his supervisor or peers is not.

The operator has a mental image of a process different from the mental image held by anyone else. The operator's interface, whether it be a console panel, CRT screen, or any other type of device, works best if it presents the proper image. A complete analysis of the operator's job, in terms of information flows and transactions which take place across the operator's interface, is needed in order to design an adequate physical interface. Mock-ups of operator's consoles frequently are used to reduce the abstract nature of this work. The operators simulate the use of the mock-up, while the engineers study the operation and try various alternatives. This produces good interaction between the operators and the engineers, helps train the operators in the use of the new equipment, and is an excellent way to get the operators' ideas on how the job should be done.

Graphic CRTs and plasma display panels, programmable slide projectors, and various mounting arrangements of more conventional devices can be used to provide images of the process in forms familiar to the operator. The flexibility of these devices, plus that of the computer, provides a powerful capability for operator interfaces.

SOFTWARE DESIGN AND MANAGEMENT

The use of software is the main difference between former engineering methods in industry and the newer application of industrial computer systems. Customized software, in the form of unique application programs, converts a collection of general-purpose hardware into a special-purpose system. This approach allows for the large-scale manufacturing of the hardware with both economies of scale and economies of specialization.

Computer application software may be viewed as an extension of the functional capabilities of a system, with computer programs being used to accomplish each function. Each program is written as a cookbook-like series of steps to be followed by the computer system. Conceptually, computer programming is a natural, straightforward, easy-to-learn activity; it is complicated in appearance and practice because of the special languages used and it is very error-prone.

Computer languages are a compromise between several factors: ease of use and training, their power to express application functions, their power over details of the computer operation, and the costs of providing translators for them. If computer programs could be written in the same languages that are used for the original system specifications, software design and management would not be much of a problem. Translators still would be needed to translate the specifications into sets of more detailed internal operations, however.

Considerable progress has been made in this direction by the development of various high-level programming languages and problem-oriented languages, which are adequate for many applications and which greatly reduce the programming effort involved. These languages replace part of the human effort of translating functional requirements into computer instructions by having a computer do part of the translation.

Organizations and individuals beginning to use industrial computers are well advised to use high-level programming languages to try to reduce the effort, training, and risk involved in the first projects, and to pay careful attention to the adequate management of the remaining effort.

Computer programming is only a small part of software design, although it is perhaps the least familiar to many engineers and managers. Most emphasis should be placed on project definition and task breakdown, so the programming later can be done in small easy-to-manage modules, which also are easy to integrate into the well-structured system. The following sections provide an overview of the tasks involved and describe some recent advances in the methods of software design and management.

Advances in Software Design and Management

Rapidly declining hardware costs have recently directed a great deal of attention to steadily-rising software costs. Software, historically, has been labor-intensive, using fairly high-quality labor at that. Translators for high-level programming languages have helped, but software costs continue to reflect a trend as shown in Fig. 6.11 toward an increasing percentage of total project cost. Absolute hardware costs, for a given amount of computing power, have declined due to volume production and lower semiconductor technology costs. Software costs have risen due to increased labor costs and the increasing complexity of systems.

Software engineering is a relatively new field. Organizations such as computer system vendors, software consultants, and large users of computers have worked for years to develop improved software engineering methods. Only recently has much significant progress been made, but this progress has been very significant indeed.

Software engineering involves much more than computer programming. In fact, anything that is not hardware may be considered to be software, such as project specifications, design calculations, engineering drawings, project

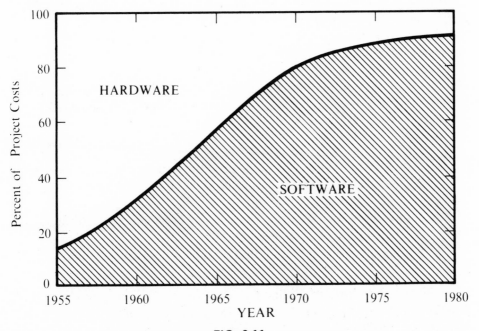

FIG. 6.11
Hardware—Software Cost Trends

management standards and policies, reporting systems, or the project organization itself. The task of computer programming is simplified greatly by careful attention to some of these other software items.

The structured functional breakdown of a project is one of the newly-discovered software design tools. In terms of actually programming a computer, this means that programs are developed in small, manageable pieces, each related to a small function within the project. This is not new since hardware design usually is done this way, but it is relatively new in software design. The previous tendency has been to attempt to write programs in overly-large segments (some systems are known to contain only a single giant program) with no means to keep track of what was being done. Small program segments can be assigned to many people and should be defined so that each segment can be written and tested without interaction with other segments.

Top-down decomposition of project segments is a key element to the new software design strategy. This focuses attention first on the overall project objectives and less on the computer itself. In terms of programming, top-down structuring also means that programs are written first to serve the overall system functions, which are those for which the project manager is personally responsible.

Programs unique to the computer itself, such as those that read in the process measurements and those that directly operate the typers, are done later. To answer an obvious question, the programs that are not done at first are simulated in order to test the top-level programs. As each program module is completed, simulation programs are devised to test it. When each module is tested and documented, it replaces the module used to simulate it and it is integrated into the higher-level module it supports. Experience has proven that system integration problems virtually disappear with this approach, and that errors within new modules are effectively isolated to those modules only.

The modular programming concept has three basic disciplinary strategies:

1. Data flows only vertically in the program structure between modules in adjacent layers of the structure used for functional decomposition.

2. Data used by various modules are defined very carefully and cataloged.

3. Each program module has only one starting point and one ending point.

The first and third rules define the interfaces between programs and aid in establishing the correctness of program behavior. The second rule effectively standardizes the rules by which data operations are performed. The third rule relates to the concept known as "structured programing," which was introduced in Chapter 4.

As an example of the modular and structured programming design concepts, consider a program to perform the following functions: "Sum the first ten digits and print the sum but stop and print a daily report if the time of day is 2:00 p.m."

Using top-down decomposition, the first level of program design can be outlined and diagrammed as shown in Fig. 6.12. This first-level sequence description does not provide much detail, but it does outline the job at hand.

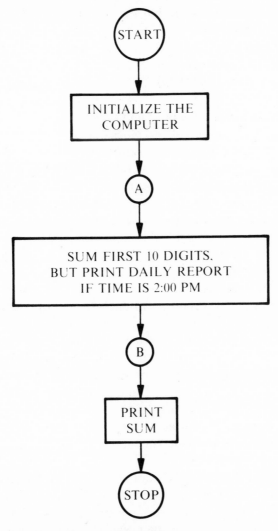

FIG. 6.12
First Level Description of Example Program

Points A and B are used for reference in the following decompositions of this small job.

As the first step in the decomposition, a program loop to perform the summing operation is detailed as shown in Fig. 6.13. Note that the original program had only a single entry point (START), and a single exit point (STOP). This is still true after the first expansion of the program details. The block between points A and B has become more complicated, but this block also remains with just one entry point and one exit point. Points C and D now identify another structure within the looping segment to provide for the 2:00 p.m. report. Further expansion provides a branching operation for this report as shown in Fig. 6.14. Note again that the report is provided without adding entry or exit points between C and D.

Two points are important about these examples: (1) Only three basic structures are needed to perform this (or any other) programming job; and (2) The data for the variable TIME which is generated by another program is disciplined.

The three fundamental programming structures introduced in Chapter 4 are shown in Fig. 6.15. Either of the blocks A or B may be missing in the looping or branching functions. Any program of any complexity can be represented using only these basic structures. (The kinds of structures to be avoided are those that make several branches without returning to a common point in the program logic.) These structures can be used with all programming languages although some languages are better suited than others. These structures also fit well into the top-down decomposition strategy, since any element can be expanded readily into any of these structures to any required depth.

In the example, another program (not shown in the flow diagram) is presumed to be running in response to signals from a time-of-day clock. This clock program prepares data for use by perhaps dozens of programs, so agreement obviously is needed on how the TIME data are structured and how the TIME data may be accessed by programs that require them. The flow chart of Fig. 6.14, showing the details of the test for the daily report, indicates that 2:00 p.m. actually is depicted on a 24-hour clock which counts hundredths of hours. Thus, checks for TIME = 2 and TIME = 1400 are two entirely different things. This emphasizes that data types and structures must be rigorously defined and must be known to all programmers on the project team.

The relationships between the example clock program and the rest of a given system might be depicted as a hierarchical structure shown in Fig. 6.16. This structure indicates that the example program is started by the main system program and exits to the main system program when the example program is completed. The example program, in turn, can cause the daily report program to run. Both the example program and the daily report

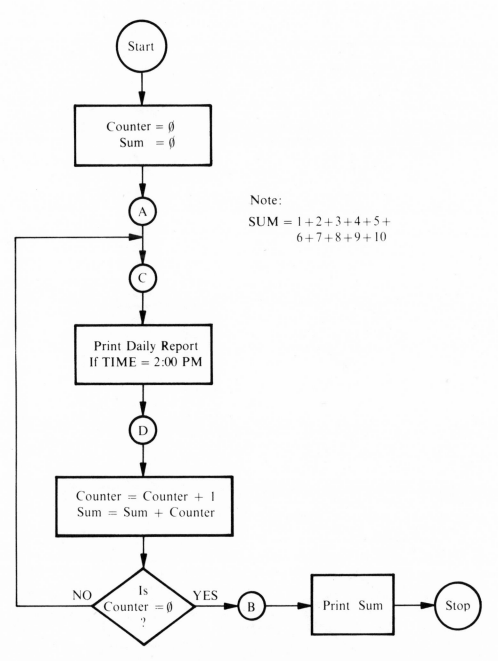

Note:
SUM = 1+2+3+4+5+
      6+7+8+9+10

FIG. 6.13
Second-Level Breakdown of the Example Program

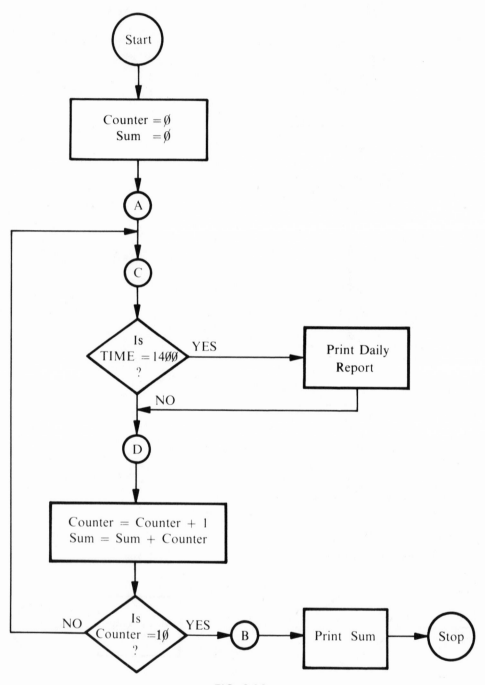

FIG. 6.14
Third-Level Breakdown of the Example Program

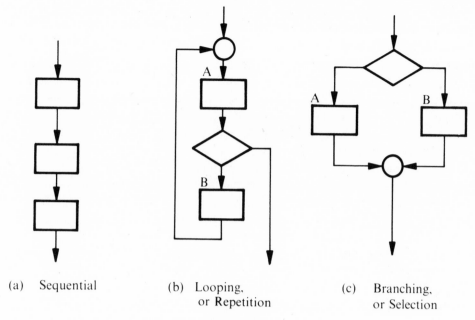

(a)   Sequential

(b)   Looping,
      or Repetition

(c)   Branching,
      or Selection

FIG. 6.15
Fundamental Programming Structures

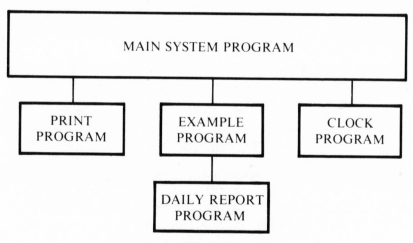

FIG. 6.16
A Hierarchical Program Structure

program make use of the print program by passing data to the main system program (up through the hierarchical structure) and requesting the print program to be run by the main system program. This type of definition of software modules, data properties, and their relationships, is the heart of software design.

In the previous discussion, graphic aids were used to illustrate the example. The graphic aspects of software design can greatly enhance human understanding. The software designer must be able to comprehend the work at hand and graphic diagrams help visualize structural relationships. Since most projects involve teams of designers, it is also important for them to be able to relate their individual modules of work with those of others. Only recently has it been realized that it is as important for people to understand the finished software as it is for the computer to properly execute it.

This introduces the concept of software readability. Programs must be able to be read by other people for a variety of reasons, including testing, maintenance, or educational purposes. An unfamiliar programming language appears confusing at first, but experience has shown that readability is improved greatly when the program is written in a structured way. The structure gives the reader some idea of what to expect and keeps small functions localized within a few program statements. Thus, programs have the properties of readability and locality and both are enhanced by good software design practices.

Readability also is improved by the generous use of comments, which are notes to the reader rather than computer instructions, and the use of the rule that program modules be sized so they can be printed on a single page. Another good rule is to use the format of a program as a guide to the program structure. Using the previous example program and the BASIC language, these principles are illustrated by the program of Fig. 6.17.

The readability of this example program is improved by indenting some statements by different amounts, as in the loop between statements 180 and 210. Liberal use of comments (REMARKS in this case) helps explain the somewhat cryptic program and relates various points in the program to corresponding points in the flow chart.

If programs are readable, another productive software engineering technique can be applied. Other programmers, or perhaps the end users of the system, can help check the programs for errors. If programs are structured into small modules that are simple enough to write in a few days and be checked readily by someone else, the programmer can manage his work individually, can meet schedules (or have an early warning of problems) and budgets, and avoid a great deal of mental anguish, confusion, and programming errors.

In summary, application of modern software engineering methods is showing a dramatic improvement in programming productivity of an order of magnitude or more. Properly managed by both project managers and team workers, software engineering need not be a mystery or an expensive and risky business venture, any more than hardware engineering. In many respects, software is easier to work with than hardware, particularly in the maintenance of old systems. In brief, the techniques mentioned here are:

1. Place initial emphasis on the overall functional requirements of the system. These requirements are the personal responsibility of the project manager or chief programmer.

2. Break the system down from the top (most general level) to the bottom (most detailed level) of a functional hierarchy.

3. Organize the work to be done around the individual functional modules at each level.

4. Size each module of work so that the actual effort to build or program the module is no more than one work-week.

5. Prepare the work on higher-level modules first and begin work on the next lower level only when all work on the higher level is complete (including testing via simulation).

6. Discipline data and information flows in the system.

7. Completely document each module with program listings, written descriptions, flow charts, etc., so as to be readily readable by others before a new module is started.

8. Assign specific responsibility for the clerical task of keeping records of complete modules, data descriptions, etc., so all finished work is available to all team workers. This should be someone trained in office or library operations such as a secretary.

```
100 REMARK – PROGRAM TO SUM FIRST 10 DIGITS, PRINT THE SUM, AND
110 REMARK – TO PRINT DAILY LOG AT 2 PM.
120 REMARK – AUTHOR: JOHN DOE            1 OCTOBER 1974
130 REMARK – PROGRAM NAME:               EXAMPLE
140 REMARK – CALLED BY:                  MAIN
150   EXTERNAL TIME                      'TIME OF DAY, XXXX HOURS AND
                                          HUNDREDTHS
160 LET COUNTER = 0                      'POINT A
170 LET SUM = 0 'INITIALIZE              'POINT C
180   IF TIME = 1400 THEN CALL REPORT    'POINT D
190   LET COUNTER = COUNTER + 1
200   LET SUM = SUM + COUNTER
210   IF COUNTER < 10 GO TO 180          'POINT B
220 PRINT SUM
230 STOP
240 END
```

FIG. 6.17
Sample Program

9. Structure all program modules so they have only single entry and exit points and use only the three fundamental program structures.

All of these techniques should be used together; omitting any one of them has been shown to greatly reduce the efficiency of programming efforts. Most programmers say they use most of these methods most of the time. The key seems to be to use all of them all of the time.

Application Software Development

Application software is the programming that is unique to a given system's functional requirements, as contrasted to the general-purpose support software described in the next section. Some applications of digital computer systems are common enough that application software "packages" have been developed, while other applications require a complete new software design for each project.

Packages may be tailored to a given application with relatively minor effort, sometimes by simply supplying the system with data describing the parameters of a given plant. In these cases no additional programming, in the usual sense of the word, is required. Examples of applications for which such packages have been developed are: petrochemical process control, spectrometer operation, injection molding machine control and monitoring, power demand monitoring, security systems, various kinds of servomechanism regulators, and logical sequencing systems. Most program packages also feature some type of "escape mechanism," so that conventional programs can be combined with the packages, or so several packages can be combined in a single system to handle a wide variety of applications.

In many cases, there are no packaged application programs available and the potential system user must either provide the required programs or obtain them from a software supplier. If the user represents an organization with well-developed software capabilities and can see a competitive advantage in keeping the work proprietary, the work might be done in-house.

Other legitimate reasons for in-house software development are the lack of suppliers with either the capabilities or the marketing interest in a given area, the use of software development as a training mechanism, the small size of the project does not justify the burden of contract administration, or perhaps the whole project is a bootleg proposition as an add-on to another system.

Small bootleg projects are usually to be encouraged. Computer systems offer a certain flexibility and fascination that generally is put to productive use by individual engineers. The ease with which an engineer can try ideas with little need for constructing hardware makes it almost impossible to prevent bootleg jobs anyway. Management's job is to try to discipline these jobs so they are done efficiently and do not consume resources committed for another purpose.

Some comments were offered in previous sections on getting software from outside sources. For in-house development of major software systems, careful attention to the material in the previous section is in order. The next section describes some specific software engineering tools that should make the job easier and the section on documentation offers some guidelines on how to preserve the value of the work that is done.

Support Software

Many programming-related tasks, such as coding, program testing, and documentation, can be expedited by means of software engineering tools. Support software also is used to help diagnose and maintain hardware, both within the computer system and in the physical plant.

Most support software is supplied as standard program packages by the computer system supplier and is used to help build and maintain the computer itself. Packages typically found to be most useful include translators for programming languages, text editors, operating systems, program loaders, linkage editors, debugging packages, hardware diagnostic programs, and libraries of programs to operate various computer system devices.

Language translators include assemblers, compilers for FORTRAN and other high-level languages, and macroprocessors. Assemblers are the most basic translators and usually translate program statements into machine codes on a one-for-one basis. They allow mnemonic names to be given to machine operations and storage locations so that programmers can remember them more easily. Compilers are more powerful and usually translate a single high-level-language program statement into several machine instructions. High-level languages usually are designed to be more readable than assembly languages and allow programmers to think in terms more nearly like the terms used to express the original problem specifications. Most compilers also can examine and optimize programs to reduce execution time or storage. Macroprocessors are further extensions of the assembler idea, but they allow considerable customizing of languages and a programmer can apply names to groups of programming statements. These groups of statements then are generated automatically whenever the group name is used by the programmer.

Text editors typically are used for maintenance of source programs; that is, those programs written by the programmer prior to their translation. They are convenient for making program changes, particularly when the same change is to be made several times within a program, or when program segments are to be rearranged. They also provide for somewhat-automated program (and revision) documentation. Some editors check the program and notify the designer whenever the rules of structured programming are violated.

Operating systems are the management programs in a computer system. They provide the means for programs to request execution of the other programs, provide required linkages between programs, and allocate the resources of the computer in such a way as to minimize conflict.

Program loaders usually are small programs used to operate just enough of the computer equipment to allow more elaborate programs to be loaded into the system. Some loaders have more elaborate functions such as those that allow programs to be loaded into any of several different storage areas. Linkage editors are an extension of loaders, in that they establish relationships between various program and variable names within separately-built program modules.

Debugging packages provide a set of program test facilities so that detailed program behavior can be observed during test runs. They usually feature adjustable stopping points and messages that can be inserted temporarily in a program being tested.

Hardware diagnostic programs are used to provide known patterns of operations to the hardware so its behavior can be observed. In some cases the observations are made by the system itself and messages are printed to provide clues for trouble-shooting purposes. These features can greatly expedite system checkout and repair.

Vendor-supplied libraries generally provide many programs used to perform commonly-used arithmetic operations and input/output functions. In some cases, elaborate collections of application-oriented programs also are included.

The value of a computer system as provided by a supplier is largely a function of the support software that is included. The support software can have a significant effect on the engineering and programming costs incurred in building and maintaining a system. Since the support software can be provided for and used by almost all systems, its cost is quite low in comparison to its value. This is why previous sections emphasized the difference between total system costs and the misleading practice of comparing only initial bid prices.

Documentation

The function of documentation is to communicate the system design to other people. A system is largely documented without special effort if the structured design approach outlined in this chapter is followed. Periodic checks by the project manager on such factors as the completeness of all functional specifications and the readability of programs aid in both project control and documentation.

Documentation is required for many reasons, but the most obvious reason is so the end-user can maintain and update the system after the original design organization is disbanded. Documentation also provides a valuable educational tool to train others in how the system was designed, and is particularly important to users who want to expand their in-house capabilities.

Many systems or modules can be reapplied in other than the original application if they are adequately documented. The actual design process itself can be aided considerably by keeping careful notes on design considerations. These notes can then become part of the system documentation and can aid in project control.

Design notes also are protection against turnover of design people and can reduce confusion and rework when the staff changes. Since computer system design skills are in demand, it is unwise for an individual to be bound to a given assignment because documentation is poor or not current.

Good documentation also facilitates design team coordination, peer review of module designs, and testing and integration efforts. Design teams, using a structured approach and documenting as they go, are reporting remarkably low error rates. The peer review process, using all available documentation, also reduces attempts at programming tricks such as the use of instructions as data, which tend to produce very hard-to-detect errors.

Until recently, documentation was usually an add-on effort to record the nature of a completed design. Sometimes documentation was provided by professional writers and artists with little contact with the actual design team. System designers also had a tendency to view themselves as too creative to bother with documenting a system for someone else. Hopefully, these people either will adapt to the newer methods or find some other form of self-expression, because the structured design approach provides both systems and documentation of a quality too good to be ignored.

Good documentation can take many forms depending on the application, the people involved, and how each is organized. Program flowcharts and listings with explanatory text have been the media of the past. Structured systems design seems to require less flowcharting, and much of the text comes about automatically from the system or module specifications. The use of host systems with their improved software support capabilities to prepare programs, and increased emphasis on program readability, have done a great deal to improve documentation via program listings.

Structured design practices result in structured systems so some documentation should be included to indicate this structure. Relationships between system modules often can be depicted best graphically as via hierarchy diagrams, decision tables, or state transition diagrams. The structure within a module can be indicated by the format of the program listing as, for example, by indenting loops.

Each functional module in a system represents some system activity and operates on defined data. Therefore, activity cell or data packet diagrams are a good way to help visualize the system structure.

Examples of each of these documentation forms are given throughout this chapter. The following is a list of considerations that can be used to form a documentation checklist for a given project:

1. Statements of system functions, in plain language, with breakdown into module functions;

2. Statements of design strategies and constraints with a minimum of technical jargon;

3. Data definitions including variable names, storage arrangements, other pertinent classifications, sources, destinations, access methods, and structures;

4. Operating procedures and maintenance procedures;

5. Design notes and test data;

6. Documentation index;

7. Graphical representations of program modules, data transfer relationships, and program structures;

8. Readable program listings and flowcharts;

9. Sequence or dependence charts;

10. Cross references;

11. Applicable standards and conventions;

12. Vendor's literature and instructions;

13. Procedures for handling and preserving the documentation.

Although it usually is not considered to be part of the documentation problem, the training of people who will be involved in the day-to-day operation of the system depends heavily on the quality of the documentation provided. The design team should test the documentation itself for its suitability as part of the system start-up.

One also must document the system hardware using the original purchase order specifications, electronic diagrams, connection diagrams, vendors' instructions and installation recommendations, test and maintenance procedures, and a list of all hardware documentation.

A system log should be maintained in the computer room to record all operating problems, corrections, and any other pertinent data, beginning when the system is accepted from the vendor and continuing throughout the life of the system. This helps to spot trends in system behavior, such as failing components, and it is a good way to record all register contents when the system suddenly dies at 3:00 a.m. for no apparent reason. It generally is conceded that computer systems are complex enough that it is impossible to remove all errors, but a good log helps to catch most of them.

As a system gets older, its documentation typically tends to suffer. Changes are made and not recorded. Sometimes part of the documentation gets lost or destroyed, but these problems can be avoided by access-controlled backup copies. Still, the time eventually comes when the system can no longer be expanded or maintained adequately and when removing one error produces two more. That is when you scrap it.

BIBLIOGRAPHY

Archibald, R. D., and Flaks, M., "The EE's Guide to Project Management," Reprinted from the Electronic Engineer, Chilton Company, Philadelphia.

Broekhuis, H., and Jongkind, M. S., "Planning and Managing Process Computer Projects," Control Engineering, February, 1971, pp. 60–67.

Dallimonti, R., "New Designs for Process Control Consoles," Instrumentation Technology, November, 1973, pp. 48–53.

Drucker, P. F., *Management: Tasks, Responsibilities, Practices*, Harper & Row, New York, 1973.

Frost, D. R., *Structured Software Design*, Honeywell, Inc., Phoenix, 1974.

Fuller, D., *Manage or be Managed*, Industrial Education Institute, Boston, 1963.

Harrington, J. J., Jr., *Computer Integrated Manufacturing*, Industrial Press, Inc., New York, 1973.

How to Increase Programming Productivity Through Software Engineering, Course Notes, SofTech, Inc., Waltham, Massachusetts, 1974.

Improved Programming Technologies: Management Overview, IBM Corp., August, 1973.

Kelly, C. R., *Manual and Automatic Control*, John Wiley & Sons, New York, 1965.

Merrill, H. F., (Ed.), *Classics in Management*, Revised Edition, American Management Association, 1970.

McCracken, D. D., "Revolution in Programming," Datamation, December, 1973, pp. 50–52. (See also pp. 53–61 for related articles.)

Ogilvy, D., *Principles of Management*, Ogilvy and Mather, 1968.

Orth, D. C., III, "Engineers are Different—or Are They?," paper presented at IEEE/INTERCON, March, 1974.

"Special Collection on Requirements Analysis," IEEE Trans. Software Engineering, Vol. SE-3, No. 1, January 1977.

Weinberg, G. M., *The Psychology of Computer Programming*, Van Nostrand Reinhold Co., New York, 1971.

Willard, F. G., "Interfacing Standardization in the Large Control System," paper presented at the IEEE Industry Applications Society annual meeting, October, 1974.

7 IMPLEMENTING THE SYSTEM

Kirwin A. Whitman, M.Ch.E., M.B.A.
ALLIED CHEMICAL CORPORATION,
MORRISTOWN, NEW JERSEY

During the implementation phase, everything that has been developed up to this point is brought together. Implementation involves installation of the equipment and software, test evaluation, and maintenance of the system.

Most of the material presented in this chapter is applicable to any industrial computer project, regardless of application. Recognizing this similarity between projects promotes lower implementation costs and, more importantly, lessens the risk of encountering pitfalls that can be avoided or otherwise overcome.

User participation is vital during implementation, just as it was during the initial specification and design period. The project team should have the philosophy that the system is built for and belongs to the user. Design and implementation must be directed primarily to serving user needs, rather than the convenience of system personnel. Gaining user participation may itself be a challenging task. However, without user involvement and acceptance, the project has little hope for success.

Once the human resources have been enlisted on the side of the project, one can address the physical problems of implementation. An effort must be made to minimize the environmental effect upon the integrity of the computer system. Two important environmental considerations are the ambient air characteristics and electrical noise. Air-conditioning to change the ambient air temperature, humidity, or dust and gaseous content may be desirable. **279**

Similarly, electrical noise control in the form of shielding and other measures may be necessary to achieve the desired system performance.

It normally is important that industrial computer systems have high reliability. The implementor has the choice of either designing higher reliability into the system and increasing initial cost, or accepting higher eventual maintenance costs and increased system downtime. Regardless of which decision is chosen, there must be provision for system maintenance. An assessment must be made of the plant's ability to support, train, and keep qualified maintenance personnel. This decision is unique for each plant and also must consider the vendor's ability to service the particular plant.

System testing involves four stages of testing: the hardware, software, on-site system, and availability tests. The purpose of the first three stages is to ensure that the system meets its specifications and that it is ready to be integrated into the total operational system. The fourth stage, availability testing, is an indication of the long-term reliability of the system and cannot be performed until after the system has been operational for some period of time, typically several months.

Quite often, documentation only begins to receive serious thought in the final stage of implementation. Actually, documentation can be an important aid throughout the project, and should not be considered only as an historic anti-climax.

However, the one task which is properly an anti-climax is the project post-completion audit. The audits increasingly are being expected by management as a means of objectively evaluating the true profitability of an industrial computer installation. In addition to benefits, other evaluation elements include budgets, specifications, schedules, efficiency, and ease of use.

PHYSICAL PLANNING

Preparation for system installation starts well before the computer system is delivered. In both new and modified plants, physical planning for the computer and its installation must take place concurrently with the design of the plant or its modification, since each may affect the other. Space must be provided for the computer equipment; electrical wiring is needed to power it; and provisions must be made for sensor and control wiring.

Site Layout

This activity involves the design of the computer portion of the control room to provide space for the system and to promote its easier use and maintenance. The operator's console or other operator input/output peripherals should be located in the control room at a place convenient to the operator's normal station. Minicomputers, with their compact size, often make it possible to locate the computer cabinet in the control room, although this may not be required or desired. The exact location should consider how the system relates to the other instrument control functions, where the control wiring is run, whether adequate space is available, and whether the traffic pattern is satisfactory. At least three feet of access space should be allowed in the front and rear of the system. If more space is available in the front, it will permit groups to receive instruction or observe the system. Consoles or cabinets with signal lights should not be placed facing direct sunlight, as this makes their observation more dificult. In addition, they should be placed so that the operator can observe the lights from the normal operating position. Site layout also should consider expansion of the system by allowing the flexibility for future growth of the system.

Attention should be given to the appearance of the system, as some people may infer that a cluttered, slipshod-looking installation mirrors the state of the hidden hardware and software, and perhaps even the very objectives of the application. Proper lighting also can play a part, adding not only to the appearance, but also to reducing operator fatigue. An average illumination of 60 to 100 footcandles, measured 30 inches above the floor, is appropriate. Diffused fluorescent lighting is preferred, as it is shadowless and glare-free.

Floor loading is not a major factor, as most industrial floors are adequate. For other than concrete floors, however, a floor loading calculation should be made. Concrete floors pose some cable routing problems, even where a recessed cable trough is provided. In this case, drainage to prevent moisture accumulation is important and future expansion must be carefully planned. A raised floor largely circumvents these two problems, but is more expensive than, for example, the use of an existing floor with cables less aesthetically routed in suspended overhead trays. Whatever floor covering is chosen should be antistatic. Concrete floors should be coated to reduce chalking, which can result in more frequent filter replacement.

Air-Conditioning

Depending on the manufacturer's recommendations, and taking into account the worst-case temperature and humidity predictions for the particular site, air-conditioning may or may not be required. Many control rooms are air-conditioned for personnel comfort or to eliminate atmospheric contaminants. In those cases where air-conditioning is required and there are no plans to include it for the entire control room, the cooling can be provided for the cabinets alone. Vendor recommendations for air temperature and humidity should be observed. Electronic components and circuits are heat-sensitive and may malfunction at very high or very low temperatures. In addition, long exposure to high temperatures reduces the operating life of semiconductor devices. Similarly, dust and contaminants can affect the performance of the system. Dust has several deleterious effects. A coating of dust on electronic components reduces heat transfer from the component to the ambient air. In addition, the dust absorbs moisture and contaminants which may lead to increased corrosion and electrical leakage.

In many industrial situations, filters which remove dust and various corrosive atmospheric contaminants are built into the air-conditioning or computer system. It also helps to keep the computer away from building entrances, through which contaminants may be entering the room. In some cases, pressurization of the room or the cabinet can be an additional anti-contaminant measure by fostering an outflow of air. Proper maintenance of particulate and contaminant filters is important to prevent reduced efficiency and air flow.

Electrical Power

Adequate electrical power is required to operate the computer and its associated equipment. The manufacturer provides specifications as to the voltage, frequency, and current which are required, as well as special requirements such as filtering. Small installations may operate directly from 120 vac service provided for regular utility use. Larger installations typically require specialized wiring. In many cases, the manufacturer may recommend a dedicated service, so as to provide some measure of isolation from electrical noise sources. In all cases, applicable local and national electrical codes should be followed.

Power protection considers the need for dependable power to the system, within allowable tolerances of voltage level and frequency. However, the need for power protection, such as an uninterruptible source or protection from transients, is not universal. In situations where it is not required, an orderly shutdown of the computer (especially involving disk transfers) should be considered in the hardware and software design. As a minimum, a diagnostic procedure should be employed upon restart to detect possible errors made during the shutdown sequence.

Isolation transformers may be recommended to insure against grounding faults occurring remote from the computer causing interference with (or finding a path through) the computer equipment. A separate earth ground should be used, along with an isolation transformer. The computer should be located as close as possible to the isolation equipment to minimize the opportunity for pickup on the line.

A more complex question is that of protection against power failure. An estimate must be made of the expected frequency and duration of power outages and a strategy evolved which is consistent with provisions for other vital electrical equipment in the process. For example, if a process unit normally shuts down on power failure, then the computer system power requirement is limited to a period which permits an orderly shutdown of the computer and process equipment. There is no purpose in keeping the computer running when the plant is shut down. It must also be remembered that without power protection, a computer may be affected by a momentary power failure, which may be almost unnoticed by the process or operator. For example, the time frame for a computer failure versus a process failure may be cycles versus minutes.

Possible methods of power protection are shown in Fig. 7.1. The purpose of the various devices in this figure are as follows:

(1) A rectifier provides regulated dc power and can be furnished with a current-limiting feature to prevent battery overcharge and rectifier damage.

(2) A battery provides backup power either for the duration of the power outage, or until another power source such as a motor generator set can be switched over to using fuel energy. The battery may float on the system input power lines or be switched in on main power failure. When in use, the battery should be disconnected as a power source before the battery is exhausted. This may be accomplished with a dc under-voltage relay.

(3) An inverter supplies ac power when supplied with dc power from either the rectifier or battery.

(4) The switching (static transfer) device causes the load from the inverter to be switched to the backup power source without interruption of computer operation.

(5) A motor-generator delivers electrical power when it is driven either by the main power source or by an engine running on a fossil fuel. The motor-generator also provides noise isolation, even for extreme cases, such as power line disturbances caused by large arcing contacts.

(6) The flywheel is driven by the motor and its momentum carries the generator for a few seconds after power fails, to provide time for the engine to start.

(7) The diode is a device that conducts current in only one direction.

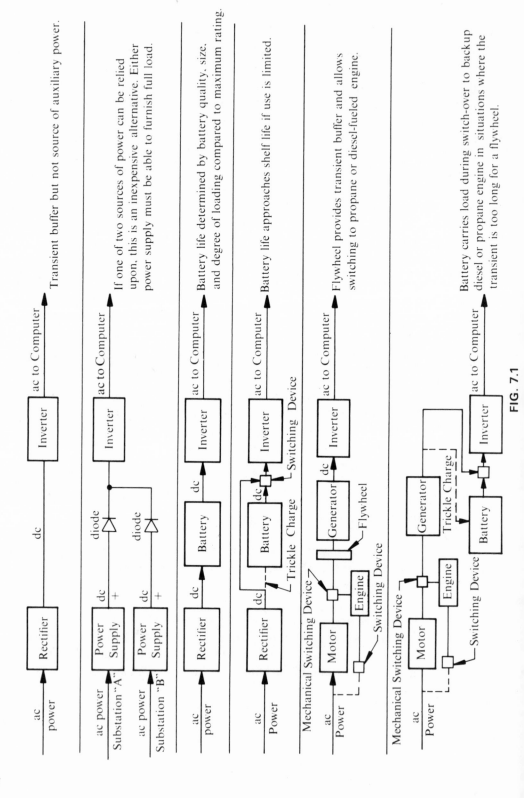

FIG. 7.1

Use of a battery as the only backup power implies that this source of power only is available during power outages of limited duration. Its use can be divided into three stages. The first is to continue normal control operation in order not to cause a shutdown during what may be a very short power outage. This period might be planned for a number of minutes. The second stage is the orderly shutdown on the expectation that the outage will be prolonged. The third stage is a longer duration maintenance of some critical control or monitoring functions and requires less power than the first or second stages.

ACHIEVING DESIRED SYSTEM RELIABILITY

A distinguishing difference between computers for industrial control and computers for non-real-time applications is the greater need for reliability. Interruption of computer operation for real-time systems means a loss, always of information, sometimes of control, and occasionally of plant operation, when the computer is not backed up. Any lost function translates to dollars or else there would have been no economic incentive for installing the computer.

Reliability factors can be considered in terms of the past, the present, and the future. The past was when the design decisions were made which, in part, affect the system reliability. There is more control over the present, because the user has certain options in hardware configuration, software philosophy, and input manipulation. The prospect of future expansion requires decisions which favor flexibility and perhaps efficiency, but which may be somewhat at the expense of reliability if not considered carefully.

A philosophy to maximize reliability contains elements of fault prevention, fault detection, and fault tolerance. Fault prevention is enhanced through design efforts to simplify hardware and software. A characteristic of minicomputers is the reduced complexity of both hardware and software when compared to larger computers. The fewer circuits and the simpler architecture inherently aid high reliability. Fault detection includes the initial factory testing of hardware and software to correct manufacturing errors and early-life component failures. It also uses on-line hardware and software analyses of computer operation after installation to continuously check for errors, so that action can be taken to minimize their consequence. Fault tolerance may employ a combination of hardware redundancy and data rejection to anticipate possible problems.

Increasing Input Reliability

In applying industrial computer control, a user must be concerned with the reliability of the plant inputs, as well as the computer itself. As discussed earlier, these inputs are available either in analog form (e.g., thermocouples, pressure and flow transmitters) or in digital form (e.g., contact closures and pulse inputs). Methods for increasing input reliability usually depend upon a combination of redundant inputs and the analysis and rejection of questionable input data.

In the simplest case, redundancy utilizes two or more independent sensors associated with the same measurand. For example, two thermocouples might be used to measure the temperature of a fluid in a vat. By attaching these two thermocouples to two analog-input points which do not have a common addressing or signal path in the analog-input multiplexer (i.e., they are associated with different switches), an additional degree of redundancy is provided in the event of a block switch failure. If only two thermocouples are used and the data differ between them, a software algorithm must be used to decide which data are valid. A third "tie-breaker" thermocouple can be used. The use of redundant inputs increases cost with no increase in information content except when a failure occurs. This additional cost must be justified on the basis of the importance of the data and the probability of a sensor failure.

Rather than merely comparing data from redundent sensors, it is often possible to use the sensors in such a way as to derive additional information. For example, it is advisable to work with at least two contacts (e.g., breaker closed and breaker open) for verification that a pump is on. This tells a more complete story than a single contact alone (e.g., breaker closed). The second contact is a reinforcement of the first contact and a backup in case the first contact fails. In addition, it provides a means of observing a pattern in the operation of the two contacts, which indicates that the equipment is in the transient state of either starting or stopping. Actually, an additional contact normally would be used to resolve conflict between the other two contacts. This is called a resultant effect contact which can be actuated, in this example, by a differential pressure switch across the pump. It not only verifies the data from the motor-starting contacts, it also detects a pump failure.

Figure 7.2 illustrates the contact input sequences which occur when a pump starts or stops. When the pump is off, the normally-open (NO) contact is closed, and the normally-closed (NC) contact is open; the resultant effect contact is closed, indicating that there is no differential pressure across the pump. When the pump start circuit is energized, the NO contact opens and a short transient period lasts until the NC contact closes. A second transient period lasts until the resultant effect contact opens and the pump operation is verified.

A normal sequence summary, as shown in Fig. 7.2, can be used to determine which contact is malfunctioning. Three additional pieces of information are used for this type analysis: (1) the previous equipment status (i.e., on, off, or transient, as determined from a previous scan of the inputs), (2) the operation being performed (e.g., whether the equipment was ordered to

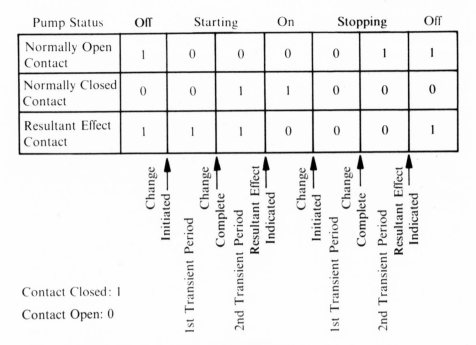

FIG. 7.2
Contact Input Sequences for Pump Start and Stop

start or to stop), and (3) data from a backup analog-input (e.g., measurement of motor power).

Another input diagnostic technique is the Verify Program (Whitman, 1966). It combines input data in as many ways as possible to ascertain correctness of analog and contact data. It verifies backup inputs as well as those being used as primary inputs and operates during the computer's idle time.

There is no need for computers necessarily to be limited by the deficiencies of input instrumentation. The only valid question is at what point is there a balance of required input reliability and the cost of achieving it. This must be determined on an individual basis for each application. In general, cost versus reliability resembles an "inverted-S" curve. Figure 7.3 approximates such a curve for input reliability and indicates that the number of inputs should be increased before increasing the sophistication of analysis.

Increasing Software Reliability

Software reliability is improved through the use of the techniques of simplification, avoidance, and testing. Simplification relies on the premise that errors occur less frequently and are easier to debug if a program is less complex. An example is the use of table-driven programs versus straight-line coded programs. Table-driven programs sacrifice some processing speed because of the need to interpret the table, but they are inherently easier to work with, especially during the debugging operation. Use of structured programming, which employs a limited number of simple program patterns as discussed in Chapter 4, leads to easing of the coding and debugging tasks.

An example of avoidance is the use of additional storage to preclude sharing storage between different programs. This eliminates possible problems when the two programs run concurrently. It also recognizes that there are occasional problems when an operating system fails to properly allocate and schedule main storage in a multiprogramming environment.

Software testing is an effective means of increasing reliability. A thorough test procedure represents a controlled effort to explore methodically the use of the programs and compare the results against expectations. It should be noted that a hurried test may allow bugs to remain which may never be corrected if

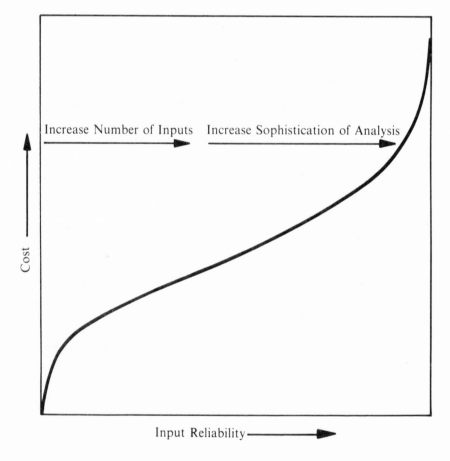

FIG. 7.3
Cost vs. Input Reliability

they occur only infrequently. It is much better to do this testing before installation because it can be costly in terms of plant outages and possible equipment damage to test the programs against the live plant. Programs containing control algorithms must be tested meticulously because they most directly affect the plant operation. They also can respond improperly to plant conditions which were overlooked during program design. After installation, frequent on-line, automatic, diagnostic checks of the software operation are recommended.

Increasing Hardware Reliability

It was stated earlier that current minicomputer design and construction results in a more reliable machine. One aspect of this is that the number of individual components in the system is decreasing drastically with the use of integrated circuits, even though the number of circuits is increasing. The reliability of an integrated circuit is much better than the aggregate of the many individual components it replaces. Furthermore, the decrease in the number of components results in a corresponding decrease in the number of connections which are responsible for a large portion of system failures.

Maintenance is improved because of the modular construction which permits rapid replacement of plug-in modules and cards. Diagnosis is eased, since failures must be isolated only to the replacement unit which, in today's design, may be a major functional unit such as the CPU. These factors decrease mean-time-to-repair (MTR), which increases availability of the system.

Equipment redundancy is often used to increase reliability, commonly by duplicating peripheral equipment and only occasionally by duplicating the computer itself. For the maximum redundancy benefit, all subsystems that affect critical inputs and outputs must be redundant. Otherwise, for example, an analog-to-digital converter, if it is not backed up, can fail and cause the system to go down. In addition, redundant hardware does not protect against software bugs. The same errors are produced with the same effect, for example, in dual computers as in a single computer.

Proper hardware tests prior to installation are essential to good hardware reliability. This testing is discussed in detail in a subsequent section.

The True Cost of Poor System Reliability

There often is an understatement in the value placed by both vendor and user on the cost of poor system reliability. A vendor usually limits his liability to waiving a portion of the monthly cost of the computer for the period of downtime in the case of a leased system and to parts and labor for a specific period of time (e.g., 90 days) in the case of a purchased system. A user is quick to realize, however, that benefits which normally are derived from using the system on the process are lost during this downtime and these often are of greater value.

There are additional factors which add to this cost. First is the value of the user manpower which is employed to detect and correct the problem. However, more significant, but less easily measured, is the cost of losing operator confidence in the system. This is a cumulative loss which gets disproportionately larger with repeated failures. The loss is manifested in the operator more often overriding computer control in favor of manual control. Therefore, the effect of poor system reliability continues to drain potential benefits long after the system is restored. The operator begins to assume that the computer is wrong whenever there is a conflict between the computer output and that of the sensor device, the board instrument, or the operator's intuition. The instinctive reaction is to take the process off computer control. Thus, the true cost of even a small loss of system reliability may be incalculably larger over a period of years.

SIGNAL WIRING PRACTICES

The wiring between signal transmitting instruments or sensors and the computer termination cabinets is a possible source of error in the system. Low-level signal circuits are a particularly vulnerable contributor to system degradation as a result of electrical interference. There are three basic approaches to reducing this interference: avoidance, protection, and compensation. Avoidance is practiced by locating the wiring at a sufficient distance from sources of electrical noise. Protection relates to minimizing the introduction of noise through proper material selection, twisting, shielding, and grounding of the wiring. It is also common to reduce noise that reaches the computer by applying analog filtering (signal conditioning) as part of the analog and digital input subsystems. Another technique is the use of digital filtering, which is a mathematical manipulation of multiple readings of a particular analog-input to attenuate the noise.

The physical location of wire runs often determines how susceptible the system is to electrical interference. Electrical equipment or power distribution lines are common contributors of noise into the system. Allowing adequate separation of the signal wiring from these sources can be a cost-effective solution. Table 7.1 provides recommended minimum separations between signal wiring and power wiring. Signal wiring can be oriented to minimize noise pickup from a strong magnetic or electric field. Runs parallel to power wiring should be avoided and crossovers should be made at right angles.

Wiring separation often is smallest at the approach to the central control area. Cable entrance space to the computer location usually is limited, resulting in crowding and the possibility of noise coupling to sensitive circuits. Planning cable entrances to buildings and cabinets is necessary and important.

Splices or joints in the signal wiring should be avoided, except at required terminal junctions. Furthermore, when wire pairs are brought to terminal strips, they should be connected to adjacent screws or lugs to reduce thermally-induced voltages (EMF's generated by temperature difference of wires contacting dissimilar metals).

Twisted wire is effective in minimizing induced pick-up from magnetic fields. Twisting causes the signal wires to stay in close proximity to each other, reducing the area intersected by an external magnetic field. In addition, twisting wires carrying higher level currents is useful in canceling the magnetic field which is generated by the current.

The use of shielded circuits minimizes capacitive pick-up. Shielding is the enclosing of a signal circuit with high conductivity metal which, in turn, is covered with an insulated sheath. The basic concept associated with the use of shielding to prevent errors due to capacitive pickup is illustrated in Fig. 7.4. In Fig. 7.4(a), a capacitive current flows through the stray capacitance C and the line resistance R to create an error potential in series with the signal voltage V_{sig}. The error potential across R cannot be distinguished from the valid signal V_{sig} and the system reads an erroneous value.

This type of error can be eliminated by shielding. Figure 7.4(b) shows that the low resistance shield causes any capacitive current to flow through the shield to ground. As a result, no error potential is developed across the resistor R and the system can read the signal voltage V_{sig} without error.

The important requirements for shielding are: (1) the shield must be grounded at only one point and (2) the shield must be insulated so that it is grounded only at the intended point. While low level analog wiring requires shielding to minimize picking up stray currents, it is also advisable to shield high level wiring (greater than 30 volts full scale) to lessen its ability to cause interference. An overall shield for multipair cable is suitable and economical for this high level wiring.

TABLE 7.1
Recommended Minimum Separation of Signal
and Power Wiring

Power Wiring Capacity	Recommended Separation (Inches)
125 V 10A	12
250 V 50A	18
440 V 200A	24
5 KV 800A	48

Proper grounding practices have the purpose of eliminating ground loops. A ground loop may be defined as a conducting path (other than primary conductors used purposely as an electrical path) between two ground points which are at different potentials with respect to the earth. Since these ground points are at different potentials, they can provide the driving force for large current flows. This electrical flow can induce noise into cables carrying analog signals and even into the computer circuits if they share a common path.

Proper grounding practices contribute both to reliable system operation and to personnel safety. Various types of circuits, such as sensitive analog

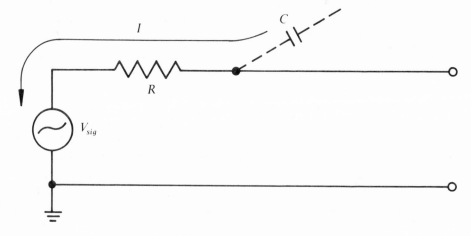

FIG. 7.4a
Capacitive Coupling Without Shielding

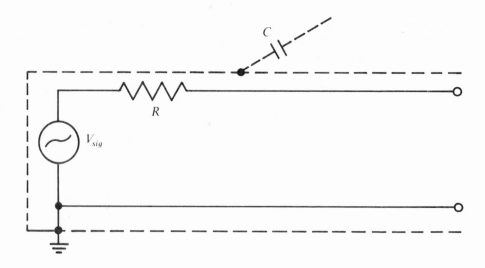

FIG. 7.4b
Capacitive Coupling Limited by Shielding

circuits, are connected to a separate ground system. This system is not intermingled with others, such as one used for peripheral devices and other noise contributors. However, if all of the ground systems were isolated, it would be possible for a person to hazardously become the conductor between two ground points at different potentials. Therefore, for personnel protection, all of the ground systems must be tied together at one point. Restricting the connection only to this point provides no return conduction path and, therefore, no noise-producing ground loop current.

Digital filtering is another means of counteracting the effects of noise entering the system, despite the techniques of avoidance and protection (including analog-input filtering circuits). Usually, noise is considered a random error which is superimposed on a given electrical signal. Figure 7.5 illustrates the variation of a physical quantity and its superimposed noise error over a period of time.

Assuming that the physical measurement has lower frequency components than the data, a mathematical averaging technique can reduce the error. It may be the simple average of a series of readings or a more sophisticated calculation, such as exponential smoothing which derives a new average based on a function of the old average and the new instantaneous value.

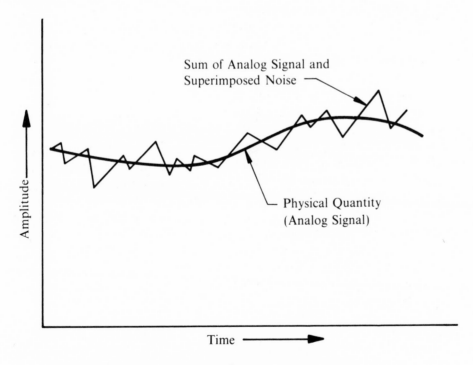

FIG. 7.5
Analog Signal with Superimposed Noise

SYSTEM TESTING

Tests for industrial minicomputers may be considered as a four-part series of tests to demonstrate system quality, workability, and reliability. Demonstration of system performance is of concern to both the vendor and user. However, there must be agreement between the vendor and user about which quantities are to be the indices of performance and how they are to be tested. The four phases of testing are: (1) hardware (pre-ship), (2) software (pre-ship), (3) on-site system, and (4) availability.

Hardware testing has become better understood, due to the publication of a recommended practice in this area by the Instrument Society of America. It identifies the tests to be considered and provides recommended procedures. Detailed specification values to define system acceptance pass/fail criteria should be negotiated between the vendor and user before the system is contracted and, therefore, are not included in the recommended practice. Most of the recommended tests concern individual subsystems, but there are also tests for the full system.

Software testing usually is performed after the system has passed the hardware test. This tends to make the diagnosis of software problems more efficient. The work which is tested in this part include standard software, modified software, and any application programs provided by the vendor.

On-site system testing is performed after the system is installed at the plant site. The purpose of the test is to: (1) establish that the system has not been degraded in transit, subsequent to testing performed at the factory, (2) verify that the machine has been properly installed, and (3) provide the first opportunity to test with live plant signals in the plant environment. The on-site tests resemble an abbreviated version of those which may have been performed at the factory.

Availability testing provides an indication of the probable long-term reliability of the system. The test provides a period of well-documented scrutiny of the computer system operation. The period must be long enough to permit recognition of the possible recurrent nature of certain intermittent problems. The larger computer systems used before the advent of the minicomputer occasionally required a formal commitment of the vendor to correct any uncovered problems (within their responsibility) during this period. There was often a penalty if the system did not achieve a certain availability. This practice largely has disappeared but there is much to be learned from this technique.

Hardware Testing

The publication of the ISA Recommended Practice RP55.1 (American National Standard MC8.1–1975) "Hardware Testing of Digital Process

Computers" provided the first consensus of ideas in this area. Not only were tests and procedures recommended, but also a philosophy of testing. RP55.1 permits the hardware tests to be performed at either the vendor's factory or at the user's site. In some cases, a vendor's normal final test location is not at the factory because of a field merge method of assembling the system, and it is costly to change this procedure. On the other hand, computer diagnosis and repair are considerably more efficient at the factory because of the availability of expert personnel, test equipment, repair tools, and replacement parts.

It is recommended that the vendor and user agree upon which hardware testing specifications are applicable before the system contract is signed. It is not the intent of RP55.1 to define rigid specifications or to set specific acceptance criteria. This recognizes that there are many differences both in vendor product design and in user requirements. As a result, the Recommended Practice is a basic nucleus of tests, but other tests may be substituted or added based on cost, established vendor procedures, and the changing state of the art.

The user must evaluate the cost of various tests versus their value to the particular installation. For example, a humidity test may be essential to a Gulf Coast installation, but unnecessary for one in central Canada. Typical factors affecting the cost of testing are:

(1) Number of separate test configurations required;

(2) Methods of compliance;

(3) Sequence, duration, and location of tests;

(4) Quantity of hardware tested;

(5) Special programming requirements;

(6) Special testing equipment;

(7) Effort required to prepare and perform tests;

(8) Documentation requirements.

The mass production methods utilized in the manufacture of today's minicomputers are significant factors in lower prices and special testing increases costs. However, the additional testing costs may be justified by reduced installation expense, more timely installation, and earlier identification of application problems.

The RP55.1 standard provides test procedures for the following subsystems and functions: (1) Central Processing Unit, including instruction complement, arithmetic and control logic, input/output adapters, I/O direct memory access channel, interrupts, timers, and main storage; (2) Data Processing Input/Output Subsystems, including the attachment circuits which furnish logic controls, along with data links to the input/output bus, the controller which provides the buffer between the input/output bus and the input/output device itself, and the input/output devices; (3) Digital-Input/Output Subsystem, including operation, signal level, delay, noise rejection, counting accuracy, timing accuracy, and interrupt operation; (4) Analog-Input Subsystem, including addressing, speed, accuracy/linearity, noise, common mode and normal mode rejection, input resistance, input overvoltage recovery, DC crosstalk, common mode crosstalk, and gain changing crosstalk; (5) Analog-Output Subsystem, including addressing, accuracy, output capability, capacitive loading, noise, settling time, crosstalk, and droop rate for sample and hold outputs; (6) Total Interacting System, including operation in a simulated real-time environment, in order to check the level of interaction or crosstalk resulting from simultaneous demands on the several subsystems which make up the system; (7) Environmental operation, including temperature and humidity, AC power, and vibration.

The required degree of test documentation also should be indicated in the contractual agreement. RP55.1 describes three types of documentation:

Type I: Statements or any evidence provided by the vendor that the hardware successfully has passed the applicable tests. It may consist only of a certificate or statement of compliance.

Type II: Itemized check list, indicating contractual tests with a certification that each test has been performed successfully. It also may include a history of successful and unsuccessful tests if contractually required.

Type III: Detailed numerical data, printouts, histograms, and other information, compiled during performance of the contractual tests.

Software Testing

Considerable preparation for software testing is required to: (1) plan for most possible results, (2) have the test conditions written into the contract, (3) have a meaningful pass/fail acceptance, and (4) have prior agreement on how the test results are to be interpreted.

Part of the advance preparation is the development of test cases and test data. The driving thought in the user's mind should be that the software must be demonstrated working properly in the context of its intended use, rather than merely working in a general way. The way to accomplish this is to make the test cases comprehensive, covering as many situations as possible. To do this, the user must simulate the use of various types of inputs, including their peculiarities and their abnormal processing demands, if any. The output from the software should be anticipated before the test is run, in order to more readily detect improper operation. This preparation is the user's responsibility.

It is well to incorporate a description of the plan of software testing into the contract. A satisfactory performance level must be defined, including how it is to be judged and by whom. A vendor commitment to correct problems by applying a certain level of resource, or to have it completed in a given period of time, is desirable. It is frustrating to watch benefits being lost because a vendor must correct uncovered problems. At this stage in the project, it is usually impractical to consider going to another vendor, so the user must rely on the integrity of the vendor. If the vendor's commitment is part of the contract, there is at least a recognition on each side of what is expected. The sense of obligation and expectation is the real value of this part of the contract. The user must realize, however, that the vendor undoubtedly has tested the system program thoroughly during its development. As a result, the vendor will not assume automatically that the supplied software is the cause of the problem. Experience has shown that the user-supplied data and software are equally prone to faults.

Watching the vendor respond to these initial software problems is a source of valuable information to the user. Not only is it educational to observe the method of tracking down the problems, but it is also an opportunity to evaluate the capabilities of the vendor personnel who are doing the debugging. In the future, the user may request that the vendor send the same individuals if other software problems develop. In addition, the user should write down the names and locations of the factory experts who are telephoned for their opinions. They also may be a resource that can be contacted in the future. The resource should be used with caution, however, since phone diagnosis is less than an exact art. In addition, local service personnel may not appreciate this apparent distrust of their expertise and ability.

On-Site System Testing

After the computer has been installed at the site, there are both old and new situations to check out. First, an abbreviated version of the factory-performed hardware and software tests should be run, to establish that there has been no deterioration during shipment. If the tests were not run at the factory, then this becomes the first opportunity for comprehensive testing. The on-site test usually is shortened if hardware and software tests were performed previously at the factory and the system probably will be sounder arriving at the site. This promotes plant personnel confidence in the computer.

The next step is to connect the process inputs and outputs. These already should have been calibrated, using conventional techniques. If not, the computer can aid in calibration, since the analog-input subsystem probably represents the most accurate voltmeter in the plant and can read raw signals from instruments more quickly than is possible manually.

Completion of calibration permits implementing scanning, logging and alarming functions, and these aid control tuning. The on-site test is the first opportunity to use live input data, which is necessary for control loop tuning and for the determination of electrical interference being carried on the input lines. Control loop tuning is facilitated (as is actual operation) if "bumpless" transfer has been designed into the programs and hardware. This means that in transferring back and forth between computer control and conventional instrument control, there is automatic rather than manual alignment of the mechanism receiving control, so that there is no jolting of the process variable.

Of the problems that are detected in the various tests, it is well to particularly follow the diagnosis of the more significant ones. Significance depends upon the consequences to the system of a reappearance of the problem. Those of greatest significance are problems which result in shutting the system down or disrupting storage. Next, are factors which affect repeatability of process information or control. Finally, factors which affect peripherals (assuming data are not lost) have a lesser effect if there is means of outputting or inputting on substitute devices.

Availability Testing

The purpose of the availability test is to establish system performance in an environment of well-documented observation, over a period long enough to permit recognition of recurring intermittent problems. Another important aspect is the continued commitment of the vendor to correct any problems (within his area of responsibility) which may be uncovered during the test period.

The end products of the availability test should be:

(1) A fairly representative index of long-term system performance;

(2) Verification of vendor guarantees with respect to availability and failure frequency (or mean time between failures), if such guarantees are provided;

(3) A better debugged and more reliable system.

Computer system requirements vary widely and therefore availability test conditions should be agreed upon mutually by the vendor and user in advance. With the greater reliability of minicomputers, there is a diminished demand for this long-term test. However, even if there is no formal contractual agreement for an availability test, some of the following procedures may be helpful. These procedures promote closer scrutiny of downtime during the first few months of operation and aid in the detection of failure patterns.

The starting date and duration of the tests must be established in advance. The availability test should not be started until hardware and vendor-supplied software are operating properly. Typical test durations are three months (2184 hours = 91 days) or six months (4368 hours = 182 days). The duration of the test should be defined as starting at a certain date and time, and finishing at a certain date and time. It is not equivalent, and should not be acceptable, to use a sliding scale of test duration. A sliding scale means running the test and sliding the three or six months period along, until a period is found which meets the availability requirement.

Downtime of the system is recorded during the period and compared to the agreed upon acceptable amount. A figure of 1% (43 hours 41 minutes for a six months test and 21 hours 51 minutes for a three months test) sometimes is used in the process industries.

Downtime is counted for all unplanned system outages, except those beyond the responsibility of the vendor, such as the following:

(1) Outages caused by equipment other than that of vendor;

(2) Outages caused by plant problems;

(3) Outages during scheduled preventative maintenance, scheduled program debugging, or user-requested tests;

(4) Outages of a peripheral, if a spare device can be substituted before loss of data or control occurs.

Test documentation procedures should require that both vendor and user verify that an outage did occur for a certain duration. The outage immediately should be entered in a log book, although the evaluation may await other information, such as storage dumps, hourly and special logs, and reports from the use of diagnostics. A meeting should be scheduled, both at the midpoint and the end of the test, in order to resolve outages that are still in question. Agreement must be reached on details of notification of the vendor's maintenance personnel, whether traveling time is exempted from downtime to a certain limit, and whether a minimum downtime (e.g., 1 hour) is charged per outage to encourage finding the cause of a problem, rather than just quickly restarting.

It should be emphasized that the comprehensive test procedures described here generally are not included in the terms and conditions offered by most minicomputer vendors. The minicomputer business is dependent on volume in building, testing, selling, and installation, to achieve the low prices which are available today. Vendors typically do their best to ensure that their systems are properly built and tested, since rejects, factory returns, and field problems increase their costs and, as a result, reduce their profit. The user must expect, therefore, that contractual arrangements requiring any additional testing or non-standard procedures will increase the contract price. This can be a significant amount because the planning and execution of special tests is time consuming and labor intensive. Before requiring such tests, therefore, the user should understand the vendor's standard tests and procedures. Based on a judgement as to their adequacy, additional testing can be included in the contract if it seems warranted.

APPLICATION PROGRAM TESTS

After vendor hardware and software have been tested, system start-up progress depends primarily upon detecting and correcting any remaining errors in the physical installation and the user generated programs.

In programming, the expression, "to err is human," is not only unfortunately an excuse: it has become a hallmark. The problem goes beyond having a certain number of errors proportional to the number of instructions written. It is compounded by the several translations that take place, not just between programming languages, but mainly in human communication. Clerical errors are introduced by the terminal or keypunch operator, or by the programmer miswriting a number. Logical errors occur when the programmer has attempted an illogical procedure or has omitted an element of logic. These errors are the easiest to detect. More difficult to detect are communication errors, in which a programmer has not properly interpreted an analyst's intent. These errors cannot be detected by the programmer, who finds the program operating exactly as expected. Such errors occur when an analyst either ambiguously states the requirements, or does not explain them fully. Consequently, it is only the analyst who can detect the resulting discrepancies.

Even after the programmer and analyst have detected and corrected their errors, there may remain a communication gap between what was intended by the user and what was perceived by the analyst. Validation is necessary to ensure that the user's requirements have been satisfied. It is seen, therefore, that with the prospect of three levels of possible error, there must be three levels of testing.

Testing for Programmer Errors

Most clerical and logical errors are detected by the programmer through use of test data that simulate the various conditions that the program has been designed to handle. Presumably, these errors are caught long before the start-up phase of the project. To reach this point, the programmer has desk-checked the coding, checked the use of instructions and subroutines, planned tests for the mainline logic and also for various routines, exceptions, and combinations of switch settings. In addition, the design and code may have been subjected to design reviews, code inspections, and analyses by an independent test specialist. Test data then are created and compared to the test plan. The programs are run, using the test data, and the results are compared to expected results obtained through manual calculation and other techniques. The less probable situations should be included in the test data, because they may not occur in actual operation for some time. Despite this approach, it still should be expected that some programmer errors will be uncovered with the use of live inputs during start up.

Testing for Analyst Errors

The next level of testing requires that the analyst verify that the program works exactly according to his understanding of the requirements. This reflects whether the analyst's instructions to the programmer were clear and properly interpreted. During this test, the analyst prepares the test data, which normally includes some random data to determine program behavior in unplanned situations.

The analyst also is interested in verifying that the components of the system work well together. This is done by using various interacting systems tests, including cases which demonstrate how man interacts with the programs. The analyst also seeks to anticipate problems, by studying the programming changes that have already been made, to determine if there is any pattern which might lead to the need for further changes. Finally, the analyst must assess whether the system as a whole is operating efficiently, according to the criteria which have been defined during the design.

Testing for User Errors

The last level of application program testing verifies that the user requirements have been satisfied. Errors remaining at this point typically are limited to conditions which were not tested previously, or which are caused by improper design. Design deficiencies at this point might indicate user oversight or poor communication with the analyst. The user normally is not interested in observing individual program operation, but rather is concerned with the operation of the complete system. The user may generate test data for certain key conditions of concern, but is more likely to rely heavily on live data. These tests consist of checking to verify that particular inputs give the proper outputs. The user closely checks the handling of manual inputs to the system, whether they are sources such as the operator, or from an off-line laboratory.

System controls, whereby invalid operator requests or unreasonable input data are rejected, also are checked by the user. A by-product of a thorough user test is the training of operators and a familiarization of plant management with the system.

SYSTEM MAINTENANCE

It has been mentioned that system availability can be increased through design and testing measures which increase the mean-time-between-failure (MTBF). Availability also can be increased by decreasing the mean-time-to-repair (MTR). Proper system maintenance can contribute substantially to this objective.

A decision must be made whether to maintain the system through the use of plant personnel, or through the use of an external service group, such as the computer vendor. Each plant is a unique situation with respect to its ability to support, train, and keep qualified maintenance personnel. Similarly, it should not be taken for granted that a vendor necessarily is in a better position to provide maintenance than the user. It is a function of the location of the plant with respect to the location of the vendor's closest maintenance person and, sometimes, whether the user is willing to pay for full-time use of the service person on the plant site.

Quick, competent response is vital to good system maintenance. Planning in advance for the maintenance of the system contributes to the success of the installation. Minicomputers generally are quite reliable; however, when a problem does occur, it is important to get the system back in service, generating benefits for the user as quickly as possible.

Internal Systems Maintenance

If system maintenance is to be supported internally, the maintenance and operational aspects of a computer control system probably can be handled best by assigning total system responsibility to one individual, usually a control system engineer. A person with a background in electronics, process operation, and process control has the ideal qualifications for a computer system engineer. It often is difficult, however, to find an individual with experience in all three areas. It probably is easier for an electronics expert to learn the required process operation and control knowledge, than for a process expert to acquire the necessary knowledge of electronics. There also should be two qualified craftsmen available to assist the control engineer with system maintenance. These craftsmen should have a good electronics background and have the capability for being trained to maintain digital computer equipment. Depending on the size and complexity of the system, this team may provide service for one or more systems.

The type of organization that is established to handle system maintenance is important and is influenced by plant policy and the availability of manpower. In the interest of efficiency, it is often decided that the craftsmen should report directly to the system engineer. This group should have the primary responsibility for all the analytical and conventional instrumentation providing inputs to the computer, as well as for the computer hardware. Because of their technical capability, this group often is assigned the responsibility for all of the analytical instrumentation as well. Qualification requirements for analytical instrumentation maintenance compare more closely to those for computer system maintenance than do those for conventional instrumentation maintenance. On occasion, the more capable analytical maintenance people have been successfully upgraded for computer system maintenance. The analytical maintenance load also helps keep the system people busy.

However, there still may be a problem initially keeping these personnel fully occupied. Once a computer control system is in service, it usually requires very little maintenance. In general, one to three days of preventive maintenance per month is sufficient for typical systems. It is a good possibility that both the analytical instruments and a single computer control system will not require two craftsmen full time. However, it is desirable to have at least two craftsmen trained on the computer in order to have a backup.

Once a computer system goes into operation, there is little opportunity to train on the job. In fact, service personnel generally work on the system so infrequently that staying conversant with the system becomes a problem. It is recommended that as much training as possible be given before installation. The control engineer and craftsmen normally attend the schools taught by the computer manufacturer or system integrator. The control engineer should attend both the programming and maintenance schools, whereas the craftsmen might attend only the maintenance school. In addition, it may be advisable for the control engineer to be at the vendor's factory during final system assembly and checkout, if the vendor provides this opportunity. This provides an opportunity to work on the system and become thoroughly familiar with its operation prior to installation. With the advent of mass-produced computer systems, however, this practice is becoming less common and, if allowed, usually involves an additional fee.

Vendor-Supported Maintenance

It is quite common for maintenance to be provided by the hardware supplier or by an external service organization. An advantage of this approach is the availability of personnel who know the computer intimately and have good diagnostic and repair experience. This yields quick analysis and correction of problems. Since these service personnel work full-time on the same or related models of the computer system, they have up-to-date skills and experience which are helpful and valuable. They also have ready access to other expert personnel who can assist on particularly difficult problems. One factor to be considered is the travel time involved. As stated earlier, rapid repair increases availability and, therefore, the longer it takes the maintenance person to get to the site, the more system outage accrues. In addition, if a reasonable amount of spare parts is not stocked locally by the vendor, then it must be kept on hand at the plant or the repair time increases. This, of course, is also true if maintenance is performed by plant personnel.

There are a variety of vendor maintenance plans available. A common plan is geared to a principal period, most commonly the normal weekday working hours, in which service calls are made with a stated normal response of between four and eight hours. This plan requires an extra charge for after-hours calls or, for an additional flat rate, the service hours can be extended for two or three shifts coverage and weekends. Another plan charges for all calls on a time and materials basis and guarantees availability of personnel. All plans should clearly state whether the service rates include the cost of replacement parts and whether the user or vendor is responsible for having the parts on hand. It should be stated whether travel expenses are additional and whether the hourly rates apply against travel time.

DOCUMENTATION

Documentation often is a much maligned and misunderstood project task. It usually is thought of as a necessary evil and almost anticlimactic in the implementation schedule. It is, however, a necessary requirement and can significantly affect the outcome of a computer control project.

The use of documentation for historical purposes is only one of its four uses. It is also valuable for communication, project control, and instruction. The communication requirement addresses the need for orderly, distortion-free transfer of project information between user, systems analyst, and programmer for all project phases and tasks. When documentation is a vehicle for this communication, it means that there is always current recorded information, less chance for misinterpretation or forgetting, and a built-in back-up remedy for the problems that may occur when a key team member leaves before project completion.

Documentation for project control should provide a project description at each phase and set the performance criteria to be satisfied in succeeding stages of the project. Management, therefore, has a standard for comparing completed work. Proper documentation also allows a quality control review throughout development, rather than relying on one final review.

The final purpose of documentation is as an instructional medium, especially for the user. Without this source of information, the user's understanding of the system is impaired and, as a result, the system may not be utilized fully.

Documentation can be subdivided into five sections: project proposal, system, program, instrumentation, and operation. These are discussed in detail in Chapter 6 and the reader is referred to that material. This brief mention of documentation is included for emphasis and as a reminder of its vital role in a successful project.

PROJECT POST-COMPLETION AUDIT

The main objective of the post-installation audit is to verify that the feasibility study objectives have been accomplished. This is a proper function of management, although quite often it is delegated downward in the organization. Occasionally, the only group with the technical competence to evaluate the completed project is the very group which did the implementation. If this is the case, lack of objectivity can be partly counterbalanced by requiring a report which contains actual data (sampled systematically) and a logical presentation of how these data can be interpreted. Management may then assess whether the interpretation appears to be unbiased and if the conclusions are valid.

The initial system proposal and subsequent documentation should provide the bulk of elements to be evaluated in the audit. The audit is accomplished through interviews, observation of the system in operation, and review of plant data derived both from the computer and other plant logs. The audit need not be only an evaluation, but can contain recommended modifications, if warranted. This recognizes that there may be weaknesses in the system that can be corrected. These may relate to improvements in the following areas:

(1) Adherence to original specifications or recommendations for changes;

(2) An approach to achieve original or modified objectives;

(3) The ability of the user to communicate with or modify the system;

(4) Operating efficiency;

(5) Documentation.

In addition to considering benefits, it is also relevent to evaluate attainment of specifications, efficiency, budgets, schedules, and ease of use. It also is recommended that less extensive audits be continued on a periodic basis to look for deterioration of system use or benefits.

Evaluating Benefits and Budgets

It may seem simple to compare achieved benefits with the predicted amount and thereby determine fulfillment of the original economic goals. In reality, the first obstacle is that the numbers themselves may be subject to interpretation. It may be difficult to find comparable before and after periods of operation when the system has been added to an existing plant. Therefore, adjustments must be made, for example, to account for a difference in plant outages, if a monthly throughput is being measured, and for different climatic conditions, if ambient temperature affects yield. Sometimes it is even more difficult to assess effects of other process, equipment, or procedural changes, which occurred coincident with the computer system implementation. Another proper question is whether the benefits could have been obtained by some other means. An example is the use of an analog instrumentation system to attain the same control benefits as the installed computer. This question also addresses whether a sufficient exploration of design alternatives was made during the project initiation phase.

The project budget should be examined to determine whether the initial project costs exceeded the estimate. Also, the future recurring annual operating costs should be updated to reflect all charges which are attributable to the system.

Evaluating Specifications and Schedules

The benefit and budget audit focuses on the achievement of the financial objectives of the project. It is always possible that the project team has been successful in solving the wrong problem! The concept of alternate opportunities states that there may have been a more beneficial computer project or other capital expenditure which was postponed or completely overlooked, while money and human resources were spent on this project. It is admittedly a difficult question to answer, especially for someone not familiar with the particular plant, other plant problems, the extent that the user rather than the system analyst determined the objectives, and whether the achieved objectives were exactly what the user understood they would be.

An attempt should also be made to evaluate whether the non-quantifiable goals are being achieved. Many project proposals include statements about benefits which cannot be equated to dollars and, therefore, are not included in rate-of-return calculations. This does not mean, however, that their achievement should not be evaluated or that it is not important to attain them.

Schedules are evaluated by comparing completion of project milestones to the original schedule. If the project was behind schedule in achieving milestone points until near the end of the project, it may indicate a hurried completion with the potential consequence of some neglected tasks or tests.

Evaluating Efficiency and Use

Efficiency and ease of use are considered together because one often is traded for the other. A very tightly-written program, for example, may be very efficient in terms of storage usage and processing time, but may be quite difficult to debug or modify. Generally, user ease of use is more important in industrial computer control than is program efficiency. An examination of the procedures and disciplines required to modify the programs on the basis of changed plant conditions and objectives, provides some insight into whether ease of use or program efficiency was accentuated in the design.

A Caution

A post-completion audit should not be a witchhunt! Its primary purpose should be an objective evaluation of the project success, with the idea that future projects can be made even more successful. It is rare that a computer control project, or any other project, achieves all of its original objectives. It is equally rare when the audit does not reveal some benefits that were totally unanticipated during the initial study and planning.

BIBLIOGRAPHY

Anon., "RP55.1: Hardware Testing of Digital Process Computers," Instrument Society of America, Pittsburgh, Pennsylvania, October 1971, reaffirmed 1975. (Also American National Standard MC8.1—1975).

Bitticker, W. R., "The Process Operator—Heart of Production," Proceedings of the International Federation of Automatic Control Symposium, Purdue University, Lafayette, Indiana, August 3–6, 1971, p. 96.

Constable, G. J., "Managerial Problems Associated with Computer Process Control," Proceedings of the International Federation of Automatic Control Symposium, Purdue University, Lafayette, Indiana, August 3–6, 1971, p. 74.

Gray, M., and London, K. R., *Documentation Standards*, Brandon Systems Press, Inc., Princeton, New Jersey, 1970.

Harrison, T. J., *Handbook of Industrial Control Computers*, John Wiley & Sons, New York, 1972.

Hodges, K. J. H., "A Fault-Tolerant Multiprocessor Design for Real-Time Control," *Computer Design*, December, 1973, p. 75.

McCracken, D. D., "Revolution in Programming—an Overview," *Datamation*, December 1973, p. 50.

Ott, H. W., *Noise Reduction Techniques in Electronics Systems*, John Wiley & Sons, New York, 1976.

Whitman, K. A., "Starting a Pump Under Computer Control," *Chemical Engineering*, January 2, 1967, p. 81.

Whitman, K. A., "Computer Monitoring and Surveillance of Process Equipment," *Instrument Technology*, July 1972, p. 50.

Whitman, K. A., "Organizing the Program for Control," *Chemical Engineering*, December 5, 1966, p. 135.

8 MINIS, MICROS, AND MISCELLANY

Thomas J. Harrison, Ph.D.
INTERNATIONAL BUSINESS MACHINES CORPORATION,
BOCA RATON, FLORIDA

The previous seven chapters have been arranged in essentially chronological order, starting with the basics of hardware and software, and proceeding through the steps involved in designing and installing an industrial computer system. Along the way, some of the jargon associated with the computer industry, such as bits and bytes, has been introduced. By necessity, however, this treatment has been incomplete and many concepts, terms, and current topics have not been discussed. The purpose of this chapter is to consider some of these additional topics which did not fit earlier in the book.

Microprocessors and microcomputers are a relatively recent development which promise to continue the rapid evolutionary growth of computer applications. Much of this evolution has been spawned by a corresponding evolution in the development of transistor circuits and large-scale integration (LSI). Coupled with this semiconductor evolution are economic factors which have a significant effect on both semiconductor developments and the use of semiconductors in minicomputers and microcomputers. These coupled effects are considered briefly in this chapter.

Microprocessors today are undergoing a rapid evolution in physical characteristics, price, and application, which is not dissimilar to that experienced with minicomputers in the late 1960's. Microprocessors are finding application in TV games, microwave oven controls, industrial controls, small computers, and big computers. They often are treated as a unique development which is radically different from the previous generations of computers. Although different and revolutionary in some ways, in other ways microcomputers are very similar to minicomputers and, for that matter, to large computers. This chapter considers the use of microcomputers in a variety of applications and discusses the similarities and differences which may affect the use of the information presented in the previous chapters.

Along with evolutionary growth and changes in the computer itself, the manner in which computers are applied in industrial applications also is evolving. A recent development, made possible by the lower price of minicomputers and microcomputers, is the use of a number of interconnected computers to satisfy an application, or group of applications, which in the past would have used a medium or large central computer. These interconnected computers, often known as computer networks or distributed processors, have advantages in certain situations. Reading the current literature sometimes gives one the impression that distributed processing is the panacea for all applications; in this author's opinion, distributed processing is merely one of a number of techniques available to the system designer to solve an application problem. This idea and some of the possible configurations of distributed processing networks also are explored in this chapter.

THE COMPUTER EVOLUTION

The events in the development of computers often have been called revolutionary. But just as the difference between a fire and an explosion is the rate of oxidation, the difference between an evolution and a revolution often is a matter only of the rate of change. The basic concepts of a computer were described several hundred years ago. The first practical application in the United States probably was the tabulating equipment developed for the 1890 census. But it was the requirements of World War II, coupled with advances in electrical and electronic technology, which spurred the early development of computers as they are known today. One of the first of the modern computers was developed to calculate the ballistic tables required for artillery. This early effort was largely government-funded. Succeeding commercial developments resulted from the recognition that the capabilities of the computer could be applied economically to the information-processing needs of many businesses. Although some of the earliest computers were installed for research purposes, almost the entire history of computer development has been driven by economics. Computers provide profits for the commercial and industrial user, either through savings on expenses or by providing a capability which cannot be realized any other way.

Obviously, the expenses associated with the use of a computer detract from the additional profit. Since the price of the computer is one of these expenses, the hardware cost is a factor in any economic evaluation of the use of a computer. From the very beginning of the modern use of computers, there has been a rapid and steady decrease in hardware cost. This has been largely the effect of competition, volume production, and the rapid decrease in the cost of the electronic circuits from which the computer is built. Each of these factors, and their interaction, is considered briefly in this section.

Advances in Electronic Technology

Tabulating machines, the forerunner of the electronic digital computer, were constructed using relays as logic elements. The relay is an electro-mechanical switch whose contacts can be closed ("on") when the relay is energized and open ("off") when not energized. Thus, it is a two-state device and can be used to perform the various digital logic functions described in Chapter 2. Relays still are used to perform simple information-processing functions in power control circuits, where the ability of the relay to handle high voltages and currents provides an advantage when compared to semi-conductor switches. Relays, however, have the disadvantages of requiring significant operating power per logic function and they are slow compared to semiconductor switches. Even a high-speed relay requires several milliseconds to operate, compared to the submicrosecond switching speeds of transistor switches.

The first electronic digital computers were constructed using vacuum tubes. Vacuum tube computers were designed and marketed through the 1950's. The vacuum tube logic circuit provided a significant speed increase over its relay counterpart. It had the disadvantages of relatively high power, high heat dissipation, and relatively poor reliability. The power consumed and the heat dissipated were largely the result of the heated filament and high signal voltage necessary for the tube's operation. Most of us can remember that vacuum tube radios and early television sets generated enough heat to become noticeably warm to the touch. The vacuum tube computer contained thousands of vacuum tubes and cooling was a major problem. In addition, although the reliability of a single vacuum tube was quite good, when thousands were combined in a computer, the resulting reliability was rather poor; early experimental computers often had a mean-time-between-failure (MTBF) of only a few hours. Nevertheless, the computational capability in even a few hours of operation was equal to several thousand man-hours of manual effort. It was this increase in performance that further spurred the efforts to develop the computer for commercial, research, and military applications.

The semiconductor transistor was discovered by researchers at Bell

Telephone Laboratories in 1947. Even prior to this time, however, it was known that certain materials, when placed in contact with a fine metal wire would produce a rectifying junction. This was the same phenomenon known since the early days of radio, which was utilized in the "cat's whisker" detector of the crystal set. The important discovery in 1947 was that two metal contacts placed in close proximity on a suitably prepared piece of semiconductor material would produce a device that exhibited current gain; that is, a small control current injected at one electrode could control a much larger current injected at another electrode. These early devices were known as "point-contact transistors." They consumed only minute amounts of power compared to the vacuum tube and showed promise for switching from "on" to "off" faster.

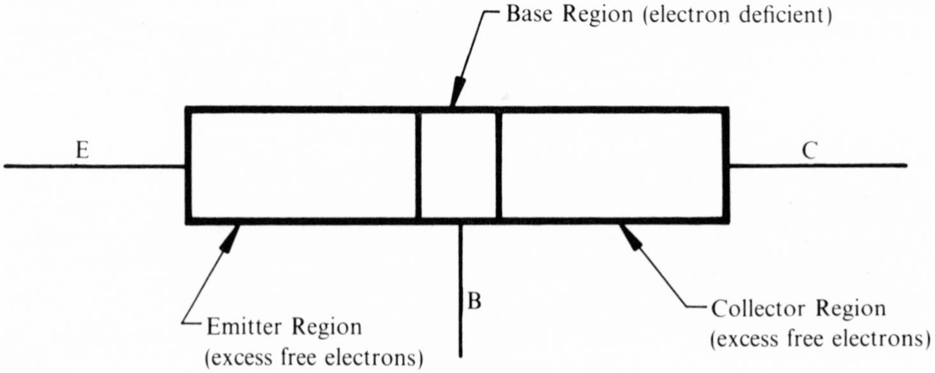

Base Region (electron deficient)

E

C

B

Emitter Region
(excess free electrons)

Collector Region
(excess free electrons)

FIG. 8.1
Basic Junction Transistor

It was not until the late 1950's, however, that the transistor was utilized in a commercial computer. By this time, a second type of transistor, known as the bipolar junction transistor, had been developed, which had significant advantages over the earlier point-contact transistor. In a junction transistor, a junction is formed as a transition between a crystalline semiconductor material (germanium in the early days, now silicon) containing an excess number of free electrons and the same material containing a deficiency of electrons. By forming a second junction very near the first, in which the transition is from material having a deficiency of free electrons back to material having an excess of free electrons, a very thin "base region" is formed. This is shown schematically in Fig. 8.1. A voltage placed across the two junctions, from the "collector" to the "emitter," causes a current to flow whose magnitude can be controlled by a current between the "base" and either the collector or emitter. The magnitude of the current flowing between the collector and emitter can be several orders of magnitude greater than the control current flowing into the base. Thus, useful current, voltage, and power gain are available and the device can be used for control and amplification of electron signals.

The foregoing explanation of transistor operation is greatly simplified.

Since the initial discovery of the transistor, thousands of improvements have been developed and put into commercial use. To a very large extent, it is these improvements which have made a major contribution to the evolution of computers. Of most importance have been improvements relating to reducing the size and cost of transistors, increasing their switching speed, and reducing their power consumption.

The initial transistors used in computers were constructed on a "chip" of semiconductor material which was about 0.1 inch (100 mils, 1 mil = 0.001 inch) square. The chip was mounted in a small metal "can" about 0.4 inch in diameter and 0.25 inch high. This represented a vast reduction in size below the comparable vacuum tube which was about 2 inches high and 0.75 inch in diameter.

The semiconductor material used today is silicon to which minute amounts of other metals (phosphorus, arsenic, boron, gold, etc.) are added to provide materials which either have an excess or deficiency of free electrons. In making a transistor, a single crystal of pure silicon is prepared by specialized techniques to provide an ingot which is between two and four inches in diameter and on the order of 12 inches long. This ingot is sliced into very thin circular "wafers," on which multiple transistor chips can be fabricated simultaneously through the use of a series of steps utilizing various photographic and chemical techniques.

Although shown in Fig. 8.1 as being bar shaped, transistors actually are fabricated on the surface of the silicon wafer by selective etching and doping. Doping is the procedure whereby the minute amounts of other metals (impurities) are added to selected regions of the silicon wafer to provide the excess or deficiency of free electrons necessary for transistor action. The regions to be treated are determined by the transistor designer and drawn hundreds of times larger than real size. By photographing the pattern and reducing it to its final size, a negative is produced very similar to the common black-and-white photographic negative. This negative is known as a "mask." Light can pass through the transparent portions of the mask and is blocked by the opaque regions.

The wafer is coated with a photosensitive material similar to the emulsion on photographic film. It is then exposed to light, using the previously prepared mask. By chemically "developing" the exposed wafer, similar to developing black-and-white film, regions through the coating can be opened to expose the silicon. By selectively etching these open regions and exposing them to the desired impurities at high temperatures, the silicon beneath the open regions can be transformed into doped silicon, having either an excess or a deficiency of electrons. By repeating the process several times using different masks, the desired configuration for the base, collector, and emitter regions of the transistor is produced. As a final step, a metallic contact, called a "pad," is deposited on each of the three regions.

Since the wafer is several inches in diameter and each transistor is only about 0.1 inch square, hundreds of transistors can be produced simultaneously on a single wafer. This is done using a step-and-repeat camera to expose a matrix of transistor images using a single mask. When all of the masking and chemical processing steps necessary to produce the transistors have been completed, the transistors are separated into discrete devices by scribing and breaking the wafer into individual chips, each containing one transistor. This is known as "dicing" the wafer. After testing, very fine wires are bonded to the metallic pads and the transistor is mounted in a "can" or similar package.

This explanation of the fabrication of transistors necessarily is simplified and, in fact, current methods use many additional techniques somewhat different from those described here. However, this simplified description has been included to provide the basis for understanding the evolution of semiconductor transistor technology, which has had a dramatic effect on the design of computers.

In the early 1960's, discrete transistors were combined with other discrete electrical components, such as resistors and capacitors, to form logic circuits similar to those described in Chapter 2. From a packaging density point of view, these circuits represented a vast improvement over the previous vacuum tube circuits. A complete logic circuit easily could be fabricated on a printed circuit card about three inches by four inches in size with an assembled thickness of less than 0.5 inch. The power consumed and dissipated as heat in the circuit was only a small fraction of the power of a comparable vacuum tube circuit.

Because of the degree of quality control which is possible in the manufacturing process and the fact that nothing is consumed in the operation of the transistor (as compared to the vacuum tube where the filament eventually is consumed by oxidation), the transistor also has inherently higher reliability when operated within its specifications. A disadvantage compared to vacuum tubes is that it is a relatively fragile device, which is affected greatly by high temperatures; it will not withstand overload conditions and high temperature to the same degree as the relatively rugged vacuum tube. As a result, the circuit and system designer must take adequate precautions if the higher reliability is to be realized.

As transistor technology developed, it was found that the wires interconnecting two or more transistors could be fabricated on the same silicon chip, using photo-chemical techniques similar to those used in fabricating the transistor. Similarly, resistors can be combined with the transistors on the silicon chip. This led to the development in 1961 of the "integrated circuit," or IC, whereby an entire logic circuit could be fabricated on a single silicon chip.

With concurrent advances in the wafer processing and optical techniques, the integrated circuit could then be produced on a chip about the same size as the previous chip for the transistor alone. The integrated circuit is mounted in a carrier or can of about the same size, so that a space savings on the order of 10:1 was achieved. The cost of producing the integrated circuit using mass production techniques remained about equal to that of producing a single discrete transistor, so a similar cost improvement per circuit was realized. Additional savings were realized because the integrated circuit eliminates the need to mount additional discrete components on the printed circuit card, a relatively time-consuming and expensive operation.

Somewhere in the continuing evolution of semiconductor technology, the term "large scale integration" (LSI) was coined, to describe an integrated circuit which contains over 100 logic circuits on a single chip. This capability was reached by 1968 and "very large scale integration" (VLSI) is a term currently being discussed. It should be noted that all of these advances have been based on improvements and refinement of previous techniques. Although there have been a few revolutionary developments, many of the improvements can be viewed as a steady, continuing evolution. The evolution is continuing, so that today microprocessors containing several thousand logic circuits, and storage chips containing 16K bits of storage on a single 200 mil chip, are being used commercially. They are being used, however, not because they merely are possible to fabricate, but rather because they provide economic and/or performance advantages.

The Economics of the Computer Evolution

The economic factors underlying the evolution of computers are extremely complex. It is clear, however, that the economic factors have been the driving force, both in terms of the user's interest in new applications and the computer vendor's interest in a higher performance, lower-priced product. The improvements in semiconductor technology, coupled with competition, have been major factors in reducing the cost of computing significantly and continually for the past several decades. An extensive and exact economic analysis is beyond the bounds of this book and the capabilities of this author. However, certain aspects of the economics of the computer evolution easily are recognized and worthy of discussion to understand the origin and current interest in minicomputers and microcomputers.

An estimate of the reduced costs of computer circuits can be derived. The vacuum tubes used in early computers were similar to those still produced today. A flip-flop required either two tubes or a dual element tube which, in quantity, can be estimated as costing about $2.00. When combined with a tube socket, a handful of discrete resistors and capacitors, and a carrier, the cost of a single computer circuit constructed with vacuum tubes would be on the order of $3.00. A microprocessor, utilizing the most recent semiconductor technology, is available in quantity for less than $10.00 in 1977. Such a microprocessor represents about 2000 logic circuits, providing a cost of

$0.005/circuit. The cost improvement, therefore, is on the order of 600:1. This comparison is simplistic, in that logic circuits comprise only a portion of the total computer cost. The cost of the package and power, specifically, have not been included. These costs also have decreased substantially due to the lower power requirements and the reduced size of integrated circuits. Despite its simplicity, however, this estimate shows that semiconductor technology improvements have been a major factor in reducing the costs of computers.

A similarly simplistic view of semiconductor processing costs provides some insight into the reasons for the reduced cost. Very roughly, the cost of processing a semiconductor wafer is constant for a given process and logic technology. The percentage of good chips on the wafer (called "yield") is a major factor in determining the cost of the good chips. Assuming a satisfactory yield which is relatively constant, the cost of the chip is relatively constant for a given chip size, whether it contains a single transistor or a complete microprocessor containing 2000 circuits. The impetus for increasing the circuit density on each chip, therefore, is primarily economic, in that the cost per circuit tends to be reduced with increasing density.

The processing of semiconductor wafers is an intricate and precision process. It requires specialized automated equipment which is extremely expensive to build, maintain, and operate. Similarly, the preparation of the masks is a time-consuming and expensive process, even with substantial assistance from computerized methods. A key factor, therefore, is that the high development and capital expenses must be amortized over a large number of chips. This implies that integrated circuits must be mass-produced to realize the maximum economic benefits.

The actual production of the computer itself is similar, in that the application of mass-production techniques is a major factor in the final cost. Early computers were produced one at a time and involved thousands of man-hours by teams of highly-skilled technicians. In today's economic environment, a similar labor expense would exceed the current selling price of a minicomputer! As a result, highly automated mass-production techniques are utilized in the construction of minicomputers. This dictates that many copies of the same machine must be produced and that any special features must bear the additional cost of individualized treatment. It also indicates that the computer designer must design the hardware in such a way that it can be used in a wide variety of applications with little, or no, modification.

This economic picture is summarized by the diagram of Fig. 8.2. Semiconductor process improvements (1) contribute directly to lower circuit cost through improvement in yields and lower processing costs. Process improvements also allow higher circuit densities per chip, as described above. The higher circuit density (2) contributes to lower circuit costs, since the processing cost at the wafer level may be approximately constant. Higher density circuits and circuit design improvements also can contribute indirectly

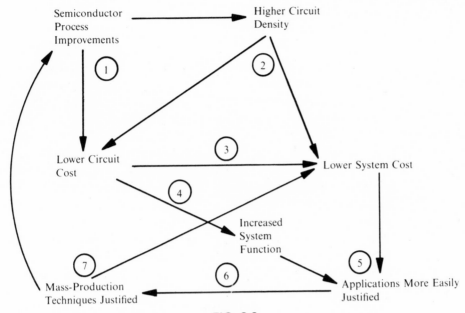

FIG. 8.2
Computer System Evolution Factors

to lower system cost through savings in packaging and power. Lower circuit cost directly contributes to lower system cost (3). It also, however, provides the alternative of providing additional hardware function at approximately the same cost (4).

Either as the result of lower system cost or increased system function, applications are more easily justified (5). This expands the number of applications in which computers can provide an economic benefit and, as a result, the demand for computers increases. This increased demand and greater number of applications provides the justification for the necessary capital and development investment in mass-production techniques and equipment (6). The mass-production techniques further lower product cost and also provide additional justification for continuing improvements in the semiconductor production processes (7).

The interrelationship between the evolutionary factors illustrated in Fig. 8.2 is synergistic, and this effect has been a primary reason for the continuing decline in minicomputer prices while, at the same time, providing an increase in performance and functional capability. It is noteworthy that sales quantity enters the diagram at a number of points and is an essential ingredient for the synergistic effect. Also important, but not indicated in the diagram, is the competitive environment which exists. Every technological advance which provides an economic benefit is seized upon by the vendors to provide products which are either better in some way or less expensive.

The Microcomputer Evolution

The technology and economic factors described above "caused" the microcomputer. The semiconductor technology advanced to the point that it was technically possible to fabricate a "computer on a chip." A large number of semiconductor products were being utilized in industry and provided the necessary volume base for the justification of the equipment necessary to build a microcomputer. And lastly, the economic factors were such that the microprocessor represented a profitable product for the semiconductor manufacturer.

"Minicomputer" was not defined precisely in this book (see the discussion in the Preface); neither will the terms "microprocessor" and "microcomputer" be defined in a rigorous and precise manner. However, a microprocessor fundamentally is a processor fabricated on one, or a small number, of chips. When combined with storage chips and other peripheral circuits to provide the capabilities of a computer, the resulting configuration is called a microcomputer.

The prefix "micro" is relative and really only indicates that the computer or processor is smaller than a "mini," in much the same way that "mini" merely implies something smaller than a "big" computer. Neither prefix implies that the functional capability or performance is "mini" or "micro." Minicomputers today have instruction sets and performance comparable to the so-called medium-scale computers; similarly, microcomputers have functional capability and performance approaching that of the small minicomputer. The microcomputer is no more than a downward extension of the total range of computers that has evolved over the past 30 years.

USING MICROCOMPUTERS AND MICROPROCESSORS

Microcomputers and microprocessors today are being used in a variety of products ranging from entertainment devices to sophisticated research instrumentation. In many cases, the user is not aware that a microprocessor is being used. Consumer products make a significant contribution to the volume requirement for an LSI microprocessor. One of the earliest examples of a consumer microprocessor product is the hand-held calculator. The arithmetic portion of such a calculator is, in reality, a special-purpose processor. It is special purpose, in that the hardware functions provided are chosen specifically to be optimum for the keyboard input, display output, and decimal arithmetic functions required in a calculator. The effect of volume and competitive pressure clearly is evident in the case of the hand-held calculator which, when first introduced, cost hundreds of dollars and today sometimes is given away as an advertising novelty.

Similar examples of consumer products utilizing microprocessors are plentiful. The TV games made popular last Christmas are microprocessor-based. Microwave ovens, sewing machines, and washing machines incorporate microprocessors as the control element. A "personal computer" application, based on the microcomputer, is growing among hobbyists at a rate far greater, for example, than amateur radio grew in its early days.

These few examples illustrate the pervasive application of micro-processors today, and new applications are being introduced every day. It is impossible and inappropriate to attempt to discuss all of these applications. However, it is instructive to consider the manner in which microprocessors and microcomputers are being utilized, both in consumer products and in computer and industrial control applications. For this purpose, the applications are categorized as controllers and "buried" micros, micros as "engines," and micros as computers.

Controllers and "Buried" Micros

A "buried" micro is a microprocessor which is imbedded in a piece of equipment in such a way that its existence is not obvious or known to the user of the equipment. Most consumer uses of microprocessors fall into this category. The user of a microwave oven, for example, is not aware that pushing the control buttons actually initiates the execution of a program in a microprocessor.

The primary justification for the use of the microprocessor in these applications is that it can provide equal or greater function at lower cost when compared to alternatives. The general-purpose nature and low cost of the mass-produced, general-purpose microprocessor provides a flexible component which can be personalized, through programming, to provide the functions required by a wide variety of products. Since the cost of additional functions is primarily the cost of additional program development (amortized over many copies) and some additional storage, it is relatively easy to provide functions which otherwise cannot be justified. The alternative of developing a custom digital or analog circuit for each product results in high development cost and a higher unit product cost because the amortization base is much smaller.

Buried micros can be utilized within the overall structure of an industrial computer system. The existence of these micros may, or may not, be known to the computer user. As in the case of consumer products, the justification for their use is economics and function.

As described in Chapter 3, most peripheral equipment used with the minicomputer processor is connected to the I/O channel by means of an "attachment." The attachment hardware performs functions related to the operation of both the channel and the peripheral device. These functions include such things as address detection and decoding, timing, and error detection and correction. Some of the functions are independent of the particular device being attached; other functions are unique to the particular peripheral device.

The microprocessor can be used as a device controller in these peripheral attachments. Functions common to all peripheral devices are provided by means of common subroutines stored in a memory associated with the microprocessor. Specialized subroutines related to the particular device also are written by the developer and stored in this same storage to provide the personalization required by the peripheral device. For example, the error recovery routines for a disk file are distinctly different from those for a printer. In addition, the general-purpose nature of the microprocessor may make it possible to eliminate specialized hardware needed to control the peripheral device. For example, the carriage control and form-feed functions of a printer may be controlled by the microprocessor with the resultant elimination of specialized analog or digital control circuits.

The use of a microprocessor reduces the development expense of such attachments by reducing the need for specialized hardware for each peripheral device. Its use, however, does not eliminate totally the individual design of each attachment. Each attachment has unique requirements so that, as a minimum, individual subroutines must be developed. In addition, it is often true that the speed of the microprocessor is insufficient to handle some attachment functions. For example, the error checking calculations used on high-speed communications lines typically are beyond the capability of today's microprocessors. In these cases, additional specialized hardware can be added. The microprocessor can provide the required initialization for these specialized circuits and handle the interpretation of the resulting data or signals.

Because of the general-purpose computational capability of the microprocessor, it often can perform some calculations which otherwise require the services of the main processor. Thus, for example, the microprocessor can perform data comparisons to detect overload conditions. Conceptually, this use of the microprocessor is a form of distributed processing, a topic discussed later in this chapter. The result is an off-loading of the main processor which frees it for other computational work. This provides a system with a higher overall performance, without the necessity for improving the performance of the main processor.

In its use as a controller, the microprocessor usually is pre-programmed by the system designer and its function cannot be altered directly by the user. Very often, the program resides in a read-only-storage (ROS) device incorporated in the attachment. Some random-access-memory (RAM) also may be required for use by the microprocessor as a "scratchpad" storage. Because of this preprogrammed approach, the instruction set of the microprocessor does not need to be known by the user, but only by the designer. The microprocessor instruction set usually is different from that implemented in the main processor.

Microprocessors increasingly are being used in various terminal devices. The amount of function provided varies greatly with the type of terminal and its price. In a simple case, for example, a microprocessor in a CRT entry device may provide for simple cursor control, screen refresh, and functions required by the channel attachment. In higher-function units, the microprocessor provides some local text editing capability, such as selective erasure or insertions.

A third example of the buried micro is its use in industrial measurement and control equipment. Process controllers, capable of implementing the PID algorithm described in Chapter 1, are available in which the calculation is performed digitally by a preprogrammed microprocessor. Similarly, analytical instrumentation increasingly is incorporating microprocessors to perform both control and computational functions. A microprocessor incorporated in a chromatograph, for example, can provide the necessary valve sequencing and timing functions required for its operation. Electronic test equipment incorporating microprocessors can provide the digital average, maxima and minima, and other statistical measures of an input signal. They also can provide conversion of raw data to scaled units selected by the user.

All of these examples are characterized by the idea that the existence of the microprocessor is unknown and unimportant to the user. As a result, the user need not be familiar with computer technology and programming to utilize the equipment. This is important, since it minimizes training requirements and provides computer capabilities to unskilled personnel.

Micros as "Engines"

In the case of the buried micro, the existence of the processor is not known to the user. But micros are computers and they can be applied in much the same way as other computers. One such application is the use of a microprocessor as the "engine" for a general or special-purpose computer. The concept of a microcoded or microprogrammed computer structure was introduced in Chapter 2. Basically, the concept involves the use of a processor with associated programming (microcoding) that "creates" an instruction set (the target instruction set) which is different from the machine-level instruction set (the microinstruction set) of the imbedded processor. This approach utilizes a simple processor with relatively simple instructions to emulate a higher-function instruction set. The imbedded processor is called the "engine" of the computer seen at the target instruction set level.

In most cases, the microcoded subroutines necessary for the emulation are contained in a ROS and are invoked as the result of decoding a target instruction. Since the execution of the target instruction requires the execution of more than one microinstruction, the performance of the emulated machine typically is less than if the target instruction set were implemented directly in hardware. However, a direct implementation typically requires many more logic circuits and a specialized hardware design. Thus, the simplicity of the microcoded engine and the ease of personalization through microcoding is a tradeoff for lower performance. In the case of using a general-purpose microprocessor for the engine, the additional economic advantage of a low cost mass-produced component also is realized.

By using the emulation approach, a computer compatible with other models of a vendor's line can be provided. With compatibility, the software developed for the other models is usable with the microprocessor-based member of the line. This provides a significant economic advantage for the user through reduced program development, education, and maintenance expenses in an application where the lower performance is sufficient. As a result, a number of minicomputer vendors offer a low-end compatible computer based on a general-purpose microprocessor.

Micros as Computers

Finally, since the microprocessor *is* a processor, it can be combined with additional I/O circuits and devices to form a microcomputer conceptually equivalent to larger computers. The microcomputer is programmed in its machine instruction set which is made accessible to the user. When used in this way, the total performance capability of the micro is made available directly to the user. Due to the fact that the number of circuits available to implement a complete processor on one chip is limited, the instruction set of the microprocessor typically is more limited than that available on a minicomputer. This, again, is a relative statement, in that some microcomputers have instruction repertoires of over 100 instructions. By comparison, the first minicomputers had instruction sets of less than 50 instructions. In comparison with today's minicomputers which may have an instruction set of more than 200 instructions, however, the microcomputer instruction set is not as rich in function.

The performance level of current microcomputers also tends to be lower than equivalent minicomputers. This is due primarily to two factors. First, there is always a tradeoff between circuits and performance. By using additional circuits, a computer designer is able to provide specialized functions through dedicated hardware. For example, more than one ALU may be provided, with one of them dedicated to address calculations. Additional circuits also provide the possibility of realizing concurrency or overlap. Thus, for example, it is possible to overlap the fetch of the next instruction with the execution of the current instruction. With limited circuits available, as is the case with today's LSI, these possibilities are not economical. When further density improvements are made as the result of advances in semiconductor technology, however, these limitations will be alleviated.

A second reason for lower performance in some microprocessors is the type of semiconductor devices used to realize the circuits. The type of transistor described earlier is known as a bipolar junction transistor and inherently is fast in switching speed. Another type of transistor, known as the metal-oxide semiconductor field-effect transistor (MOSFET), is somewhat easier to fabricate and permits higher density. The unipolar MOSFET also has a slower switching speed under equivalent circumstances. Recent developments, however, have resulted in the realization of MOSFET switching speeds approaching those of junction transistors. In both the case of the junction and the MOSFET transistors, switching speed can be increased by increasing the power utilized by the circuit. This, however, has limitations beyond a certain point. Although each individual circuit may consume only a fraction of a milliwatt, the concentration of several thousand circuits on a chip only 200 mils in size results in a significant heat density. This heat must be removed from the chip or the resulting temperature increase will destroy the device operation. The net result has been a tradeoff in favor of higher density and lower power, thereby limiting the performance of microprocessors to a level lower than the ultimate potential of the circuits.

When used as a computer, the microcomputer can be provided with the same level of peripheral and software support as the minicomputer. The low cost of the microcomputer, however, often results in a situation where the cost of the peripheral equipment far exceeds the cost of the microprocessor and a reasonable amount of storage. This results from the fact that the peripheral equipment, and particularly that which involves electromechanical equipment, has not benefited from the cost advantages provided by LSI to the degree possible in totally electronic equipment. In recent years, some peripheral equipment has been developed which is less expensive and which is designed specifically for use with microcomputers. These peripherals generally have a lower level of performance, but this often is of little concern with the current performance level of most microcomputers.

Software support comparable to that used with minicomputers can be developed for microcomputers. Some language translators for high-level languages currently are available. Similarly, some elements of operating systems are being marketed. In general, however, the level of software support is limited due, in large measure, to the fact that microcomputers are a recent product. Assuming that developers can devise a satisfactory means of recovering their software investment, there is reason to believe that substantial software support for the most successful microcomputers will be developed.

WHAT'S THE SAME, WHAT'S DIFFERENT

The primary emphasis in this book has been on the minicomputer, but the current interest in microprocessors and microcomputers suggests that the information in the previous chapters should be re-examined to determine its applicability to microcomputers.

Chapter 1 was primarily concerned with process control theory and modeling. The existence of the microprocessor does not affect this theory or approaches to modeling. What it does affect, however, is the manner in which the theory is implemented and the ease of implementation. As mentioned previously, controllers utilizing the PID algorithm and incorporating a microprocessor currently are available. It is expected that even more will become available as the microprocessor technology matures. Similarly, analytical instruments, both on-and off-line, are incorporating micro-processors for control and preprocessing of data. These trends are expected to result in controllers which can implement some of the advanced control strategies which are either impractical or uneconomical to implement with analog circuits. Secondly, since the instruments contain a digital device, one can expect that the communication techniques between the instruments and the industrial computer system eventually will be digital, rather than the current analog methods. Finally, the capability of preprocessing in the instrument or controller will off-load the central system, resulting in higher overall system performance.

Chapter 2 on computer principles is directly applicable to micro-processors. The details of implementation and the tradeoff between circuits and functions differ between microprocessors and minicomputers, but the principles remain the same and essentially the same architectural structures are used in both. Similarly, the material in Chapter 3 applies when the microcomputer is used as a computer rather than as a controller.

The use of microprocessors as controllers for peripheral devices has been mentioned previously. This trend will result in some cost reductions but, more importantly, probably will result in increased function in the peripheral device. Obvious functional improvements include improved error detection and recovery, and the possibility of limited preprocessing of data.

The microprocessor also provides the opportunity for remote subsystems; that is, subsystems which are capable of performing calculations and control without the intervention of the main system processor. These are being implemented widely in the case of terminals of all types. In the industrial computer area, the extension to remote process I/O subsystems is natural. A remotely-located subsystem can be placed close to the portion of the process under control. In a semi-autonomous manner, the subsystem can collect data, perform limited processing, and communicate the results to the central computer system via digital communication lines. Available subsystems of this type generally are preprogrammed and fall into the category of the buried micro discussed above. Conceptually, however, the remote subsystem can have the capability of executing user-written programs which are transferred to the remote subsystem via communication lines. None of this requires new concepts of technology, only a different application of the information provided in Chapter 2 and Chapter 3.

The software concepts and programming techniques discussed in Chapter 4 are applicable to microcomputers. In the case of the buried micro and the micro engine, most of the programming is imbedded in a ROS. Nevertheless, the concepts and the techniques apply. Since the amount of software associated with a microcomputer often is limited and an operating system, *per se*, may not be used, some of the techniques, such as the chief programmer team, are unnecessary, since the entire programming task can be performed by a single person. This fact, however, should not be used as an excuse for less than adequate documentation and good programming practices. Once a program is imbedded in ROS, it is difficult and relatively expensive to change. In any case, maintenance over a number of years may be required and proper attention to the details discussed in Chapter 4 is necessary.

Chapters 5 and 6 on economic justification and project management apply when microcomputers are being used, but they must be scaled down to be appropriate for the usually smaller project size. Clearly, it is not necessary, or wise, to conduct a two or three month economic survey to justify the installation of a microcomputer costing a few thousand dollars. On the other hand, it should not be assumed automatically that a microcomputer-based solution is the only possibility, and an economic study, appropriate to the anticipated expenditures, should be performed. The sources of justification are essentially the same for the minicomputer and the microcomputer project.

Similarly, the project planning and management activities should be scaled appropriately for the microcomputer project. Most of the topics discussed in Chapter 6 remain applicable and many are just as important. For example, the top-down design technique is valid, and the availability of the microprocessor and microcomputer offers the additional possibility that some of the decomposed modules can be implemented as semi-autonomous portions of a total system solution. Documentation remains an important subject and should not be slighted.

Installing a microcomputer system involves most of the considerations discussed in Chapter 7. Wiring practices, physical installation considerations, and test methods, are all important. The difference again is that the effort must be scaled to the size appropriate to the microcomputer project. The installation of a device with a buried microprocessor fundamentally is no different than that for a similar piece of equipment which is not micro-processor-based.

In summary, the microcomputer is a computer, and most of the material discussed previously applies to some degree. Probably the biggest difference is one of philosophy: The microprocessor is a relatively inexpensive digital component that can be customized, through programming, to perform a specialized task. Its existence as an inexpensive device changes the manner in which solutions can be designed and implemented. One no longer needs to think only about computer *systems*; rather, the designer has a computer as a *component* for use in a system solution.

MULTIPROCESSORS

Multiprocessors are computer configurations which involve two or more interconnected processors. Each processor may have associated I/O devices for its exclusive use, or some or all of the I/O devices may be shared. In some manner or another, depending on the physical configuration and the design of the programming system, the multiple processors cooperate in satisfying the requirements of the application. Multiprocessors are used in industrial computer applications primarily as a means of increasing system reliability, although they also have other advantages which are discussed in subsequent paragraphs.

Physical Configurations

There are a number of means by which cooperating processors in a multiprocessing configuration can be interconnected. Each method has advantages and disadvantages in any particular application. Two example configurations are discussed here to illustrate several of the possible options. The configuration shown in Fig. 8.3 utilizes a shared file as the communication means between the two processors. Requests from one processor to the other are posted in queues maintained on the shared file. The scheduling program in the operating system periodically checks the queue to determine if a request is pending. If it is, the request is scheduled according to the particular scheduling algorithm implemented by the operating system. It should be noted that, since a disk file is a serially-reusable device, both processors cannot access the device at the same instant. This contention problem generally is resolved by circuits in the file attachment.

Figure 8.3 also shows one method of connecting I/O devices. In this case,

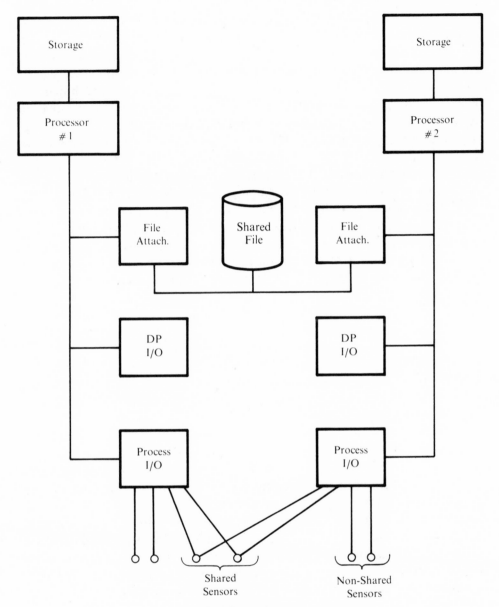

FIG. 8.3
Shared File Multiprocessor

each processor has its own set of DP I/O devices and a process I/O subsystem. Some of the sensors from the process are connected to both sensor I/O subsystems, whereas others are connected to only one subsystem. Generally, the shared sensors are those which are critical to the process operation. In the case that one of the processors is inoperable, the other processor now has access to those sensors necessary to maintain control of the process.

A second method of connecting two processors is illustrated in Fig. 8.4. In this case, the connection is through a channel-to-channel attachment. The channel coupler is similar to a device attachment and is connected to the I/O channel of the individual processors. The transfer of information takes place at the data transfer rate of the slowest processor. Typically, the attachment has minimum buffering capability, so that the receiving processor must be interrupted before the transfer can take place. If cycle stealing or direct storage access capability is provided, the subsequent transfer of information can continue by this means.

In this configuration, each processor has some I/O which is dedicated to its use. In addition, however, some shared I/O is available. This might be a specialized piece of equipment, such as a high-speed printer or a color graphics console. The process I/O subsystem in this example configuration is not duplexed, but rather is connected to one or the other processors by means of a switch. In the case of a failure of the primary processor or for some other programmed reason, the process I/O subsystem can be switched to the other processor.

Operational Modes

There may be several modes in which a multiprocessor system can operate. In one situation, the processors may cooperate in the solution of a particular problem which requires more computing power than is available from a single processor. For example, each processor might control a portion of an overall process and the necessary coordination between the control strategies is effected through the processor interconnection means. In this type of application, both processors are of equal importance in maintaining control of the process and both must be operating to obtain optimum performance.

A more common mode of operation in industrial control, however, usually is called duplexed operation. The purpose is to increase the reliability of the total system. A primary processor normally performs the control task. In the event of a failure, however, the second backup processor takes over. The primary processor can then be taken offline, repaired, tested, and returned to service without interrupting the control of the process.

In a duplexed operation, the backup processor continuously must be aware of the status of the process or have access to these data. In the case of a shared file interconnection, this is done by maintaining the necessary information in a shared file accessible to both processors. In the case of a channel-to-channel connection, the primary processor periodically posts the status of the process into the storage of the backup processor. If the posting is done frequently enough, switching from the primary to the backup processor is accomplished with only minor upsets in the process.

In order to maintain operation, the backup processor must have access to

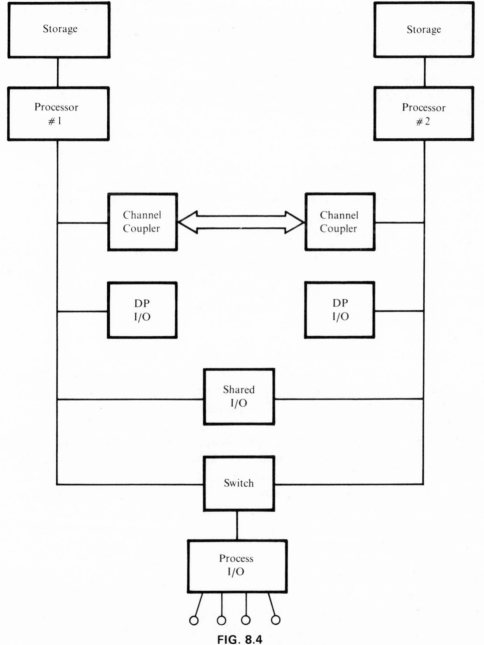

FIG. 8.4
Channel-Connected Multiprocessor

the process inputs and outputs required to control the process. This can be provided by means of shared sensors, as in Fig. 8.3, or through a switched process I/O subsystem, as in Fig. 8.4. A primary difference between these approaches is cost. In the case of duplicate sensor inputs, the additional instrumentation may represent a significant cost and two process I/O subsystems are required. The use of a switched process I/O subsystem adds the cost of the switch, but saves on subsystem and instrumentation costs. However, if a failure takes place in the shared process I/O subsystem, control of the process may be lost, since neither processor has access to the necessary data and control points in the process.

One problem in utilizing duplexed processors is determining when the backup processor should be activated and notifying it to take over. Several methods are available. If the primary processor has detected that a critical subsystem is malfunctioning, it can issue an order to the backup processor to take control. Sometimes, however, the primary processor itself may not be aware of the error or may not be able to issue such an order; for example, if the primary processor is in a non-interruptable state and is executing a loop continuously, it cannot notify the backup processor of its problem. A common solution to this is to have the primary processor set a timer in the backup processor on a periodic basis. Failure of the primary processor to reset the timer before it interrupts causes the backup processor to assume that the primary processor is "hung up," to take control, and to notify the operator to disable the primary processor. This approach sometimes is known as a "watchdog timer" or a "deadman's handle."

The use of duplexed processors essentially provides twice the necessary computing power, since either processor must be capable of separately controlling the process. The excess computing power often can be utilized for non-critical or optional tasks. For example, the backup processor might be used to run an optional optimization program which is desirable, but not absolutely necessary, for control. Thus, if the backup processor takes control due to failure of the primary processor, the optimization program is not run. The resulting control of the process may not be optimal but, at least, control is maintained. In some cases, the programs run on the backup processor may be unrelated to the process and its control. For example, payroll or scientific computations can be run on the backup processor when it is not needed for control. In this way, the investment in the second processor can be justified more completely.

Multiprocessor Justification

The primary justification for the use of duplexed processors in industrial control applications is increased availability. Increased availability is the result of a higher level of reliability for the total system. For example, if the mean-time-between-failure of the processor and its associated I/O necessary for control is 1000 hours, the probability of a failure during any given hour is $1/1000 = 0.001$ or 0.1%. Assuming identical systems and a purely random failure mechanism, the probability that both processors and their associated I/O would fail simultaneously is $0.001 \times 0.001 = 10^{-6}$ or 0.0001%. This represents a failure once every 1,000,000 hours. In an actual case, the calculation of the resultant reliability is considerably more complex than this example. However, the concept of increased reliability due to substantially reduced probability for simultaneous failure of the processors is valid.

It should be noted that the mere existence of two processors in the configuration does not guarantee higher reliability. For example, in the configuration of Fig. 8.3, a failure in the shared file attachment results in a total system failure. Similarly, a failure in the shared process I/O subsystem of Fig. 8.4 results in a total system failure. Thus, the entire system must be examined to determine what will happen as the result of a particular failure. Similarly, the software support for the duplexed processors must be designed in such a way as to take advantage of the higher potential reliability of the hardware.

Other reasons exist for the use of duplexed processors, although increased reliability is the primary reason in industrial control applications. In some cases, two different processors are interconnected in order to take advantage of their special characteristics. For example, the second processor might be designed specifically to perform a particular calculation, such as the Fast Fourier Transform or floating point calculations. When such a calculation needs to be performed by the primary processor, the required data are sent to the special processor for the calculation. When the calculation is complete, the results are returned to the primary processor.

Multi-Microprocessors

The advent of the microprocessor has resulted in computer configurations which are, in reality, multiprocessor configurations. To the user, however, the configuration appears to be that of a uniprocessor. Several of these configurations were discussed earlier in this chapter in the sections dealing with microprocessors and microcomputers. The best current examples are the use of microprocessors as I/O controllers in channel attachments. In this application, the microprocessor is microcoded and, typically, the code is stored in a read-only-storage (ROS). The primary reason for using the microprocessor is to save development cost, but its generalized capability allows the designer to substantially increase the I/O function without a corresponding increase in hardware cost.

The second current use of microprocessors which is beginning to emerge is a channel-connected special purpose processing unit. In essence, this is the configuration shown in Fig. 8.4, except that the special-purpose processor normally does not have associated I/O equipment. These special-purpose processors currently are used to provide functions which are not included in the basic design of the minicomputer because the increased cost is not justified in all anticipated uses of the minicomputer. Thus, for example, a channel-connected processor (sometimes called an "outboard processor") can be provided to provide floating point calculations. The outboard processor, in the case of today's minicomputers, is very often a microprocessor which is microcoded for the necessary floating point functions.

At this point, multiple microprocessors have not displaced the application processing functions of the minicomputer. However, research is being pursued in which multiple microprocessors are used to provide a configuration that could replace a uniprocessor minicomputer. Although not yet demonstrated, the goal is to provide the computing function and performance of a minicomputer at a significantly lower cost by utilizing low-cost, mass-produced microprocessors. It also is possible that the multi-processor nature of the configuration might provide unique advantages for some applications.

DISTRIBUTED PROCESSING AND COMPUTER NETWORKS

Distributed processing currently is a topic which is being discussed extensively in the literature. It does not have a precise definition and some of the debate in the literature concerns its definition. It is really a concept which can have many embodiments. Within a single computer configuration, the use of microprocessor I/O control units and channel-connected outboard processors is a form of distributed processing. In this case, the processors can be called "tightly-coupled," in that the various microprocessors are under intimate control of the primary processor and are specifically dedicated to off-loading the primary processor. All of the processors in the configuration typically are applied concurrently to the solution of a specific problem in a coordinated manner.

Another form of distributed processing utilizes computing elements which are physically separated and less tightly-coupled; that is, they act as semi-autonomous units. This is typically the case, for example, in the use of so-called intelligent terminals or remote subsystems in industrial control applications. Intelligent data collection terminals or process I/O subsystems may be distributed throughout an industrial plant to capture data near their source. In the distributed processing concept, these remote units have some processing capability, although they may not be user-programmable processors. Limited data processing is performed by the remote units and summary or exception results are transmitted to the host computer system through communication lines.

Several advantages are claimed for distributed processing. One which has been discussed previously is that the computing capability of the remote units off-loads the processor at the next higher level and provides an increase in the performance of the total system. The distribution of computing capability can also simplify the operating system at the central system. Although the central system typically must still be a multiprogramming system, the degree of multiprogramming is reduced, since some functions are handled directly by the remote computing units. Time responsiveness may be increased, due to less overhead in the system and due to the fact that simple high priority functions, such as scanning and alarming, can be executed by the remote units without waiting for the availability of the central system.

Distributed processing systems also offer a degree of modularity which is sometimes difficult to achieve with a single control system. As additional portions of an industrial plant are automated, for example, remote units can be added as needed. This eliminates the need initially to install a system large enough to handle all anticipated applications. Of course, the system initially must be designed with the idea that this manner of expansion will be used.

Depending on the design of the total system and the computing capability of the remote units, the distributed processing concept may contribute to greater system reliability. If the capabilities of the remote units are such that they can sustain operation for some limited time independent of the central system, a short failure in the central system may be tolerable. Similarly, since the data collection and preprocessing may be distributed among a number of remote subsystems, it may be possible for the central system to maintain control during limited outages of some number of remote units. Just as in the case of duplexed processors, this advantage does not happen automatically and specifically must be designed into the system hardware and software configuration.

Computer networks are really an extension of the distributed processing concept. In reality, networks have been used in various applications since the early days of computers. The differentiation between a distributed processing system and a computer network is ill-defined and, to a certain extent, a matter of degree. Typically, computer networks consist of one or more complete computer systems which are geographically distant. The distance may be hundreds of feet, as in the case of an in-plant network, or thousands of miles, as in the case of a corporate network of computers connected by common-carrier communications facilities covering the United States.

Networks are logically and physically organized in a number of different ways. In most cases, the design is such that the computers in the network are loosely-coupled; that is, they are capable of standalone operation and communicate with other computers in the network in an autonomous manner.

Network Logical Configuration

The logical configurations of the network may be categorized as being master-slave, hierarchical, or peer-connected. The logical configuration is an indication of the manner in which the network is controlled and how responsibilities are delegated between processing units. In a master-slave relationship, a single computer in the network has control and determines which of the slave computers performs a particular task. Communication from one slave computer to another is controlled by the master and, in most cases, takes place only through the master computer.

The master computer has the overall responsibility to satisfy the needs of the application. When the execution of a task is required, the master assigns the task to one of the slave processors. It also provides the necessary data, if such data are retained in the master computer's files. If the required data are to be obtained from the process, the slave unit must have the necessary data collection subsystems. Once the task has been assigned to the slave, it proceeds asynchronously with respect to the master until the completion of the task, or until it needs services controlled by the master. Comparing this to the operating system concepts discussed in Chapter 4, the master computer is analogous to the operating system module which provides the task scheduling functions. The master system may, of course, utilize its own resources for any particular task.

The master-slave configuration primarily is used to provide coordinated control over a number of computers and to provide for load sharing. If properly designed, it can be expanded modularly by adding additional slave units. Thus, the computing power can be increased incrementally, or the system can be expanded to provide for the coordinated control of additional units within an industrial plant.

The hierarchical network configuration is similar to a multi-level master-slave network. The primary difference is that various levels in the network have assigned responsibility for certain functions. The concept is analogous to the organization used for the management of many commercial concerns, where the highest level of management is involved in policy decisions and the lower levels have operational responsibilities for increasingly specific functions.

Figure 8.5 illustrates a possible division of responsibility in a hierarchical computer network. At the lowest level (Level 1), minicomputers or microcomputers are utilized to provide unit control. The functions performed at this level typically include the monitoring, alarming, and loop control functions introduced in Chapter 1. With the advent of microprocessors and "intelligent" subsystems, some of these functions might be performed semi-

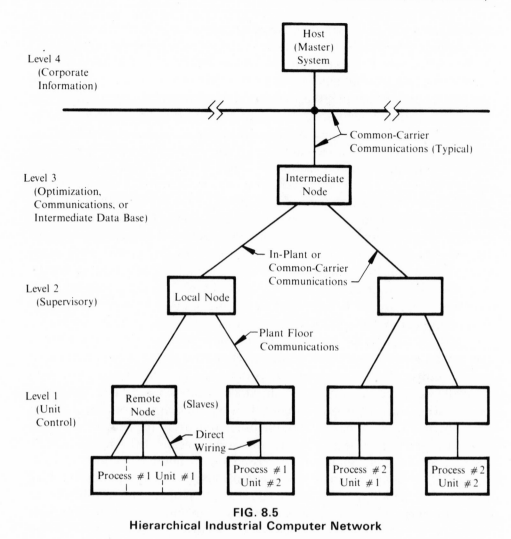

FIG. 8.5
Hierarchical Industrial Computer Network

autonomously by computing units below the Level 1 computer; if used, such units could be considered as Level 0 processors, responsible for specific functions or for a limited number of control loops.

The Level 2 computers are responsible for the establishment of the set points for the various loops under the control of the Level 1 computers. As such, the Level 2 computer provides the coordination between units within a single process. Optimization between several processes within the same related industrial complex may be provided by a Level 3 processor. This processor provides strategic, long-term direction for the various processes under its control. Summary results and high-level management information for the industrial complex is provided by a corporate-level information system which may include diverse functions, such as summary information from inventory control computers, financial analysis computers, and all of the other functions involved in an industrial enterprise.

It should be noted that the level of responsibility with respect to the total corporate operation increases with each level. The time response requirements also decrease by level. At the Level 0 or 1 computer, the time response may be measured in fractions of a second to satisfy the requirements of loop and unit control; supervisory functions may require a time response of minutes, optimization may be required every hour or less, and the corporate system may provide new direction to the lower levels on a daily or weekly basis. This reduction in required time responsiveness generally is beneficial in that the number of calculations and data manipulation required at each level tends to increase, due to the increasing interactions of the many factors involved in managing an industrial enterprise. It also is generally true that the size of the computer system increases at each level. Levels 1 and 2 are typically computers that are considered as minicomputers, Level 3 may be a medium-sized computer system, and Level 4 may be a large-scale system.

Both the master-slave and the hierarchical networks imply a top-down control philosophy, with the higher level having more responsibility and overall control than the lower level(s). A third logical configuration consists of mutually cooperating computers, in which there is no defined master or precedence of one system over another. This type of peer network requires that each operating system be aware of the other systems in the network and that the scheduling algorithm provide for some means by which work is distributed. Once a job has been passed on to another computer in the network, the originating computer essentially loses control. Without adequate precautions, the job may be lost since no single system is responsible for its execution. Typically, such systems operate in a manner that, if a computer is busy and unable to handle a new task, the task is passed onto another computer. When an available computer is found, it executes the task. It may also happpen that some computers in the network have special capabilities (e.g., a Fast Fourier Transform processor). In this case, another computer in the network can direct a task to the specialized computer.

In the peer network, each computer has considerable autonomy and there must be a prior agreement—usually incorporated in the design of the operating system—as to how the computers will cooperate. Time response is difficult to predict, since no single computer knows the workload of another and there is no master which can impose preemptive control. Nevertheless, peer networks have been implemented and they provide a means for the user to have access to specialized facilities not available on the originating computer. They also provide a method whereby the computing load can be shared; this results in more efficient use of the total computing facility.

Network Physical Configuration

The physical configuration of the network refers to the actual physical connections between the computers in the network. There are a number of possible configurations, some of which are illustrated in Fig. 8.6. In the star network, one of the processors is connected by a single line to each of the other processors. This configuration is typical in the small system master-slave logical relationship.

In the multidrop configuration, all computers in the network are connected to a single communication line. The communication line may be a multiplexed channel or a serial "Data Highway." Due to the shared nature of the communication line, only two processors may communicate at any given time. This configuration may be used in any of the logical configurations described previously.

In the loop configuration, all computers are connected to a loop communication line, which begins and ends at a loop controller, and which typically is a computer that maintains control over all communications. Messages between computers typically are handled as a string of words or bytes containing information as to the originator and the addressee. When a computer recognizes a message being addressed to it, it accepts the message and leaves a blank "frame" on the loop communication line. In some cases, each computer inserts a unit delay in the message transmission timing, so that it can insert a message on the line prior to forwarding an incoming message. Loops are difficult to control and have the fundamental disadvantage that all messages are sent past all computers, thus requiring higher line data rates.

In the point-to-point unswitched physical interconnection, each processor in the network is connected to every other processor. The notation $n(n-1)/2$ refers to the number of interconnections required when there are n processors. It easily is seen that the number of interconnections increases approximately as $n^2/2$; for $n = 3$, there are three communication links; for $n = 5$, the number of links grows to 10; and for $n = 10$, the number of links is 45. Thus, the number of required communication links quickly can become excessive. The advantage of the network is that every processor has direct access to every other processor. If some of the links are broken due to equipment failure, many alternate paths between any two processors exist if messages can be forwarded.

It is important to note that the physical and logical configurations are relatively independent; that is, any of the logical configurations discussed above can be implemented by the various physical configurations. This is shown in Fig. 8.7, where the first figure shows a point-to-point multipoint physical configuration. Due to the design of the network software, however, one of the computers has control over the others in a master-slave relationship. This

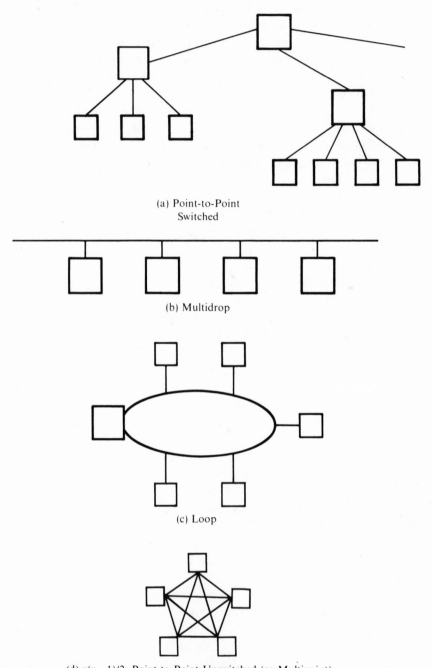

(a) Point-to-Point
Switched

(b) Multidrop

(c) Loop

(d) $n(n-1)/2$: Point-to-Point Unswitched (or Multipoint)

FIG. 8.6
Physical Configurations

provides a logical configuration equivalent to that shown in Fig. 8.7(b).

The actual physical interconnection between processors is dependent on a number of factors. The interconnection may be established by a channel-to-channel connection similar to that described earlier in discussing duplexed systems. Due to the number of physical wires in the channel, the limitation on the driver circuits, and the time delay associated with the transmission of

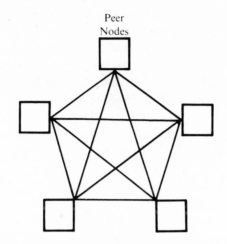

(a) Physical Configuration

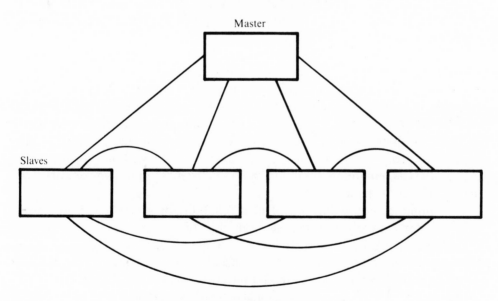

(b) Logical Configuration

FIG. 8.7
Logical vs. Physical Configuration

electrical pulses, such an approach only is applicable to computers which are located physically close to each other. Geographically distant computers usually are interconnected by serial communication systems in which the messages are transmitted one bit at a time. The serial path may be a dedicated pair of wires or coaxial cable which is permanently connected to the processors, or it may be a common carrier (telephone) line in which the connection is established through a switching center only when required. In either case, the transmission rate may range from a low of about 150 bits per second (Baud*) to a high of several million bits per second. As the transmission speed increases, the cost of the communication facility increases.

The speed of transmission is a fundamental design parameter in the network design. In the case of systems requiring fast time response or the transmission of large quantities of data in a fixed time period, a high performance communication line is required. If the design of the network does not require either of these conditions, lower performance (and lower cost) communication facilities may be utilized.

Justification

Distributed processing and computer networks are the result of evolving computer technology and the requirements of various applications. Many of the justifying factors have been mentioned in previous sections, but it is worthwhile to summarize them here. They can be categorized as increased reliability, access to specialized resources, load sharing, and system simplification.

Increased reliability is the result of not concentrating the total computing capability of the system in a single processor. With a single centralized processor, a failure in the processor results in the complete loss of the system. The loss of a peripheral device may or may not result in a complete loss, depending on the design of the application system. In a distributed processor or network, the total system can be designed such that one or more of the individual processors can fail or be taken off-line without losing total capability. The remaining capability can be sufficient to maintain some level of activity useful to the application.

It should be noted that the intrinsic reliability of a distributed processor or computer network may be less than that of a uniprocessor. Hardware reliability is dependent primarily on the number of electronic components in the system, and the number of interconnections between these components. The number of components and interconnections in a distributed processor, or in the aggregate of all the computers in a network, generally is greater than in a

---

*The Baud is defined as the rate of coded symbol transfer. In a communication coding method which involves only binary symbols, 1 Baud is equal to a transmission rate of one bit per second.

single comparable uniprocessor. Thus, the intrinsic reliability can be expected to be less. The key to increased reliability, therefore, is the manner in which the application functions are divided among the various processors, and the provisions which are made through the sofware to provide backup for a failing computing unit.

The availability of specialized resources is an advantage of distributed processors and networks. This was mentioned previously in the case of specialized outboard processors for minicomputers performing such functions as floating point arithmetic or storage management. A similar situation exists in a network, where a particular computer in the network may have specialized resources or characteristics applicable to a particular type of problem. For example, the network may contain an "array" processor, particularly suited to some kinds of array-oriented calculations. Or, the processor may have a large storage size or performance level, which contributes to the easy and economical solution of a large problem. In such a case, a user at another computer in the network can transmit his program and data to the particular computer for processing.

The computing load on an individual computer often varies with time. For example, in a commercial application, a billing period at the end of the month may represent a time when the computer is overloaded, simply because of the quantity of work which must be accomplished. Similarly, in a control application, an upset in the process can require all of the resources of the control computer. In a computer network, some of the overload can be assigned to other processors which have excess capacity at the time. This results in the work being completed in a more timely fashion and the more efficient use of the other computer, which would otherwise be operating below capacity.

Simplicity often is cited as an advantage of distributed processing and computer networks. This claim, however, must be examined carefully in order to appreciate its meaning. There is a well-known "law" in computing, known as Grosch's Law, which states that computer performance is proportional to the square of the price. This implies that computing capabilities should be concentrated in large machines in order to realize the most economical computing. On the other hand, it is well known that effective utilization of the performance of a large machine requires a complex operating system and that the complexity and overhead of this operating system increases rapidly with machine size. Thus, some people argue, there is a point where the gain in performance of a centralized machine is outweighed by the additional complexity necessary to use it. The alternative, the proponents say, is to break down the system into smaller computing nodes, either as a network or as a distributed processing system. Each of these nodes can be dedicated to smaller tasks and, therefore, do not require the complex operating system of the centralized approach.

What is sometimes neglected by the advocates of distributed processing is that dividing the computing responsibility among many processors or independent computers increases the amount of coordination which is required. It creates, implicitly or explicitly, the need for a "manager," in exactly the same way that controlling the activities of a group of programmers or engineers requires a manager, whose primary tasks revolve around the coordination of the work of independent and intelligent people. Thus, although simplicity may be achieved at any given node in the distributed processor or computer network, complexity again may result for the total computing facility. Careful design and management are required to produce a successful system, just as in the case of uniprocessor applications.

An Observation

The computer industry has had its share of "fads" throughout its history. In the initial enthusiasm following the first report of a new hardware device, software technique, or computer application, the technical literature often contains papers which sound as though the new development is the panacea for all known problems in computing. As the development matures and is better understood, its limitations become known, it is found not to be the answer for all problems, and it takes its place in the system designer's "bag of tricks."

The current literature on computer networks and distributed processing appears to be at this stage of initial enthusiasm. Enthusiastic papers by the proponents abound. Time will tell, but it is likely that these approaches to computing will become merely another possibility for the design of a system. Distributed processing and computer networks will not displace all uniprocessors, and they will not be the optimum solution for all applications. Thus, centralized and decentralized systems will coexist in control applications and in other commercial applications. The choice between them will be made by the skillful system designer by comparing the alternatives to the requirements of the application.

BIBLIOGRAPHY

Barna, A., *Introduction to Microcomputers and Microprocessors*, John Wiley & Sons, New York, 1976.

Blanc, R. P., and I. W. Cotton, Eds., *Computer Networking*, IEEE Press, New York, 1976.

Computer Networks: A Tutorial, Revised, IEEE Computer Society Publications Office, Long Beach, CA, 1976.

"Distributed Processing—What the Experts Say," Data Processing, November, 1976, pp. 45–47.

Grimsdale. F. L.. and F. F. Kuo, Eds.. *Computer Communication Networks.* Noordhoff International Publishing, Leyden, Netherlands, 1975.

Klingman, E., *Microprocessor Systems Design,* Prentice-Hall, Englewood Cliffs, 1977.

Martin, J., *Future Developments in Telecommunications,* 2nd Ed., Prentice-Hall. Englewood Cliffs, 1977.

McGlynn, D. R., *Microprocessors—Technology, Architecture, and Applications,* John Wiley & Sons, New York, 1976.

Peatman, J. B., *Microcomputer-Based Design,* McGraw-Hill Book Co., New York, 1977.

Reynolds, C. H., "Issues in Centralization," Datamation, March, 1977, pp. 91–100.

Soucek, B., *Microprocessors and Microcomputers,* John Wiley & Sons, New York, 1976.

Wagner, F. V., "Is Decentralization Inevitable?", Datamation, November, 1976, pp. 86–97.

INDEX